Reading Beyond the Boc

Reading and sharing books remains a significant activity for many people in a digital age. Literary culture has become a form of popular culture over the last fifteen years and opportunities to share reading with others have multiplied during an era of converged media and changing technologies. Mass reading events, such as televised book clubs and community-wide reading initiatives, are among the new cultural formations designed to attract, educate, and entertain groups of leisure readers. Based on extensive research, including original interviews and surveys with readers and event organizers in the UK, US, and Canada, this volume offers the first critical examination of mass reading events. The authors explore the social practices inspired by the sharing of books in public spaces, alongside the exclusionary features of events in order to challenge the assumption that books are everywhere and accessible to everyone. Through a consideration of the major actors, institutions, and materials that shape contemporary cultures of shared reading, this study identifies and interrogates the complex ideological investments made by readers, cultural workers, government agencies, and the mass media in the meanings of reading at the turn of the twenty-first century.

Danielle Fuller is Senior Lecturer in the Department of American & Canadian Studies at the University of Birmingham, UK.

DeNel Rehberg Sedo is Associate Professor in the Department of Communication Studies at Mount Saint Vincent University, Canada.

Routledge Research in Cultural and Media Studies

For a full list of titles in this series, please visit www.routledge.com

Reading Beyond the Book

The Social Practices of Contemporary
Literary Culture

**Danielle Fuller and
DeNel Rehberg Sedo**

Routledge
Taylor & Francis Group

NEW YORK AND LONDON

First published 2013
by Routledge
711 Third Avenue, New York, NY 10017

Simultaneously published in the UK
by Routledge
2 Park Square, Milton Park, Abingdon, Oxfordshire OX14 4RN

First issued in paperback 2015

*Routledge is an imprint of the Taylor & Francis Group,
an informa business*

Library of Congress Cataloging in Publication Data

Fuller, Danielle.
  Reading beyond the book : the social practices of contemporary literary
culture / by Danielle Fuller and DeNel Rehberg Sedo.
    pages cm. — (Routledge research in cultural and media studies ; 49)
    Includes bibliographical references and index.
  1. Books and reading—Social aspects—History—21st century.
2. Books and reading—Social aspects—United States. 3. Books and
reading—Social aspects—Canada. 4. Books and reading—Social
aspects—Great Britain. 5. Group reading—Case studies. 6. Book
clubs (Discussion groups)—Case studies. 7. Reading promotion—Case
studies. I. Rehberg Sedo, DeNel, 1965– II. Title.
  Z1003.F863 2013
  028'.9—dc23
  2012041620

ISBN13: 978-1-138-92993-7 (pbk)
ISBN13: 978-0-415-53295-2 (hbk)

Typeset in Sabon
by Apex CoVantage, LLC

To Brent and Julie—our favorite readers

Contents

Figures, Illustrations, and Photos

Tables

Acknowledgments

Too much wine, or too much sun? Certainly, both were present on the day that we began to design the research study that informs this book. Our enjoyment of them may have encouraged us to think about investigating shared reading events on a much bigger scale than we had first envisaged. But we were, to our credit, following the words of advice offered by wise guides in the form of Research Officers at our respective universities. Because of Patrick O'Neill, Tony Davis, Brenda Gagné, and Big Jim, we dreamed and planned big. Our indefatigable project advisory board counseled us and helped to shape what became the *Beyond the Book* project. Thanks do not seem sufficient for what we have learned from Professors Dick Ellis and Jenny Hartley. We appreciate, too, all that Drs. Maureen Bell and Anne McDermott shared with us. This book is a result of that sun-drenched patio planning session, but undertaking the work that informs the analyses that we offer here was a collaborative endeavor.

Dr. Anouk Lang was the tireless and talented Postdoctoral Research Fellow whose contributions to the collecting and organizing of data, the discussions of initial analyses, and the editing of an inspiring volume of essays about contemporary reading practices, represent several, but by no means all, aspects of her valued labor on the *Beyond the Book* project. Anna Burrells, who was the Administrative Assistant to BTB while also working on her PhD, shared with us her extraordinary organizational and creative skills. She not only helped the core research team to produce a successful project conference, but she also worked diligently with the entire transatlantic project workforce to ensure effective data collection in each of the research sites. Anna also did a bang-up job as a Research Assistant with her attention to detail and her witty sense of humor. In fact, *Beyond the Book* was blessed with efficient and fun-to-work-with Research Assistants. We appreciate the transcription work, the proof-reading, the searching, and the laughter that the following individuals shared with the project: Corinne Jones and Cristina Ivanovici (UK); Julie Van Huyse and Amelia Chester (Canada). In her own way, our stats consultant, Lindsay Engel Marchand, is also a translator. Right up to the end we depended on her to help us with the translation of formulas and numbers, and her skill with statistics meant that we could tease as much meaning out of the data as possible.

She helped us to make sense of similarities and differences and to confirm our conclusions. We are grateful for her expertise.

In each of the research sites, we depended on local graduate students to help us recruit study participants, organize media advertising buys, and get a better "lay of the land." We appreciate the efforts of LaDonna Saunders, Amy Laurent, Cathy Collett, Kimberly Walsh, Lesley Mulcahy, Lori Theissen, Sara Beadle, Claire Brown and Ross Cohen, Diana LaChance, Felice Atesoglu, and Mitogo Ondo Ayekaba. Because of these energetic young people, who are readers themselves, we were able to "hit the ground running" with comfort and knowledge that may not have been possible without their efforts. Each of the fieldworkers also worked to promote participation in online surveys. In some cases, the surveys had to be translated into French or Spanish. We feel fortunate to have worked with Dominique Belkadi, Aiora Jaka Irizar, Louise-Marie Bédard, and Claire Wood.

The plethora of qualitative data that we collected and recorded via interviews and focus groups needed to be transcribed. If you've ever done this task, you understand that it can be interesting but that it can also be very arduous and exasperating when working with multiple voices, accents, and excited readers talking over one another. Fortunately, we employed Rich Langley, Brett Birks, Amelia Chester, Bronagh Clarke, Julie Van Huyse, Hanni Bouma, Patricia Smith, Mike Dunn, and Michael Burns. Careful consideration of each word and utterance is a trademark of these workers.

In late summer 2007, we hosted a successful project conference at the University of Birmingham. In addition to the hard work of Drs. Lang and Burrells, Dr. Cristina Ivanovici, Olivia Chambers, and Ann Bower, more than 120 scholars and practitioners came together from 19 countries to meet, discuss, and share ideas about contemporary cultures of reading. It was an exciting and exhilarating few days.

Throughout the project, the faculty and staff at our respective universities were nothing short of exemplary supporters. We feel grateful to work with such people. As departmental administrators, Margaret (Mags) Conway, Gaye Bye, and Kathryn Britten run our departments—and sometimes they (mercifully) run us. Fiona Gilyead, Sheena Robertson, Sue Bowen, Julie Tonks, Bali Shergill, and Bob Bushaway from the former School of Historical Studies, University of Birmingham, were always supportive of the project, and we are thankful. We also want to acknowledge members of the School Research Committee for Danielle's teaching relief and the MSVU Research Committee and Deans Mary Lyon and Kim Kienapple for their financial support and unwavering belief in *Beyond the Book*. Our faculty colleagues have had to live through the many ups, downs, and sideways movements of the project in the hallways at work and over late-night glasses of wine. Our appreciation for the ability to listen and to give wise advice freely goes to: Michele Aaron, Adriana Benzaquén, Francesca Carnevali, Kevin Davison, John Fagg, Roni Gechtman, Steve Hewitt, Wade Kenny, Helen Laville, Scott Lewis, Karen Macfarlane, Allan Nielsen, Lorri Nielsen Glenn, Katherine Side, James Walters, and Sara Wood.

We not only met fabulous librarians in each of our research sites, but we also work with some. Karen Jackson, Jill Russell, Denyse Rodrigues, Peter Glenister, Stan Orlov, and Donna Bourne-Tyson each played a special role in helping our research process, from finding sources to managing them, to making all of our quantitative data available to researchers around the world. Their work—and ours—is facilitated by kind and patient IT service workers. While we are in awe of them, we are also thankful for Spencer Webb, Mark Connop, Trevor Batchelor, Greg Pretty, Christine Schumacher, Rob Carr, Andrew Carr, Payne Nickerson, Bill Powell, Neill Penny, and the University of Birmingham Arts IT technical support team, especially Ravinder Ghuman. Our website and logo were designed by the creative folk at Nemisys. Several years on, John Horne and Grant Burton helped us to refresh the pages and update the interface. We are grateful for their ideas, technical know-how, and all-round professionalism.

Beyond the Book was funded early on by MSVU, the British Academy, and the Department of Foreign Affairs and International Trade (Canada). The larger project was funded primarily by Arts and Humanities Research Council UK (2005 to 2008, ID 112166), and, through the provision of research space and equipment on the North American side of the Atlantic, by the Nova Scotia Research Innovation Trust and the Canadian Foundation for Innovation. We remain humbly appreciative that our project was selected from among the many as worthy of funding. Of course, we are grateful to our institutions for the research leave that gave us the opportunity to make sense of the data and to present our conclusions in this book.

Ideas, data, hypotheses, and theories were initially tested out on various conference audiences, at symposia, and in workshops. There are too many of these events to list here, but we would like to thank everyone who has ever sat through one of our presentations or participated in a workshop. The questions that have been posed to us have been intellectually stimulating and the generous responses that have been offered very encouraging. Editors and reviewers of various journals and book collections also helped us to focus our analyses and to hone our prose. We are grateful for their

www.beyondthebookproject.org

Figure Ack.1 BTB Logo
Beyond the Book logo designed by Nemisys
Source: Authors' image.

careful attention to our work and to the publishers of articles and book chapters for granting permission to reprint and/or revise extracts from these publications. Within Chapters 1, 6, and the Methods Appendix are parts of Fuller and Rehberg Sedo, "Mixing It Up: Using Mixed Methods to Investigate Contemporary Cultures of Reading," in *From Codex to Hypertext: Reading at the Turn of the Twenty-First Century*, ed. Anouk Lang (Amherst: University of Massachusetts Press, 2012), pp. 234–51. Chapter 2 contains several paragraphs extracted by permission of the publishers from "Suspicious Minds: The Richard & Judy Book Club and its Resistant Readers," in *The Richard & Judy Book Club Reader*, ed. Jenni Ramone and Helen Cousins (Farnham: Ashgate, 2011), pp. 21–42. Ideas from Fuller, Rehberg Sedo, and Thurlow's "More Than 'Just a Little Library Program'" *Logos* 20 (1–4): pp. 228–40, appear in the Methods Appendix and in Chapter 5. Small sections of the following appear as parts of Chapters 2 and 3: Rehberg Sedo, "'Richard & Judy's Book Club' and 'Canada Reads': Readers, Books and Cultural Programming in a Digital Era." *Information, Communication and Society* 11 (2), (2008): 188–206, by permission of Taylor and Francis (http://www.tandfonline.com) and from Rehberg Sedo, "Cultural Capital and Community in Contemporary City-wide Reading Programs." *Mémoires du livre/Studies in Book Culture* 2 (2), (2010), available at: http:// www.erudit.org/revue/memoires/2010/v2/n1/045314ar.html. Extracts from Fuller and Rehberg Sedo, "A Reading Spectacle for the Nation: The CBC and 'Canada Reads.'" *Journal of Canadian Studies* 40 (1) (Winter 2006): 5–36, resurface in Chapter 3. Chapter 6 contains a small adapted extract from Rehberg Sedo, "Twentieth- and Twenty-first-century Literary Communities," in *The Cambridge History of the American Novel*, ed. Leonard Assuto in association with Clare Virginia Eby and Benjamin Reiss (Cambridge: Cambridge University Press, 2011), pp. 1159–60. Thanks to the Eccles Centre for American Studies at The British Library for allowing small sections of the following to be reproduced in revised form in Chapters 3, 4, and 6: Fuller, "Citizen Reader: Canadian Literature, Mass Reading Events and the Promise of Belonging," *The Fifth Eccles Centre for American Studies Plenary Lecture and Pamphlet Series*, 25 (London: Eccles Centre & The British Library, 2011). Also available at: http://www.bl.uk/eccles/pdf/ bacs2010.pdf#zoom=80.

In spite of this long list, the vast majority of material in this book has not been previously published, and a wonderful group of colleagues cheered us on during the writing process. Earlier versions and drafts of various sections and chapters were shared with our advisory committee, and also with our scholarly mentors: Elizabeth Long, Janice Radway and Christine Pawley. We are downright lucky to have their support and sage advice. We would also like to thank David Hesmondhalgh and David Wright for their good-humored support. We are indebted to our "clever friends," each of whom read a chapter and provided invaluable feedback, with only the moniker as a thank you. We give a "shout out" to: Jan Campbell, Simone Murray, Marnina

Gonick, Isabelle Szmigin, Nancy Duxbury, Ann Steiner, James Procter, James Walters, and Alla Kushniryk. Our very special clever friends, Julie Rak, Brent Sedo, and Claire Squires read the manuscript in its entirety. More than once. To say that we are thankful is not sufficient. We are indebted.

Skype facilitated our transatlantic partnership in ways that we could not have imagined when we began working together. To creators Janus Friis and Niklas Zennström, we raise a glass. And while weekly meetings made the project possible, yoga kept us grounded and sustained us—in our respective homes and on the road. To James Critchlow, Claire Hatchell, Rene Johnson, Cathy Guest, Mario Corella, and Kine Röst, we say "Namaste." The same could be said for our furry friends Tashi, Mr Thomas, Sancho Panza, Coyoacán, Lyle, and Autumn. They are each muses in their own right. But we would not have had anything to write about if it were not for the thousands of readers who shared their experiences with us, and who continue to intrigue, inspire, and motivate us. We send a big thank you to each one of you.

DeNel Rehberg Sedo and Danielle Fuller
Hubbards, Nova Scotia, Canada & Birmingham, UK

Introduction

Reading is the new rock n' roll.
                    —Mary Worrall, Birmingham Readers' Day, 2003

One Book, One Community gives our city props.
                    —Teen Book Club member, Chicago, 2005

Let the battle commence!
                    —Host of CBC Radio's *Canada Reads*, 2006

Excitement, entertainment, and city pride—but not because Birmingham City won a championship soccer game or the Boston Red Sox won the World Series, or (to briefly enter the realm of fantasy) the Toronto Maple Leafs beat the Chicago Blackhawks in the NHL Stanley Cup finals. All the people quoted above are referring to the pleasure of reading and sharing books on a scale and in ways that contemporary mass media and new technologies make possible. At the turn of the twenty-first century, this kind of excitement signals a resurgence of interest in sharing the experiences of book reading with other people. That level of interest has inspired television producers, librarians, and arts administrators to create new cultural formations, or models, for what we call *shared reading*. These manifestations of contemporary cultures of leisure reading, or mass reading events (MRE), as we have named them, are the focus of this book. They deserve careful scrutiny because investigating their production, promotion, circulation, and reception suggests why a feeling for reading and sharing books persists in North America and the United Kingdom in a digital age. During a time when it became possible for those with Internet access to share the minutiae of their everyday lives—their photographs, political opinions, and homemade movies with a few clicks of a mouse—why did some people choose to share their reading experiences?

For those of us whose lives have been closely bound up with books and reading, professionally and personally, the increased media visibility lent to print culture during the first decade of the twenty-first century can hardly have gone unnoticed. Thanks in part to big-box stores, online retailing, film adaptations, and televised book clubs, books appeared to be everywhere. But they were not, in fact, appealing or accessible to everybody. Obtaining books, sharing reading experiences, and engaging with different media depend on the possession of particular skills and material resources. Cultural events that focus on or adapt aspects of print culture exclude people who do not possess those competencies or assets. As a leisure pursuit, reading books is considerably less popular than playing sports, listening to music, and watching television. Why then, would community organizers and gov-

P.1 Bookmark for *A Raisin in the Sun*

One Book, One Chicago highlights *A Raisin in the Sun* for its Spring 2003 season

Source: Beyond the Book project: Artefacts and Ephemera, available at: http://epapers.bham. ac.uk/1469/

ernment agencies choose shared reading? In *Reading Beyond the Book*, we explore the social practices inspired by the sharing of books in public spaces and reveal the complex ideological investments made by readers, cultural workers and managers, institutions, and the mass media in the meanings of reading. From the belief in reading as an individually transformational, educational, therapeutic, creative, and even "civilizing" experience, to the ideal of shared reading as a way of building community and improving cross-cultural understanding in urban centers, the reading and sharing of books is an activity that is variously inscribed with the dreams, anxieties, hopes, and political goals of those who promote it. *Reading Beyond the Book* explains why, paradoxically, literary reading can never be popular on a mass scale within societies that invest books with significant amounts of cultural value and social power.

Our title invokes both our methodology and subject of scrutiny. *Reading Beyond the Book* is our analysis of the meanings of shared reading at the beginning of the twenty-first century. In particular, it is about book reading pursued and promoted as a social practice through the vehicle of reading events that operate on a citywide, regional, or national scale. We offer a series of insights into the ideological work performed by a specific aspect of contemporary literary culture as it has developed in the United States, Canada, and the United Kingdom. We consider how and why people come together to share reading beyond or outside of their solitary encounter with a text, or how they might participate in an organized event without even having read the featured book. We explore the pleasures to be experienced beyond rather than between the covers, as a book is mediated through a series of live activities, broadcast and staged entertainments, public spaces, and other people. Enthusiastic declarations such as "reading is the new rock n' roll" and "[One Book, One Chicago] gives our city props" are indicative of how some readers are emotionally invested in reading, and feel thrilled to share their love of it with others. The ideals, desires, and motivations of organizers, funders, and participants are an abiding concern of this book. Achieving a greater understanding of what such events mean to those involved in them contributes a human dimension to a critical picture of the meanings of shared reading in a digital age.

"SUPER-SIZING" SHARED READING: MASS READING EVENTS

In 2002, from our respective home bases in Canada and the United Kingdom, we began to notice the emergence of a "new" cultural formation of shared reading on both sides of the Atlantic. As researchers interested in popular culture, reading communities, cultural production, and mass media, we were intrigued by broadcast book programs such as the radio series *Canada Reads*, and by televised book clubs such as The Richard & Judy Book Club (RJBC) in the United Kingdom. The phenomenal success of Oprah's Book Club, the first series of which aired in 1996 on *The Oprah Winfrey Show*, was a direct inspiration for both shows, and also for the inception of the One Book, One Community (OBOC) model. Nancy Pearl and Chris Higashi, professional librarians working at the Center for the Book in Seattle, Washington, initiated the first citywide reading program of this type in 1998. As the name suggests, a book, often but not always a work of literary fiction, is selected as the focus for a series of activities in which the citizens of a community, city, region, or even nation, are invited to participate. Some activities such as book discussions assume that participants will read the book, but others, such as author events, craft workshops, and even campouts, canoe trips, and pub crawls, do not. Screenings of film adaptations, theatrical dramatizations, and staged readings of extracts from the books by professional actors or local celebrities are common to various iterations of the model. The opportunity to participate online is offered by most programs, but, in the mid- to late-2000s, when we were investigating events, the extent of interactivity was frequently limited by budget constraints. The OBOC model has been widely replicated and adapted, not only in the United States and Canada, but also in the United Kingdom, continental Europe, Singapore, and Australia. Although it is impossible to provide an exact figure, we estimate that more than 500 "One Book" programs take place annually around the world.[1] In the spring of 2010, OBOC even entered the "Twittersphere."

When we began to research OBOC, we were particularly fascinated by the ways that these twenty-first-century versions of shared reading took the concept of people reading and talking about a book, "super-sized" it (to borrow the term originally used by fast-food restaurant giant McDonald's to describe the option that increased the customer's portion size), and transported it into public places and spaces. Significantly, these spaces were not confined to those where the meanings of reading have traditionally been made within northern industrialized societies such as the US, Canada, and the UK—spaces such as public libraries, schools, and city halls. Whereas these locations were—and remain—common places to hold activities associated with citywide reading programs, work places such as offices, and leisure spaces such as pubs, ice rinks, and parks have also become temporary sites for shared book cultures. Sometimes these sites host activities such as singing, acting, making artwork, debating, or even eating a picnic or listening to a talk about Italian wine, none of which depends on anyone reading a book.

What, we wondered, was going on? Why did people come together for these events? What cultural meanings about books and reading were being promoted and negotiated by organizers and by participants? Who were these events for, whose interests did they serve, and were they capable of generating any kind of social change—as some organizers claimed that they could? These were among the questions that quickly sprang to mind as we identified more examples of initiatives for sharing reading. What we chose to reference through the use of the phrase, "mass reading event," is not only scale ("mass") and spectacle ("event"), but also the idea that an event promoting reading and the sharing of reading usually engages with one or more aspects of the mass media, whether in print, broadcast, or digital form. Two of the case studies that we subsequently chose to investigate depended on broadcast media for their primary delivery. The first of these, RJBC, forms the focus of Chapter 2, "Television," whereas the Canadian Broadcast Corporation's *Canada Reads* grounds our exploration of radio's suitability as a medium for shared reading in Chapter 3, "Radio."

Adaptable in terms of format, medium, and scale, OBOC is a model that appeals to different agencies with specific ideological agendas, as the case studies featured in Chapters 4 to 6 of this book reveal. A striking example is the adoption of the OBOC model by the National Endowment for the Arts (NEA) in the United States. In 2005, encouraged by the organization's Chairman Dana Gioia, employees at the NEA used the OBOC as a ready remedy for the "decline in literary reading in the US" (2004, vii) reported in their "Reading at Risk" study. As we explore in more depth in Chapter 4, "Money," press statements and publicity for the Big Read program (the umbrella term for the NEA's rollout of the model) make explicit links between being a reader of literary fiction and becoming a well-informed citizen. On the program's website, meanwhile, the sharing of ideas and experiences inspired by reading books is promoted as more culturally and socially valuable than sharing thoughts about television programs. Keen to steer Americans away from watercooler chat about *Desperate Housewives* and to make "classic" books such as *To Kill a Mockingbird* the focus of office banter instead, the NEA gave over 1,000 Big Read grants to communities in the US between 2006 and July 2012. The title of their 2009 report, "Reading on the Rise," suggests that the organizers of the Big Read believe that the "quick fix" worked. In a sense, the NEA has been using the OBOC model as a form of extramural learning or cultural uplift. Educational institutions, on the other hand, have adopted it to help new students feel part of a community. In both Canada and the US, and, more recently, in the UK, colleges and universities have employed the OBOC model as a means of inducting university freshmen into the sometimes bewildering experience of higher education (Fister 2011). Offering a new cohort of students an experience in common that involves reading a book may well provide some individuals with an original conversation opener, and thus smooth their way into forming new friendships. Beyond this social use, however, reading and discussing a book also aligns with the ideological premise of a liberal arts education to which the practices of reading and critical thinking are fundamental. In some instances, such as Western Reads in London, Ontario, OBOC was viewed by organizers as a means to extend a learning community beyond the campus, and to publicize the university's 125th anniversary.

Although there are far fewer annual Canadian and British versions of OBOC than American events, citywide reading programs have taken place in diversely located cities of different sizes. Some of these, for example, One Book, One Vancouver and One Book, One Kitchener-Waterloo-Cambridge in southern Ontario have been running annually and continuously since 2002. Even earlier than this, the Southern Ontario Library Association supported First Nations Communities Read throughout the province, beginning in 1999 (Fuller 2011, 9–10). In the United Kingdom, Liverpool Reads, and Bristol's Great Reading Adventure, the first two British versions of the model both began in 2003, and were followed by (among others) One Book, One Edinburgh, which began in 2007 after the city became the first UNESCO-designated City of Literature. Longevity is one measure of success, and the OBOC model has certainly lasted longer and traveled further than we initially expected. At the time of writing, adaptations continued to emerge close to our respective homes. A province-wide version for Nova Scotia was being planned by public librarians to coincide with Canadian Library Month in October 2012. Meanwhile, Transworld publishers "in partnership with the Reading Agency" in the United Kingdom, identified Birmingham public library services as their public sector partner for Big City Read (Birmingham City Council 2012). In an overtly commercial twist to the model, Big City Read featured S. J. Watson's novel *Before I Go to Sleep*, a Transworld publication. Of course, publishers nearly always benefit from MREs in terms of sales and publicity for their authors, as we explore in Chapter 4, "Money," but we believe that this is the first example of a publisher-led OBOC program. Transworld's partnership with the Reading Agency, an independent charity funded by a mixture of government-funded organizations and corporations, also indicates how the promotion of reading as a public good has been handed over to private agencies by the central government in the United Kingdom.

MREs may serve various ideological, social, and commercial purposes for a range of agencies, but they are not universally applauded. To return to our opening analogy with sports, in common with different teams, broadcast events such as *Canada Reads* and iterations of the OBOC model have their advocates and their detractors. For Hal Niedzviecki, a media commentator, *Canada Reads* is a dumbing-down of Canadian Literature and the "middle-browing" of the Canadian Broadcasting Corporation (CBC) (2002). Ditto for the United Kingdom's RJBC for books in general, according to writer Andrew O'Hagan, who accused the television book club of "over[selling] a reduced, unimaginative notion of what people's literary enjoyment might be" (quoted in Boztas 2008). Meanwhile, American professor of literature Harold Bloom, referring to the OBOC model, pronounced, with overt disgust: "I don't like these mass reading bees. It is rather like the idea that we are all going to pop out and eat Chicken McNuggets or something else horrid at once" (cited in Kirkpatrick 2002). Cheering for the opposition, the former Mayor of Chicago, Richard M. Daley, publicly championed his city's twice-yearly shared reading program as "cultivat[ing] a culture of reading and discussion by bringing our diverse city together around one great book. Reading great literature inspires us to think about ourselves, our environment and our relationships. Talking about great literature with friends, family and neighbors can add richness and depth to the experience of reading" (2002).

Rather like the fans of opposing teams, what these promoters and critics share is an unquestioned belief that the object of their strong opinions and focus of their passion is worthy of their time and emotion. What their comments also reveal is the persistence of the idea that books are a "special" kind of commodity (unlike Chicken McNuggets), and the assumption that reading them is good for you. The common ground among these commentators fractures along the fault line of taste with regard to their differing attitudes toward the iterations and adaptations of literary culture within contemporary popular culture. Not everyone, it seems, wants book reading, let alone shared or "mass" reading, to be the "new rock n' roll." Rowdy crowds of supporters having fun may be the dominant practice for popular music and sport, but, heaven forbid that reading should be openly enjoyed in public (in Bloom's case, at least, reading is clearly something that you should do alone and in private). Bloom's horror of homogenization, of everybody reading the same mass-produced book "at once" (cited in Kirkpatrick 2002), echoes a much older debate about the polluting effects of commerce on culture, and even an anxiety about "the masses" themselves (Carey 1992; Brantlinger 1998). A suspicion of blatant commercialization and commodification also inflects Andrew O'Hagan's telling remarks about RJBC. Combine the hard-sell with the popular genre of the daytime magazine show, and you inevitably promote a limited version of reading pleasure, lacking in reflection and literary sophistication—so the logic of O'Hagan's comments would seem to suggest. Made in the context of the high-profile and high-culture environment of the Edinburgh Book Festival, his response also speaks to the media hierarchies that still structure dominant notions about cultural consumption and taste in the UK. Within this hierarchy, watching television is below reading a book or going to the cinema, a play, or a concert; "lifestyle" television is a lowbrow genre bereft of intellectual content. At least, it is for some of those who, like O'Hagan, Bloom, and Niedzviecki have a professional investment in the business of evaluating books. Their role as cultural arbiters of literary taste is not of much account for many nonprofessional readers who have developed their own methods for determining which books to buy, borrow, read, and share.

Nonetheless, the vehemence with which these detractors write is itself an indication that MREs are worth investigating. When a cultural formation, event, or artifact provokes dramatically different responses, closer examination can tease out the ideological investments, cultural anxieties, and power relations that inflect those opinions. The academy, newspaper reviewers, and media institutions, such as the CBC and BBC, no longer wield as much cultural authority as they did before the media landscape and its audiences digitized, fragmented, and segmented. MREs cut across that contemporary media context in practical terms, borrowing from both well-established and new media. Organizers and producers are well aware of the coextensive nature of the codex with more recent technologies. In other words, they know that for many people, the printed book has not yet been replaced by its digital version, or by mobile devices such as the e-reader, but exists alongside them, just as other types of online content expand the opportunities for a user to engage, sometimes interactively, with information in a variety of formats. More than this, digital media, such as radio and television, can be used to create dynamic relations among print and nonprint media. Hence, event producers employ formats and stage activities that will appeal to confirmed readers, but also try new ways of engaging people who are not already into the book-reading and -sharing habit. For these reasons alone, then, MREs need a closer examination. As we argue throughout this book, they are a product of their time, not only in terms of their organization, delivery, and reception, but also in terms of their emergence within nation-states where the neoliberal political climate underscores the civic, social, and economic function of public culture and the arts. Rather like sports teams, city governments often hope that MREs will attract out-of-town visitors and generate revenue as well as give their cities "props," as the enthusiastic young Chicagoan exclaimed.

Our comparison of shared reading and sport, although intended to have a defamiliarizing effect, is more resonant than it might at first appear. MREs, as Mayor Daley's comments demonstrate, are frequently promoted as a means to create community by bringing people together to read a selected book (or series of books). Similarly, sporting events are often credited with the capacity to create imagined community on local or national levels. Soccer, baseball, and hockey are games that invoke powerful emotions in those that follow them, and each sport is inscribed with culturally specific ideas about masculinity, class, physical strength, and the virtues of being a team-player. These values persist whereas more girls and women are involved at both amateur and professional levels than ever before, even in the face of the commercialization and corporatization of professional major league sports, processes that have made transfer fees and billionaire club owners lead media stories. In common with soccer, hockey, and baseball, specific kinds of reading such as the reading of fictional genres, and particular practices, such as the sharing of reading among groups of people, are frequently coded in gendered terms as feminine pursuits regardless of who actually engages in them. Commercialization and corporate convergence likewise play a role in terms of which books reach readers, with a small handful of writers receiving substantial and widely reported advances from publishers, rather like star sportsmen. In the first decade of the twenty-first century, stories about the buying and selling of players and clubs migrated from the sports pages of newspapers to the business pages, appearing alongside reports about the runaway sales resulting from television book clubs such as Oprah's Book Club in the US and the RJBC in the UK.

There is another aspect of the industrial-scale and mass-mediated production of sports and reading events that makes the analogy worth pursuing just a little bit further. In North America and the United Kingdom, many followers of major league sports are prevented from attending games in person because of exorbitantly high ticket prices, so television, radio, and the Internet offer access to the "live" event, and bars and living rooms are among the sites where enthusiasts gather to share their passion for sport. Similarly, different media have prompted readers to find new venues for sharing reading—online through blogs, virtual book clubs, reading challenges, and LibraryThing, as well as continuing with older forms of sharing, such as face-to-face book clubs, some of which also take place in bars and living rooms. The analogy breaks down somewhat because readers do not have to buy books in order to read—they can borrow them from libraries or download out-of-copyright titles for free. But both of these activities presume access to resources: either to a public library system or to a broadband connection. Although, unlike major league sports games, many citywide reading events are free to attend, watch or visit, they all assume some economic means are available to potential participants who have to travel to a venue. Despite the differences in the economics and the size of audience for "live" events, sports and mass reading require their followers to have recourse to some money. Who can participate in these leisure events can also depend on the possession of other cultural assets, such as print literacy in the case of reading.

Beyond entertainment, serious benefits are believed to accrue from being involved in sports and reading, and the cultural reproduction of these beliefs occurs at home, in school, and in the mass media. Many people encourage their children to play sports because they believe they will learn about cooperation, commitment, and competition, while (hopefully) having fun and keeping physically fit. Even when there is no money for equipment, it is possible to play versions of all three games with a little creativity, some ice, a patch of ground, or an empty street. Such adaptations sometimes fuel their own mythologies about the sporting hero whose talent took him or her from the street (or frozen pond) to wealth, and then the Hall of Fame. There is an equally compelling history of book reading as a form of class mobility and of liberation from gender and race oppression for individuals and for groups: those histories, like their sporting versions, underpin dominant cultural norms about the value of these pursuits.

THE STRUCTURE OF THIS BOOK

We explore aspects of the history of reading in the introductory chapter as part of our explanation for how and why we conceptualize shared reading as a social practice. But we begin by examining the material and ideological contexts within which MREs occur through a consideration of the ways that reading has become part of popular literary culture in a digital age. We introduce our concept of "the reading industry" and outline the evolution of MRE models, paying particular attention to the aims and desires of the event organizers and media producers who developed them. We then go on to situate our study of mass reading events within a series of intellectual contexts that foreground our methodological priorities as feminist scholars, and as researchers of nonacademic reading cultures. The scope of our primary research, an account of our methods, a brief profile of the readers whom we encountered as a result of these methods, and our engagement with notions of taste and cultural capital form the final section of our introduction.

Our consideration of shared reading includes a discussion of literary culture as a form of popular culture, histories of shared reading, feminist analyses of contemporary readers, and theories of reading and readers. We deliberately move among the conceptual frameworks of our analysis, and the ideological and material concerns of our investigation. In doing so, we hope to render visible the parameters of our empirical study alongside our own intellectual and personal investment in the research and analyses of contemporary cultures of shared reading. We were—and are—thoroughly interested in why and how people share reading. We are both "interested" in the Bourdieusian sense of the professional benefits and symbolic profit to be gained from our work (1993), but we are also interested because books and reading have shaped the contours and values of our own lives. If we had not ourselves experienced versions of the "passion for reading" and for sharing reading that many of the readers and event producers we met articulated, then it is doubtful that we would have had the energy or desire to undertake a transnational study on such a large scale.

The following chapters review the component parts—the agents, institutions, individuals, ideologies, economics, and practicalities—that together produce MREs. Each chapter draws upon the case studies that we undertook as part of our original research project, "Beyond the Book: Mass Reading Events and Contemporary Cultures of Reading." We make some comparisons within and across various media and models while also situating each event within its cultural and local situation: both strategies tease out the various meanings attached to shared reading within the contemporary cultures of the UK, Canada, and the US. The five chapters following the introduction each detail a key element within the production and reception of MREs. In Chapter 2, "Television," we consider how television mediates the experience of shared reading in our analysis of the RJBC. We examine how the daytime television book club disrupted the ideological assumptions of reading as a high-culture activity but produced a mixed reaction from readers regarding its popular format and democratizing messages about who could be a reader. We then move to a consideration of a medium that has a much longer association with books and reading than television in Chapter 3, "Radio." The CBC's annual series, *Canada Reads*, provides a focus for our exploration of radio book programming. With its overtly nationalist project of selecting a book for "all Canadians to read," the show frames shared reading in terms of specific ideas and ideals of Canadian identity that appeal to some listeners, but appall others as reductive and oversimplified versions of what it means to be a citizen of a multicultural and multilingual nation-state. In common with television book clubs such as those featured on *The Oprah Winfrey Show*, and RJBC, the producers of *Canada Reads* have successfully exploited the communication strategies of the show's primary medium of delivery while experimenting with other media platforms—with varying degrees of success.

What is without dispute is that both the RJBC and *Canada Reads* increased book sales, thus creating their own versions of the "Oprah Effect." In Chapter 4, "Money," book sales and the economic organization of the contemporary book publishing industry are among a number of factors and agents that we examine in our exploration of the relationship between the economic and ideological imperatives that inform MRE production. We consider aspects of cultural policy in the three nation-states of our study and illustrate the ways that cultural policies shape funding priorities and funders' notions of what cultural activities—in particular shared-reading programs adopting the OBOC model—are expected to achieve. The labor and creative work of the event organizers charged with the task of producing events comes under scrutiny in Chapter 5, "Worker." As cultural intermediaries, these cultural workers manage institutional expectations about shared-reading programs while also bringing their own "passion for reading" to bear on the style and staging of events. Taking that passion seriously, we examine the ideological, physical, and emotional labor that they perform, and assess its costs and benefits. Cultural workers are also readers, of course, but, in Chapter 6, "Reader," we focus on those nonprofessional readers who take part in the different activities that constitute an MRE. Focusing on specific case studies of the OBOC model as it occurred in several different locations, we explore the meanings and value that readers derive from shared reading when it is mediated through various kinds of activity and "live" events. Attending to readers' commentaries about their participation, we analyze the different notions of community constructed and experienced through events, and reach a more nuanced understanding of the ways that feelings of intimacy, "belonging," and social connection are significant to some readers. Finally, in Chapter 7, "Book," we reinstate a material object that our previous concentration on different media and the organizational agents has placed into the background: the book. As part of our conclusions to the meanings of reading in a digital age, we reconceptualize the book as a social artifact and as a cultural mediator.

As we argue throughout this book, the notion of a community reading a book together plays into a range of contemporary desires and anxieties in an extremely powerful way, in particular, concerns about cohesive community, levels of educational achievement, the globalized economy, technological change, and the loss of print-based skills (and the cultural capital associated with book culture knowledge) in a digital age. Subsequently, shared-reading programs are often overladen with expectations, including hope that they can effect social transformation such as improving literacy and cross-cultural understanding. But, as we have indicated in this introduction, these tensions, cultural anxieties, and competing political agenda are part of what makes the study of large-scale reading events worthwhile. In the early twenty-first century, a feeling for reading books, feelings about books, and a desire to share reading with others provoked a range of conflicted but creative responses—as the following chapters reveal.

P.2 Readers Guide for Seattle Reads *The Namesake* by Jhumpa Lahiri

Reader's Guide for the 2007 season of Seattle Reads featuring *The Namesake* by Jhumpa Lahiri

Source: Beyond the Book project: Artefacts and Ephemera, available at: http://epapers.bham. ac.uk/1469/

1 Reading

When Mary Worrall, a Reader Advisory librarian from Solihull in the United Kingdom declared that "reading is the new rock n' roll" at a Readers' Day held in Birmingham in 2003, she expressed the excitement that many members of her profession, and keen readers, felt about the situation of book reading in the early twenty-first century. Suddenly, it seemed, reading was fun and sharing books with others was in vogue. Books and book clubs certainly appeared to be everywhere, or, at least, they were represented in places other than just branch libraries, bookstores, and people's homes. Supermarkets and newsagents sold books alongside groceries. The Starbucks chain of coffee shops hosted book clubs across the US, whereas in the UK shelves of books that could be borrowed or swapped started appearing in pubs, doctor's offices, and home hardware stores. These shelves were often stocked by groups of readers who had come to know each other in person because of their involvement in the practices associated with BookCrossing. By registering a book on the BookCrossing website, downloading and attaching to it a label showing a unique identification number, and then "releasing" that book into the public domain, a BookCrosser could track the journey of a specific book through several readers' hands and sometimes across considerable geographic distances. Additionally, online forums within the BookCrossing website enabled readers to share reading suggestions, and to interact socially both on- and off-line. Even as the corporate world jumped on the book club bandwagon, eager readers continued to find innovative means of sharing their love of an activity that has often attracted denigrating labels to its enthusiasts, such as a "book worm." Whereas some journalists continued to scorn book clubs and the readers who joined them, the media outlets they worked for were using them to sell newspapers or keep listeners tuning in and visiting their websites. By adapting the book club format, the mass media of television, radio and newspapers substantially increased the visibility of shared reading as a cultural activity.

Meanwhile, the adaptation of literary best sellers and prize-winning books for the screen, while not a new practice, became more lucrative for production companies, literary agents, and—in some cases—authors (Collins 2010; S. Murray 2011). In addition to face-to-face, online, and mass-mediated book clubs, readers could access "literary experiences" in various nonprint media through cinema-going, by visiting book festivals, or attending One Book, One Community (OBOC) activities. All of these bookish encounters occurred outside the academy, which, as Jim Collins convincingly demonstrates, was no longer viewed by nonprofessional readers as a source of expertise about which books to read and how to read them. Instead, new media authorities such as Oprah helped to legitimate the "personal reading" strategies already pursued by many readers within book clubs (2010, 44). Literary culture had become part of popular culture in terms of its cross-media presence and in terms of the reading practices advocated by readers from media stars to amateur book reviewers posting online. Reading may not have acquired the subversive or counter-cultural appeal of rock n' roll by the first decade of the twenty-first century, but it certainly seemed to have shed its popular image as a serious, solitary, and academic pursuit.

Reading was also on-trend in the sense that at least some of its practitioners kept pace with online media practices that enabled them to share reading via blogs (Pedersen 2008), fan sites (Skains 2010), customer reviews (Steiner 2008), virtual communities (Pinder 2012; Rehberg Sedo 2003, 2011b), and social media such as Facebook and Twitter (Gruzd and Rehberg Sedo 2012; Lang 2012). As the decade progressed, new digital devices such as e-readers, tablets, and smartphones enabled those readers who could afford them almost instant access to books. Far from disappearing, as some late twentieth-century doomsayers, such as Sven Birkets (1996), had predicted, the book was (at least partially) remediated, the codex remained a significant material form for many people, and more books were published in North America and the UK than ever before (see Chapter 4, "Money"). Certainly, the "late age of print"—to coin Ted Striphas's (2009) phrase—operated differently for both producers and consumers of books than it did in earlier periods of the twentieth century. The ability to reproduce content across multiple media platforms, and the facility of the largest publishing and media companies to pour millions of dollars into the branding and marketing of select lead titles contributed significantly to the outstanding success of some books, most famously the *Harry Potter* and *Twilight* series (Larsson and Steiner 2011; Striphas 2009, 141–74). Strategic marketing campaigns also played a role in the creation of several "cross-over" best sellers that found both an adult and a younger audience of readers. These included Mark Haddon's *The Curious Incident of the Dog in the Night-Time* (2003), and the Potter series, all of which were published in "adult" and "teen" editions (Beckett 2009; Falconer 2009 Siebert 2011; Squires 2007, 147–75). The scale of popularity of these books suggests that, for a sizeable portion of younger people, reading was not entirely uncool. Perhaps only a minority of such readers, however, would proudly declare themselves to be "book geeks"—even to researchers investigating reading events. Members of the Teen Book Club at the Kenwood Academy High School on the south side of Chicago were enthusiastic participants in the city's OBOC

Chicago program, treasured the books they were given as part of the city's Teen Book Club network, showed great skill at running a book discussion, but told us that they had, nonetheless, to defend their hobby against the occasional taunts of classmates. Reading, especially the reading of fiction, may have become a part of popular culture, but the older cultural values that are attached to it appear to be in tension with its more recent cultural forms.

Mass reading events (MREs) are one of these forms and part of a popular literary cultural arena that positively bristles with various media practices, technologies, and opportunities to interact with other readers. Like all cultural producers, those involved in the design and delivery of large-scale shared reading events have to compete for their audience with many other cultural activities, entertainment options, and leisure pursuits. As will become clear as our chapters unfold, the quest for audience share is driven by both economic factors and struggles over symbolic capital. From the inception of our study, we have been intrigued by the ways that the various agents involved in MREs (including readers, event organizers, publishers, media producers, government representatives, arts organizations) promote, contest, and negotiate the value of shared reading. At the same time, our past professional lives in communications, marketing research, and book publishing, and studies of cultural and media industries produced by book historians and cultural studies scholars, made us keenly aware of the need to take commercial concerns and the influence of cultural policy into account. Meanwhile, structural changes in the cultural and media industries have transformed the field of literary production so that Pierre Bourdieu's (1993) model of restricted and large-scale production no longer adequately conceptualizes how books are made and how literary value is brokered. In order to situate MREs within the contemporary literary cultural fields of the twenty-first century, therefore, we need to reframe the terrain. Our notion of the reading industry enables us to make better sense of contemporary cultures of leisure reading in general, and of MREs in particular. We therefore follow our explication of the reading industry below by mapping the evolution of large-scale reading events within the context of popular reading culture. Our discussion then turns to our conceptualization of shared reading as a social practice, and the methodologies and methods that we used to investigate a specific iteration of that practice: MREs.

FROM THE LITERARY FIELD TO THE READING INDUSTRY

Throughout *Reading Beyond the Book*, our analyses are indebted to Pierre Bourdieu's theories, and to the scholarship that has updated, complicated, and problematized the insights and methods of his original studies into cultural production and consumption. As our brief discussion of our own methods later in this chapter and, more explicitly, in the Methods Appendix, make clear, we did not set out to investigate the logics of a particular field or to replicate Bourdieu's actual methods. However, one aspect of Bourdieu's (1993) theory of the field of cultural production that remains conceptually compelling in the context of our study and of contemporary media production is his formulation of the literary field as "a space of literary or artistic position-takings" by "social agents" (30). Whereas these social agents (individuals, institutions, groups) can exercise some agency in terms of decision-making, their actions and position-taking occur within the context of a structured set of economic, political, and social relations (23–73). Although this description appears to constitute a system, Bourdieu is careful to make a distinction between his method of analysis, which requires him to delimit the object of enquiry, and his notion of the system as "the product and prize of a permanent conflict" (34). It is, as he argues forcefully in *The Field of Cultural Production*, the "struggle" that is "the unifying principle of this 'system' . . . with all the contradictions it engenders" (ibid.). In other words, alliances may be formed between agents but these are tactical arrangements in a competition for varying degrees of economic profit and cultural status. Whereas relations of power derived from economic or symbolic capital can be realigned by the actions of agents, their interests drive the conflict. Key to our analysis in *Reading Beyond the Book* is our effort to understand the interests of the agents who create and participate in MREs.

However, as our opening image of reading as "the new rock n' roll" intimates, twenty-first-century popular literary culture and contemporary practices of leisure reading are not easily locatable within one field of production or consumption. Moreover, there are several complications that arise from the reality that, increasingly, fields of cultural production intersect. In her study of the literary "adaptation industry," for example, Simone Murray (2011) offers an incisive analysis of the transactions among multiple agents operating within the fields of film and literary production. Although films that adapt literary texts are trading on the cultural value of prestige markers such as literary prizes in order to target the "well-educated and affluent urban" audience demographic who bought the book (167), these same connotations of cultural esteem can have a huge commercial impact. That is, whereas at first glance the marketing and branding of arts-house films such as *The Reader* (2008) seem to locate them within a restricted mode of production, they can end up capturing a sizeable box-office (169–84). At the same time, the media industries keep "cultural hierarchies . . . alive" by, on the one hand, "push[ing] audiences to consume near-identical content across multiple media platforms" and on the other, "by constantly reiterating a filmmaker's respect for a content property's prizewinning literary pedigree" (18). Playing at both ends of the field, as it were, is a paradoxical but increasingly common practice for the producers of contemporary literary experiences.

Intersecting fields of production also complicate critical attempts to delimit where one field begins and another ends. Television and books offer another convincing illustration of this situation. Far more agents are hustling for profit and shaping notions of cultural value within the field of contemporary English-language literary production than Bourdieu could envisage given his own temporal and geographic location, as David Wright (2007) observes in his critique of the British Broadcasting Corporation's 2003 television series *The Big Read*. It is not simply a matter of producers of television book clubs and book-focused programming influencing the sales of featured books, or blurring the boundaries of literary and popular books by championing eclectic lists. Rather, production companies, media giants such as Oprah Winfrey, and even nationally recognized television personalities, from gardeners to cooks, are able to wield "metacapital" (symbolic capital accrued in non-literary fields) that mediates positions and the organization of social space in the literary field (Wright 2007, 10). A further complication to the dynamics of the literary field is produced through the many "assemblages and linkages" forged by producers of mass-mediated events such as the BBC's *The Big Read* with a variety of institutions within and outside the book industry (Wright 2007, 4). Our own research concurs with Wright's: the relationships among for-profit organizations, and agencies with policy interests in libraries, schools, and "cultural" provision for local communities, "are emblematic of a particular orientation to the production of culture from policy-makers, a belief that 'culture' can do civic work and contribute to social goods" (5, see our Chapter 4, "Money"). Iterations of the OBOC model tend to adopt this orientation more explicitly than broadcast MREs, as our analysis of the National Endowment for the Art's Big Read program illustrates. Contemporary literary production is thus shaped by cultural policy discourse as well as the organization of media corporations and interlocking fields of cultural production. In order to represent this early twenty-first configuration of book production, we have adopted the term "the reading industry." More than a descriptor, it is also an effort on our part to move on from the anachronistic aspects of Bourdieu's ([1979] 1984, 1993) analysis, such as restricted and large-scale production.

For our purposes, the reading industry is primarily a useful conceptual framework that enables us to focus on the various agents and agencies that produce MREs. In this book, we examine the relations among them, paying particular attention to the kinds of power that various organizations and individuals possess and deploy. In an important sense, the reading industry is our way of giving a name to the various social and economic structures that together produce contemporary cultures of reading. However, the reading industry is not simply an abstraction. In other words, although it cannot be identified as one coherent material entity, its working parts are visible. For us, the reading industry refers to the organizations, institutions, and businesses that produce a series of cultural artifacts and events. Our choice of terminology is deliberate. "Industry" connotes the production of material goods for profit, large-scale manufacture, and the presence of a market. It also suggests that labor and capital are required for the industry to function. But when we think about the ways that money is dispersed across the organizations that make up the reading industry, it is clear that we are not only referring to activity in the private sector. That said, we consider the reading industry to include for-profit organizations such as book publishing and book-selling. But it also includes not-for-profit agencies, such as public library systems funded by the state and arts organizations, many of which are financed by a combination of private and public monies. So, the reading industry's primary product is not books (they are the primary product of the book publishing and retail industries) but the artifacts, programming, events, and literary adaptations that represent books (both fiction and non-fiction). The "market," or target audience for these products, are ordinary, or, nonprofessional, readers.

An important resonance that we want to convey through this notion of "the reading industry" is the specificity of its temporal situation. By using a new term we want to register the "here-and-now," contemporary aspect of the forces that constitute and circulate reading cultures. The reading industry has emerged in part from the late-twentieth-century/early twenty-first-century formation of the entertainment industry, itself a conglomeration of media organizations and companies, that produces a variety of publications and events across a range of platforms (Collins 2010, 1–35; Murray and Weedon 2011). The reading industry's "business" is to make leisure reading entertaining and to do so using any of the delivery methods, formats, and sites (both physical and virtual) that contemporary and older forms of media technology and communications enable. Unlike the directors and producers of the entertainment industry, many of the reading industry's producers and managers are not working for commercial companies, and so profit margins are not always their primary concern. Nonetheless, as we explore in Chapter 4, "Money," securing funds, brokering deals with for-profit organizations, and accounting for money spent in terms of audience participation, artifacts distributed, and media visibility form a central part of their "business." As we argue in Chapter 4, "Money," commercial profit coordinates with neoliberal cultural policies in the funding of MREs, specifically those that adapt the OBOC model. Along with the economic configuration of the entertainment industry, then, neoliberal cultural policies provide an important context for the emergence of the reading industry in the three nation-states of our study.

Our analysis of the production, circulation, and reception of MREs in this book is thus informed by our desire to interrogate the social and material relations among the reading industry's agents and agencies. Our original research investigation examined the institutions and the individuals who fund, organize, and participate in these shared reading events. Only by disaggregating the constituent processes that produce this cultural formation while attending to the economic, ideological, and social contexts of its proliferation could we approach what we felt would be a sufficiently multilayered appreciation of its function. The organization of this book into chapters, focused on two forms of mass media (television and radio), money, workers, and readers, allows us to consider the platforms, processes, and people involved in MREs. Approaching our subject in this way also enables us to make connections between case studies occurring in diverse locations, while also maintaining a sense of their cultural, political, and historical specificity.

Fun, and Other Reasons to Share Reading with Strangers: A Brief History of a Model

What all the events in our study have in common is an unquestioned acceptance by those producing and managing them of the idea that reading and sharing books is a worthwhile pursuit. None of the events that we analyzed were designed to test whether sharing reading was preferable or more appealing to people than other types of leisure practices that can be shared, such as gaming, for example. Rather, driven by their own "passion for reading," their professional involvement in the reading industry, and, sometimes by commercial goals, producers of events implicitly reconfirm the cultural legitimacy of reading and sharing books by making these practices center stage. The MREs that they create and deliver may vary in size, scale, medium, and degree of spectacle, but, as our analyses in this book reveal, the messages that are communicated to the public about shared reading through publicity, support materials such as reading guides and online resources, the event frames, and the activities that constitute the events themselves are inflected by historically persistent ideas about the socially transformative and civilizing effects of book reading. To varying degrees and with different emphases, MREs engage with these ideas, while promoting a third: the sharing of reading is pleasurable, fun and entertaining. In an important sense, then, it is the style of MREs, and their situation within what Elizabeth Long calls a "new matrix of mass communication," rather than their aims and ideals that are new (2003, 217). That said, as we argue throughout this book, the meanings of shared reading in the twenty-first century are imbricated with imperatives that are specific to this era, and inflected by the locations (in terms of space and place) where MREs unfold.

Whereas some event organizers may hope to create social change through programs that contextualize, historicize, and explore complex issues, many, such as Nan Alleman, the first director of OBOC Chicago, are pragmatic in their aims. As a professional librarian with a strong public service ethic, Alleman remarked in an interview with us that her main goal for the twice-yearly program was to publicize the work of Chicago Public Library as "fun and intriguing" (pers. comm., 2005). She also noted, on several occasions, the influence of the Mayor's office as the reason why the program runs twice a year (pers. comm., 2004). Indeed, in 2005, the beginning of the Fall run of OBOC was delayed because Richard M. Daley, then Mayor of Chicago, had to appear in front of a federal grand jury that was investing allegations of corruption over job hiring practices in the city. The overt association of the city-wide read with the Mayor's focus on increasing literacy, and the necessity of waiting for the indicted Mayor himself to launch the selected book (ironically, it was Jane Austen's *Pride and Prejudice*), signpost the ways that publicly funded reading programs can be framed by institutions and powerful political individuals as civic projects. That does not mean, however, that other agents involved in them, including participants, understand MREs as civilizing in their effects. Other hopes, desires, and goals centered on other meanings of reading can also be realized or explored— as we examine through our case studies. MREs are employed by different reading industry agents with sometimes apparently divergent aims and different forms of investment in the process and its outcomes. It is the tension between these forms of investment, or "interestedness" to use Bourdieu's (1993) term, that propelled our original research investigations and that tension informs our analyses throughout this book. What becomes clear, as we scrutinize the component organizational parts of MREs in the following chapters, are the ways in which this contemporary iteration of shared reading becomes overcharged with desires: from utopian dreams of democratizing access to reading and connecting cultural groups to each other, to functionalist goals about increasing print literacy.

It is worth reflecting further on the evolution of the OBOC model, because it directly influenced all the examples of shared reading that we explore through our case studies. In 1998, when Seattle librarians Nancy Pearl and Chris Higashi first tried out their idea for a city-wide reading event focused on one book, they were responding to a local enthusiasm for shared reading in the city's many book groups. Undoubtedly, the growing success of Oprah's Book Club, which first broadcast in 1996, was an encouraging sign that there was an appetite among readers to share books and reading on a larger scale than a conventional book group. But, as we explore in more depth in Chapter 5, "Worker," the initial motivations inspiring Pearl and Higashi included a pragmatic and modest aim: to use shared reading to connect Seattle's book club readers to each other. Because both women were public librarians responsible for creating reader-centered programs at the Seattle Library, and both had considerable experience as leaders of book discussions, developing an event program that could create a network among existing groups while offering opportunities for others to participate made professional sense. This is one reason why their OBOC model was so attractive to their colleagues when they spoke about If All of Seattle Read the Same Book . . . (as it was originally called) at American Library Association (ALA) conferences—sometimes alongside Nan Alleman. By 2002, a "how-to" pack had been produced by the ALA and was being sold online, and a One Book, One Conference version ran as part of the combined American and Canadian Library Association annual meeting held in Toronto in 2003.

The format appealed to library professionals because it was very flexible in terms of the types of activities that it could include: from book discussions, to pub crawls, to craft workshops and public lectures and film screenings, or indeed any activity that tied in to the context or content of the selected book. Crucially, the scale of the programming could be adjusted depending on available funds, staff resource, and facilities. Ideologically, the model coincided with the "outreach" ideals and practices of professional librarianship that have for decades brought books and information services to patrons outside of library walls and institutional sites via book mobile services, for instance (Knight 2004; Pawley 2007). Further, as a model that expanded a reading practice and social formation (the book group) often perceived to be pursued for social as well as intellectual reasons by women, it is probable that many public librarians in the US and Canada, and shortly thereafter in the UK, could envisage a core audience of participants who would make it viable in their own community, city, or region. In advancing the model, they were themselves performing labor that could be conceived of as gendered. As historians of libraries and librarianship have demonstrated, women in the late-nineteenth-century US were viewed as acceptable "cultural guardians" and thus well-suited to the job of public librarian (Eddy 2003, 159). The ALA itself was among the professional bodies that adopted gendered rhetoric to rapidly advance university training for female librarians and as a way of enhancing the status of the public library between 1880 and 1920. Historical analyses of libraries and library workers remind us that the number of women working in the sector of public service librarianship in all three countries steadily increased from the late nineteenth century onward (Eddy 2003; McNally 2004, 287; Valentine 1992, 198–200; Van Slyck 1995, 160–73). Many of the library workers and managers in our study are grappling with ideological tensions and institutional imperatives that have a gendered history.

Outside the professional networks and publications of public librarians, the word about OBOC spread via the mass media. Journalist Patrick Reardon wrote a feature article about the Seattle program for the *Chicago Tribune* that Nan Alleman remembers as a significant influence on the decision to employ the model in Chicago (pers. comm., 2004). Meanwhile, the much vaunted failure of New York City organizers to settle on a book choice (e.g., Burkeman 2002; Haberman 2002) gave almost as much publicity to OBOC as the expansive newspaper, television, and radio coverage given to Chicago's first version of the model in October 2001. In "the city that works" (a phrase replete with double meanings about local politics), OBOC was efficiently branded, marketed, and lent the imprimatur of the mayor. Thus, it was Chicago, the former second city, and still the third largest city in terms of population in the US, and not the left-leaning West coast city of Seattle, that caught the attention of reading industry agents north of the border and across the Atlantic. In an interview with us, Mike Poole, the producer of the British Broadcasting Corporation's *The Big Read*, a televised search for the nation's one hundred favorite books, told us that he happened to be in Chicago during October 2001 and saw the local advertising and mass-media reports (pers. comm., 2005). Similarly, the initiators of Bristol's Great Reading Adventure (see Figure 1.1) were also on vacation in Chicago during

Figure 1.1 Flyer for The Great Reading Adventure

The One Book, One Community model traveled from the US to the UK. In both nation-states, organizers attempt to attract readers by using popular culture icons. In the case of Bristol's 2006 Great Reading Adventure, Aardman Animations' characters Wallace and Gromit share the spotlight with Jules Verne's classic novel *Around the World in Eighty Days*.

Source: Beyond the Book project: Artefacts and Ephemera, available at: http://epapers.bham. ac.uk/1469/ Image titled Flyer The Great Reading Adventure

the first OBOC in the city and inspired to take up the model in the UK (M. Kelly, pers. comm., 2005). Although public librarians continued to play an important part in the proliferation and delivery of the model in these three nation-states, and, subsequently, in other regions of the world, other reading industry agents and affiliated organizations began to reconfigure the model through mass-media and local adaptations.

As it traveled, the model accrued different goals and ideals, which were foregrounded by organizers. As we explore in Chapter 5, "Worker," it caught the imagination of Jane Davis, self-styled "Reading Revolutionary" (2009), because of her commitment to a democratic vision of shared reading, and her conviction that literature is for living. In Bristol, by contrast, the model fit a local government-oriented agenda to promote the city as a creative and cultural hub (see Chapter 4, "Money"). Whether the agenda of organizers was to "build community through reading," as one Canadian organizer expressed it (T. Siemens, pers. comm., 2003), or to create a better-cultivated citizenry, as the rhetoric of the National Endowment of the Arts Big Read program framed it, OBOC could be pressed into service. It is, as this brief history makes clear, a model that can be adapted—or co-opted—to express ideologies of reading as liberating or as civilizing. As Wendy Griswold has noted:

> "One Book" programs have proven to be irresistible, for they tap into readers' desires for intelligent discussions, libraries' desires to increase visibility in the community, and mayors' desires to associate their cities with the prestige of literature. (2008, 58)

But these are not the only desires that MREs satisfy. By the mid-2000s, Chris Higashi envisaged Seattle Reads as a means of cross-cultural connection among different communities in the city (see Chapter 5, "Worker"). If the OBOC model was being made by some local governments to do their ideological (and neoliberal) work at a lesser cost to their budget than the social and cultural programming that they were cutting, then it was also being employed by others, like Higashi, to advance a more transformative discourse about shared reading.

If this brief history of the evolution and serial adaption of the OBOC model in various locations suggests how powerfully it reproduces the cultural legitimacy of book reading, it does not account for the passion that all organizers of MREs—including the mass-mediated broadcast versions— expressed to us about books and the sharing of books. For all of her savvy as a television producer, the woman behind The Richard & Judy Book Club (RJBC), Amanda Ross, described herself to us as a keen reader who was bewildered by the amount of books available (pers. comm., 2006). Certainly, as a media professional she was looking to add a repeat feature to a magazine-style daytime show in order to increase audience share (ibid.). But the broadcast book club was partly inspired by her experiences of trying to make last-minute choices in a bookstore before going on summer vacation. Sitting in an office full of books and posters advertising the Book Club, but with few signs of her career in television, Amanda Ross looked more like a publisher or editor when we interviewed her. Like Talin Vartanian, the producer of *Canada Reads*, who told us, "I'm not a literary maven" (pers. comm., 2003), Amanda Ross does not claim to be a literary-cultural authority, but she loves books, and understood how to make them work in a nonprint medium. In Ross's words: "if a book is entertaining to read, it's going to make entertaining TV, and vice versa, so that is the key—the key is to make sure the book's entertaining in the first place and then you're home and dry. It's gonna work" (ibid.). In common with all MREs, regardless of how much celebrity sparkle and multimedia interactivity the organizers can afford to produce, making shared reading fun and pleasurable is, it seems, "the key."

Reading as Popular Culture?

Making entertaining television and radio programming focused on books requires considerable skill and imagination, as we demonstrate in Chapters 2 and 3, "Television" and "Radio." Success is never guaranteed. The audience share for broadcast events, and the numbers of participants who take part in OBOC activities, are small in comparison to those for other forms of entertainment. As a leisure activity, book reading and shared reading are not pursued by "masses" of people when compared to playing sport, for example (Bennett et al. 2009, 94). Sales of featured books, especially those from broadcast events that usually carried stickers and were often prominently displayed in stores (and libraries) alongside colorful advertising posters or in branded book containers, appeared to tell a more spectacular story about popularity, however. British journalists were generally in a state of jaw-dropping awe at the capacity of the RJBC to make best sellers of many titles that were selected (e.g., K. Allen 2009; Dugdale 2006; Farndale 2007; McQueen 2006). But, as Jenni Ramone's (2011) interview with Andrew Smith, author of one of the 2006 choices *Moondust* indicates, at least some of the club's books sold at levels predicted by their publishers prior to their selection for the show (179). Rather, Smith's publishers noted that the paperback of his book sold much faster than it would otherwise have done had it not been selected for the RJBC.

In this instance, partnerships among members of the reading industry—a television book club, its corporate sponsors (a confectionary company), publishers, libraries, and high-street retailers—intensified the commercial process. The reading industry produced a high-visibility, multiplatform campaign that had what we might call a Formula One effect: there was a great deal of (media) noise and high-speed (selling), but not all contenders made it over the finish line in terms of increased *volume* of sales. The Formula One effect also applies to citywide reading events. Sales of the featured books increase for the few months when programming and publicity is at its most intense according to booksellers and publishers whom we interviewed (e.g.,

D. Gibson, pers. comm., 2003; K. Schwarz, pers. comm., 2004; T. Siemens, pers. comm., 2003). Library lending statistics, meanwhile, show that loans of the selected book increase significantly and are sometimes sustained at above-average levels for more than a year after the program ends (Alleman, pers. comm., 2004; M. Kelly 2007, 8). For the agents who constitute the reading industry, then, MREs can help to make a few books "popular" for a short time.

There is little empirical evidence to suggest that the OBOC model or the mass-mediated events that we investigated create significant numbers of new *readers*. Leisure readers constitute a niche audience in many respects, and John Frow's assessment of late-twentieth-century literary culture as "a pocket within commodity culture" (1995, 86) bears remembering. The shape and content of the "pocket" may have altered during the early 2000s, and the audience for its content certainly became a more recognized and well-defined "target" of the reading industry. The proliferation of the OBOC model, of book festivals, book cities, and Readers' Days across the three nation-states of our study are among the compelling indicators of this change. Although reading for pleasure became a more widely represented activity, however, the normative meanings of book reading persisted. In Ted Striphas's words, "The value of books would [still] seem to lie, first and foremost, in their capacity for moral, aesthetic, and intellectual development" (2009, 6). Not surprisingly, most readers we interviewed or who answered our online questionnaire believed that encouraging more people to read books was a "good thing." Any attempt to make books and reading "accessible" (a favored term) to more people, won their approval, regardless of the medium or format employed.

In researching city- and nationwide configurations of shared reading, then, we were less focused on the size of their audiences as a measure of popularity than on how readers perceived and evaluated them. Did readers regard MREs as popular and acceptable forms of contemporary book culture? What did they believe such events achieved? Why did they choose to participate or not to participate? For some of the readers in our study, television book clubs were too imitative of other popular nonprint cultural forms that they considered to be rather lowbrow—although most people we met were reluctant to use that exact categorization. For these readers, possessing the competencies to read books and to talk critically about them is a valued skill and can be understood as a form of cultural capital. As we discuss in more depth in Chapters 2 and 7, "Television" and "Book," books are still viewed as "special" objects, or even as "sacred product[s]" (L. Miller 2006, 19) by many keen readers. To view books and book reading as part of popular culture was a step too far for those readers we met who (implicitly) wanted to retain a distance between commerce and culture. These readers sought to maintain hierarchies of value that separate popular or low-brow books from "good quality" (for example, prizewinning) tomes. Listening to readers talk about why and what they read has been a salutary reminder that, whereas as academics we might be happy to declare the contemporary irrelevance of "brows" as applied to cultural artifacts, and to dismiss the high/low culture binary as a false dichotomy, these distinctions and the tastemarkers they connote have not yet entirely disappeared from the value systems of nonprofessional readers. The definition of "what constitutes a quality reading experience" has clearly shifted (Collins 2010, 18), and is no longer confined to the reading of canonical literature. For readers outside the academy reading books for pleasure and sharing reading is often pursued for a range of motivations and fueled by multiple desires to learn, to escape from the everyday world and yet to form social connections with others. In Chapter 6, "Reader," we explore the pleasures expressed and experienced by readers who choose to participate in OBOC events, in order to reach a more nuanced understanding of their desires and their sense of "what constitutes a quality reading experience" (ibid.).

We are more cautious and less celebratory than Jim Collins (2010) in his assessment of how literary culture became popular culture. He claims that "cultural life" in the United States of America changed "fundamentally" in the last decade of the twentieth century (19). We do not dispute his argument that the identity and location of the taste-makers has altered profoundly from the days when professors of literature were viewed as cultural authorities. We agree, too, with his analysis of how "changes within culture industries" (ibid.) and convergence culture have transformed the ways in which literary experiences can be represented, delivered, and consumed. However, to declare that readers access books and information about them "within a thoroughly destigmatized popular literary culture" (ibid.), is, as our case studies in this book will repeatedly demonstrate, to overlook or discount the unease that some keen readers appear to feel in relation to the media, artifacts, and practices of popular literary culture. Their discomfort with, and in some instances, outright rejection of the new cultural authorities such as Oprah or Richard and Judy, and of their book selections indicates a need to distinguish themselves as serious readers (Lang 2010). It also suggests an attachment to older yet persistent cultural hierarchies of genres and media.

No reader or event producer featured in this book proudly declares that they love middlebrow culture, for instance. Yet popular literary culture is shaped by middlebrow formulations of literary taste. We understand the "middlebrow" to be a series of historically specific formations, rather than a category that expands its terms of reference, or its contents, across time. The term is most often associated by book historians with the production and consumption of mass-market novels and magazines in the interwar years and the 1940s, when "middlebrow moderns" offered a more widely read alternative to texts by (avant-garde) modernists (Blair 2011; Botshon and Goldsmith 2003; Harker 2007; Rubin 1992). Meanwhile, Janice Radway's analysis in *A Feeling for Books* (1997) demonstrates in detail how the editors and reviewers of the Book-of-the-Month Club adeptly assessed the expectations and desires of America's newly minted and rapidly expanding professional middle class in the late 1920s. Oprah and her production team, Amanda Ross (the producer of the RJBC), and the organizers of OBOC events have contributed to the construction of a contemporary iteration of middlebrow taste. No one ever utters that term, of course, because of its historical association with gendered practices of novel reading, and its denigration as an outcome of mass production (Driscoll 2008, 141–42; 2011, 111–12). Nevertheless, contemporary producers and cultural intermediaries have developed intricate and careful modes of evaluating what educated readers want to read for pleasure. The books selected for MREs, for example, must never be too "difficult" to decode in terms of their formal elements, so avant-garde and experimental texts are rarely chosen. Contemporary fiction in a realist genre or "classic modern" novels such as *To Kill a Mockingbird*, which was also a successful Book-of-the Month-Club selection during the 1960s, are the most selected book types for OBOC programs. At the same time, featured books must be "discussable," as we examine in Chapters 2 through 5 as part of our consideration of the values that event organizers attribute to shared reading. One way of understanding our analyses in *Reading Beyond the Book*, then, is to regard them as a critical, if incomplete, account of contemporary middlebrow cultures of reading.

In their presentation of books through different media, event organizers, television producers, and radio show hosts promote not only books that can both entertain and inform readers, but also particular ways of reading that often mimic the social practices of book talk employed in reading groups. As we demonstrate below, our conceptualization of shared reading as a social practice is informed not only by the history of shared reading, but also by the scholarship of book historians, cultural studies' specialists, and scholars of library science. Research focused on reading communities, especially contemporary formations of shared reading such as book clubs, also influenced our methods of investigation, which we introduce in the final part of this chapter.

SHARED READING AS A SOCIAL PRACTICE

In this book we understand shared reading to be both a social process and a social formation. Reading is a social process, because, as book historian Roger Chartier observed, it "is always a practice embodied in gestures, spaces, and habits" (Chartier and González 1992, 51). Thus, even solitary book reading can be understood as a social practice because the action of reading always takes place somewhere, whether in what we discern to be a domestic and private space such as the home, or in a public space like a library or on a bus. In fact, even conceptualizing spaces as public or private indicates one way in which socially constructed ideas about the everyday world through which we move tend to shape normalized ideas about the act of reading. The "habits" of reading, as many book historians, sociologists, and education specialists have demonstrated, are also socially produced (see, e.g., E. Long 2003; Norvel 1973; Rose 2001). As D. F. McKenzie reminds us, "the technical and social dynamics, of transmission and reception" are "processes" involving "human agents" as well as "structures" (2002, 31). Whereas reading has to be "embodied," that is, enacted and experienced by an actual living reader in order for any kind of reading to occur, whether that reading is solitary, shared, silent, or spoken, all reading requires a "social infrastructure" (E. Long 2003, 8). Within Western Europe and North America, that "infrastructure" is supplied by the material conditions of book production (such as book publishing and the mass media), by the educational training of readers, and by the institutional promotion of literacy (by libraries and governments, for example).

The social infrastructure of reading is differently constituted at different historical moments in time, and is also inflected by cultural and geographical location. Recent scholarship that approaches book history "through postcolonial eyes" (Fraser 2008) has shown how contingent the processes and habits of print cultures are on particular industrial practices and the "powers, events and systems entirely outside [national] geopolitical boundaries" (Shep 2008, 22). These include, for instance, the making, shipping, and selling of paper; the availability of print technologies; and the facility with which books can be distributed (exported from imperial centers to colonies by ship via various nodes within trade networks, for example). The promotion—or enforcement—of print literacy as both a skill-set and an ideological imperative played a fundamental part in Western Europe's colonization of people in other regions of the world (see, for example, Gauri Viswanathan 1989). Indigenous cultures of writing, print production, and reading "struck back" at the actors, values, and products of empires in diverse and symbolically powerful ways, through gestures, practices, and habits that continue to challenge Eurocentric constructions of literacy, print, writing, reading, and literature (Shep 2008). It would be wrong to suggest that books and reading are now somehow cut free from a deeply racialized and political past. Indeed, scholarship by Sarah Brouillette (2007), and by James Procter (2011) and the "Devolving Diasporas" research team (2007–2010), is among work that demonstrates how the legacies of colonialism continue to affect the production, circulation, and reception of fictional texts by "postcolonial" writers, especially in the marketplace of English-language print texts (Hofmeyr 2004; Joshi 2008; Low 2010; Lyons 2001; McDonald 2009; Van der Vlies 2007). The complex relationships between print and oral cultures in locations where colonialism and multiple linguistic traditions coincided is also highlighted by research into the histories and contemporary uses of print in, for example, South Africa by Archie Dick (2011), West Africa by Karin Barber (2007) and Stephanie Newell (2006a, 2006b), and India (Desai 2011).[1] By conceptualizing reading as a social practice, then, we also wish to acknowledge the troubled histories attached to Western European constructions of the habits of reading. At times, our analyses of MREs foreground the effects of those histories, for instance, in our discussion of the exoticizing of racial difference during on-air interpretations of *Half of a Yellow Sun* (2006) by Chimamanda Ngozi Adichie in the RJBC (Chapter 2, "Television").

Book historians have not only been paying increasing attention to the relationship between the artifacts of print culture and colonial—and postcolonial—geographies. The history of reading as a subfield of book history has expanded especially rapidly since the late 1990s, with scholars taking up a range of methods in their study of "actual readers" and "specific reading communities" situated in particular times and places (Fischer 2003; Howsam 2006; Pawley 2002; Price 2004). Especially valuable to us, as researchers working on shared reading practices in the contemporary period, are the social histories of reading communities that offer insights into how and why members shared books and reading. As several anthologies, essay collections, and contributions to multivolume national histories of the book illustrate, the sharing of reading in salons, coffee houses, study clubs, faith groups, literary societies, and political associations has a rich history in North America and the United Kingdom.[2] Aspects of that history have been ably examined by, among others, Elizabeth McHenry whose work focuses on African-American literary societies from the nineteenth century onward (2002); and, in Canada, Heather Murray (2002) and Fanie St-Laurent (2007) who have investigated the literary societies of nineteenth-century Ontario, and francophone groups such as the Société d'étude et de conférences founded in Montreal in 1933, respectively. Many of the readers profiled in Jonathan Rose's (2001) history of working-class English readers were autodidacts who reflected on their individual reading habits and acts in diaries, memoirs, and autobiographies, but some also belonged to factory debating societies, or were accustomed to listening to a reader while he or she worked. As book historians continue to demonstrate, people have been coming together to share reading and discuss print texts of various genres, for several centuries. When literacy rates were low, members who could would read aloud to others. As literacy rates increased in North America and the United Kingdom from the mid-nineteenth century onward, people from nonelite groups began to use study clubs, reading groups, and debating societies as a means of self-education, and political empowerment.

In terms of purpose, the parallels between the historical formations of shared reading described above, and contemporary models, such as Get Into Reading (Liverpool, UK, see Chapter 5, "Worker"), Literature for All of Us in Chicago, or prison book groups, are especially striking. The notion of reading as a means of self- or group-liberation remains ideologically powerful within the nation-states of our study, although it is now rarely associated with social movements such as feminism or civil rights. Nevertheless, the consciousness-raising effects of print literacy are promoted by some educators, and by self-styled "reading revolutionaries" such as Jane Davis, the founder-director of Get Into Reading (see Chapter 5). Whereas the religious connotations of reading as a form of liberation have become widely secularized, book groups focused around the study of sacred texts continue to play a significant role within many faith communities and families (Boyarin 1992b; Coleman 2009; E. Smith 2007, 2008). Enlightenment through reading has long been regarded not only as a spiritual goal but also as an epistemological project in the West. Like their historical counterparts in literary and factory debating societies, contemporary readers are often motivated to share their reading by a desire to acquire new knowledge (Rehberg Sedo 2011b, 11). Moreover, as histories of reading communities underline, the acts and habits of individual and shared reading are not mutually exclusive (Hartley 2011; Hochman 2008; Kelley 2003; B. Ryan and Thomas 2002; Schellenberg 2011). The upper-class American women readers of the Gilded Age analyzed by Barbara Sicherman (2010) used a combination of solitary and shared reading in family or friendship circles to educate themselves in specific disciplines of science or the arts. The women in Sicherman's case studies also employed their reading practices to negotiate a sense of their own identity within cultural contexts that sought to define—and confine—them. Again, there is an almost palpable connection with the ways that contemporary readers in our own study undertake forms of identity work by participating in shared reading events. A major difference, of course, lies in the increased access to education afforded to women in the contemporary period. As our online survey results indicated, the more formal education a reader has acquired, the more likely they are to get involved in MREs.

Friendship, like education, is a shared "signifier" for "reading communities across time" (Rehberg Sedo 2011b, 11). From the Bluestocking network of eighteenth-century Britain (Schellenberg 2011), to National Home Reading Union circles in South Africa, Australia, and Canada (Snape 2011), sharing reading has enabled socially and culturally isolated people to retain intellectual contact through reading (Rubin 2007, 302–3). But the intellectual aspects of belonging to a reading community are not always viewed by members as their primary benefit. Jenny Hartley and Sarah Turvey were the first researchers to ask non-academic book groups in late-twentieth-century Britain to describe their practices, motivations, and pleasures (2001). Like many historians, Hartley and Turvey pay attention to the social aspects of reading by concentrating on the discussions that take place within groups; their reading lists; and the details of where, when, and how shared reading unfolds. The latter aspect reveals another sense in which shared reading can be thought of as a social practice, because for many book groups the social rituals of sharing food and/or beverages are integral to their members' investment in the sociability of group behavior. Similarly, for some readers, off-topic discussion is not only enjoyable, but also contributes in very significant ways to the friendly relations among members. At the same time, as Ian Collinson, in his study of "everyday reading" notes, not all readers seek, need, or prioritize sociability, particularly in relation to book talk (2009, 85). Our study develops the notion of sociability in relation to contexts of shared reading that do not depend on group membership or regular meetings. In Chapter 6, "Reader," we explore how sociability, locality, and spectacle combine to produce an enjoyable shared reading experience for some MRE participants.

There are some historical consistencies to be noted when it comes to the content of these publicly staged reading events. In the lyceums of the nineteenth century and early twentieth century (Snape 1995), readers would gather to hear about a timely topic or listen to an author reading, for example. Literary societies and factory debating societies alike hosted guest speakers, discussions of pamphlets and books, and debates about political issues of the day. Versions of these activities are typical features of the OBOC model. However, there are some marked differences with events of the contemporary period in terms of how books are represented in creative programming such as outdoor excursions and the presentation of film adaptations. Whereas the study group model of shared reading proliferated in the nineteenth century via religious reading groups, literary societies, and more formally organized programs such as the Chautauqua summer camps or, in the twentieth century, via the Great Books program (Born 2011), shared reading is often constructed as a multisensory experience and as an entertainment, rather than primarily as a form of instruction and learning. Nevertheless, the variety in the social formations of reading in the late nineteenth and early twentieth centuries represents a further comparison with the contemporary period. Historically, increased rates of print literacy and the introduction of methods of mass reproduction meant that more people could read and access reading materials. At the turn of the twenty-first century, these changes were echoed by others as new media technologies and digital literacies opened up new spaces for reading and different means of accessing or constructing reading communities.

Whereas the evolution of book programming has embraced new technologies and sociological changes such as increased literacy rates, the ideological arguments that are used to garner financial support and to promote contemporary reading events often echo those declarations of library and reading advocates of the past two centuries (Pawley 2010). Public libraries and library professionals have also been involved in the generation of ideological notions of reading as a civilizing and a social good in the three nation-states (Augst 2003; Augst and Carpenter 2007; A. Black 1996; Lamonde, McNally, and Rotundo 2004; Pawley 2007, 2009; Sheldrick Ross et al. 2006; Van Slyck 1995; Wiegand 2009, 2011). Of course, libraries are not the only institutions through which advocates for the civilizing effects of reading have operated, because educational and government agencies have also played their part, for example, through the promotion—or alternatively, banning—of particular books. But, as Christine Pawley argues, public libraries are among the agencies that create "institutional sites of reading," spaces where, especially in the late nineteenth and early twentieth century, readers could encounter (and sometimes produce) texts (2009, 74). In *Reading*

Beyond the Book, we take up Pawley's invitation to pay greater attention to this "middle layer"—the institutional layer—that mediates the production, circulation, and consumption of books. We consider, in particular, the nation-building mandate of a public broadcaster (the Canadian Broadcasting Corporation, Chapter 3, "Radio"), the role of public library systems and government agencies in sponsoring and organizing events (Chapter 4, "Money"), and the creative and ideological labor performed by library professionals (Chapter 5, "Worker"). We also lend some consideration to the various sites and spaces in which readers encounter each other—some of which are also institutionally inscribed scenes of reading, whereas others are not (Chapter 6, "Reader").

The Politics of Reading: Feminist Analyses of Contemporary Social Practices

If the spaces and habits of reading are socially and often institutionally produced, specific habits, for example, novel reading, the consumption of "chick lit," and participating in reading groups, have also been inscribed as gendered at different historical moments within North America and the United Kingdom (Ang 1996; Berg 2008; Kiernan 2011; E. Long 2003; Radway [1984] 1991; Travis 2003). Our understanding of reading as a social practice has thus been particularly informed by the feminist analyses of women readers, scholarship on late twentieth-century book groups, and early-twenty-first-century research into the sharing of reading among vulnerable social groups such as prisoners (Sweeney 2010). Preeminent among feminist scholars of adult readers in the contemporary period are Elizabeth Long (1986, 1992, 2003) and Janice Radway ([1984] 1991, 1997). Radway's (1991) seminal work on the readers of romance fiction pays special attention to the meanings that the act of reading genre fiction held for the women readers themselves. As a result, whereas her analysis of the romance texts demonstrates their promotion of heterosexuality and their perpetuation of unequal gender relations, her critique of the women's acts and habits of reading—where, when, and why they read the books—tells a different story. For Radway's romance readers, time spent reading offered them a literal and imaginative space, and the opportunity to indulge in fantasy, explore desires, and to rest from the gendered duties of housework and child care. Like Radway, we are interested in how dominant gender norms and expectations may be embedded within or challenged by media practices and texts. Our focus also falls upon those people (mostly women) who engage with an older medium: the printed book. The shared reading of books now coexists with the newer media practices of blogging, online fan-fiction, and social media studied by feminist scholars such as Catherine Driscoll and Melissa Gregg (2011). Whereas it is beyond the scope of our current study to offer an analysis of how readers might move among these different media practices, our data offers a few suggestive glimpses into the ways that keen readers turn to online sources for information about books, events, and other readers. What emerges more strongly from our investigations are the complex pleasures that readers can derive from sharing reading through the various activities and media that constitute an MRE. In that regard, our study echoes Radway's efforts to take seriously the ways that readers use reading, their articulations of what shared reading means to them, and their opinions of contemporary book cultures.

As Elizabeth Long observes in her groundbreaking ethnography of women's book groups (2003), reading can be considered as a social practice in terms of the cognitive, intellectual, and self-reflexive processes that it inspires in the individual reader. These processes are social because they constitute relationships between reader and text, reader and author, and in relation to a reader's comprehension of her own identity, or sense of self.

The notion of the private and solitary reader is itself a social construction, and belongs to an ideology that privileges and romanticizes the creativity of the lone and isolated actor (writer or reader). Elizabeth Long begins her analysis by dismantling the dichotomies between private/public and solitary/shared reading (2003, 2–12). Her detailed account of the ways that women in Houston, Texas, came together to share their reading in book groups during the late twentieth century is a fine illustration of how "the 'doing' of culture" is always part of a "web of social relationships" (17). The women in her study move through that web, not as passive consumers of books, but as agents whose acts of cultural consumption are "implicated in the 'doing' of gender, class, race, and social development" (ibid.) even when they read alone.

Our work shares Long's (2003) feminist conceptualization of the social world as observable in everyday interactions. Like Long, we view shared reading as a process and formation that takes place within a "web of social relationships" (ibid.) and is, in turn, constituted by it. Whereas we use the term "public" in our analyses of MREs, it is usually with reference to formally organized gatherings of people, to broadcast networks (e.g., National Public Radio), or to monies that are raised through taxation (public funding). We do not intend that "public" invokes "private" as its binary opposite. Rather, our references to public spaces and groups of people in this book often serves to highlight the assault wrought upon collectively owned spaces, cultural resources (such as arts funding and social programs), and institutions (such as public libraries) by the policies and economic decisions of neoliberal governments (discussed in more detail in Chapter 4, "Money"). More intricately, in Chapter 6, "Reader," we draw on Lauren Berlant's (2008) notion of an "intimate public sphere." Her elaboration of shared spheres of affective identification helps us to account for the social dynamics and cultural significance of reading event participants' feelings of belonging to local or regional communities and even to the nation-state. Berlant's (ibid.) theorization of the "intimate public sphere" is important to feminist analyses of the role played by cultural formations and artifacts that are especially attractive to women, such as particular genres of books or book groups, in the early twenty-first century. This, after all, is an era when the private individual has been increasingly charged with taking on responsibility for maintaining and financing the social well-being of the self and family—labor that often falls to women.

In her explication of the "intimate public sphere" (ibid.), Berlant recognizes these circumstances as both ideologically and materially constraining. At the same time, she acknowledges, through her theorization of affect, that the feelings provoked by the cultural texts of women's culture such as melodramatic films, and the circulation of such texts, produces in many spectators and readers a sense of being connected to others, even when they are strangers and "may share nothing of the particular worlds being represented" (2008, ix). By playing to "people's desires for reciprocity with the world" (x–xi), intimate publics hold out a "promise of belonging" (ix). In other words, "participants in the intimate public *feel* as though it expresses what is common among them" (5, emphasis in original). In the intimate public sphere created by women's culture, "the first . . . mass-marketed intimate public in the United States of significant scale" (5), feeling and emotion are afforded a "critical intelligence" (2). Berlant's analysis demonstrates how this emphasis on affect is marked by the consumer's fantasy that feeling something important about everyday life could contribute to social change (2). But that fantasy is also generated and "mediated" by the market because of the profit to be won from selling commodities such as books and films. Participants in MREs, we argue in Chapter 6, "Reader," sometimes enact their attachment to an intimate public when they articulate the affective dimension of their reading experiences to others. Especially compelling are reader-participants' expressions of belonging to communities, both locally realized and more broadly imagined, that are saturated with the desire for social connection. Berlant's (2008) notion of the intimate public sphere helps us to understand the wider cultural and political implications of these desires and shared reading practiced as a social act.

Feminist scholars of reading have been especially interested in how readers' transactions with books and with other readers shape an individual's self-awareness about their subjectivity (Griffin 1999; Howie 1998; Pecoskie 2009). Another connected preoccupation is the intersubjective relations that shared reading enables (Howie 2011, 143; Rehberg Sedo 2011c, 107–13). In addition to Long's (2003) study of women's book clubs, other scholars focusing on contemporary book groups have teased out some of the intricacies of reader-text and reader-reader relationships. An early example was Lynn Pearce's (1997) investigation and theorization of the "dynamic, interactive and implicated relationship between text and reader" as it emerged from the interpretative practices of feminist readers (220). Pearce's case study analyzed the reading practices of several feminist academics reading both alone and in groups in the UK and Canada (220–49). More recently, Kimberley Chabot Davis's (2008) exploration of cross-racial empathy within white American women's book clubs where African-American fiction is read, tests the limits and possibilities of an ethically "implicated" relationship between readers and texts. Chabot Davis (ibid.) suggests that sociopolitical change can begin with a reader changing her opinion or questioning her own privilege, but she also demonstrates how readers in groups sometimes discuss texts in ways that quash and ignore social difference. In the twenty-first century, book groups are rarely the site of overt political consciousness-raising as they were for some North American and British women in the 1960s and '70s, as Rehberg Sedo (2004) confirms in the conclusion to her study of women's book groups in Vancouver.

Similarly, Elizabeth Long does not make any grand claims for the political agency of contemporary women's book groups (2003). On the contrary, her analysis of her data demonstrates how difficult it can be for book group participants to challenge dominant norms about gender and race, even when confronted by textual representations of sexism and racism, or by group members' life experiences of social oppression (183–86). But, as Long also points out, the conversations, the sharing of interpretations, and the connections that members draw between the text and personal experience can sometimes lead to a reader changing her opinion, articulating an understanding of her social identity differently, or even questioning the operation of social structures that uphold inequalities of power (186). These insights about the practices and effects of book group behaviors suggest that we cannot only think about social change in terms of structural or organizational transformation. At the same time, in *Reading Beyond the Book*, we are alert to the risks of overprivileging agency or change at the level of the individual. The contemporary emphasis on reading as a source of self-transformation has arisen within a sociopolitical context in which the ideology of individualism often trumps the politics of collective action. In her historical survey of the "enduring reader" (2009), Joan Shelley Rubin comments that, by the mid-1970s, shared reading by American women was "less an occasion for exposure to communal vision than for the enhancement of individual skills and identity" (423). Rubin relates changes in the meanings of reading in the US to the demise of the social movements that focused on equal rights for women, African-Americans, and other minority groups.

From her perspective as a feminist cultural historian, Rubin (2009) offers an important analysis of a series of significant contexts for reading, especially for women's reading. Like Long (2003), she reminds us that social and cultural practices are always political in their constitution and effects, even when they appear to be personal. During the last two decades, for example, therapeutic culture has been an important aspect of popular culture, from Oprah's discourse of self-recovery promoted throughout the artifacts produced by her media empire, to the proliferation of self-help books. Nevertheless, the social functions and political implications of reading and shared reading have continued alongside this emphasis on individual well-being. For nonelite groups of people, that is, for those who are not privileged in terms of their socioeconomic status, and/or who experience discrimination because of any aspect of their identity, such as gender, sexuality, ethnicity, or physical ability, access to books and the opportunity to share reading with others can have profound emotional and social consequences.

Jenny Hartley's and Sarah Turvey's (n.d.) work on reading groups in British prisons, for example, demonstrates how shared reading can be a means through which participants not only build confidence in their ability to express their thoughts and feelings out loud, but also acquire "an inquiring and critical sociability" (3). In other words, talking about books within a group offers a means of gaining experience in respecting and questioning their own viewpoints and those of other people (Hartley and Turvey 2008, n.d.; Howie 2011). Similarly, Megan Sweeney's (2010) ethnography of women's book groups in US American prisons focuses on "the specific ways in which reading enables some women prisoners to gain self-knowledge, . . . and develop an understanding of the limits and possibilities of individual agency" (6). Sweeney's (2010) work makes a significant contribution to contemporary studies of shared reading for several reasons. She answers Elizabeth McHenry's call to foreground the print literacies of African Americans as a counter-history to the racialization of book reading as a white activity (2002, 15); she demonstrates how the history of prison libraries in the US have shaped the contents of collections, authorized censorship practices, and inflected the ways that reading is viewed by prison officials, and she identifies a series of different reading practices as they emerge through readers' engagements with different book genres, such as urban fiction and self-help. Rather than idealizing the therapeutic effects of shared reading, however, Sweeney points out the social significance of being able to express compassion toward others within a context where caring and being cared for are not always well supported in terms of access to formal resources like counseling and education (2010, 8). At times, the sharing of reading becomes empowering for the women, not only in personal terms, but also as a group of people who together are able to recognize and negotiate with some of the social and political relations structuring their lives. Sweeney's (2010) study thus underlines the importance of regarding reading as a situated act as well as a social process.

As this brief overview of recent scholarship suggests, book groups are the primary mode of shared reading among adults that have caught the attention of academics working in the contemporary period, including the best-known book clubs: Oprah's Book Club, and the RJBC.[3] Much of the critical work focused on Oprah's Book Club has analyzed the rhetoric of the show (Penfield Lewis 2008; Rodriguez 2008; Travis 2007, 2009), and the reading practices that Oprah advocated through her television broadcasts (Frampton 2010; Stow 2008; Striphas 2003, 2009), or has evaluated her book selections (M. Hall 2003, 2008). Only a few scholars scrutinized the practices of the readers featured on-air or of those who joined discussions online (Chabot Davis 2004; Kiernan 2011). In that sense, what emerges most strongly from the body of work on the world's most famous book club is a detailed sense of how Oprah's project to "get America reading again" coincided with her ideology of self-transformation and self-healing. Although, as Joan Shelley Rubin notes, Oprah's Book Club assumed that "good reading must be empathic and affective" (Konchar Farr 2005, 47; cited in Rubin 2009, 428). We concur with Rubin's (2009) argument that: "Winfrey balanced her understanding of reading as self-exploration with a keen awareness of reading's social aspects" (428). Oprah's inclusion of the dinner party with the author of the featured book and a small group book discussion within each Book Club show mimicked elements of contemporary book group practices. As we discuss in Chapter 2, "Television," recreating the "social aspects" of shared reading on television was crucial to the success of both Oprah's Book Club and the RJBC. Both productions not only lent cultural legitimacy to book groups by modeling face-to-face book group talk on-screen, they also employed the social practices of reading in order to create a sense of intimacy with the viewer. What the producers and hosts of both shows understood was that, outside the academy, many readers enjoy talking about books as a way of understanding their own lives. In the book-reviewing pages of broadsheet newspapers and literary magazines, however, professional readers such as Andrew O'Hagan (quoted in Boztas 2008) have frequently sneered at this practice. O'Hagan, as we noted in the introduction, accused RJBC of "over[selling] a reduced, unimaginative notion of what people's literary enjoyment might be" (ibid.). For critics such as O'Hagan then, "literary enjoyment" depends on a model of interpretation shaped by an aesthetics of form and style associated with an academic training in literary reading and canonical literature. Within the academy itself, experiential uses for reading have often been overlooked or dismissed in favor of textual hermeneutics, as we explore below.

Reading Beyond the Academy: From Active to Actual Readers, from Response to Experience

Our conceptualization of shared reading as a social practice and a social formation owes much to the work of book historians, anthropologists, and cultural sociologists investigating reading communities. By employing a range of empirical methods to reconstruct the groups that form around texts of various genres in a range of spaces and periods, they shift critical attention from text to reader and encourage the analysis of interactions among readers. Subsequently, "reading" can be understood as involving more processes and actions than a hermeneutic practice or a reader-text transaction. Readers, themselves, meanwhile, are not only conceivable as active, meaning-making individuals, but also as embodied, situated subjects. These definitions and theorizations of reading and readers challenge the primacy of the literary text as an object of study. But they also lead us, as scholars of shared reading, to reject the imagined and ideal readers who are often constructed from or "read off" the text within the discipline of literary studies when the method of close textual analysis is employed by the scholarly reader as the primary means of producing an interpretation. Indeed, in its Euro-American institutional formation, literary studies have tended to privilege a synecdochical relationship to the reader. Whether this has been articulated through theories of the ideal or implicit reader of a text (Eco 1979; Iser [1976] 1978, [1972] 1980), or by naming the operation (reading the words of a text) in the stead of the actor (the reader), one reader has often been made to stand in for the many (Price 2004, 304–5). We do, however, owe a debt to the notion of the active reader promoted by reader-response theory—an area of literary studies that, despite problems that we identify below, posed important questions about how reading occurred. Nevertheless, in *Reading Beyond the Book*, we are concerned with analyzing the "uses" that readers make of shared reading practices and MREs. Here, our understanding of "use" is informed by the intellectual traditions within communications and media studies that recognize audience members as active agents (Ang 1990; S. Hall 1980; Morley and Brunsdon 1978, 1980). More specifically, we investigated readers' "experiences" of MREs, rather than their "responses" to books—as we might have done if we were conducting a reception study of book reading. Redefining "response" as "experience" is also helpful because it steers between the hermeneutic and affective definitions of reading favored by reader-response theorists (H. Murray 2002, 163; Price 2004, 305). Certainly, many participants in MREs engage in the operation of reading in the sense of "doing something with the words" in a book (Price 2012, 5), but they also engage with other media as well. Recent scholarship, which explores subjects' participation across a range of contemporary media, illustrates how "media experience" extends "media use" to include multiple responses to multiple media (Gentikow 2005a, 2005b; Ytre-Arne 2011). Finally, beyond the academy, an important aspect of contemporary "media experience" for many readers is the adoption of a "personalized" orientation to literature and art. The "personal response" has been widely employed since the late twentieth century (with both positive and negative connotations) by media commentators and by nonprofessional readers. As we noted above, but explore in more depth below, different readers, from Harold Bloom (2011) to the members of book groups, have different motivations for promoting and using "personalized" ways of reading.

One of the ironies of reader-response scholarship is that much of it actually reinstates the text as its primary object, even as critics strive to lend interpretative agency to the reader. Even in the introduction to what became a landmark anthology of Anglo-American criticism, Jane P. Tompkins comments, for example, that the author of the first essay, Walker Gibson— writing in 1950—produces an "idea of the reader as a means of producing a new kind of textual analysis" (1980, xi). In the 1960s, critics such as Wolfgang Iser and Roman Ingarden ([1931], 1973) focused more acutely on the processes of reader-text interaction. But they, like Gibson before them, and in common with the early work of David Bleich (1975, 1978) and Norman

Holland (1968, 1975) that employed a psychoanalytic model of interpretation, tended to adopt a formalist notion of aesthetic response. The result was a reader who was, to all intent purposes, imagined. In Iser's ([1976] 1978) *The Act of Reading*, for example, the reader was "implicated in" the text because they had been moved by it to synthesize "perspectives" derived from formal features (such as plot, characters, and narrator). At this point in time, then, reader-response scholarship was nonsociological: no "real" readers were questioned or harmed in the making of these theories!

The "curiously bloodless and disembodied" readers of this early phase of reader-response theory were often a stand-in, not only for all other readers, but, more specifically, for the professional reader (Felski 2008, 16). Even poststructuralist critics, such as Jonathan Culler (1980), produced an ideal reader by elaborating how institutional conventions about literary theory and hermeneutics tutored the reader to interpret the text. Nevertheless, although the reader-response theory of the 1960s to early 1980s rarely dealt with actual or non-academic readers (and tended to focus on literary texts rather than popular genres or visual media), these theories offered various explanations for the reader's interpretative role in making meaning from texts. In doing so, these scholars challenged "the opposed formal and historical approaches" that had dominated the Anglo-American tradition of literary studies (Goldstein and Machor 2008, xxiii). Even if they were often more successful at theorizing the process or operation of reading, or showing how textual aesthetics produced particular responses from or positions for the imagined reader, rather than dwelling on the actions of a "real" actor, reader-response scholars offered the discipline of literary studies a way out of "textual or authorial essentialism" (xxii).

Whereas the reader begins to emerge as a historically situated agent in these theories, there is little attention to reader-reader interaction and no sense of the ways that nonacademic readers might employ various reading practices as part of their everyday lives as social beings. Even Stanley Fish's (1980) famous notion of an "interpretive community," a group of readers who share a set of ideals, norms, and interpretative conventions, refers somewhat narrowly to academic readers trained within schools of thought such as feminism, Marxism, and Freudianism. As Janice Radway notes in her critically nuanced account of the limitations of reception study, *Is There a Text in This Class?* by Stanley Fish is best understood as "an elaborate and ingenious defense of the critic's role as an informed, authorized reader" (2008, 330). Radway makes a convincing case in her essay for why the role of the expert reader and the authority of the literary text have been reaffirmed at specific historical moments within the discipline of literary studies. She even suggests that *Reading the Romance* and other studies that tried to analyze the "ways that actual readers made sense of texts," in fact, "did not entirely manage to displace the practice of textual exegesis, nor did they alter in the end the role or authority of the critic" (334). As Elizabeth Long has also noted, part of the problem has been a tendency to assume or install a linearity in which the writer and the text always precede the reader and the act of reading (2003, 21). Reading studies like Long's (2003) own sociology of book groups are designed in opposition to this model and they refuse to "subordinate the reader to the text" (Pawley 2002, 143).

Our study of MREs contributes to these efforts to disrupt the linear model in which the consumer (reader) is always the receiver of the product (book). We set out to put actual readers, rather than the texts that they read, at the center of investigation. Rather than viewing readers as the end-point or only as an audience for a specific form of cultural entertainment, we enquired about their personal reading histories, involvement in other types of book-inspired activities, and opinions about the cultural resources where they lived. But, our examination of this contemporary cultural formation of shared reading could not stop at readers' practices and their own accounts of them, because large-scale reading events are a formation shaped by industries, institutions, economic systems, and cultural values. By studying the situation or circumstances within which shared reading practices occur, we were moving toward a description of reading formations, which, in Tony Bennett's (1987) conceptualization, consist of "a set of discursive and intertextual determinations that organize and animate the practice of reading" (70). In other words, *Reading Beyond the Book* is not an audience study nor, strictly speaking, is it a reception study. Analyzing the ways that people talk about books or other media texts such as television shows, as we do in this book, is partly a legacy of reception study work within audience and media studies. David Morley and Charlotte Brunsdon's (1978, 1980) work on the British television program *Nationwide* and its audience, Ien Ang's *Watching Dallas* (1985), and Joke Hermes's (1995) study of women magazine readers have been particularly influential because of their emphasis on the uses that people make of media within their everyday lives. Reading studies takes up that legacy through research that explores "the practices and positions adopted by readers in the real (which is to say, the social) world" (Allington and Swann 2009, 220). In alignment with our own emphasis on reading as a social practice, recent work by some linguistics scholars attends to the wider "social and institutional explanations and implications" of how readers read (ibid.), not just the processes of co-constructing meaning within a specific group (e.g., Benwell 2009; Benwell, Procter, and Robinson 2011; G. Hall 2009). As we have noted, cultural sociologists, anthropologists, and cultural studies scholars have been particularly aware of the wider social and political situation in which acts of reading have occurred. The ethno-methodologies that they have developed often combine participant-observation and analysis of readers' accounts of their reading lives in an effort to achieve a more in-depth analysis (or, "thick description" in anthropological terms) of the cultural values and identifications being negotiated within groups of readers (E. Long 2003; Reed 2011; Sweeney 2010). Meanwhile, Radway's (1997) investigation of the Book-of-the-Month Club and Laura Miller's (2006) history of bookstores in the US are examples of cultural studies' influenced research that examine reading in terms of the industries that perpetuate it, rather than in terms of the individuated or imagined reader.

Our research project design and the way we have organized our analysis are informed by the tradition of cultural studies that emerged from the Birmingham Centre for Contemporary Cultural Studies. The methodologies developed by Stuart Hall, Paul Willis, and Angela McRobbie among many others, not only "displace[d] texts and textuality from the starting-point of the enterprise," but also began by considering "social communities, their histories, and their external and political relations" (Radway 2008, 335–36). Specific cultural practices were therefore not conceived of as discrete phenomena, but "had to be approached as a contingent aspect of a larger, more complex social process and formation" (336). Conceptualizing shared reading as a social practice and MREs as a social formation requires, we believe, paying critical attention to the organizational components of events, and trying to understand their historical, economic, ideological, and social situations. For that reason, as we explain below, and in our Methods Appendix, we examined the roles played by the mass media, cultural policy and funding issues, the producers, and the readers. Readers and the practices of shared reading are central to our analysis because without them there would be a branded product but no "event." For us, then, reading is a social and political act performed by embodied individuals. By this we mean that reading is a cultural activity and all cultural activities have ideological effects.

In Harold Bloom's (2011) terms, we are the unfortunate scholarly products of the "New Cynicism (a cluster of critical tendencies which are rooted in French theories of culture and encompass the New Historicism and its ilk)" (8). Worse, from a Bloomian viewpoint, we are not concerned about how "great literature works," although we do care about how professional readers, institutions, and the media construct particular ideas about what "literature" is, why some of it is "great," and by the "work" various agencies would like it to do. Bloom's position is an extreme one: he claims that he is both post- and antitheory. He describes his book *The Anatomy of Influence* as "a last-ditch defense of poetry, and a cry against being subsumed by an ideology," arguing that "the aesthetic demands deep subjectivity and is beyond the reach of ideology" (5). Bloom's stance is relatively unusual within the contemporary academy where few literary critics, let alone cultural studies scholars, would ever declare their methodological approach to their subject to be "beyond . . . ideology." Indeed, Bloom describes himself as "isolated" and "a department of one" (ibid.). But his antitheory, antipopular culture stance is in fact part of a popular contemporary regime of value that trumpets the authority of the personal response. In that regard he is very much in step with nonacademic books about reading published from the late 1990s onward in North America and the United Kingdom.

With titles such as *Good Books Lately* (Moore and Stevens 2004) and *Book Lust* (Pearl 2003), these manuals of book advice, differed from earlier versions of the genre by being "more personal than prescriptive" (Rubin

2009, 427). Joan Shelley Rubin attributes this change to the greater legitimacy lent "to personal feelings . . . in textual explication," resulting from a number of academic theories (including reader-response theory and poststructuralist theories of language) that have foregrounded how meaning is unstable (2009). Rubin also argues that feminism, multiculturalism, and postcolonialism also multiplied—as well as deconstructed—canons, so it is no longer possible to reach a consensus about what it means to be "well read" (ibid.). But the wave of advice books, which was clearly an industry response to the resurgence of book groups, might also be construed as part of a backlash against academic theories about books that foregrounded ideas or political positions over textual aesthetics and the pleasures of reading. Jim Collins comments in relation to Bloom's (2000) own book advice volume, *How to Read and Why*, that Bloom "begins with [a] diatribe against professors of literature in order to present personalized reading as the only legitimate authority" (Collins 2010, 23). Bloom goes on in his guide, as he does in *The Anatomy of Influence*, to present his idea of the "reader's Sublime" a form of "secular transcendance" that depends on the reader's ability to open themselves up, emotionally and cognitively, to literary writing (Bloom 2000, 29; cited in Collins 2010, 22). He believes, of course, that only "great literature," aka the classics, can move the reader in this spiritual way. Meanwhile, guides by nonacademic experts such as Nancy Pearl nominate a more eclectic mix of classics and contemporary fiction and nonfiction, but are equally passionate about the personal benefits of reading such books (Pearl 2003).

In an era when readers no longer look to the academy for reading recommendations, Bloom is a bestselling author of literary guides and criticism. Although he would probably be the last person to agree, his emphasis on the literary as something that is "personal and passionate" (2011, 4) connects him to guides of popular culture such as Oprah Winfrey and Nancy Pearl. The difference is that Bloom presents himself as the ideal reader, the priestly figure who wants to show other people how reading ought to be done, whereas Winfrey and Pearl are far less prescriptive. In their self-presentation, they model how to be a passionate reader, but ultimately they act as guides or coaches who encourage readers to trust their own interpretations. Similarly, personal ways of reading, such as identifying closely with the protagonists of a novel, are also often validated within contemporary book groups (E. Long 2003, 151–56). Questions posed in the reading guides produced by publishers to accompany contemporary novels also tend to invite the reader's participation, for instance, by asking her how she might have acted in a situation similar to those described in the book (Ivy 2011, 166; McGinley and Conley 2001). Such practices are a well-established part of popular reading culture then, but they have attracted some sneering and dismissive remarks within the mass media. These include American academic Dennis Baron's parody entitled "I Teach English—and I Hate Reader's Guides" (2002; cited in Ivy 2011, 162), and the claim that book clubs "coarsen literary debate" in a 2005 article written for *The New Statesman* by Nicholas Clee, former editor of *The Bookseller* in the UK. The inference that such unschooled ways of reading are decidedly low-brow becomes more overt in a piece by Canadian journalist Kate Taylor (2005). In her critique of the reading practices exhibited on-air during *Canada Reads* 2005, Taylor accuses the show of "accelerating the trend toward the personalization of all criticism; the notion that artistic value lies mainly in our personal interaction with art, one particularly heightened if the art echoes our own memories or experiences" (R1).

These opposing attitudes about the value of personal response form part of the popular and intellectual context within which MREs have proliferated. As the case studies in our chapters illustrate, the events themselves often reproduce these contests over value, taste, and the benefits of book reading, sometimes in unexpected ways. Investigating how actual readers use a contemporary formation of shared reading like MREs thus involves engaging with Pierre Bourdieu's ideas about taste, cultural hierarchies, distinction, and symbolic forms of capital, albeit with some qualifications that we discuss in the final part of this chapter. Because we conceptualize reading as a socially situated act, we understand cultural value and distinction as being brokered by a series of agents—including readers—who are differently invested in the material and ideological production of reading events. How and why we designed our research methods and determined the scale and scope of our enquiry in order to investigate these issues is our next concern.

INVESTIGATING MASS READING EVENTS: QUESTIONS, METHODS, AND SCOPE

In addition to our questions about how and why people come together to share reading via an MRE, we particularly wanted to investigate the type of cultural work that these large-scale event models were performing. What, we wondered, were these events really about? We were intrigued by this development in the history of shared reading and also somewhat skeptical about the ambitious rhetoric employed to describe and promote events. At best, the goal of bringing people from different parts of a city or nation-state together to share reading in order to promote better understanding of social difference seemed utopian. At worst, focusing on book reading as the skill that can create community appeared to be utilitarian, not to mention out-of-step with the realities of peoples' leisure time pursuits in North America and the UK. Whereas we were aware of the creativity of many reading event organizers and their commitment to reach out to diverse groups within their localities, we were concerned that, in ideological terms, the OBOC model in particular reinforced the primacy of print literacy as a civilizing skill. In the context of three neoliberal states, where governments were increasingly withdrawing their support from social programs and arts and cultural funding (even before the economic crisis of 2008), this interpellation of the citizen as "s/he-who-shall-possess-advanced-print-literacy" struck us as somewhat sinister. Thus, a key concern guiding our research design and methodology spoke even more explicitly to the politics of culture: simply put, who are these events for—who benefits? These are questions posed within a tradition of feminist cultural studies that attends to the unequal power relations that inflect access to cultural production, to cultural practices and to the ability to render visible the symbolic meanings of cultural artifacts (Driscoll and Gregg, 2011).

As we noted above, attention to the social aspects of reading is most evident in scholarship focusing on communities of readers, such as research into Oprah's Book Club and face-to-face and online reading groups. These studies tell us a great deal about ideology and identity work. Particularly relevant to our own study of shared reading are the processes of acquiring, representing, and articulating cultural capital, cultural literacies, and cultural tastes—processes influenced by social and educational structures as well as by the media and publishing industries. To access these, we combined quantitative and qualitative methods, including an online questionnaire, participant observation and textual analysis, to reveal examples of individual and collective agency, and to determine levels of access to texts and events. We also explored readers' own narratives about the social and cultural factors inflecting interpretative practices—such as gender, ethnicity, and age—as they emerged in focus groups and in responses to open-ended questions within the online survey. Interviews with event organizers and with selected teachers, writers, guest speakers, and invited performers who took part in some of the activities that constituted various MREs were another important qualitative method. The attitudes, experiences, and actions of event producers offered particular standpoints on the material processes of event production and the ideological factors shaping the desires of workers and managers whose professional and personal passion for reading generally coincide. Each of these methods brought a degree of insight to our analysis of contemporary cultures of reading.

We wanted our research methods to render some of the cultural specificities that inflect class, race, and gender formations and attitudes to literary culture within and across the three nation-states. For that reason, we decided to undertake context-specific case studies of selected MREs. We chose our fieldwork sites either because we were familiar with the local print cultures in the selected locations (Vancouver [One Book, One Vancouver], Birmingham, UK [focus groups for RJBC], and the Canadian Maritimes [focus groups for *Canada Reads*], for example); or because of their significance to the OBOC "movement" (Seattle was the first program, whereas Chicago was the model encountered and adapted by the first Canadian organizers in Kitchener-Waterloo-Cambridge and the first British organizers in Bristol); or to establish a range in the scale of events and communities studied (large cities located at a distance from metropolitan centers such as Liverpool, alongside smaller cities such as Huntsville, Alabama). Two sites were national in terms of potential audience because the MREs employed broadcast media as their primary means of communication. The radio series *Canada Reads* and RJBC on UK television not only offered us the opportunity to investigate two fascinating analogues to (and adaptations of) Oprah's Book Club, but also provided case studies of highly successful mass-mediated shared reading events that were deeply imbricated in the reading industry.

Several compelling reasons influenced our transnational approach to three northern, industrialized nations. For complex historical reasons, the US, Canada, and the UK share a number of similarities between their educational cultures and the institutions through which cultural authority and literary taste is constructed and promoted. It is beyond the scope of the current study to detail these similarities, but the multivolume histories of the book in Canada, the US, and the UK, map and analyze the colonial history of print cultures, the establishment of public library systems in all three nations, the history of publishing, and book-reviewing practices, among other factors (e.g., Kaestle and Radway 2009; F. Black, Fleming and Lamonde 2005; Suarez and Turner 2009). The dominance of English-language in these multicultural societies represents another aspect of common ground, although other languages are important to the operation of government services and to the everyday lives of significant sections of their populations. Spanish in the US, French in Canada, and the languages of the Indian subcontinent in the UK, have different degrees of visibility. Of the three nation-states, only Canada is an officially bilingual country, for example. Nonetheless, these languages (and others, such as indigenous languages in Canada) are supported by various educational programs, and by locally produced and published (as well as imported) print and digital media in languages other than English. What is striking to any student of contemporary print culture, however, is the importance since the early 1990s of transatlantic co-publishing practices and the transnational ownership of key publishing houses (see Chapter 4, "Money"). In this regard, the production and circulation of English-language books is often supranational at the level of financing and company ownership, even as the ownership of the content of books is nationally defined in terms of intellectual property law and with relation to the sales of rights within different territories of the world. The globalized structures of production—and even of evaluation in relation to book prizes such as the Impac or the Man Booker prizes (Roberts 2011, 39–43)—led us to consider the flow of contemporary print culture and the spread of shared cultures of reading as no longer strictly "national" in operation. The transnational mobility of models of MREs such as televised book clubs and of the OBOC program underline this observation.

We employed mixed methods in our multisite project, including an intentional mixing of language and concepts from realist and interpretative paradigms.[4] Our quantitative questionnaire ran online for six weeks in each of the ten fieldwork sites, in English in the UK, and in three languages in the USA and Canada (French, Spanish, and English). In the case of *Canada*

Reads and RJBC, we advertised the questionnaire across Canada and the UK, respectively (see Methods Appendix). In total, we gathered data from more than 3,500 questionnaire respondents (see Methods Appendix). We ran sixty-two qualitative focus groups with over two hundred readers, and conducted seventy-two individual interviews with event producers and other agents involved in the promotion, funding, or delivery of MREs. Participant observation of over sixty MRE activities, alongside textual and content analysis of promotional materials and event ephemera informed our efforts to generate and attend to a range of viewpoints on this cultural formation. In sum, we wanted to avoid simply taking a bottom-up (readers first) or top-down (funders and producers first) approach to our investigation. In the tradition of cultural studies we were concerned to elucidate "*all* the relations among *all* the elements in a whole way of life" (Grossberg 2010, 323; emphasis in the original). We are not, however, claiming that our version of mixed methods offers a whole, true, or complete picture of reading as a social practice. Rather, we advocate mixed methods research as an approach that can benefit reading studies, while avoiding the positivism of social science and the relativism that can characterize text-based humanities disciplines (Fuller and Rehberg Sedo 2012). The scale and scope of investigation was ambitious for a small team of researchers and there were several definite limitations to our research design and process. These limitations are discussed in our Methods Appendix. As we have explored elsewhere (Fuller 2012; Fuller and Rehberg Sedo 2012), there are also generative aspects to working as interdisciplinary researchers in a multidisciplinary core team consisting of members whose original training is in literary studies (Danielle Fuller, Anouk Lang) and communication studies (DeNel Rehberg Sedo). Above all, the scale of our study meant that we could identify interesting continuities and differences in social attitudes to the role that book reading is believed to play in people's lives.

The Reading Class in an Undistinguished Age: Introducing Our Readers

Our investigations, in particular our quantitative survey and our focus groups, tended to engage people who already identified themselves as readers. That is, they read for pleasure not only for work or study. We always intended to focus our efforts on this constituency in the sense that readers, rather than reluctant or nonreaders, were the prime subjects of our research. We wanted to hear about their perceptions and opinions of contemporary shared reading and book cultures, in particular, about what attracted them (or not) to MREs. We invited them in both the survey and focus groups to reflect on the role that reading played in their lives, and on the ways that might have changed through different life phases. The predominant demographic profile in both our focus groups and quantitative datasets consists of university-educated women whose first language is English, over a third of whom read for more than five hours a week (see Methods Appendix for statistics and discussion). In addition to these keen readers, however, we also sought out groups of people who did not fit this demographic. These people included teen readers in high schools and groups of readers and non-traditional reading groups who had been brought together by formal programs such as Get Into Reading (Wirral, Liverpool) and Literature for All of US (Chicago). We did this in part because of the difficulties we encountered in recruiting focus group participants who reflected the population demographic of the large urban field sites (e.g., Chicago, Vancouver). At the same time, as we discuss in the Methods Appendix, some of the practical limitations within fieldwork helped to make visible the formal and informal networks through which culture is made and evaluated. For instance, the difficulties of recruiting to focus groups also indicated to us which groups have most cultural capital within particular cities and who has the time, leisure, and social confidence to participate in cultural activities centered around print texts (as well as focus groups constructed by researchers) (Fuller 2012, 91–92). In the Methods Appendix, we present an account of our readers and provide detailed tables that, taken together, offer a portrait of those whom we met in focus groups (Table A1), and producers and organizers, along with other cultural managers and workers, such as authors and publishers whom we interviewed (Table A2). We also describe how we recruited people to our study and offer a rationale for the tactics that we employed.

In many respects, our readers correspond to sociologist Wendy Griswold's definition of "the reading class," that is, "those people who read for entertainment constantly" (2008, 37):

> A reading class has a stable set of characteristics that include its human capital (education), its economic capital (wealth, income, occupational positions), its social capital (networks of personal connections), its demographic characteristics (gender, age, religion, ethnic composition), and— the defining and non-economic characteristic—its cultural practices. (ibid.)

Drawing on various sources for readers' demographic characteristics, Griswold advances that "affluent people read more, although not all affluent groups are heavy readers," that the "racial/ethnic configuration varies from country to country," and that "more women read than men" (47). Education, rather than social class, tends to be another predicator for membership of the reading class. Class, as Tony Bennett and his colleagues have argued, is "muted" in twenty-first-century Britain (2009, 2), and, as we discuss in the Method Appendix, is not necessarily connected by British readers to their financial wealth as it is for many of the Canadians and most of the Americans in our study. Other social factors, such as ethnicity and gender, can affect access to formal education, which represents a resource for the learning of skills and knowledge that shapes choices about both work and leisure activities.

Education is an especially significant resource for twenty-first century book readers because to actively participate in contemporary cultures of reading in the three nation-states of our study requires more than just basic literacy skills. Griswold's (2008) differentiation between "a reading culture" and a "reading class" is pertinent here: "A reading class is a social formation, while a reading culture is a society where reading is expected, valued, and common. All societies with written language have a reading class but few have a reading culture" (37). In her investigation into the relationships between regionalism and reading culture in the United States, Norway, and Italy, Griswold observes:

> If a people are developing, or seem likely to develop, a reading culture, pressures for mass education emerge, for literacy starts becoming a requirement for full social participation. In an established reading culture, there is a rough but direct association between the prestige of a job and the amount of reading it requires. Moreover, reading for entertainment takes place at most social levels, with reading materials stratified from *belles letters* for the highbrows to comics, pamphlets, and *fotonovelas* for the semi-literate. In a reading culture, what one reads is a way by which people gauge social status. (165)

Even whereas some readers in our own study may be busy side-stepping the process of evaluating others on the basis of what they read for fear of appearing ungenerous or a culture snob, their dance of distinction suggests that Griswold is correct: cultural hierarchies of taste still adhere to reading materials, at the very least across the broader purview of reading that incorporates more than just books.

In an era when it is no longer easy to define what "good taste" might be within any specific field of cultural consumption (Bennett et al. 2009, 259), possessing knowledge of books may only be a visible and valuable asset to other members of the reading class. In this regard, MREs provide opportunities for readers to display to others their cultural competencies around book reading, such as interpretative skill, the ability to engage in book talk, knowledge of specific or various book genres, and of resources for finding out about books. Alongside the chance to demonstrate cultural capital, MREs offer readers a chance to negotiate with slippery notions of good taste—sometimes, as we shall see, by rejecting outright the organizer's idea of what counts as a "quality" book. Paradoxically, then, MREs are produced as part of popular culture but are often consumed as an aspect of a reading culture in which residual meanings about "quality" (or "highbrow") fiction and canonical ideas about aesthetics linger on. These notions coexist alongside more recent constructions of what constitutes a "good read" such as a discussable book, or one that the reader can connect to her own life experience. As we note in several of the following chapters, contemporary cultural producers of book-related events and media often deploy elements of the popular *and* the prestigious markers that connote "quality" in their branding and marketing strategies.

From the perspective of event producers like Amanda Ross, the initiator of the RJBC, there is also transferability between the entertainment derived from reading the "right" book, and the pleasure of a viewer watching the television book club (A. Ross, pers. comm., 2006). But, as we explore in the next chapter, books are not at all easy to remediate through television. Rather, event producers often assume transferability across and between media because they long to reproduce what for them personally is a special experience of reading. Paradoxically, they attribute qualities to reading and sharing books that they believe are not available from other forms of cultural consumption, and yet they seek to represent and remediate those experiences using nonprint cultural forms, media, and contexts. Certainly, emotional intensity can be reproduced across media to some extent, and forms of intimacy can be established whether an event is "live," local, or broadcast nationally. But, as we shall see, the success of these large-scale models for shared reading in terms of generating entertainment and feelings of social connection among strangers is never guaranteed. For all the skill, savvy, and alliances available within the reading industry, media sometimes clash rather than converge. At other times, the ideological imperatives attached to events by their organizers or funders limit the audiences they can reach. After all, reading is not everyone's idea of rock n' roll.

2 Television

There's a certain thread running through a lot of novels that have sold well in the UK in the last few years. They share nothing so exact as a genre or type, but they have exotic titles, a powerful story and a literary bent. Oh, and a badge. A badge that says "Richard and Judy."

—Rohrer 2009

They're always full of praise for the book—I haven't seen much criticism. I know criticism isn't always bad—there can be good criticism, but they're not very deep in what they say about it, are they? I think it's sort of a bit surface: this is fabulous, you must go out and read it, and here's our celebrity who really, really liked it, too, so if you like them, then you must enjoy it.

—Ben, Richard & Judy FG, 23 Jan 2007

In 1996, Oprah Winfrey introduced a segment on *The Oprah Winfrey Show* called Oprah's Book Club. As Winfrey herself said, the club was designed "to get America reading again" (Teather 2002). Winfrey's decision to create a book club for television and then to encourage her viewers to start their own book groups proved to be momentous. At a single stroke, Winfrey became a marketing force for books in her own right, as titles that she chose for discussion rocketed to the top of bestseller lists in the United States and around the world. Pundits weighed in on Winfrey's selections, alternately praising her choices and criticizing the ways that she selected books and shared them with others. But one thing is inarguable: Oprah Winfrey not only changed the reading habits of many Americans, but she also helped to bring book groups and shared reading to a new medium: television. The success of Oprah's Book Club has meant that it has received sustained scholarly attention from a number of quarters (Konchar Farr and Harker 2008; Peck 2010; Striphas 2009). But, although the role of television in the promotion of mass reading may have started with Oprah Winfrey, it did not end there. In this chapter, we examine a televised book club that has received less attention than Oprah's Book Club: The Richard & Judy Book Club, one of the most successful televised MREs ever produced in the United Kingdom.

In 2004, on the heels of the successful British Broadcasting Corporation's *The Big Read* program (2003), television talk show hosts Richard Madeley and Judy Finnigan began a book club segment on their hugely popular UK late afternoon program, *Richard & Judy*. Building on fame that had been growing since the late 1980s, the married couple, along with their producer, Amanda Ross, became important players in the reading industry. Publishing industry insiders and the popular press alike marveled at the golden touch that the book club's endorsement gave to a book and its author: approval by the RJBC brand on a book could mean an increase in sales by 1,000 percent (Jones 2008).

What was it about Madeley and Finnigan's version of a book club that proved that books and television can work together? Reading books and watching television—and especially daytime television—are not viewed in the same way as worthwhile leisure activities, so how were the celebrity couple able to straddle the two different sides of the cultural hierarchy divide? We believe that the unique personalities of the hosts, their on-and-off air relationship, and effective television production combined with a multifaceted branding campaign to ensure the book club's economic success. But this success resulted in a schism between readers. On one side of the divide stood readers who were skeptical of blatant commercialization and who perceived themselves as distinct from any popular form of reading recommendation. On the other side were readers who saw the couple as worthwhile cultural authorities advocating the fun aspects of reading and the accessibility of various book genres. Such opposing views arose, in part, because of the genre and format of the *Richard & Judy* show itself, its temporal location in the television schedules, and because it was broadcast on a commercial channel rather than by the BBC. The BBC, funded by the British public through the annual payment of a license fee, has traditionally been the television "home" for arts programming, including shows featuring books and writers. By the time that the RJBC began in 2004, however, British television had undergone a series of structural, organizational changes that contributed to the blurring of historical differences between commercial and noncommercial television. As we note below, Richard Madeley's and Judy Finnigan's careers map on to these changes in fascinating ways. Understanding the context for their television careers as well as the denigration of genres of daytime television helps to explain the differing responses of readers to the popular and economic success of the RJBC and its hosts.

BEYOND THE BOX: A BRIEF HISTORY OF BRITISH TELEVISION BROADCASTING

Britain's unlikely team of reading champions began their television careers as journalists and met while working on *Granada Reports*, a news show made by Granada Television (now known as ITV Granada). Granada was one of the original four franchise holders for commercial or "independent" television (ITV) in the United Kingdom, a regional system set up by the British government in 1955 as a result of the Television Act of 1954 "to counterbalance what was seen as an essentially London-focused BBC" (Crisell 2006, 24). Based in the northwest region of England, the broadcasting company originally promoted a strong northern identity through its programming, epitomized by its long-running soap opera, *Coronation Street*, which first broadcast in 1960. Although Granada was originally conceived as a "regional" company, the shows its employees produced were generally broadcast throughout the UK, so that presenters as well as particular programs became nationally well known. By the early 1980s, when Richard Madeley and Judy Finnigan met at the Granada studios in Manchester, the company had won a reputation for innovation and quality television production in several fields and genres. Notable critical successes included current affairs programming, such as the highly regarded *World in Action* (1963–1998), and serial drama such as *Brideshead Revisited* (1981) and *The Jewel in the Crown* (1984). Alongside the other ITV companies, such as Thames and Yorkshire television, Granada rivaled the BBC in exploiting the values of "quality" television (Brunsdon 1990). In the field of literary adaptation, for instance, *Brideshead Revisited* was an example of the "highly exportable 'heritage television' of the 1980s," which brought ITV commercial success as well as critical plaudits (Wheatley 2003, 80). Such series garnered substantial audiences, as did the BBC's adaptations of the "classics" of British literature known colloquially (and often affectionately) as "the Sunday tea-time serial" because of their early evening slot in the schedules. But, in spite of its association with prestige genres and "high culture," the BBC has never had a stranglehold on either "quality" television or on innovation. From its inception, in fact, ITV has pulled audiences away from the BBC because its programs have tended to more closely reflect changes in popular culture (Crisell 2006, 25). During the 1960s, for example, its producers were more open to American influences than those at the BBC, resulting in an energetic and visual style of presentation on news shows made by the ITV companies (Wheatley 2003, 78). It was within this environment of well-made television where production teams were responsive to emerging televisual styles that Madeley and Finnigan learned their trade, first as television reporters, and, later, as the presenters of shows that combined serious news features with items about pop stars and phone-in quizzes.

In many senses, the blend of integrity and enthusiasm that was to characterize Madeley and Finnigan's on-screen style reflected the mix of commercial aims with a public service broadcasting ethos instituted by the policies informing the original structure of the ITV companies. ITV came under the control of a government-mandated regulatory body, first known as the Independent Television Authority (ITA), and then, from 1972 (when radio broadcasting was also included), as the Independent Broadcasting Authority (IBA). Part of the ITA/IBA's role was to ensure that the ITV companies offered a range of programs that would appeal to the entire television-viewing public, not just to the advertisers who paid for "the spot advertising—'commercial breaks'—which occurred within and between the programmes" (Crisell 2006, 25). Editorial content and advertising were to remain distinct, and it was not until 2000 that advertisers were permitted to sponsor specific television programs such as *Richard & Judy*. The structuring of British television broadcasting as a duopoly serving the public interest contributed to a situation in which the BBC was forced to broaden its appeal, whereas ITV was reminded by various government committees in the 1960s and '70s to maintain quality and range. In other words, by the time that the fourth terrestrial channel, Channel 4 (future home of *Richard & Judy*) was launched in 1982, the distinctiveness of the BBC's programming profile from those of the independent channels was already significantly blurred. The following year, for example, both the BBC and an independent company, TV-AM, launched lightweight, magazine-style breakfast shows—the format that was to make household names of Madeley and Finnigan just a few years later.

The launch of Channel 4 expanded rather than ended the BBC-ITV duopoly, because, through a complex series of policies and agreements, ITV sold the advertising airtime for the new channel. For at least its first ten years, Channel 4 was, in effect, subsidized by ITV, and free to experiment in terms of program-making. The channel also hailed the beginning of a different model of UK television production, in which programs were commissioned from a range of independent production companies. Channel 4 (not unlike BBC2) was intended to cater for minority (or underrepresented) audiences, although, top of the schedules on its launch-day was one of the staple genres of ITV's success as a popular and populist broadcaster—a soap opera set in Liverpool, *Brookside*. Nevertheless, Channel 4's first decade included a substantial amount of politically challenging and socially controversial television-making, and, as John Ellis suggests, "defined many of the terms for British television in the emerging era of availability. It was the crucible in which programme-makers learnt to address niche or target audiences" (2003, 96). This was to become an important skill in the late twentieth-century, as the British television industry and broadcasting landscape began to look increasingly similar to its North American counterparts.

During the 1980s and '90s, a series of policy changes, especially those influenced in the years of Margaret Thatcher's right-wing government by American-style "deregulation," resulted in the "marketization" of British broadcasting (Hesmondhalgh [2002] 2007, 123). These changes initially made a big impact on the organization of ITV, but eventually also led to the creation of "internal markets" for program-making within the BBC (Garnham 1998, 216). Commerce and competition became more intense, as the structures of the industry changed. Shows became anchored to key television personalities like Madeley and Finnigan, rather than to specific channels like the BBC or ITV, and well-known presenters were able to move among them. New technologies, like cable and satellite television, also increased the availability of television broadcasting and further diluted the dominance of the public-service broadcasting ethos, because these wholly commercial companies were not obliged to follow the rules of a regulatory body like the IBA. Although initially slow to take hold in the United Kingdom, cable television (which began in 1983) became increasingly popular with subscribers in the second half of the 1990s. Rupert Murdoch's media empire launched the influential satellite company BSkyB in April 2001 and rapidly monopolized pay TV in the UK. Murdoch's company contributed significantly toward "the American style of *structuring* television as an ad-driven industry not a public utility" (Gray 2008, 100; emphasis in the original). The presence of BSkyB is a significant context for Madeley's and Finnigan's success with *Richard & Judy* on Channel 4, because the existence of a blatantly commercial channel alongside the terrestrial, public service–oriented channels, contributed to a more complicated set of symbolic relations among them. Within this nexus of cultural value, Channel 4 was positioned as overtly commercial yet able to deliver programming that retained something of the public service mandate, whereas the BBC, once identified by both the general public and the government as the bastion of everything non-commercial, was the focus of anxious debates in the media about slipping standards (G. Born 2003; Maggiore 2011; McGuigan 1996, 22). Launched in 2004, the RJBC could in many respects be understood not only as the product of a restructured broadcasting industry in which entertainment was key, but also as a perfect expression of Channel 4's position between the cultural authority of the BBC and the economic power of BSkyB.

As the first decade of the new century advanced, the expansion in the delivery of digital broadcasting meant that the television landscape altered significantly. In April 2003, for example, the combined ratings of the smaller specialist channels available through cable and satellite operators (including the BBC's own digital channels such as BBC4) surpassed those for the five traditional channels (BBC 1, BBC 2, ITV, Channels 4 and 5) for the first time (Crisell 2006, 37). Between 2008 and 2012, the UK "switched off" its analogue systems and British television "went digital" (Hesmondhalgh [2002] 2007, 263). As Madeley and Finnigan were to discover when they decided to leave Channel 4 for UKTV in 2008, the large audiences of over two million that they drew for *This Morning* (ITV) from 1988 to 2001 and for *Richard & Judy* (Channel 4) from 2001 to 2008 were no longer attainable in a multioperator, multichannel digital environment. In an era of television "overflow," when "television can be found on or in cell phones, DVDs, TiVo hard drives, PSPs, iPods . . . clothes, toys, videogames . . . official websites, spinoff websites . . . YouTube and iFilm, magazines [and] newspapers" (Gray 2008, 73), Richard Madeley and Judy Finnigan's Book Club is to be found online and in the windows of retailers (Figure 2.1).

As ever, the couple's careers have matched the trajectories of television broadcasting in Britain even to the point when "what it means to engage with a television programme, to 'follow' a specific show" (Brooker 2001, 457) may have little to do with watching a broadcast event on a television set.

Figure 2.1 Waterstones' Window
The RJBC's summer titles garner prime real estate in a central London Waterstones bookstore
Source: Authors' photo.

Madeley and Finnigan's television careers to date thus span a period in which deregulation brought about by government policy produced fierce competition among broadcasting companies operating within—and thanks to satellite technology—outside the United Kingdom. Their long tenure at Granada/ITV, in which they moved from reporting as journalists on a serious news program to presenting a popular morning television magazine show, was made possible, in part, because the structural changes in British broadcasting demanded new formats that would entertain viewers and win ratings wars. Broadcast mid-morning, *This Morning* (1988–2001) was an extension of the formats of breakfast television that emerged in the UK only in the early 1980s. Thus, in 1988, when Madeley and Finnigan began their new show, daytime television was something of a recent phenomenon in the UK. In many respects, the couple and the show's production team set the standard for live British daytime television by creating a dynamic mixed-genre magazine show. Significantly, it was a show anchored by highly capable hosts who could turn seamlessly from talking about breaking news with an expert to introducing a humorous feature centered on an ordinary member of the public. Their professional skill, combined with their friendly on-screen style, won Richard Madeley and Judy Finnigan many fans. At the same time, their popularity, celebrity, and their association with the often-derided genres of daytime television made them seem highly suspect to some viewers, and especially to the keen readers of our study.

Setting the Standard for Daytime TV

After marrying in 1986, much of Richard Madeley's and Judy Finnigan's subsequent life as a couple was lived out in public and subject to media attention because of their self-presentation on-screen. *This Morning*, a show devised by Granada, was originally broadcast from a studio in Liverpool, and aired on ITV. The show, which ran for two hours each weekday until 2001, included serious interviews with experts and politicians—Prime Ministers Tony Blair and Gordon Brown included—that drew on Madeley's and Finnigan's experience as journalists and their earlier news-oriented careers at Granada. However, *This Morning* mimicked the format of breakfast television by integrating serious interviews and news items with more entertainment-focused discussions with actors and comedians among features about cooking and healthcare advice, make-overs, and phone-ins. In visual presentation and tone, the show drew on the informal and energetic style of American daytime television, especially shows with charismatic hosts like *The Oprah Winfrey Show*, *Donahue*, and *Kilroy* (BBC1, 1986–2004). In fact, the ability of Madeley and Finnigan to project their own personalities on-screen led to many viewers referring to *This Morning* as "Richard and Judy." The program also illustrated the ethos of ITV scheduling during the late twentieth century, which was to offer viewers a bridge between serious "news" and the less serious soap operas and quiz shows featured on afternoon television (Brunsdon 2000, 8). The popular couple were described as "the most pervasive faces on television" and Finnigan as the "country's best-loved TV presenter" (McLean 2000). According to *The Guardian*'s Gareth McLean, the couple's early popularity lay mostly with Finnigan, because "she is real," and "she is One of Us on the telly":

> Judy isn't a cosmetically-altered dolly bird whose career will last as long as her looks. There is nothing manufactured about her. At times she looks fantastic, at others she looks terrible. This is life-affirming. With a background in journalism, she is, at 52, an attractive older woman who successfully combines having a family ("Jack, Chloe and the twins") and having a career. As such, she is testament that working hard and climbing the ranks—in television and, by extension, everywhere else— pays off. And she has suffered.

The "normal" persona that Finnigan presented to the UK viewing public, along with the entertaining banter between the husband-and-wife team, attracted much media attention. In a 2001 profile piece for *The Independent*, subtitled "Richard loves Judy, Judy loves Richard, Richard loves Richard. Which is why everybody loves Richard and Judy, television's golden couple,"

Cole Moreton begins with the lead sentence: "When Richard Madeley ejaculates he prefers to rest his 'equipment' for 25 minutes before attempting to make love with Judy Finnigan again."[1] Such intimate public talk, along with information about Finnigan's hysterectomy and other family secrets made the couple popular among viewers—but an easy critical target for others, including the British tabloid newspapers. Attracting upward of two million viewers, *This Morning* was successful because, in the words of Moreton, "it offered the ultimate in voyeuristic television . . . *This Morning* had the real-life, real-time spectacle of a married couple arguing, sulking, flirting, teasing and sometimes weeping, on camera, every morning, day after day, for year after year."

This Morning won the National Television Awards for the "Most Popular Daytime Show" in both 1999 and 2000. Nevertheless, Madeley and Finnigan left Granada Television in 2001 for Channel 4, to begin an afternoon magazine-format program that was to replace the American-imported *Ricki Lake* show in the schedules. Appropriately, given their now established national public profile as a celebrity couple, their new vehicle was called *Richard & Judy*, and was produced by London-based Cactus TV, a production company run by another husband-and-wife team, Simon and Amanda Ross. Over the next seven years, the couple's show garnered three million viewers (Jeffries 2009; Tivnan 2008) and maintained their popularity, despite, or perhaps because of, media coverage that was occasionally unfavorable, such as reports about the "You Say, We Pay" scandal in the popular press.[2] Key factors in the program's and couple's continuing success included their celebrated tenure on *This Morning* and the increasing omnipresence of the RJBC brand once the Book Club became a feature on the show in 2004.

As a magazine program, *Richard & Judy*, in common with *This Morning*, combined elements from various talk show genres. Neither show had a studio audience or featured audience discussion, but both were broadcast live and combined in-studio conversations with a range of interviewees with video-taped features and occasional live broadcasts from reporters on location. Whereas there was no audience present to provide "the applause and laughter" that "create[s] the sense of a live event" (Livingstone and Lunt 1994, 37), *Richard & Judy* offered viewers various forms of "active participation," including phone-in competitions, and, in the latter years of the show, live web chats with selected guests and the opportunity to buy featured books. *Richard & Judy*, in common with talk shows, blurred the "distinctions between entertainment and current affairs, ideas and emotions, argument and narrative" (37). Contributing to the "fuzzy and evolving" (37) aspect of genre boundaries on television through the inclusion of a dizzying range of features in each broadcast, *Richard & Judy* also embodied Channel 4's profile as a commercial channel with a public service ethos. Many of Madeley's and Finnigan's guests were on the show to publicize films, books and other current forms of entertainment and the show's website reflected the mix of information and commerce by offering visitors factual features alongside opportunities to purchase selected items—including the books featured on the RJBC. At the same time, advertising regulations forbade Madeley and Finnigan from explicitly encouraging viewers to go online in order to buy the books or other products (A. Ross, pers. comm., 2006). Both aspects of *Richard & Judy*—the mixing and blurring of genres and its blend of information and hard sell—unsettled a number of readers in our study, many of whom were invested in maintaining perceived differences between British television channels, as part of their belief in the relative cultural and educational value of television viewing and book reading.

Another aspect of *Richard & Judy* that shaped its reception by cultural commentators as well as viewers was the gendered association of daytime television, especially talk shows, as television made for housewives "concerned with gossip and story-telling" (Livingstone and Lunt 1994, 42). Scheduled into a late afternoon slot (5–6 p.m.) before most British people who work outside the home have returned from their workplace, Madeley's and Finnigan's afternoon television program was targeted at a primarily female audience, although, unlike *The Oprah Winfrey Show*, it was not deliberately intended "to empower women" (Squire 1997, 99). Amanda Ross, the producer of *Richard & Judy*, was hesitant to articulate actual demographics in an interview (pers. comm., 2006), but the audience can be assumed by the types of products promoted in advertisement breaks: cleaning solutions, pre-packaged dinner and diapers, for example (Meehan 2002). The content of the afternoon television program, however, did not necessarily adhere rigidly to topics that might be deemed interesting only to women. The eclectic issues tackled on *Richard & Judy* could range from strife in the Middle East to a case of stolen undergarments showing up in public places, with an interview with a famous actor positioned in between these features. The range of content and tone within one broadcast was typical of a magazine show (Brunsdon 2003, 9–11; Casey et al. 2008, 7; Moran and Malbon 2006, 36; 129). Indeed, the content and format of *Richard & Judy* meant that it could be "browsed" rather like a print magazine, instead of requiring the constant, focused attention of the viewer. Popular with students and retired people, as well as with women who were at home in the late afternoon (A. Ross pers. comm., 2006), the range of issues and recurring segments such as the "You Say, We Pay" phone-in quiz and the Book Club were skillfully brokered by Madeley and Finnigan.

The success of television talk shows depends in part on the point in the program where the guest and/or host(s) show ranges of emotion that "ordinary" people experience (Grindstaff 2002). One of the main reasons that the RJBC succeeded was because the Book Club segments allowed the two hosts an opportunity to express their own personalities. Their live, on-air reactions to the books mimicked how "regular" readers might respond. Rather than representing themselves as professional reader-critics who possessed specialized knowledge of narrative strategies and literary aesthetics, Madeley's and Finnigan's responses to their selections—and those of most of their guest reviewers—promoted reading as a pleasurable and accessible activity. In other words, Madeley and Finnigan, like Winfrey, made the books and book clubs "fit" the genre conventions of their daytime television shows as well as their personalities. They acted, as we noted in the introduction, as trusted guides rather than as authorities.

The cultural status afforded to television talk show hosts is an evolving process, however, and long-time presenters such as Madeley, Finnigan, and Winfrey have had to earn their role as lifestyle guides through various iterations of their shows by adapting their styles of self-presentation to the changing tone, demands, and reputation of daytime television programming. Madeley and Finnigan survived the denigration of "tabloid TV" as "talk trash" (Manga 2003, 222), largely because their shows avoided the sensationalism associated with American talk shows. During the 1990s, daytime television talk shows, especially the second-generation American talk shows such as *The Jerry Springer Show* and *Ricki Lake*, were constructed to reach out to younger audiences than the more serious "confessional" shows such as *The Oprah Winfrey Show* and were "based on the sheer pleasure of breaking social taboos" (Shattuc 2008, 169). All three shows were broadcast on British television, but *Ricki Lake* was eventually replaced by *Richard & Judy* in the aftermath of the negative criticism leveled at the genre. In 1995, and again in 1998, Senator Joseph Lieberman denounced "US daytime TV talk shows as sites of 'moral rot' and 'cultural pollution'" (Glynn 2000, 184, 223). Other cultural commentators focused on the negativity and violence promoted by the "real" people who appeared as guests on these programs during this period (Grindstaff 2002).[3] In the same year as Lieberman's initial accusation, Oprah Winfrey went on-air and "renounced the tabloid nature of talk shows," pledging that she would "go on 'a spiritual quest of moral uplift'" with her program (Shattuc 2008, 168). During the late 1990s, *The Oprah Winfrey Show* became "more respectable" as its production team, in common with those making other American talk shows, tried to differentiate themselves from "trash" by concentrating on the format of host, "celebrity" panel and guests, and an active audience (Haag 2003). This configuration of the genre was less confrontational in style and the conversational elements provided an excellent format for talk about uncontroversial topics such as books. Of course, Winfrey's mimicking of "real-life" book-club talk in American living rooms is the most famous example of making books and book-talk work well on television. Across the Atlantic, however, Madeley and Finnigan adopted similar tactics and communicative strategies with equally impressive results.

BADGING BOOKS: THE POPULAR SUCCESS OF THE RICHARD & JUDY BOOK CLUB

The RJBC aired as a thirteen-minute segment on the Wednesday afternoon edition of *Richard & Judy* each winter and summer from 2004 until 2008.[4] During the winter months, nine to ten books were highlighted and in the summer, six to eight were featured. Each week during the Book Club segment, the hosts were joined by two celebrity guest reviewers who discussed one of the selected books that were chosen from more than seven hundred sent to the show's producer Amanda Ross by UK publishers (pers. comm., 2006). At the end of the season, and in conjunction with the British Book Awards, the Book Club would culminate in viewers choosing The Richard & Judy's Best Read Book Award. Borrowing from, but adapting key elements of Oprah's Book Club, such as the in-studio book discussion and the opinions of "real" face-to-face book clubs, the husband-and-wife team became important players in contemporary print culture, but not through the medium of print. In the autumn of 2008, the show moved from terrestrial television to a cable channel, UKTV. There, the program's viewing figures fell dramatically, and the hosts ended their on-screen presenting partnership in July 2009.

Through the RJBC, Amanda Ross, Madeley, and Finnigan became agents within the reading industry. In fact, the Book Club exemplifies the contemporary realities of converged cultural media where books, television, and the Internet do not displace one another but, instead, coexist and interrelate. Subsequently, the function and status of each technology, including that of the printed book, shifts (Collins 2010; Jenkins 2006) and, we argue, should be problematized. Within this contemporary media landscape, the roles of television cultural workers converge in new ways with those of workers operating in book publishing. As the producer of a successful daytime TV show, Ross had the skills, agency, authority—and the dynamic duo of Madeley and Finnigan—to influence not only which books and authors would benefit from their exposure to a huge audience of potential readers, but also the messages that the show would construct and disseminate about those particular books, and, thus, about the meanings of reading more generally. Employing her economic and symbolic capital, Ross was a taste-maker as well as a money-maker for book publishers whose marketing budgets could never buy the type of exposure that the Book Club represented. Assisted by clever marketing schemes, the production team created branding through an easily identifiable logo, partnership advertising, and book-cover stickers.

With this "badge," as Finlo Rohrer (2009) recognizes in the opening quotation of the chapter, *Richard & Judy* endorsements helped to sell hundreds of thousands of books. Through the wide-ranging and eclectic titles selected for each year's lists, Madeley and Finnigan also effectively promoted books that might not otherwise have had mass-market appeal (Squires 2007, 174). The 2005 season of the RJBC, as an example, has been credited with generating £58,000 in sales of David Mitchell's *Cloud Atlas* (2004, 174).[5] In this way, the Book Club created a British equivalent to "The Oprah Effect," a phrase that captures how Oprah Winfrey's endorsement of a book could turn it into an instant best seller (Kinsella 1997; Max 1999). In the beginning of 2009, the British bookseller industry publication *The Bookseller. com* reported that the "value" of the RJBC was "more than a quarter of a billion pounds. Since it launched, 100 books have been selected, with 30.3

million copies sold for a total value of £180.4m. If the books were sold at full price, the value would be £255.6m" (K. Allen 2009). The figures for the Book Club's commercial power are as comparatively jaw-dropping as those for Oprah's Book Club, which, at its peak, moved an average of 1.5 million copies of an Oprah title into bookstores (Zeitchik 2002).

By the time that each Book Club became part of their well-established shows, viewers *trusted* Richard and Judy, just as Oprah's loyal audience trusted her. The emphasis within the UK show on the private lives of Finnigan and Madeley even led some viewers to perceive the couple as neighbors or friends. The kind of trust they inspired won Finnigan and Madeley the respect of viewers who were prepared to recognize them as lifestyle guides and cultural authorities who could help them navigate the field of consumption whether it involved wine or books.[6] But not everyone wished to follow their map. For some keen readers, print does not refer to "trashy" novels, popular genre fiction, or celebrity biographies—all types of books that have featured on RJBC summer and winter lists. Whereas book discussion on television talk shows may help some readers access fiction and nonfiction, for others, celebrating diverse genres of books, as Madeley and Finnigan did on-air, did not fit into the taste hierarchies that they envisioned for either the medium of television or print. According to our habitual readers, the combination of the "hard sell" of books with the (to them) unquestionably popular genre of the daytime television show inevitably promotes a limited version of reading pleasure, and one that is lacking in reflection and "literary" sophistication. These readers perceive television as a commercial medium that commodifies the lifestyles and objects that it represents, although, interestingly, they do not view radio in the same way. As we demonstrate in Chapter 3, "Radio," from the viewpoint of keen readers, radio and books might mix, but television and books do not. Disrupting the common perception that books and television should not be combined was thus not an easy task for the husband and wife celebrity book reviewers.

The aesthetic construction of the program, that is, the "look" and "sounds" of the RJBC, enabled the presenters and producers to reconfigure the meanings of reading as a solitary pursuit conducted in private into an interactive and social process that could benefit from the audiovisual aspects of television. In order to achieve this, the production team used genre markers that helped the viewer of *Richard & Judy* to recognize other modes of successful television production and also analogues with print media as they watched the show. Helen, one of our focus group participants, described the RJBC as "like an article in a magazine. You know, you have your keep-fit page and your cookery, then you've got a page about books and reading . . . I was excited when there was a book programme on because there are no popular book programmes" (R & J FG 2 P, 2007). The Book Club was one of several segments in the magazine format, which allowed this reader and others to position the club and the selected books within the genre of daytime television talk shows.

As we have argued elsewhere, the producers of the RJBC successfully employed the medium of television and the celebrity persona of the husband-and-wife team and of their guests "to make books accessible, fun and entertaining" (Fuller and Rehberg Sedo 2011, 39). The Book Club celebrated reading as both an interactive and interpersonal experience. Rather than promoting reading as instructional, reading was framed as a joyful, pleasurable activity. Richard's and Judy's personalities, and their interpretation of the selected books, also helped to make books accessible. Whereas the production of the Book Club segment was not as sophisticated—or as expensive to produce—as that of Oprah's Book Club, Madeley's and Finnigan's influence and popularity was evident through their media exposure and viewing figures, and the highly visible Book Club marketing always included photographs of the couple posing with books. The successful branding process included celebrity guests who may not have been known to the general public as readers, but whose enthusiasm on-air illustrated the accessibility of books and book talk. Their presence on the Book Club contributed to the production of a successful and entertaining daytime program. Nevertheless, the genre conventions of daytime television and the cultural status afforded to book reading are historically informed, and disruption of these conventions and codes is not easily achieved. To a large extent, however, *Richard & Judy* was successful not only in its efforts to combine elements of different talk show genres, but also in its translation of books to the medium of television.

MAKING "GOOD TV": CONNECTING WITH READERS ACROSS MEDIA

The Oprah Winfrey Show was the model broadcast book program that inspired producer Amanda Ross to create a UK version. In our interview with her, Ross told us: "I'd seen the success of Oprah Winfrey, and really wanted to do something like that, but for a British audience, and to do it for a British audience you have to do it in a very [different way] than you do for Americans, because theirs is very schmaltzy" (pers. comm., 2006). Despite Ross's declaration, some UK readers would consider the resulting RJBC to be "schmaltzy" television, given the propensity of Richard and Judy to express their emotional responses to books on-screen. Furthermore, both OBC and RJBC could be understood as programs that translate books and reading into a consumerist lifestyle paradigm (Collins 2010; Moody 2011).

In order to be successful, producers of shows that borrow formats from overseas need to be cognizant of the different cultural expectations of their audiences. Whereas the format is largely transferable, the style and especially the self-presentation of the host(s) must fit different national sensibilities. As we discussed in the introduction, Winfrey's self-help narrative speaks to the discourse of individualism dominant in the US (Peck 2008, 2010). Her confessional style and emotionally responsive performance, however, was uncomfortable for a UK audience, according to our focus groups. Madeley and Finnigan, on the other hand, were enthusiastic in their presentation style while following cultural codes about emotional expression. If there were tears, for example, they happened off-screen. In the show featuring *The Girls* ([2005] 2006), Judy reported that the book had "made her cry" (7 Feb 2007). In this way, the RJBC segments allowed the personalities of the hosts to anchor the interpretation of books and reading by deploying culturally appropriate forms of self-presentation.

The show's communicative strategies were also successful in disrupting elitist notions of reading and who could be a reader. The book selections made by the producers were a vital element in this process, and were also crucial to their skill and success at translating the narratives of print culture into audiovisual forms of storytelling. From the hundreds of book synopses sent by publishers each year, Ross chose eight to ten titles that would ensure that the on-screen book talk could fill eight minutes of airtime, and that the topics would make for "good" TV (see McCrum 2006). Season lists (Ramone and Cousins 2011, 201–20), including the Winter 2007 season, which we evaluated in particular, illustrate the eclectic nature of the titles that Ross chose. Table 2.1 is a list of the books selected for the Winter 2007 season.

The Book Club selections included wide-ranging choice of genres, which reflects the genre preferences of our surveyed readers in the UK: the top choices were Contemporary Fiction (36 percent), Mystery (17 percent), Science Fiction (9 percent), followed closely by Classical Fiction (5 percent), History (5 percent), Romance (5 percent), and Biography (5 percent). The

Table 2.1 The Richard & Judy Book Club's 2007 Book Club Picks

Title (Air date)	Author	Publisher
The Interpretation of Murder (31 January 2007)	Jed Rubenfeld	Headline
The Girls (7 February 2007)	Lori Lansens	Knopf Canada
Restless (14 February 2007)	William Boyd	Bloomsbury
Love in the Present Tense (21 February 2007)	Catherine Ryan Hyde	Black Swan
Semi-Detached (28 February 2007)	Griff Rhys Jones	Penguin Books
This Book Will Save Your Life (7 March 2007)	A. M. Homes	Penguin Books
Half of a Yellow Sun (14 March 2007)	Chimamanda Ngozi Adichie	Harper Perennial
The Testament of Gideon Mack (21 March 2007)	James Robertson	Penguin Books

selections reinforced the show's framing of reading as entertaining, and also as a nonelitist activity. One cultural commentator went so far as to declare: "Amanda Ross has created a revolution in the nation's reading habits, democratising the world of books so that readers with non-literary backgrounds can enjoy literature without feeling intimidated" (Farndale 2007). Part of that enjoyment, we argue, was in the visual representation of the books and the hosts' and guests' interpretations of them.

The making of Ross's "good TV" included "live" studio conversations with celebrity guests who described their reading experiences and often articulated emotional responses to the books. These responses were discussed and valued on air, and became part of up-beat introductions to the Book Club books. Viewers were also taken on a tour of the book's setting by its author, and they saw members of face-to-face book clubs offering sound-bites of opinion in two edited sequences shot on location. Each weekly Book Club segment began with Madeley or Finnigan introducing the book and its author. Within the first three minutes, the host provided a personal judgment of the book that set the tone for the upcoming discussion. In introducing the 2007 edition of the Book Club, for example, Madeley opened the show with a trailer statement introducing Jed Rubenfeld's (2006) *The Interpretation of Murder* as a "sexy, gripping murder mystery" (31 Jan 2007). Each trailer, whether presented by Madeley or Finnigan, was an enthusiastic endorsement of the book. "One of my favourite authors," Madeley claimed as he introduced William Boyd (14 Feb). About *Half of a Yellow Sun* ([2006] 2007), he said, "[i]t's everything that a good book should be; exquisitely written, easy to read, utterly absorbing and profoundly moving" (14 March 2007). Finnigan introduced *The Girls* as "one of the most wonderful books I have ever read" (7 Feb). The hosts also provided viewers with genre classifications of the featured books. *Restless* (2006) was classified as an historical spy novel (14 Feb 2007), Ngozi Adichie's book as "consecrated" literary fiction via a reference to its prize-winning status (14 March), and *The Girls* was framed as contemporary fiction (7 Feb).

The Book Club segment formula continued with audiovisual strategies that connected viewers to the book's author. Playing into a notion of the celebrity writer whose domestic and personal life secures the value or meaning of their written work, viewers would be taken to the author's home, workplace, or homeland. The four- to seven-minute personal account of the book's characters, setting, or plot usually included a nod to the author's writing process. Through the creation of these kinds of audiovisual intimacies, the authors contributed to what social psychologists call *para-social relationships* with readers and potential readers (Giles 2002; Harris and Watson 2007). During the show (31 Jan 2007) that featured Jed Rubenfeld's *The Interpretation of Murder*, for example, the author is on location in New York City. Short, edited sequences of archived film footage, photograph stills and head shots of the author talking highlighted the setting, and reminded the viewer of infotainment documentary television. One shot even captured the author with his head down in large tomes of supposedly important historical documentation, as if to verify the "serious" nature of his historical research. In another segment (7 Feb 2007) for Lori Lansens's novel *The Girls*, the viewer is shown the author's home in rural Ontario. The author's voice was complemented by a country tune as background music. Between shots of Lansens looking pensively across rolling farmland or over rugged wilderness, historical still shots worked to create a sense of place and time that situated the main characters of the book, conjoined twins Rose and Ruby, but also helped to orientate viewers in the UK who might never had set foot in Canada. Sometimes, the segment producers and directors would attempt to mimic the book's genre or tone with the author's voice as narrator. A. M. Homes's (2006) *This Book Will Save Your Life* was introduced with footage (7 March 2007) that was edited with a series of extremely fast shots and loud and changing House music, all of which conveyed the sense of hurriedness one assumes of life in the book's setting of Los Angeles. Meanwhile, misty and moody shots (21 March 2007) of the Scottish landscape provided the backdrop for James Robertson's (2006) *The Testament of Gideon Mack*.

The segment (14 Feb 2007) that highlighted Boyd's *Restless* was a good example of the producers' attempt to translate genres across media. Using cues from film-noir, the mini-documentary clip began with the author sitting in a parlor in front of the fireplace at dusk. Boyd's baritone voice carried the visuals from shot to shot, and viewers saw reenactments of pivotal scenes in the book that included original World War II–era video and audio clips. The dramatization was augmented with shots of Eva the spy, and the book's main character, on a bridge on a foggy evening. She was also seen meeting clandestinely with a man who must have been the character Lucas Romer, a mysterious Englishman who recruited Eva to espionage, and was played by the author himself. The use of color also references film noir, but with a visual twist, which highlights the romance narrative in the book: whereas the sequence is shot in black and white, Eva's lips and coat are colored bright red.

While the "documentary" clips and dramatizations told their own story utilizing viewers' visual and televisual genre competencies, the importance of storytelling was evident in all of the RJBC segments. In trailers for upcoming weeks, Madeley or Finnigan often commented on an author's ability to tell a story. In introducing *Restless*, for example, Finnigan called the book a "fascinating spy thriller" by "master story-teller William Boyd." Griff Rhys Jones's *Semi-Detached* (2006) is described as a "warm and witty account of growing up in middle-class household" (28 Feb 2007), and *This Book Will Save your Life* by A. M. Homes is introduced as a "compelling account . . . charming, funny and profound" (7 March 2007). Another communicative strategy of the Book Club, the celebrity book discussion, made the books even more inviting and accessible, as viewers were invited into the book discussion as part of the ongoing storytelling process.

CELEBRITIES ON THE SOFA: BOOK TALK ON
THE RICHARD & JUDY BOOK CLUB

Most of the interpretive book talk portion of the Book Club segments lasted no longer than six minutes. Whereas the sustained discussions possible on other broadcast book programs—or in "real" book clubs—were missing, viewers were provided with glimpses into the plot, characters and settings of the highlighted books. The short clips not only help us better understand why the RJBC was so successful, but also how the Book Club talk perpetuated and also disrupted common assumptions about shared reading practices. The composition and conversation of the celebrity book club was especially effective in reconfiguring perceptions of reading and book clubs. Instead of calling the two invited celebrities "book club members," Madeley and Finnigan referred to them as "guest reviewers." In this sense, they were given cultural capital while also maintaining the status of "regular readers." Each episode featured two popular personalities, at least one of whom had acquired cultural authority in a different cultural field. News broadcaster John Humphries and actor Olivia Williams joined in for the discussion of *Restless*; soap opera star Michelle Collins of *Eastenders* and popular television actor Jason Merrells discussed *Love in the Present Tense* (2007); and, Alan Davis and Fay Ripley—both comic actors—reviewed *This Book Will Save Your Life*. The celebrities chosen by the producers elected to review the selected texts indicate an effort to position reading as an antielitist activity. The choices suggest an awareness on their part to reach their assumed audience and to try to position reading—or at least, reading in or with the program—as a popular activity. Most broadcast arts and book programming in the UK, such as BBC 2's *Newsnight Review* (weekly 2000–2009, now broadcast as *The Review Show*), tends to include highbrow, expert commentators, or as one of our focus group participants called them, "overclass[ed] people" (Una, R & J FG 6 P, 2007).

Regular guests on the Friday night *Newsnight Review*, for example, included Germaine Greer who was always introduced as a "well-known feminist author and academic," "poet and literary critic" Tom Paulin, and "journalist and director of the Institute for Contemporary Arts" Ekow Eshun. Intriguingly Bonnie Greer appeared on both *Newsnight Review* and the RJBC. Perhaps Greer was chosen by Amanda Ross because her association with the BBC 2 arts program, which was broadcast as a late-night, once-weekly strand of a heavyweight news show, and which, moreover, was produced by the public broadcaster, brought an aura of "high art" authority to the daytime Channel 4 program. Introduced by a well-established BBC journalist as well-respected writers, critics and denizens of the arts, the reviewers on *Newsnight Review* were framed as leaders in their cultural fields of production. The aesthetics of the show emphasized this framing: guests and presenters sat in a semi-circle on individual chairs in a small studio against the background of a screen onto which images relating to the book, theater production or film under review were projected. Although short video-taped films (VTs) offered brief introductions to the cultural product or its author in common with the RJBC format, the *Newsnight Review* VTs exempted presenter and guests from summarizing the content of the book or film. Rather, the VTs functioned as a means of clearing the way for the guests' evaluations that were underwritten by their well-informed references to analogous works of art. Hotly debated disagreements about the intellectual and artistic merits of the various items selected for review were also a typical element of this and several other BBC-produced arts and book shows. By contrast, the celebrities on the RJBC, including Madeley and Finnigan, avoided representing themselves as experts because they personalized their reading experiences rather than employing specialist knowledge or language. After the introductory minidocumentary for *The Girls*, for example, Finnigan began with a personal endorsement of Lansens: "She's really nice, and I'm really glad because when you love the book, you really want to like the author." Of course, the inclusion of celebrity panelists on the RJBC also reflected the producers' astute appreciation for the production of media spectacle (Fuller and Rehberg Sedo 2006; Kellner 2003).

To further simulate a "normal" book club, the broadcast discussion took place in a living room set, but the talk did not usually sound like most book club talk. Similar to the conventions of all talk, which differs according to the social situations in which it takes place (Fiske 1987), book club talk usually finds readers talking in patterns that have been negotiated over time (Hartley 2001; Long 2003; Rehberg Sedo 2004) instead of in the polished discussion necessary in a staged setting. The manner of book talk in a "real" book club varies; it might include all members speaking at once, or it might sound like a talking circle in which each member has an opportunity to voice her or his opinion and interpretation (Rehberg Sedo 2004). Whatever the talk sounds like, members in most "real" book clubs are able to voice dissenting opinions of the selected book. This was not necessarily the case on the RJBC. Whereas the mood changed according to the book being featured and also with the personalities occupying the book club sofa, very rarely did anyone say anything negative about the book, and never about its author. The discussion might have been upbeat and frivolous as it was with comic actors Alan Davis and Fay Ripley's take on Homes's *This Book Will Save Your Life,* or serious and moody as it was when dramatic actors Hugh Bonneville and Brenda Blethyn discussed with the hosts Robertson's *The Testament of Gideon Mack.* If any celebrity guest said something negative about the book, it was contrasted with an endorsement. We see this, for example, in a comment made by newsman John Humphries in his interpretation of Eva, the spy character in *Restless.* "She is too perfect," Humphries insisted, but ended with the caveat: "It's still a terrific story . . . a page turner." Similarly, although actor Brenda Blethyn endorsed *The Testament of Gideon Mack* as an excellent choice for book clubs, her fellow celebrity book-club member and actor Hugh Bonneville was not satisfied by the book. He claimed that the "first portion of book was riveting, but by the time it got to the devil episode" he "felt a bit lost." Later in the conversation, Bonneville tries to bring out the ironies and religious ideas he saw in the story, but there was not sufficient time to fully develop his ideas in order to produce the deep analysis that some viewers might expect of book talk. In this way, then, the conversation plays into the marketing and promotional process of the Book Club.

Still, in eight minutes or less, the celebrity guest reviewers provided personal responses to the text, which supported the building of para-social relationships between the viewers and the celebrities. Almost every discussion began with one of the hosts asking one of the guests what he or she enjoyed about the story. "What about it did you particularly like?," Finnigan asked soap opera actor Amanda Holden of Lansens's *The Girls*. To bring in the other guest reviewer, actor Colin Salmon, Finnigan asked him if, while reading the book, he had to remind himself that it was fiction. Salmon responded positively and continued by referring to his childhood reading experiences. He positioned *The Girls* as a book that he would give to his own children because it is "really responsible, honest storytelling" (7 Feb 2007).

The personalization of subject matter within the RJBC is not unlike that of talk show guest experts (Grindstaff 2002, 228–29; Holderman 2003). As Grindstaff has demonstrated, producers attempt to validate the knowledge of the viewers: "Talk shows reject criticisms of the ordinary person as incompetent or ignorant, question the deference traditionally paid to experts, and assert instead the worth of common opinion" (2002, 228). In the case of the Book Club guests, the "experts" were positioned as everyday readers who might have cultural authority in one field, but who do not necessarily have the same authority in the print culture field. In this way, the viewers could imagine they had the same level of knowledge and skills as the celebrities.

By including one male and one female guest reviewer in each segment, the producers also challenged common assumptions about the gender composition of book clubs. Whereas the talk tended to be gender neutral, both *The Girls* and also *Love in the Present Tense* allowed for direct confrontation of assumptions about the books based on the titles and on the covers. Whereas both books would appeal to a female audience, they were not positioned as Chick Lit. The talk about these books, and *The Girls* in particular, followed normative gendered expectations with the men speaking about the craft of the author's storytelling and the women speaking to the novel's connections to and representations of mothering, womanhood, and sexuality. Still, in discussing the quality of the storytelling, Salmon exposed the gendered aspects of the discussion and of the book's marketing by appealing directly to male viewers: "the title, unfortunately, *The Girls*, does exclude me. I wouldn't take it off the shelf, but we're going to change that this afternoon. Boys, buy the book. It's great!"

There were other instances in the 2007 book discussions where the talk disrupted the assumptions that some audience members might have held about mixed-gender-group book talk. In the segment that highlighted

The Interpretation of Murder, for example, theater reviewer Bonnie Greer speaks to the writer's technique, his use of the thriller genre, the pace of the story, and, the style of writing. She classified the book as a "really brilliant" interpretation of Hamlet, and claimed that Rubenfeld's story kept the reader "enthralled." Lest the viewer should be intimidated by references to Shakespeare's *Hamlet* or the book's main characters Sigmund Freud and Carl Jung and their ideas of psychoanalysis, Greer was quick to qualify Rubenfeld's skill: he "makes it accessible and you can understand these big ideas," she claimed. Madeley, on the other hand, demonstrates his own level of interpretive expertise or makes a tacit judgment of the priorities and abilities of his audience by asking the comedian and writer Richard Herring if he found the book to be "sexy." Herring, shifting his position on the sofa as if he was taken by surprise at such a question, responded by saying: "it is sexy in a perverse sort of way." He continued with an interpretation of the women in the novel as being portrayed as sex objects. Greer disagreed and saw the female characters as catalysts for change. In this segment, it was the women who carried the scholarly discussion about Freud, Jung, and psychoanalysis. They deconstructed Freud's theory on the interpretation of dreams and his Oedipus complex, which runs as a current throughout the historical novel. It was also the women who identified Rubenfeld's engagement with issues of the class system in New York at the turn of the twentieth century. Madeley, however, tried to reduce the talk to "sex," and titillation.

There were instances during the book discussions when assumed gendered reading preferences were directly confronted. We noted this above with Lansens's *The Girls*. In discussing *Love in the Present Tense*, the final moments of the conversation also played out in distinctly gendered recommendations:

Jason Merrells:	I think the novel for me is basically sentimental. What I mean by sentimental is that it paints in very broad brushstrokes. I never quite got away from the fact that these characters were sort of illustrating a point that she wanted to make. I never quite got away from that. And, I think that Leonard is almost too good to be true. This little Moses. This little Solomon.
Michelle Collins:	But isn't he supposed to be?
Richard:	I mean, apart from his eyesight, which is flawed. Do you know what I mean?

[discussion continues]

Merrells:	If Hollywood were to make this film, you wouldn't have to add any sugar.
Collins:	Brad Pitt, what do you think? Brad Pitt [as] Mitch?

[laughter]

| Judy: | Ahhh. Ohhh. |
| Richard: | I do think it's a wom— [starts again] I do think it's a book more for women than for men. |

[shot of Collins disagreeing with the assessment]

| Richard: | It's not my favourite in the list we've had so far, but I do think it's beautifully written. |
| Merrells: | Ya, so do I. |

The reference to the emotional elements of the book warned the male viewers that they might not like it, although Michelle Collins gave a nonverbal cue of disagreement and Madeley tried to endorse the author's style. In the final wrap up of the segment, Madeley closes with a warning: "I think people with a sensitivity to sentiment might not like it as much as the others." So whereas the subject matter of the novel is discussed in terms of the story it tells, the final take-home message for male viewers is that *Love in the Present Tense* is a "woman's book."

The recommendations targeted specifically to women or men were less evident in the other discussions. In the Book Club featuring Griff Rhys Jones's memoir *Semi-Detached*, for example, the conversation focuses not on boyhood or fatherhood, and the book's appeal to men, but more generally on memories. Actress Geraldine James set the stage for this book's discussion. Madeley begins the conversation by saying "you feel as if you're swimming in another man's dreams . . ." and James continues with: "But isn't it funny when somebody writes as accurately as this that it actually sparks off your own memories?" Prompted by this first interpretation, and the genre of the memoir, the discussion then concentrates on each member of the Book Club recalling their own memories of childhood in a fairly serious, yet celebratory tone. The discussion mimicked those "real" book club discussions in which memory work becomes part of the readers' interpretive process. In the case of the televised book club discussion, viewers are given glimpses into the intimate lives of the celebrities, thus providing another way to further nurture para-social relationships with them (Giles 2000, 2002, 2003; Greenwood and Long 2009; Haag 2003; Livingstone 1992; Rubin and McHugh 1987).

The perception of intimacy between presenters and viewers was part of the success of the RJBC. The appearance or performance of a nonthreatening middle-class (white) identity was, at least for some viewers, an attractive aspect of the show. Reading was presented as something that anyone, with any level of education, could do, whereas books seemed less "special" and less distinct from other forms of leisure culture. Amanda Ross herself was aware of this, commenting that "book programming in the past has categorized people too much . . . it's decided who its viewers are, and decided who would be interested in hearing about books, rather than thinking 'This book could be interesting to anyone"' (pers. comm., 2006). The Book Club segment that highlighted Chimamanda Ngozi Adichie's *Half of a Yellow Sun* (14 March), the final segment of the 2007 season, illustrates well our arguments about how the RJBC worked to make reading fun, and books accessible through visual and oral storytelling techniques. The segment was consistent with the format of the previous shows: the scene began with an enthusiastic endorsement from the hosts; the careful production of a minidocumentary about the author drew upon the genre of infotainment television; and, the segment also disrupted and perpetuated common assumptions about book club composition. Nevertheless, the discussions, and the knowledge that was created in the book talk, illustrate the limitations of book interpretation within the short time frame available in a television magazine program.

Madeley began the segment with an effusive introduction: "It's everything that a good book should be; exquisitely written, easy to read, utterly absorbing and profoundly moving." While listening to Madeley's voice, viewers see a close-up shot of the twenty-nine-year-old author of the novel. The host positions the book as accessible and attractive to both men and women by calling the book "a Nigerian version of *Gone with the Wind*."[7] The minidocumentary then takes viewers to the 1960s Nigerian Civil War, commonly referred to as the "Nigeria-Biafra War." The book is framed as serious and historically important with black-and-white film footage and a loud soundtrack of the war in the background. A close-up shot of Adichie clad in African fabric dress makes the exotic accessible to viewers, and this process is extended by the author's narrative about her emotional connections to the content of the book:

> Writing *Half of a Yellow Sun* I would often stop to cry because I realised I wasn't just writing a book, I realised I was recording the memory of people who had actually lived through this. I would sometimes think about my grandfathers and think, "Am I doing them justice by writing this book?" (14 March 2007)

In the course of using her own description and interpretations of the book's characters, setting, and plot, viewers were able to connect with the author through her articulations of emotions that the readers might feel themselves and a personalization of the writing process that they could appreciate. Adichie's narrative is also framed as appealing to both a female and male audience through the author's referencing of the romance plot: "For me," she said, "this is a book about love . . . , it's very intense. And, I wanted it to be very sexual and also be full of betrayal and distrust, and also to watch how war changes love." In these opening filmed sequences, viewers can learn about the author's connections to the conflict, while also potentially being exposed to new knowledge through the presentation of the historical background material about the Biafran War. The film also elucidates Adichie's goals for the novel and suggests connections between the fictional story and her own family history. By explaining her family's involvement, Adichie is able to evoke empathy for the characters in her book. Her narrative is complemented with extremely vivid images of the war that show the suffering of the people and the destruction of the land. At the end of the segment, the author invites the potential reader to share her emotions: "I hope *Half of a Yellow Sun* is a book that makes people cry, and makes them laugh, and makes them think. And, most of all, makes them remember that all of us are human." This universal emotional appeal is an important maneuver aimed at reducing the "otherness" of the experiences that Adichie describes in the novel and the minidocumentary, but one that it is open to misreading. "One human" erodes cultural differences in ways that are problematic, as Helen Cousins (2011) identified in her study of reader responses to *A Thousand Splendid Suns* (Hosseini 2007) and *Half of a Yellow Sun*. According to Cousins, positioning readers as "one" can lead to the perpetuation of generalized assumptions about a place and its people, which often adhere to negative stereotypes:

> Whilst the familiar is frequently expressed in terms of the universal, often it is a familiarity of those (post)colonial recognitions whereby a sense of "us" as different from "them" is evoked; where the "insight" is not empathy for people like "us" but a sympathy based on reader's assumptions about that other culture and its people, mediated through difference. (2011, 142)

In the *Half of a Yellow Sun* segment, a good example of this problematic was evident in the closing shot: a clip of a young, starving African child with tears in her eyes. Ideological stereotypes in which white viewers are positioned as those who pity the starving poor people of Africa negate the emotional appeal that Adichie extends via her narrative. That the producers chose to use this visual image is perhaps not so surprising in that the conservative nature of the Book Club generally did not complicate ideas about cultural differences in either its book choices or during the book discussions.

Unlike all of the other celebrity Book Club members, the guest reviewers for this segment were two men, both of whom have a significant amount of cultural authority. Scottish-born stage actor, educator, and writer, Brian Cox, along with Rageh Omaar, a Somali-British news reporter and writer, represented the more "serious" celebrity guests of the 2007 series. Other "serious" guest reviewers that season included the BBC journalist, John Humphries, and Bonnie Greer, who is a highly sought-after arts reviewer. The solemn nature of the book's themes perhaps motivated the producers to choose two guests who could discuss the content in a manner that would represent expert analysis and yet not disenfranchise the viewers. The choice of these specific guests extends our discussion of the dominant gender assumptions evident in the Book Club. On the one hand, the guest might represent the "seriousness" of the book, translated here into the gendered notion that it requires men to discuss it. On the other hand, the choice might also construct a message about the book that emphasizes war rather than the love story aspect, which recodes it as "not a woman's book." Either analysis supports our argument that the RJBC was active in constructing interpretive frames for the selected books. Books and genres were coded or recoded in "gendered" or counter-gendered ways in a continuous—and complicated—way.

The book's discussion began, as usual, with Madeley setting the tone about the accessibility of the novel. Although the themes might be dark, he set the audience's mind at ease, by declaring:

> I don't know about you guys, but when I started this, when I read the jacket, and started, I thought, "ok, this is going to be a bit like home-work. I'm going to get a bit of a lecture about [the] Biafran [War] and stuff. And, I'm going to be reading about a culture and a world that I'm not familiar with." But actually, within three pages, I felt as if I was reading about something that happened here in Britain. The parallels between all of our lives are so identical, aren't they? (14 March 2007)

His question invites Omaar to respond with his own interpretations of the universality of the characters. Omaar personalized the theme of humanitar-ian love during times of war by using illustrations from his own experience as a war correspondent. Cox chimed in with his agreement by providing a synopsis of a scene in the book when the value of black/white human life is debated, adding that the book rings "a universal bell." Finnigan jumped into the conversation with the qualification that the war does not enter into the story until later in the book. Gesticulating with her hands while seated on the edge of the sofa, Finnigan's enthusiasm for the novel reached out to viewers who might be put off by the topic of war. "So you're bowling along in this wonderfully warm story of communities, and sisters, and lovers, and all the rest of it. And, I loved all that. I loved that community."

The disruption of the community and the upheaval of the middle-class character's lives were discussed briefly before Madeley started to wrap up the conversation with a seemingly self-deprecating "it certainly stops you feeling smug about your own culture. Because I was thinking slightly smugly at one point 'thank God these things don't happen on our continent.' And then, I thought, 'What are you talking about? Think of France, think of Central Europe in the last war' . . ." All of the Book Club members mur-mur sounds of agreement, and then the discussion allows for Cox to articu-late his identification with a character in the book. Like members of "real" book clubs, Cox's confession of understanding a boy character who rapes a girl illustrates the intimate nature of the televised book-club setting. It also demonstrates how, even in a very short period, the Book Club talk could sometimes sound like that which takes place in "real" living rooms, because the talk moves from the declaration of universal themes, to the collapsing of differences, toward a more considered recognition of them. Madeley draws the conversation to a close by calling the book a "masterpiece" and the guests agree, with Finnigan claiming that the book is one of the best books she has ever read in her life. By the end of the energetic discussion, it is difficult to determine what kind of knowledge is facilitated in thirteen minutes, when the topics that the novel raises are so complex. Perhaps, as Fuller and Procter (2009) have concluded through their study of several face-to-face book clubs, the talk might not result in overt political action, but it might have acted as an entry point to conversations about race and class for some readers.[8] For other readers, it might just be that the talk prompted them to buy and/or read the book. What is certain is that Richard's and Judy's treatment of the book talk helped to communicate to their audience that, no matter which genre of literature was discussed, the books would appeal to their viewers. Furthermore, the careful (and costly) production of the Book Club segments worked to create trust between the viewer and the hosts.

THE "TRUSTED OTHERS": NEW CULTURAL AUTHORITIES AND TASTE-MAKING ON TV

As we mentioned above, part of the success of the Book Club lay in the personalities of each member of the husband-and-wife team. Because their talk show had, by 2009, been on air for twenty-one years, viewers had many opportunities to create and strengthen their para-social relationships with the hosts. We saw evidence of these kinds of relationships among our focus group participants who were work-at-home mothers or retired people. Wendy (60), a lower-middle-class reader who is retired and living in Birmingham, describes the consistent dependability of seeing the couple on television:

> . . . when the book thing came along that was a sheer stroke of genius and I think they're only what you'd regard as minor celebrities, but they're out there and, well, a lot of people are aware that they're there and I think having known them through the years like a lot of people, I think, you gain respect for the fact that (a) they're still together (b) they're still going and that they do have some interesting things to say, and when they bring in other people to discuss these books, either celebrities or the authors themselves, it ripples out, doesn't it, and you all gain from something that they've started and I don't think it'll ever go away because I think it's brought it into the national consciousness and psyche that, you know, reading is good. (R & J FG 6 P, 2007)

In para-social relationships, an intimate bond forms over time between a viewer and the media personality or fictional character. It is not uncomfortable, then, for regular viewers of the show to see Richard kiss Judy as a way to apologize for not including her opinions in a summary of what the featured readers thought of *Love in the Present Tense*. As Rubin and McHugh note, "[A]s time goes on, predictability about the character is increased. The character is reliable. The fan is loyal" (1987, 280). In this sense, Madeley and Finnigan became trustworthy sources for book recommendations to a certain set of television viewers. Of those readers we surveyed, one-third (33 percent; 492) of those who watch the Book Club segment did so because it motivated them to read or encouraged them to read books they would not normally read. In other words, Richard and Judy acted as "trusted others" whose book selections were reliable. Typically, readers place their friends and family in this role (Rehberg Sedo 2004), and for members of book clubs, their fellow members can also come to occupy that position. Rather cleverly, the RJBC television feature always included a "real life" book club in order to develop its role as a "trusted other."

Each Book Club segment ended with a two-minute review of the book from a featured book club. The formula included a one-minute, videotaped clip of the club meeting and discussing the book. Only in the *Half of a Yellow Sun* segment did the Book Club include members who are not white. Instead, the perception of book clubs as a white, middle-aged, middle-class women's activity was largely supported through the producers' choice of featured book clubs (Hartley 2001; E. Long 2003). The very short snatches of conversation to which viewers were privy made for successful television production, but they included only supportive comments about the book. A still image of a pile of books—the selections for the 2007 Book Club—were superimposed on the right-hand side of the screen during the sequence of rapid-fire reader's comments. In common with the enthusiastic tone of the studio discussion, the opinions offered in all the book-group films tended to be positive, focusing on sections of books, themes, or characters that had engaged the reader's attention. Two members of the BookCase book club, for example, commented on how the research underpinning *The Interpretation of Murder* made Rubenfeld's representation of New York City very "evocative." A female member praised the character of Littlemore as "well drawn," and a male reader admitted that some of the "twists and turns" of plot were predictable, whereas others caught him out. Finally, three people explicitly recommended the novel as "a light read with an academic edge" (male reader), with a middle-aged female group member declaring, "It's fantastic! Any reading group would have a good time reading it . . . ," "and discussing it," added Finnigan in almost *sotto voce*, as the clip ended and the segment returned to the studio. Finnigan's quick-witted reaction to the final taped reader's comment not only provided a seamless word bridge back to the live broadcast, but it also foregrounded the producers' declared purpose of including "real book club" footage within the Book Club feature. Amanda Ross told us enthusiastically: "I think that's the thing that inspires [viewers] most, at the end of the [segment] you think, 'Well, they look like me, I could be like them, I will go out and try this book'" (pers. comm., 2006). Following on from the studio book discussion that employed celebrities to pique the interest of viewers, the "real book club" readers were meant to secure the audience's confidence that they, too, could be readers capable of engaging with the selected books and, perhaps, of sharing their responses with friends.

In the final moments of the segments, one or both of the hosts invited viewers to the Richard & Judy website (http://forum.richardandjudybook-club.co.uk/), where they could participate in a discussion forum and link to information about a book's author, publisher, and plot. After several of the 2007 book club segments, reader-viewers could talk with authors and each other in a live web chat. According to Ross, more than a thousand people participated in each discussion (per. comm., 2006).[9] Through the website, the producers were trying to capitalize on the coexistence of different media by extending the viewer experience, and according to our data, it worked. Visiting the website did have an effect on whether individuals read the RJBC selections. Forty-five percent (710) of the UK readers who participated in our online survey indicate that they had visited the Richard & Judy website. One quarter of those readers (178) indicated that they at least sometimes read the books selected by the television couple. People are more likely to read the selections when they have visited the website ($p < 0.05$, $R^2 = 0.48$).

Through the website, clever marketing schemes, and successful television production, the RJBC became a power player in the contemporary reading industry in the UK. The Book Club celebrated reading as an interactive and interpersonal experience that could occur across different media technologies. It also communicated the messages that reading books could be both an enjoyable and worthwhile learning activity. Perhaps most impressively of all, the show's production team overcame the challenges of translating a print medium to an audiovisual one and, as television, the Book Club worked. However, many of the readers we spoke to were suspicious of this success, as we explore below.

THE DANCE OF DISTINCTION: RESISTING READERS RESPOND

The RJBC is significant because it was successful in achieving the popularization of literary culture in Britain. As Jim Collins has recently argued with regard to literary culture becoming part of popular culture in the United States, ". . . refined taste, or the information needed to enjoy sophisticated cultural pleasures, is now easily acquired outside a formal education. It's just a matter of knowing where to access it, and whom to trust" (2010, 8). But how do actual flesh-and-blood readers respond to this apparent increase in the availability of "refined taste" and "literary" books? In his earlier work, Collins argues, "[T]he popularization of good taste—or more precisely, how to get it—is a manifestation of consumer culture but it is also a complex phenomenon which complicates many of the basic assumptions about how 'taste,' whether it be popular or elite, is recognized as such in contemporary cultures" (2002, 1). The readers in our study often refused to watch or were dubious about the merits of daytime television, were uneasy about the books selected for the program, and were suspicious of the brand that has become the RJBC. These readers' commentaries represent an interesting articulation of Bourdieu's (1984) conceptualization of taste as distinction, a conceptualization that is complicated by television becoming an agent of the reading industry. Whereas the "Richard and Judy Effect" has had a profound influence on twenty-first-century British publishing—at the very least in terms of the number of bestsellers it has created—some readers actively reject and distinguish themselves from exactly the elements that made the Book Club work so well.

Bourdieu's analysis of the "vendors of symbolic goods and services" ([1979] 1984, 310) identified a group that he named "the new taste-makers" (311)—a category that could arguably include the producers and hosts of the RJBC. As the creators of symbolic goods, they are part of the new service industries and white-collar jobs of the new bourgeoisie, a new bourgeoisie that, according to Bourdieu, have a "hedonistic morality of consumption," which creates a society that "judges people by the capacity for consumption, their 'standard of living', their life-style" (310). The petite bourgeoisie—those workers at lower levels in the same industries—play into extant class anxieties because their own class position is insecure. As Beverly Skeggs comments, "the constant supply of new, fashionably desirable goods, or the usurpation of existing marker goods by lower-status groups" (2004, 136) produces an effect in which people want to distance themselves. In order to maintain this distinction or social distancing, according to Skeggs, knowledge becomes essential: not only knowledge about the products themselves, but also their social and cultural value, and "how to use them appropriately" (136). The focus group readers in our study could be classified as part of the petite bourgeoisie, because many of them worked in education and in publishing and communication companies. Many of them also possessed cultural knowledge about how to "use" aesthetic objects, especially books, and they valued their acquired knowledge. These were the readers, who, as we will discuss below, were most suspicious of the success of the RJBC.

Branding Books

The readers in our focus groups demonstrated uneasiness toward the popular artifacts and processes of commodity culture, which, to them, was actualized through the omnipresent Book Club brand. The "brand," that is, the "specific identities, images, and values [that] contribute to an individual's feelings about and attitudes toward the company" (Argenti and Barnes 2010, 113) illustrates the disconnection these readers felt between the commercial nature of the book club and literary fiction.

Life-size posters, stickers on the selected titles, and complete sections in major bookstore chains, such as Waterstones and WHSmith, illustrate the marketing partnerships enjoyed by the Book Club and booksellers (Figure 2.2). Other relationships communicated the commercialization and commodification of the Book Club, as it is evident in the photo of a sponsorship poster associating the Book Club with the candy manufacturer Galaxy. The juxtaposition of books with commercialization and popular culture, while certainly not a new phenomenon, is what has continuously

Figure 2.2 Galaxy Chocolate and The Richard & Judy Book Club Poster

Shared advertising with companies like Galaxy Chocolate works to increase readers' suspicions about the quality of *Richard & Judy*'s selections

Source: Authors' photo.

created distrust among readers who want to distinguish themselves from the masses. Reading books, especially those books that have been consecrated as "literature," is thought by some to be a worthy leisure pursuit because reading within North America and the UK is inscribed as having moral and "civilizing" purposes and effects. Television, on the other hand, has often been thought to be exempt from these kinds of moral imperatives and is connected—with the exception of public television—to profit-generation rather than to the advancement or preservation of high cultural ideas. Partly because they are the products of educational systems that promote these meanings of reading, readers who participated in the focus groups found it difficult to be categorized alongside readers who might watch daytime television, even if the program promotes the same books that they would choose to read. Our readers found it difficult to rationalize the influence of the Book Club, in part, because of its financial success.

Participants in both our survey and in our focus groups who identified as participating in the Book Club may not necessarily watch the program, but they seem to be well aware of the branded book list. Whereas the stickers on the selected books' covers serve as a deterrent for the non-participating readers, they act as an emblem of a tested and trusted recommendation for others. We see this in Viv's explanation of her involvement in the Book Club:

> I was told about it by a friend and I thought what a good idea. I've never managed to watch it very often, because of the time it is and maybe not wanting to watch it enough to record it, . . . having said that, when I go into Waterstones I look for the *Richard & Judy* recommendations and I've read *George and Arthur* [sic], which I thoroughly enjoyed, . . . So, yes, I'm aware of it, but haven't seen the programme very much, but am always aware of the books. (R & J FG 2 P, 2007)

From 2006 until 2009, the visibility of the RJBC brand was omnipresent in UK bookshops and libraries (Figure 2.3).

"I've seen the stickers in bookshops—you're sort of bombarded with them aren't you, as soon as you walk into the bookshop," said Sonal, one of our readers when we asked about her awareness (R & J FG 1 NP, 2007). By the end of 2008, the Book Club had become larger than its televised segment. Industry insiders claimed that the economic success lay in the relational marketing efforts with both book and nonbook organizations. Nikki Crowther, WHSmith's controller for fiction commented in a *Bookseller.com* article that the Book Club "reached a point that [the book club books] are totally outside the show. The 'Richard & Judy' brand is strong enough to carry the book promotion forward. Our customers really trust their recommendations" (Jones 2008). The same article quotes Tesco supermarket's category manager claiming that the *Richard & Judy* sticker works as a promotional tool before, during and after the Book Club segment is broadcast.

Figure 2.3 The Richard & Judy Book Club Display Inside News Shop
The RJBC's selections are sold in news shops, alongside bottled water
Source: Authors' photo.

The branded pervasiveness of the Book Club seemed to unnerve those readers who were apprehensive about the economic relationships among authors, publishers, and television producers:

> I don't actually look for the Booker because I'm slightly suspicious of the prize stuff and I'm suspicious of *Richard & Judy* as well, I have to say. Let's be honest. I was tempted to read a couple of their books, but I think they may have another agenda. Perhaps we'll discuss that. (Ann, R & J FG 4 P, 2007)

Whereas Ann's response may seem overly suspicious, her unease demonstrates a common theme of distinction. Disavowing Book Club selections may even secure a reader's claim to good "literary" taste. Here, Ann seems to feel that commercialization has tainted the literary value of the lists. In common with a number of other readers, Ann also believed (incorrectly as far as we have been able to surmise) that the producers were receiving money from book publishers and that this shaped the Book Club selections.

Sybil, a forty-seven-year-old freelance writer, told us that she did not watch *Richard & Judy*, but she was nonetheless quite passionate in her articulation of what she felt was the homogenizing potential of the program:

> I mean it's an interesting idea that whether the money could push or is being channelled, you know generated by extra sales. I mean, like, kind of *Harry Potter* means that Bloomsbury is doing quite nicely. But my impression is that . . . although more and more books are published, fewer and fewer people are reading, and it gets a bit . . . divided between the books which are very heavily promoted and which do sell and the other things which fall by the wayside. It's a lot of stuff to do with the book trade as well and 3 for 2 offers and so on, and I think I just feel, you know, huge efforts need—*Richard & Judy* alone isn't going to transform the way people read. (R & J FG 1 NP, 2007)

Sybil is articulating concern over the access to books that might not be chosen for review in other media, for book prize short lists, or the like. She also infers her own disdain for reading what everyone else is reading. Not only might she have personal interests at stake as a professional writer who earns part of her living from book sales, but she also seems to be concerned that everyone is reading the same books—those that are promoted—at a cost to those books that might not get the same coverage.

The conversation that followed Sybil's comment is interesting in that it demonstrates that our focus group readers have a general suspicion of the larger economic structures of the book industry in the UK:

Sonal: I think that's true because people only have a certain amount of time and if they're lucky enough to be home to watch *Richard & Judy* and they've got some books to recommend then I think that they'll choose them. I mean, if they're going to watch *Richard & Judy* . . .

Sarah: Well I watched it and I didn't choose the book that they had on, but I watched it, but I suppose . . .

Sonal: But I think the majority of people watching it are going to choose those books if they're going to pick up a book, and they will go to Waterstones and do the 3 for 2 instead of sort of going to independent bookshops, so I sort of think that that's what would happen.

Sarah: It gets somebody into a bookshop that maybe wasn't going to go into a bookshop then maybe . . .

Sonal: Yeah, but it's expensive to all the independent bookshops who sort of go out of business because Waterstones are making an

Sibyl: I guess people don't feel they've got, if they're not very experienced or regular readers, is a lack of guidance, and I suppose Richard and Judy function as guides. I mean, your average person behind the till at Waterstones hasn't really got the time or you know, given the awful pay, they can't necessarily do guidance. People who often don't go into libraries or have a sort of relationship with librarians so I guess it's a big bewildering competitive world of bookselling and I think people kind of get quite lost in it. So maybe that kind of personalisation via so and so's book club makes people feel they've got a bit of a base or a safe place.

The exchange illustrates not only Sonal's and Sibyl's sophisticated understanding of print culture, but also how the concepts of cultural capital and distinction are at work.[10] There is an assumption that people who watch the program need to have their books recommended to them. Meanwhile, Sarah admits to watching the program, but suggests that Madeley and Finnigan do not have enough cultural authority to choose the books she reads. She hesitates in her articulation of who is worthy to suggest books, but reiterates the moral imperative we heard from many of our focus group readers who were screened as nonparticipants in the Book Club. Like Sarah, other readers expressed their opinion that if Madeley and Finnigan get people to participate in a reading culture, then that is "a good thing." Sarah ends with, "But it's like someone mentioned earlier on, it's the idea that if it gets people reading, if it introduces people to books maybe that they weren't interested in before that can only be a good thing." The lasting message inscribed in readers' qualifying statements was often something along the lines of "but I don't need them." The "dance of distinction," which we have identified elsewhere (Fuller and Rehberg Sedo 2011), is subtly evident here. Readers articulate the idea that reading is good for you or that "[p]eople are nicer when they read" (Sue, R & J FG 4 P, 2007), while also reinforcing their own cultural capital by using phrases that work to draw out their own distinction. These exchanges illustrate well how reading has worked its way into popular culture and yet, readers can still find ways to distinguish themselves as "authentic" consumers of books who are removed from the masses.

The articulation of a moral imperative for *others* is illustrated again in another focus group, which was made up of readers who did participate in the Book Club.

Sam: I think it's great because they're not appealing to people that are widely read, they're people that are watching television—otherwise they'd be reading a book. So, if you're capturing a new audience . . .

Ann: Yes, but you can do that, because we all watch it, don't we, and read books as well. We don't read books instead of watching *Richard & Judy*, we do both, don't we . . .

Sam: But we're a certain kind of audience.

Ann: We're a certain kind of audience?

Sam: Yeah. There are people that don't read and if a single one of them then turns to a *Richard & Judy* book, then I think that's fantastic. (R & J FG 4 P, 2007)

In this exchange, we can see that the readers want to distinguish themselves from the audience who watch afternoon television. Although they admit to watching the program, they, and Sam in particular, consider themselves outside of the intended audience but attempt to mitigate any class "snobbishness" that their comments might infer. In the next section, we analyze how reading books is still perceived by many of the readers in our study as a high-culture activity. When this activity is presented through a medium or a popular television genre that is perceived to be low culture, readers work to maintain their own distinctiveness through articulations of taste.

"Not One of the Lemmings": Taste Hierarchies On- and Off-Air

Of those we surveyed specifically about the RJBC ($N = 1549$), 81 percent identified as participants in the broadcast book club (Table 2.2). This included watching the book club segment on the afternoon television program, registering in the discussion forum, going to the website, or reading at least one of the picks.

Obviously, members of the British public watched the program (Holmwood 2008). The sales of the books, however, increased exponentially beyond the audience of the program itself (Fuller and Rehberg Sedo 2011, 23; Ramone and Cousins 2011, 8), so the club's successes in both ratings and in resultant book sales suggest that branding efforts worked to bring the selected books into the public consciousness. This "branding" is what caused our focus group readers the most unease.

Table 2.2 Participating in The Richard & Judy Book Club

Activity	Percent	*n*
At least sometimes watch the RJBC	56	1,478
Registered on Richard & Judy's website	4	1,462
Visited the RJBC website	45	712
Read Richard & Judy's book(s)	26	1,477

(Respondents could participate in more than one way.)

When we showed the readers a list of the books selected for the 2005 through 2007 (Winter) seasons, most of them were surprised at the diversity of the selections. Before being presented with the lists, readers articulated a distancing from what they perceived of as Madeley and Finnigan as television hosts and from the Book Club lists, believing them to be much more lowbrow than they actually were. When we presented the titles, the readers remembered or realized that some of the books on it were Booker Prize winners or titles that had been nominated for other literary prizes. The lists, they recognized, also included some books that they themselves had read. The important point then becomes not the books on the list themselves, but rather, the readers' identification of *Richard & Judy* as daytime television and a magazine-format program. Because they associated this genre with popular culture, they perceived the Book Club as a popular cultural product and worked actively to distinguish themselves from it, so that they would affirm their own identities as readers of "serious" literary fiction or nonfiction. In the following exchange, Frances (R & J FG 3 P, 2007) admits that her opinions about the Book Club selections are based on her preconceived notions of the television program:

Anouk: How do you characterise the different attitudes in your groups to *Richard & Judy*? I mean, do people explicitly talk about it, because you have quite strong views about it?

Frances: Yes, but I will now eat my words thoroughly because I had never watched the program and I just had this vision of this incredibly light and rather silly program that is on at a time of evening that I don't tend to watch television. Anyway it's not convenient, so I had never put myself out to see it. The only time I watched it was when they ran a first novel competition, uhm, and the person who won was going to be on, so I made a point of sticking that on to record. Then, watching it later, uhm, but mainly it's because the library gets multiple copies, which means that we can get enough copies for the reading groups and so on, and I must admit that they picked some stunning books, so I do eat my words thoroughly. [laughs][11]

Frances's discomfort in admitting that she reads the Book Club choices—if only for her face-to-face book club—was a common response among our focus group readers who were screened as participants in the Book Club. Admitting to reading or watching the program for many of the readers was usually qualified by excuses so as to not to be judged harshly by their peers or by us as researchers. Barry, a male reader from Bristol, explained why very effectively, when he told us that, even if a reader is intrigued by the books discussed on the Book Club, it is best not to admit it:

. . . and they were discussing really sort of serious books, last year sometime, but, no, it wouldn't put me off. I just sort of sit there and sometimes a topic comes up and when it's the books I listen to and, like you, I wouldn't be put off but it might cause you to be taken as less than you are if you follow them because I think a lot of people, if Richard and Judy told you to read the telephone directory then you would. Not that you would, but you wouldn't want to be thought like that. You're not one of the lemmings or the sheep. (Bristol Great Reading Adventure (GRA) FG 1 P, 2006)

Barry's explanation of his response to *Richard & Judy*'s picks suggests that many of our focus group readers were not rejecting the RJBC on the basis of the book choices. Indeed, a substantial number of them were ignorant about the actual composition of the lists. Instead, through their assumptions, they were demonstrating their discomfort with the transformation of literary culture into popular culture. Arguably, if the RJBC had been broadcast on the publically owned BBC rather than on the commercial Channel 4, the readers would not have exhibited the same reaction because the Club and its list would be differently situated[12] within their sense of taste hierarchy.

Instead of articulating a taste preference, readers in our online survey gave lack of time (19 percent) as a top reason for not participating in the RJBC. So, are those readers who participated in the Book Club more likely to participate in any other broadcast book programming? According to our online survey, Book Club participants were not more likely to participate in other broadcast book programming. In fact, the opposite relationship was true. Those who *were not members* of the RJBC were more likely to participate in other clubs (Beta = –0.10, $p < 0.05$). Table 2.3 illustrates that there is a distinct level of participation in certain programs that are perceived to be part of high culture such as the BBC 2 (short-lived) television program *Page Turners*, or BBC TV's *The Big Read*, which selected the top 100 favorite UK books in 2003. Many of our readers could conceivably have the same amount of cultural capital as Madeley and Finnigan.[13] However, for those who did watch the program at least sometimes (56 percent), Madeley and Finnigan may have performed a pedagogical role.

Table 2.3 Participating in TV Book Programs

Activity	Percentage	n
Watched BBC's *The Big Read* at least sometimes	52	1,486
Read any of the top 100 of *The Big Read* selections	37	1,470
Watched *Page Turners* at least sometimes	12	1,478
Read any of the *Page Turners* selections	9	1,434
Watched *Oprah* at least sometimes	8	1,475
Member of Oprah's Book Club	1	1,467
Read any of *Oprah* selections	1	1,459

Part of the articulated taste hierarchy of the book broadcast landscape lies in the authority appointed by viewers to the networks themselves. The following exchange highlights the kind of discussions we heard around notions of a fixed hierarchy among the different television channels in the UK.

Anouk: Could you explain to me what the difference might be between BBC programmes, because a few of you have mentioned these other programmes and the programmes which are being disseminated on Channel 4? Can you explain that to me, as someone who doesn't have your cultural background?

Clare: I think anything that's going to be on BBC2 you automatically think was going to be slightly more highbrow. Now, whether that's true, certainly anymore, I don't know, but I think that's the—and possibly also on Channel 4, Channel 4 is a bit more arty almost. I mean its way of doing things is slightly—I mean you get the complete rubbish on Channel 4, but you get some interesting things on Channel 4 as well, so they're not necessarily . . .

Ben: And potentially more daring as well, I suppose. (R & J FG 1 NP, 2007)

The learned genre expectations of the programs and the television channels inflect the readers' perceptions of the types of books that appear on the programs themselves. As a case in point, consider Sarah's positioning of "difficult" books (a code for "literary fiction") within the genre of daytime television:

> . . . and I suppose I'm aware of The Richard & Judy Book Club thingy, and I'm not normally at home in time to see *Richard & Judy*, unfortunately. But that's been quite an interesting change, I suppose, because suddenly they've kind of, you know, they're seen as kind of lowbrow in terms of "Oh God, you watch *Richard & Judy*, do you?" But you know, the books I'm aware some of the books they have put on, have been maybe more difficult to access [than] what I've heard and read. I think *Cloud Atlas* was one of them, you know, the reviews were saying that was quite a difficult book, and that was quite refreshing to think that they'd pushed that one. (R & J FG 1 NP, 2007)

Not only does Sarah articulate well the positioning of the program within a perceived cultural hierarchy of contemporary British taste, but she also illustrates a common reaction among our readers, namely, their attempts to distinguish themselves against popular culture by reiterating that hierarchy even in the face of its apparent dissolution. Confirming Squires's argument that in "*Cloud Atlas*, the contemporary British book marketplace had found a title which ultimately combined cultural and economic capital, thereby fusing the 'literary' and the 'popular'" (2007, 174), Sarah's comment also hints at the complexity of reader responses to what Squires conceptualized as "crossover" novels—those pieces of literary fiction that also appeal to the mass market as a result of "forceful interventions of marketing" (175). For Sarah, it is "book reviewers," the traditional consecrators of literature and cultural authorities who are still primarily associated with a print medium, classifying *Cloud Atlas* as a "difficult" book that leads her to categorize the novel as a boundary-pushing choice for the comparatively "low-brow" Book Club. Thus, the legitimation of the book's selection outside the realm of the television club secures its literary value for Sarah, and trumps any anxieties that she might have about books with mass appeal (and massive sales) being stylistically unsophisticated.

The lists created by Ross for the RJBC included books that were always recently published and those that, because of their genre, might never be short-listed for major literary and nonfiction prizes. While not always the case, many of the picks' authors were not widely known when their book was chosen for the club. In this way, Madeley and Finnigan had the potential to avoid reproducing existing hierarchies around literary taste, because the authors and the recently published books had not yet been consecrated. However, because the books were chosen for the RJBC, the readers in our focus groups who did not identify as participants were unsettled by the collision course that the Book Club seemed to represent between the individual, private act of reading "literary" books, and the increased accessibility to book culture that the mass media was offering.

CONCLUSIONS: *BOOK TALK REMEDIATED*

As we have argued throughout this chapter, economics tell only part of the story of the RJBC. To play on the title of our own work, the importance of the phenomenon lies beyond the book. The book talk and the context in which that book talk takes place has important cultural meanings that illustrate the perseverance of cultural hierarchies in contemporary book culture even while the media structures and delivery platforms have changed. The twenty-first-century dance of distinction is articulated by the keen readers who assess the RJBC as worthwhile because it "gets people reading," but who then qualify their approval by disavowing their own connection to the program. The readers appear snobbish about their reading preferences, but they try to legitimize their condescension in politically correct ways that reflect contemporary neoliberal sentiments that reading is a social good. Helen, a forty-three-year-old reader from Birmingham, summed up the ideas we have discussed in this chapter when she commented:

> I've picked up the *Richard & Judy* leaflets in the library and looked to see what books they're recommending, and I have seen the programme

a couple of times, you know, when they have a guest on, like a celebrity to talk about it, which is always interesting. And I have read some of the books they've recommended, including *Cloud Atlas*, which they actually named as their book of books kind of thing, and I really enjoyed it, actually. But it is a bit of a strange book, I agree, and I also read [2005 Winter season] *The Time Traveler's Wife* (Niffenegger, 2004), which I really enjoyed. And my mum always reads them and so it gives us—we talk about them together. But I have to say, my book group that I come to here [at her local library], whenever we're trying to make recommendations and if I suggest something, [like] *The Time Traveler's Wife*, which was one of *Richard & Judy*'s—when I said it was one of *Richard & Judy*'s they wouldn't have anything to do with it and they all poopooed it. There's a real snobbery there and I was not impressed. (R & J FG 2 P 2007)

Helen obviously found pleasure in the celebrity panelists' discussion of the books. She learned to trust Madeley and Finnigan and the guest reviewers sufficiently to choose a book that they recommended and went so far as to recommend it to her face-to-face book club. Her reaction to their highly illustrative response suggests that the bifurcations between the brand of the RJBC and the genre of literary fiction can leave contemporary readers in unsettling positions vis-à-vis taste hierarchies. Whereas she wanted to resist the cultural hierarchy of taste imposed by her book club, we can assume that the book club's response troubled her. The club's response echoes that of the different readers in our focus groups who were non-participants in the television book club, and whose perceptions about the Book Club were explored above.

In addition to the low place in the cultural hierarchy generally appointed to daytime television, we believe that the type of book talk featured on the RJBC segments might have led some readers to respond as they did in our focus groups. The broadcast book talk did not mimic the reading and discussion practices expected by some of the readers who were accustomed to the more in-depth discussion encountered in a face-to-face book group. Associations of class with specific cultural artifacts and media practices also play into readers' understandings of contemporary taste formations. Our readers' unease with the Book Club suggests that the meanings of reading that circulate within contemporary culture—in this specific case, within English-speaking British culture—are associated with and inflected by the medium in which reading is portrayed. Shared reading practices that are produced for and consumed (or not) by television viewers are thus perceived as lower-class reading practices. Each articulation of readers' discomfort with the televised book talk is attached firmly to their perceptions of the cultural authority of the hosts and that of the celebrity reviewers. The book reviewers represent a mixture between popular and high culture personalities; however, the television program's genre and format allows for only limited book talk because of the brevity of each feature within the magazine genre. Readers also assume that the commercial realities of contemporary broadcaster, publisher, and advertiser relationships inform what will be said about a book in the discussion. In sum, our readers understand the convergence of television and books within the context of commodity culture, and the result for them is "caveat emptor."

The inclusion of aspects of contemporary celebrity culture in the TV show also represents another difficulty for book readers who associate having a literary experience with reading a book, not with watching television. Historically, books have not been associated with nonliterary celebrities, so there is a disjuncture between being a good actor, for example, and reading. The tension that matching books with celebrities produces represents one of the risks entwined in the RJBC producers' engagement with celebrity culture. In terms of viewing figures, media coverage, and the production of entertaining television, however, the risk paid off. Readers might be dismissive, but without the celebrities, the Book Club feature would probably not have worked.

The readers in our focus groups generally have high levels of education and are habitual readers, and this may prompt them to express higher levels of skepticism about celebrity culture than people who are less invested in reading printed books or who have lower levels of formal education. In general, the readers were resistant to the very ways in which we consider Madeley and Finnigan to have been successful. *Because* the RJBC made literature entertaining and accessible to the masses, readers in the focus groups felt that they had to push back against an idea of reading that was quite different from the one they had been educated to adopt. Rather than embracing the dismantling of cultural taste hierarchies that the show facilitated, these readers were quite articulate about maintaining the high/low divide. Why were they so invested in making such distinctions? We think this can be explained by their struggle to maintain the hard-won cultural capital that comes with high-level literacy in the face of media convergence and the shifting position of the printed book in a digital era. To recall Raymond Williams's (1977) conceptualization of cultural practices and discourses, our suspicious readers may be seen as clinging tenaciously to the "dominant" elements of a disappearing print-centric society in which cultural capital could be acquired by reading "good" books that had been legitimated by well-established authorities such as academics, educators, and the literary reviewers of broadsheet newspapers. The celebrity television book club disrupts the "special" character traditionally afforded to reading books twice over: by making the symbolic capital associated with book reading available on a mass scale, and by altering the identity and social position of cultural authorities, who no longer need to belong to the formally educated elite groups, but may now be drawn from the ranks of celebrities whose own symbolic capital has been accrued in an entirely different cultural arena. The readers were unsettled, in other words, precisely because the successful mixing of books and television so thoroughly represents the disruption of traditional understandings of high and low culture brought about by media convergence (the emerging cultural form in Williams's terms).

The symbolic status of reading as a high culture practice persists within contemporary British culture and so keen readers, like many in our study, articulate anxiety about books losing their "special place" in the hierarchy of cultural artifacts. Their anxiety also raises questions about how readers understand class and about how notions of class distinction persist, despite popular claims that the UK has become, in former Prime Minister Tony Blair's words, a "classless society" (Toynbee 2011). Ironically, the RJBC legitimated reading and book talk as an enjoyable leisure activity, available to anyone who wanted to participate, as if reading books was indeed a "classless" pursuit. Moreover, because the show foregrounded the message that books provide entertainment and prompt enjoyable conversations with friends and family, there was no moral imperative that reading would make a reader more intelligent or a better person. These ideals of reading as fun and of books as part of social experiences attainable through a variety of media technologies belong to a newly minted version of popular literary culture that is gradually changing the structure of "feeling for books" (Radway 1997). But cultural values, like the remediation of the printed book, alter slowly. The RJBC's democratic, classless, and often gender-neutral messages about the meanings of reading were not, as it turned out, to every reader's taste.

Just as many of our British readers were uneasy with the RJBC's adoption of celebrity culture and the situation of book talk within a daytime television show, so their Canadian peers felt similarly perturbed when their trusted national broadcaster changed its approach to promoting Canadian books. In the next chapter, the Canadian Broadcasting Corporation's annual series, *Canada Reads* provides a focus for our exploration of radio book programming. In common with television book clubs like Oprah's Book Club, and the RJBC, the producers of *Canada Reads* have successfully exploited the communication strategies of the show's primary medium of delivery while experimenting with other media platforms—with varying degrees of success.

3   Radio

In this annual title fight, five celebrity panelists defend their favorite work of Canadian fiction. One by one, books are voted off the list, until one panelist triumphs with the book for Canada to read this year . . . This year, the rules have changed: readers across Canada have been asked to submit their picks for the ESSENTIAL CANADIAN BOOK OF THE DECADE!

—Promotional message from Anansi Press 2010;
emphasis in the original

The e-mail announcing the first "bout" of Canada's public broadcaster's tenth annual reading program arrived in our in-boxes in early Fall 2010. The note did not come from the production team in Toronto, but rather from the House of Anansi press, an independent publishing house whose books were part of the 2011 competition. We were on the mailing list of this press, and in its special anniversary year, the producers of *Canada Reads* had invited publishers to help them promote public participation in the Survivor-style MRE—a change from earlier series. From 2002 through 2009, *Canada Reads* involved a small group of radio producers working with a preselected list of Canadian books and a carefully chosen panel of celebrities, each of whom "championed" one of the books during a weeklong radio program. Another striking aspect of the 2011 version of *Canada Reads* was that the show promoted Canadian national identity even more than in previous years. Extending an explicit invitation to readers to interact with the production process of the series, the e-mail message set the tone for the subsequent Tweets, public service announcements, and web copy promotion employed by the producers to engage—and perhaps to expand—the audience of the long-running national competition.

As these strategies suggest, the coextensive nature of print books with other media, such as television, radio, and social networking sites is particularly well illustrated in the production and delivery of the *Canada Reads* program. Since 2002, the producers have experimented with various modes of audience engagement and promotional practices in their attempts to fulfill the CBC's mandate to promote Canadian culture. Achieving this mandate might not seem to be a major task, considering that the CBC has consistently and explicitly taken on the role of facilitating national identity by broadcasting programs made by and about Canadians. Even more pertinent to our discussion of the relationship among mass media and print is the fact that the CBC has a history of acting as a publisher of Canadian writing, especially of short stories. Moreover, a radio show celebrating books should not, you would think, be a hard sell to Canadians who are, by contemporary standards, avid readers. According to a 2005 Canadian national survey, 87 percent of the population reads, and, of those polled, more than half (54 percent) read virtually every day (Créatec and Canadian Heritage 2005, 4). On average, Canadians read seventeen books for pleasure each year (66), supporting the findings of the "CBC Arts Study and Culture Research Study" (2005), in which three in four Canadians say that "books are an important part of their lives" (5). However, the convergence of books and radio, and the added interactivity enabled through the Internet affect how readers think about books and reading. Readers participate in new ways of mediation via various platforms, and yet the situation also demands that readers possess cultural literacy acquired through engagement with traditional channels of communication. In Canada those channels include the national broadcaster and its book programming.

Debates about the cultural value of book reading are as emotional for Canadians as they were for many of our UK readers. Our analysis of the RJBC demonstrated that broadcast book programs play a large role in shaping the ways that contemporary print culture is mediated by readers within their reading lives. Like the RJBC, *Canada Reads* is a broadcast MRE that has achieved popular success on a national scale and, also in common with the television show, the annual series has sent book sales soaring. But the cultural nationalist tenor of the radio series, the authoritative status of the CBC and the fact that its primary broadcast medium is radio offer a series of different insights into the circulation of contemporary reading cultures.

The content of *Canada Reads* and the RJBC is similar in that both feature celebrity reviewers who engage in literary book talk, but the listeners who tune in to the Canadian national broadcaster are different from the viewers of the afternoon television talk show. The audience for the CBC is one that could be considered "higher class" or what American sociologist Wendy Griswold calls "the reading class" (2008, 1)—those people with the time, education, networks, and money to read (37). These listeners are the latest in a long line of avid readers to appreciate book programming on public radio in Canada. The focus on Canadian-authored texts continues CBC radio's well-recognized tradition of promoting Canadian literature, but *Canada Reads* is a deliberate attempt on the part of its producers to break with conventional radio book programming. Currently hosted by CBC radio personality and ex-musician Jian Ghomeshi, and broadcast over CBC's Radio1 for one week each spring, the pretaped program airs in edited half-hour segments.[1] As we have argued elsewhere, the producers conceived the program in part to attract a "younger, hipper audience" (T. Vartanian, pers. comm., 2003; cited in Rehberg Sedo 2008, 50), and see the program as a "fun" way to facilitate the CBC's explicit ideological imperatives as a public broadcaster to educate, inform, and represent Canadians (Fuller 2007, 3, 12; Fuller and Rehberg Sedo 2006, 6–7, 31). A five-person celebrity panel, which is usually comprised of well-known Canadian actors, musicians, and politicians, debate and ultimately choose one book that over the years has been promoted as the book that "All Canada Should Read." Eliminating book choices over a five-day period in a *Survivor*-style format, the lively and sometimes argumentative book discussion is augmented by summaries, author interviews, and podcasts of the radio broadcasts on the show's website (www.cbc.ca/canadareads). In addition to the celebrity competition that in 2006 became "a spirited quest to find a homegrown book for all Canadians to read," the website includes a link to the CBC store to purchase the chosen books, and an online and moderated letters section titled "Your Say" (*Canada Reads* 2006). By 2009, the program's website offered links to YouTube videos that showed clips of the book deliberations of the five different broadcast segments.[2]

Changes in the type and amount of interactivity extended to the potential and actual listeners of *Canada Reads* reflect not only rapid advances in technology over the past decade, such as the increased popularity of mobile devices with Internet access, but also the demographic challenges faced by the CBC. The CBC management has recognized the necessity of engaging a younger audience in traditional media and programs, while maintaining the satisfaction of traditional, older audiences (Canadian Heritage and Créatec 2005, 4–5)—a tricky, some might say, impossible, balancing act. As part of their own efforts to engage across the different age demographics, the producers of *Canada Reads* use new technologies and social networking to reach younger audiences (K. Walsh, pers. comm., 2007), and it does appear that many reader-listeners engage with the program online. Altering the style and tenor of arts programming on CBC radio was another tactic employed in an attempt to rejuvenate the schedules—and the audience. However, the strategy of adopting and adapting formats successful in other media, such as the elimination contest that is central to many reality TV series, has not been an entirely winning formula. The listener-readers in our study, for instance, offered nuanced commentaries about their aversion to the use of popular genres in CBC television and radio programming. Their responses illustrate that, for many Canadians, public radio maintains an elite position within a hierarchy of cultural forms in Canada—at least, for the listener-readers we met and surveyed who are older than forty-five years, middle-class, and well-educated. The cultural authority that some of these readers accorded to the CBC, and the special status that they lent to public radio have their roots in the inception of the national broadcaster.

The mixed response of readers to the show suggests that the function of traditional cultural authorities and taste-makers such as the CBC are, in fact, changing in an era of new and converged media. In part, this is because producers of radio shows for the national broadcaster face specific challenges as they seek to reposition the CBC within a multiple channel and multimedia environment. Readers are divided in their responses to the "older" medium of radio and its "newer" incarnations, and their stories about *Canada Reads* provide important insights into the meanings of reading in an era of media convergence. Their articulations are informed by the historical foundations of public radio broadcasting in Canada. That history helps to explain how and why the readers in our study tended to either closely identify with the ideological aims of *Canada Reads*, or felt patronized by them. The history of CBC book programming, in particular, contextualizes readers' feelings of either alienation or excitement inspired by the *Canada Reads* book choices, as well as some readers' rejection of the popular-culture elements within the series, such as the show's engagement with celebrity culture.

"THE MOTHER CORP": THE CBC AND CANADIAN CULTURE

From its inception at the turn of the last century, Canadian radio policy and development has been illustrative of the identity work that happens at the national political level. For nearly a century, the Canadian Broadcasting Corporation (CBC/Radio-Canada) has produced programming whose aim is to "foster Canadian cultural identity" (Vipond 2004, 260). The perpetual narrative that informs communication policies has concerned the protection of Canadian culture and cultural products from the influence of the United States. Cultural sensitivity, then, works to fulfill all Canadian broadcasters' legislated mandate to work toward "the enhancement of national identity and cultural sovereignty" (Jackson 2004, 276). Both philosophically, and practically, radio has always been an important communication tool in Canada. With a land mass of 9,976,140 square miles (World Statistics 2011), and a population that has always been relatively small and linguistically diverse, and in which nine out of ten people live within ninety miles of the US border (Pagé and Spencer 2004), communication networks and policies have a complicated history and existence (Vipond 2004, 257; 2009, 235–36). Unlike the UK or the US, radio in Canada played the role "of contact between settler and civilization through the 1930s" (Kuffert 2009, 305). Often referred to as a link across the miles, radio in Canada—and in particular, CBC/Radio-Canada—is not only a cultural institution, but it is also considered by many Canadians to play a part in their understanding of national identity.

CBC/Radio-Canada broadcasts in English and French (*Société Radio-Canada*) via radio, television, the Internet, digital audio, and satellite radio. It also provides programming in eight different Aboriginal languages in Canada's territories [Northwest Territories, Nunavut, and the Yukon] and in Northern Québec and Labrador (CBC/Radio-Canada 2012).

Advertisement-free Radio1 offers news and current affairs; comedy and variety; telephone call-in programs; feature programs; programs about science and the environment; and dramatic, sports, and cross-cultural programs (C. Miller 2004). The attempt to reach out to a broad listenership is a legislated mandate of the network: Section 3 of the Broadcasting Act (1991) identifies the CBC as Canada's public broadcaster. This mandate includes the CBC's obligation to be distinctively Canadian and reflective of the country's cultural, racial, and regional diversity. According to the Act, the CBC has a distinct responsibility: it "should serve to safeguard, enrich and strengthen the cultural, political, social and economic fabric of Canada" (3.1.d.i). The Broadcasting Act also states that the CBC must endeavor to be equitable in its focus on English and French cultures and ". . . through its programming, [provide] a public service essential to the maintenance and enhancement of national identity and cultural sovereignty" (3.1.a.).

The motivation to protect Canadian identity through its media and cultural products is neither recent nor unproblematic. Before World War II, nearly all radio programming came from the US (MacLennan 2005; Vipond 2004) with a few BBC programs rounding out the lineup (C. Miller 2004; Pagé and Spencer 2004). Although the Liberal government of MacKenzie King established the Royal Commission on Broadcasting—commonly referred to as the "Aird Commission"—in 1924 to address the worries expressed by English-Canadian cultural nationalists, it was not until 1932 with the passing of the Radio Broadcasting Act that the Canadian government had its own national network. Through the Canadian Radio Broadcasting Commission (CRBC), the government collected licensing fees and regulated Canadian broadcasting. As Canadian Broadcasting historian Mary Vipond illustrates, "in its brief existence, the CRBC ran into many organizational, financial, and political problems. But it was successful enough in regulating and enhancing the national distribution of Canadian programming that in 1936, rather than killing it, the King government replaced it with a structurally sounder successor, the Canadian Broadcasting Corporation (CBC)" (2004, 259).[3] In 1938, the CBC became a full crown corporation. Operating at once as a competitor and a regulator of its private counterparts, the CBC was continuously under scrutiny. The CBC's role in cultural life was publicly acknowledged in 1949 thanks to the federally appointed Massey-Lévesque Commission, which was charged with investigating the cultural and intellectual life of Canadians and required to make a series of recommendations about the future funding of arts and culture in Canada. The Conservative government of the 1950s, however, acquiesced to the private broadcasters and removed the regulatory function of the CBC with the establishment of first, the Board of Broadcast Governors, and then, in 1968, with the Canadian Radio-Television and Telecommunications Commission (CRTC) (Armstrong 2010; C. Miller 2004; Vipond 2004), which had "a much stronger national mandate" (Pagé and Spencer 2004, 270). The CRTC dictates the amount of Canadian content that must be broadcast on television and radio programs each day.[4]

Working against the pervasiveness of imported cultural products and media to create distinctive Canadian programming with nationwide reach is a gargantuan and, perhaps, idealistic task. Whereas the cultural tradition in Québec has paved the way for distinct programming (Pagé and Spencer 2004, 266), public broadcasting regulation and initiatives in English Canada have been largely unsuccessful at establishing national unity (Filion 1996a). Imported television programs, movies, books, and music are more economically viable than the homegrown counterparts (Filion 1996a; Savage 2009; 2010). Despite Canadian ownership and content regulation, foreign cultural influences remain strong, and imported products and programs are still in high demand (Filion 1996a, 1996b). For some Canadians, as for a number of readers in our study, foreign media content is perceived as an ongoing threat to Canadian cultural autonomy, even while they enjoy US television shows, films, music, and books. Throughout the first decade of the twenty-first century, for example, US-produced television and cinema consistently topped weekly Canadian viewing figures (Savage 2009). Anxieties about the "Americanization" of Canadian media and culture, thus sit alongside a keen appetite and desire for US-American cultural products.

The popularity of foreign content informs contemporary debates about the value of the CBC, or "the Mother Corp"[5] as it is sometimes called because of its historical foundations as a broadcaster and regulator. The contentious arguments hinge on the economic costs of running a national network, and on its cultural role. Unlike BBC television and radio in the UK, which are funded by a license fee paid by all UK television viewers, the CBC has had a hybrid public/private funding format because license fees were abolished in 1953, and thus depends for its income on a mixture of advertising revenue and government subsidy. Appearing on the public agenda most often during election periods, disputes about the function and future of the CBC are mired in questions of the institution's ability to "unify" the country through programming (Adamson 2005; R. Lorimer 1992; Watson 1999) and its relevance in the contemporary milieu of citizen journalism and alternative audio programming. Similarly to their counterparts at the beginning of the last century (see, e.g., Spry 1931), supporters of the (partially) state-funded network perceive the CBC as the alternative to for-profit, multinational media conglomerations (R. Lorimer 1992). Because CBC Radio is less infiltrated by American programming than is CBC Television,[6] proponents view the CBC, and particularly CBC Radio, as a vital Canadian cultural institution—a publicly funded medium that has historical roots and that is imperative to a shared national consciousness.

As a cultural institution, the CBC's symbolic historical roots run deep in English Canada. Indeed, in an article announcing the digitization of CBC Radio content, Chris Conrath writes that "[O]f all things Canadian, few are more tied to our history than CBC Radio" (2001). According to a representative of the private Internet companies vying to host the public radio's archives, the cultural value of the CBC is no less significant than the historic nation-building role of the Canadian Pacific Railway: "CBC Radio was the link that brought Canada together much the same way the railroad's ribbon of steel joined the country." To make this comparison is to invoke a powerful popular narrative of nation-building that has achieved the symbolic status of national myth (albeit a myth that is masculine and highly racialized). Industry experts and media scholars (Filion 1996a, 1996b; R. Lorimer 1992; Savage 2010) alike argue that the goal of "national unity" through CBC television is too lofty an aim, but one that is still achievable via radio. National unity, however, should logically include the assumption that all Canadians listen to CBC Radio. This is not the case.

Canada Reads is broadcast on CBC Radio1, which, according to the Friends of Canadian Broadcasting (2010), draws only 11.1 percent of the Canadian radio audience.[7] This is not surprising, considering that CBC Radio began to gradually lose much of its audience as early as 1952 when television was launched in Canada (C. Miller 2004). Today, the audience is a "highly fragmented" one (Attallah 2000, 184) that overwhelmingly watches mostly American television programs (BBM 2011).

Although the majority of the CBC's budget appears to be devoted to providing popular programming on CBC English TV,[8] it is CBC Radio programming that, according to Savage, is "really at the center of the CBC's dynamic cultural identity reshaping in Canada" (Savage 2010, 283). Savage's argument is that whereas many American talk shows are broadcast through syndicates, CBC's radio content mainly originates in Canada. In particular, he argues, the CBC has been lauded by supporters for its Arts programming, which highlights Canadian content. *Canada Reads'* panelists and book lists, then, not only illustrate an interdependence between print and broadcast media, but they can also be regarded as material and ideological manifestations of culturally protectionist Canadian content policy.

One particular aspect of the CBC's programming history helps to contextualize the high expectations and strong opinions that readers in our study articulated about *Canada Reads*. Simply put, book programming on the CBC is nothing new. Indeed, books on radio have a unique history in Canada. Unlike early radio programming in other nation-states that generally featured adaptations of already published work, Québec radio was innovative in that authors created works specifically to be broadcast over the air waves (Pagé and Spencer 2004, 268). According to media historians Pierre C. Pagé and David R. Spencer, "Between 1930 and 1970, half a million pages of literary texts were written for radio by about 1,000 authors. The serial or radio-novel, because of its structure, based on chapters broadcast over many years—often ten or twenty—became a major building block of the collective imagination" (ibid.). *Anthology*, which aired in English from 1954 until 1990, featured literary documentaries, interviews, and the short stories and poems of new and established Canadian authors (Latham 2007, 155). During its run it was commonly called "Canada's most important publisher" (CBC Digital Archives n.d.). In addition to these programs, the long-running *Writers & Company*, and the more recent *Between the Covers* (1993–2010) and *The Next Chapter* (2008-present) illustrate CBC Radio1's involvement within the literary print culture field. The institution's efforts as an active agent in the field of Canadian literature have earned it a high place on the cultural authority hierarchy with many contemporary Canadian listener-readers. But who are these readers?

According to historian Len Kuffert (2009), the conception of audience make-up has always been problematic for the national broadcaster, and the struggles have always centered around the question of high/low culture programming and the tastes of the Canadian public. Of the early years in Canadian broadcasting, Kuffert writes:

> The norms re-inforced by the Canadian Broadcasting Corporation (CBC) and its antecedent the Canadian Radio Broadcasting Commission (CRBC) echoed those of the educated Canadian elite . . . Popular tastes seemed less genuine or relevant to the public broadcaster because they shifted rapidly, seemed less rooted and more open to influence than those of elites. The audience could look dangerously fickle. (304)

While writing about a much earlier era, Kuffert (ibid.) could have been writing about the contemporary scene at the CBC, where the struggles between high culture and popular programming preferences are played out internally (CBC/Radio-Canada 2005, 8–13) as well as in the public sphere. A published self-study shows that nearly 70 percent of CBC staff perceives Arts & Culture programming as being skewed to traditional "High Arts" (8), to the exclusion of popular culture or mainstream entertainment. As noted by one staff person, this perception is important, because "it is the public broadcaster's responsibility to speak to and reflect the country as it lives today—the priority on 'high' culture does not reflect the majority of Canadians' cultural reality" (9). Some of the readers in our focus groups also perceive the CBC, and thus *Canada Reads*, as too pretentious. Still, 64 percent (731) of the Canadian respondents to our online survey identified as participants in *Canada Reads*.[9] Where is the disconnection then between reader-participants and *Canada Reads*? Whereas the CBC producers try to reach out to readers through various platforms, the readers with whom we spoke demonstrated unease with the CBC's use of a format adapted from the popular television reality show subgenre of the "vote off" contest. As we explore below, reader discomfort is bound up in cultural expectations about CBC Radio, their desire to learn about Canadian culture and literature, and doubts about the authority of the panelists.

Canada Reads works for some readers because, generally speaking, books work better on radio than they do on television (Fuller and Rehberg Sedo 2006, 12–13; Rehberg Sedo 2008, 200–2). In part, this is because the formats of book talk shows on radio allow for the sustained discussion of selected texts. The drama of *Canada Reads*, for example, is conveyed chiefly through debate, whereas the context for the chosen titles is provided by panelists' verbal presentations and audio clips of the selected authors making comments on their craft. These are typical of the communicative strategies that radio, a medium dependent on auditory signs, employs in order to establish a context for the broadcast content. In this way, radio mediates "the risks of ambiguity or complete communication failure [which] are high" (Crisell [1986] 1994, 5). By varying the verbal text through changes of speaker and pace, and signposting the structure of the show (via announcements, such as "previously on *Canada Reads. . . ,*" and repeated explanations of the debate format by the host), the radio version of *Canada Reads* attempts to engage and retain both the attention and the imagination of its listeners. Because radio listeners may be highly mobile and busily occupied within a variety of domestic, work, or leisure spaces while they listen, radio constantly has to guard against the fact that it can readily become "like wallpaper" within everyday life (Laycock 1992, 1). Although television is also "part of a larger environment with which we remain connected even while we watch" (R. Allen 1992, 13), the TV viewer is more likely to remain in one space than a radio listener—not least because TV employs visual as well as auditory and textual codes to convey meaning. However, these communicative strategies also make book television more difficult to produce successfully in ways that capture the full attention of the viewer. Oprah's Book Club and the RJBC are rare examples of well-produced television book shows that fully exploited the visual techniques (moving images, camera-angles, range of shots) and editing strategies like prerecorded on-location film intercut with talking heads (some "live," others prerecorded), dramatizations, and interactive studio discussion that make book television engaging for viewers. Too often, as was the case with the television version of *Canada Reads* in 2004, book television is not sufficiently visually dynamic, relying too heavily on more or less static images of seated interviewees or reviewers talking about a static material object (a book). The reviewers of the literature highlighted on the radio version of *Canada Reads* are neither traditional nor static.

CELEBRITIES DUKE IT OUT FOR CANADIAN LITERATURE

Placing celebrity reviewers and the reader-participants' responses to them at the center of our analysis of *Canada Reads* is imperative because the panel is a carefully constructed lineup of Canadian personalities who are not necessarily known for their literary prowess. Instead, they are people, such as track-star Perdita Felicien and d.j. Cadence Weapon, who have been successful in television, music, comedy, and, sometimes, in law, journalism, or sports. Using celebrity judges as a bid to promote accessibility to literature is not unique to Canada nor is the condemnation of celebrity judges—Jerry Hall and Lilly Allen were criticized in the UK press when they acted as judges for the Costa Book Awards and the Orange Prize, respectively, for instance (Street 2005)[10]—but the CBC panelists are not judging a literary prize. In order to play into the popularity of reality television formats, the producers pit the celebrities against one another with the books as their weapons. They each "defend" a selected title with the goal of having their book come out on top in a competition that is advertised in libraries, bookstores, and in national newspapers. Nevertheless, the marriage of celebrity readers with Canadian literature contributes to some mixed messages about the symbolic role and value of "reading Canadian" together with other people that are also evident in the publicity for the series.

In Figure 3.1, for example, the promotional copy is at odds with the program itself: the image of the program promoted on-air is of an urban production, a shared reading experience, and a pugilistic "battle of the books." The visual image chosen for the *Canada Reads'* homepage, however, ignores the shared reading experience offered (and, indeed, enacted by) the panel, in favor of a classic image of an individual reader having an immersive experience with a book—and, moreover, reading in an apparently rural setting. The visual image on the homepage references the historical role of reading in Canada and the part that the CBC has played in it, while also attempting to gesture toward the new, funky tenor of shows like *Canada Reads* via the photo of a young, male reader with his back against a VW camper-van. The contradictory messages about who is reading, with whom and where, echo the tension that runs through the program. The CBC's traditional role as a promoter of highbrow Canadian literature and the sounds of the *Canada Reads* broadcasts are at odds with one another, and with the desires and expectations of some of the reader-listeners, as we discuss below.

Whereas the messages about reading promoted by the show and its publicity are mixed, the production values of *Canada Reads* are consistently high. The program reflects substantial market research knowledge about popular television programming, but also takes into consideration production costs and network expectations. The result is a reading program that attempts to mimic face-to-face book talk at the same time as it is trying to create what we call "a reading spectacle" (Fuller and Rehberg Sedo 2006). At times, it is the spectacle aspect of *Canada Reads* that disconnects the show from the lived experiences and expectations of our readers about how book discussion should proceed. According to media studies scholar Doug Kellner (2003), who coined the term "media spectacle," the late twentieth and beginning of the twenty-first centuries saw the emergence of "a new form of *technocapitalism* marked by a synthesis of capital and technology, and the information and entertainment industries, which [produced] a new form of 'infotainment society' and spectacle culture" (17; emphasis in the original). In Kellner's account, "media spectacle" constructs star status for politicians and pop stars alike, and Canadian politicians and musicians have regularly appeared on *Canada Reads* as panelists. Media spectacle also inflects the format and visual codes of all media from reality TV programs to epic Hollywood films.

Figure 3.1 CBC *Canada Reads* 2006 Season Transit Poster

Source: This image was created and is owned by The Canadian Broadcasting Corporation, and is used with permission.

Depending for its success on media saturation and the capacity of consumers to become addicted to their interaction with "multimedia extravaganzas" (14), media spectacle fetishizes the visual image, thereby obscuring the labor and hierarchies of its capitalist and transnational production from the consumer. As we have argued elsewhere, the CBC does not have the resources to achieve media saturation and thus produce a "true" media spectacle with *Canada Reads* (Fuller and Rehberg Sedo 2006, 10). Nevertheless, the conception of the program is symptomatic of the "infotainment society" that Kellner (2003) describes. An aural medium borrows a TV-game-show-cum-reality-TV format, which has been franchised and reproduced around the world, in order to promote explicitly a nationwide shared act of reading and learning about a "national" cultural product—Canadian literature. Digital technology enables radio producers to add visuals (static in the early years, moving image in more recent editions) to the radio broadcasts on the show's website, before turning it back into a television program for series three and four (in 2004 and 2005). When the television version failed, in part, because of the disjuncture between the drama of debate that is evident on radio and the flat delivery of author interviews and traditional book talk on television (Fuller and Rehberg Sedo 2006, 12–13), the producers focused on developing an enhanced web experience suitable for those accustomed to the environment of Web 2.0. At first glance then, *Canada Reads* could be characterized as a clever adaptation of a global product to more local needs: an evaluation that even lends the series a resistant purpose if one recalls the contexts of technocapitalism, namely, transcontinental market expansion, the shrinking public sector, and the diminishing significance of the nation-state (Kellner 2003, 17–19).

If we examine the production process of *Canada Reads* more closely, however, its engagement with the culture of spectacle and celebrity threatens to obscure the producers' nationalist project—and creates a disjunction between style and purpose in the eyes and ears of many listeners and readers. Right from the start, the producers have proven that they are sufficiently adept readers of media culture to realize that some aspects of "media spectacle" (ibid.) can be imitated for relatively few dollars. *Canada Reads* on-air and online employs the glamour of celebrity participation; the frisson of "the playful and unexpected" produced by the "right chemistry" among the panelists (assisted by scrupulous prepping, scriptwriting, and editing) (T. Vartanian, pers. comm., 2003), and a cliff-hanger structure to each broadcast. The website, meanwhile, extends the event beyond the temporal and spatial limits of the broadcast schedule, offering the listener-participants opportunities to interact with the broadcast debate and with each other. The CBC's adoption of spectacle and "infotainment"—a style and format associated with for-profit broadcasters and television networks owned by multimedia conglomerates—does not always sit well with our readers who see the CBC as a national institution that ought to operate differently from commercial business models of for-profit broadcasting.

The mixing of popular genres borrowed from successful television shows might be troublesome for some reader-listeners of *Canada Reads*, but it is often used as a hook to attract new participants. Now in its eleventh year, anecdotal evidence suggests that Canadians—especially those who read and fit a middle and upper-class demographic—know about the program.

As a state-sponsored radio program, however, *Canada Reads* is not a popular culture product that is consumed by the masses. The attempt to attract a wider audience through a format borrowed from a popular television genre is commendable, but the content of the program tells another story. The texts selected for the yearly contest—usually fiction and sometimes poetry—exemplify the culturally consecrated status of Canadian literature (Fuller 2011, 3–20) even while the format of the program mimics a reality-TV competition, and captures the glitz of our celebrity culture.

In the pretaped five- to eight-hour discussion, the *Canada Reads* producers chose to broadcast exchanges that create drama, which make for interesting radio, and also tap in to the emotional conflicts that are reminiscent of television reality competitions, such as the *Amazing Race* and *Big Brother*. During the 2006 season, *Deafening* by Frances Itani (HarperCollins Publishers) was championed by feminist lawyer and author Maureen McTeer; *Cocksure* by Mordecai Richler (McClelland & Stewart Ltd.) by comedian and novelist Scott Thompson; *Three Day Road* by Joseph Boyden (Penguin Group Canada) by memoirist and filmmaker Nelofer Pazira; *Rooms for Rent in the Outer Planets: Selected Poems, 1962–1996* by Al Purdy (Harbour Publishing) by poet Susan Musgrave; and *A Complicated Kindness* by Miriam Toews (Random House of Canada, Alfred A. Knopf Canada) by musician and publisher John K. Samson.

Popular radio personality and author Bill Richardson hosted the program in 2006. As a writer, Richardson has the cultural capital necessary to lead the discussions. He also has a charismatic personality that plays into the game nature demanded by *Canada Reads* producers (T. Vartanian, pers. comm., 2003). In the "sneak preview" broadcast during the week leading up to the competition on the radio and on the web page, Richardson's booming voice invites listeners to join him in the "ever-popular battle of the books on CBC Radio."[11] In a playful style, Richardson provides listeners with a "handy-dandy guide" to this year's competition—"the books, the authors, the plots, the *scheming* and the personalities" (emphasis in original). Thus, he sets the tone of competition, and is supported by the panelists for the next minute with individual quips about their combat style. "It's basically preparing for battle. I'm preparing for battle," says Musgrave, whereas Thompson follows with "I will be taking no prisoners." Not known for her comedic talents, Musgrave says "I will either kill them with humour or with my sword." The preview also provides snapshots of the panelists' personalities and the performative traits that will come into play during the subsequent five-day show. We hear from the soft-spoken Sampson, whose selection actually wins the competition. He is presented as the level-headed musician who, as a publisher, has cultural authority across two cultural fields. Yet Sampson introduces himself as a laid-back pacifist: "I'm terrified of my opponents," he says, "but I'll have to hide it somehow . . . I don't really have it in me to be especially political. I'll probably be one of those panelists that other people pick on." Prize-winning filmmaker Pazira pipes in with a calm announcement: "I'd like to not call myself a fighter. I'd like to believe I'm a debater. I believe in the power and persuasion of words." Before the broadcast program begins, the "battleground" and its players are set.

Elsewhere we have argued that *Canada Reads* on-air book talk "frequently favours interpretive practices shaped by canonical aesthetics and formalist hermeneutics" (Fuller 2007, 13). However, by season four, broadcast in 2005, there was a marked similarity to the kinds of vernacular book talk and social dynamics found in face-to-face book clubs (E. Long 2003; Rehberg Sedo 2004),[12] which was peppered with the language of competition. An extensively edited discussion between the celebrity panelists found them frequently overtalking and joking with each other, and sometimes being malevolent toward one another in their arguments. Passionately promoting the titles they were "defending," the *Canada Reads* panelists would often play up the competitive nature of the "game" while also providing pedagogical interpretations of the book they were "championing."

Books as Tools for Learning and Weapons of War

Canada Reads can be interpreted as a response to the contemporary popularity of book clubs and the concomitant increase in interest in best-selling literary fiction (Fuller and Rehberg Sedo 2006). Eleven years running, the titles selected for the program were consistently identifiable as components of the culturally consecrated body of literature known in Canada as "Can Lit." Although the book lists suggest otherwise, some commentators view *Canada Reads* as further evidence of the "middle-browing" (i.e., downgrading of quality and intellect) of the CBC (Niedzviecki 2002; R. Smith 2004). Part of the critical reaction to the lists might in fact lie in the framing of the book talk that is broadcast on the airwaves, which tends to merge the perceived high-culture status of books with the popular culture status of reality television in the form of a "battle of the books."

Consider the 2006 list as an example of the consecration of the literary quality of the books chosen for *Canada Reads*. For instance, *Rooms for Rent in the Outer Planets: Selected Poems, 1962–1996* (1996) is a collection written by Al Purdy, who has been called Canada's "unofficial poet laureate" (Brooke 2000), whereas Mordecai Richler's 1968 satirical novel *Cocksure* was awarded the Governor General's Award the same year it was published. The more recently published *Three Day Road* (2005) by Joseph Boyden and *A Complicated Kindness* (2004) by Miriam Toews had both won national book competitions before they were featured on *Canada Reads*.[13] The lists over the years actually ignore the preference for mass-market genre fiction

Table 3.1 Top Five Genre Preferences

	Canada Reads	
Genre	Most preferred	%
Contemporary fiction	344	36
Mystery	157	17
Science fiction	86	9
Biographies	51	4
Classical literature	47	5

N = 961

articulated in a Canadian study of readers (Créatec 2005). That study found that "the mystery, suspense, detective, spy, adventure genre" is the most popular genre for Canadian readers: 62 percent of Canadian readers had read at least one book in that genre in the last year, and 20 percent of Canadian readers read that genre most often (66). Table 3.1 illustrates which genre *our* survey respondents chose when asked to select the type of book they most prefer. The readers in our study demonstrate a slightly different taste preference,[14] with contemporary fiction leading the choice preference and better reflecting the *Canada Reads* target audience.

The producers of *Canada Reads* have to walk the delicate line of appealing to a wider audience, while honoring the historical culture of the CBC "to inform and educate" its audience. Contemporary fiction allows for successful book talk on radio in ways that book discussion of mysteries or science fiction might not.[15] That is, contemporary fiction generates more familiar book talk unless the target audience is science fiction or mystery fans, who would not find the book talk pleasing. Outside of those fan groups, genre fiction is often viewed as being too formulaic and repetitive. As the Alabama MRE producer, Mary Wallace notes in Chapter 5, "Worker," the very elements that seem pleasurable to one group are distinctive elements to another group of readers. Genre fiction generally does not work well in MREs but, interestingly, the long-running and well-established reading programs do sometimes chose science fiction.[16]

As a conduit for discussion, the book on *Canada Reads* garners special attention when it is held up as a tool for learning. The voices of Musgrave and Pazira start Day One's broadcast likening the upcoming discussions to classrooms and exams, and McTeer follows with her comment that "Canadians should try and read them all because it's through reading that we begin to understand different points of view, different places, different perspectives." Sampson's edited-in retort counters McTeer with "I don't think books should be didactic. You shouldn't read fiction because you want to learn something, it should be the other way around. You should *happen* to learn something because you love the book" (emphasis in the original).

These introductory sound bites invite listeners to evaluate their own reading practices. They also illustrate the oftentimes blatant message that listening to *Canada Reads* can be informative.

The discussions begin with a symbolic bell clang, and Richardson announcing "let the games begin." *Rooms for Rent in the Outer Planets: Selected Poems, 1962–1996* by the late Al Purdy is the first book that the panel discusses. Musgrave tells the listening audience that she chose this book because she hopes "that by giving Canadians a taste of poetry, that they'll go on to read not just Al Purdy, but me!" After the jovial, if uncomfortable, laughter subsides, she continues with a list of contemporary poets who, in her words, "speak to who we are as Canadians." The book talk in each program differs from year to year, depending on the celebrity book reviewers. Consistently, however, the talk about the role of the program in the Canadian literary consciousness always works its way into the discussions.

Thompson criticizes Canadian literature while choosing world-renowned author Mordecai Richler's *Cocksure* (1968) because it is "hilarious." He says, "I think Canadian letters are very devoid of comedy and I think there's a prejudice in this country towards comedy." Identifying what constitutes humor is debated during other segments, but McTeer dismisses the novel right away with "I'm not a prude, I just think we should just try to have more words than the F word and the S word. And I think one of the things we are trying to do here is have Canadians read . . . and it is a book I would not be recommending to anybody" (Day 1). McTeer articulates the role of *Canada Reads* as instructional, and she suggests that Richler's book is not up to the task.

The book that McTeer defends, *Deafening* (2003), is a narrative about World War I and Canadians' reactions to it back at home. McTeer describes the book as a "romantic epic, [one that] deals with all of the great issues . . . Issues of relationship, of family, or war remain powerful." She continues by setting up the affective connection readers often seek with the books they read for pleasure: "Set in rural Ontario, the real power comes, I think, with the juxtaposition of World War I and its impact on all of their lives, not just the minuscule—the family—but also the whole community, the whole country." By identifying the locale of the book, McTeer specifically addresses the intentions of the *Canada Reads* producers who try to represent Canada's diverse regions and provinces. Efforts are also purportedly made to represent a range of cultural and historical experiences through the book selections. In 2006, however, there were three books on the list that were set in Ontario and two that take place during the war: *Deafening*, *Three Day Road*, and *Rooms for Rent* are set in Ontario, and *Deafening* and *Three Day Road* are World War I narratives.

Pazira's introduction of *Three Day Road* is the longest of all the celebrity preambles, suggesting that the editors needed her contextualization for future debates that would support the educational tone and combative tensions that would play themselves out in subsequent days. When Richardson tells the listening audience that the book is another WWI story, she is quick to retort that the book is "different." Illustrating the national identity project that *Canada Reads* supports, Pazira says in a passionate voice:

> This book is different . . . it taught me something about Canadian history that despite the fact that coming from outside and being very, very sort of thirsty for wanting to know about this country, I had never heard about it before . . . Our war against the Natives [was a] covert war that we hardly talk about but if we do, we do it in such a rhetorical way out of guilt . . . It's not only that it's a great piece of literature—as it is—but it's also something about the history of this country that we—most of us—ought to know about. And it's not just about "let's acknowledge it" but try to understand it from the perspective and the point of view of those who enlisted in the Canadian larger army to go and fight for this country and then they came back and they were betrayed . . . If Canadians are going to take time out of their busy schedules to read a book, it should be this. I felt quite connected to it not just because of my own experiences with war and all of that but because I also feel, as a Canadian, I feel responsible that there are things that one ought to know. (Day 1)

As a member of a visible minority who acknowledges her new Canadian status, Pazira fulfills the role of representing a "multicultural" nation-state with a population that has been growing by about 250,000 people each year during the first decade of the twenty-first century (Chui, Tran, Maheux, and Statistics Canada 2007). Such representations are ideologically significant because they counter the French-English dual identity so often represented as the national identity of Canada (Fuller and Rehberg Sedo 2006, 22–23). In this introduction, Pazira articulates a responsibility for Canadians to acknowledge histories that have not been given their due. This argument carries through the entire season, with Pazira repeating her reasoning that this is the book that "all Canadians should read this year."

Introductions to the books and their celebrity proponents continue on Day 1 in order to contextualize the competition. Sampson defends his friend and fellow Winnipegger Miriam Toews's *A Complicated Kindness* (2004), which he promotes as a "rare book that . . . alters the way you see the world and your own place in it. It addresses all these themes that I think are timely and important. Things about, you know, family, religion and community." The book is set in a Mennonite community in Manitoba, which, according to Sampson, is unique and "the uniqueness is so universal . . . primarily it's the voice of Naomi Nikel, the narrator, and it's the voice I've been waiting for in Canadian literature. I think it's a voice that captures all the weird and hilarious and sad beauty of who we are." Canadian national identity for Sampson is engendered by a teenager whose religious community offers both safety and constriction. His opening introduction, during which he rapidly conflates what is individual and "unique" with what is "universal" and "Canadian," reiterates the program's nationalist project and the desire of both producers and the on-air celebrity readers to unify the country through reading. Indeed, the choice of Canadian books, the selection of celebrity panelists who hail from different regions of the country, and the topics highlighted by the editing of the book discussions frame literary book talk as a celebration of Canadian cultural production. However, the competitive nature of the program still maintains the assumption of a hierarchy of literary value. After all, the merits of all the books are discussed, but only one comes out on top.

Throughout the 2006 season, we hear the panelists give short messages of congratulations to the CBC for producing *Canada Reads*. On Day 5, however, an explicit discussion of the value and role of the CBC in supporting print culture in Canada and its value in nurturing a national identity is given airtime. McTeer begins with her accolades after she explains that she is sad for her author (Itani) because the book was voted off. Of the program itself she says, "I enjoyed it. I enjoyed being here, I enjoyed doing the French [books] as well, because I find you meet new people. But also the whole process and I think that this is something you should be very, very proud of. Susan [Musgrave] mentioned the role of the CBC in Canada writ large and I think you do us all a service when you do this kind of thing." Richards responds: "Well, on behalf of my colleagues I say thank you." The blatant promotion of the CBC during the final day of the competition may have sounded to some listeners like a plea for popular and political support in the face of media segmentation and audience fragmentation. However, for many of our readers, the authoritative role that the CBC plays in advocating for Canadian culture, especially Canadian print culture, is unquestionable.

CONTRADICTIONS AND CONTINGENCIES: READERS' REACTIONS TO *CANADA READS*

Generations of Canadians have learned through school, the media, and their parents that the CBC exists, in part, to support Canadian cultural products. Similar to the divergent views that are played out in various public venues—such as national newspapers and in Internet chat rooms—readers across Canada are divided in their perceptions of how well the CBC does this. In Halifax, for example, we heard everything from "I love CBC, I have it on all the time" from Marie, a sixty-year-old professor, and "I'm a CBC junkie, and I think it's for everyone" from Beth, a young marine scientist in her mid-twenties, to "I just can't stand to listen to it, I find it, it is sort of patronizing in a way . . ." from thirty-nine-year-old Kim, who volunteers her time. The task of addressing a mass public, who are as diverse as these voices indicate, might seem daunting, but the part that *Canada Reads* plays in maintaining the CBC's cultural authority is illustrative of high- and popular-culture debates of decades past. Consider, for example, that 64 percent (464) of the readers in our online survey participate in *Canada Reads*. Of those readers, 35 percent watched and/or listened to the program; 20 percent have read at least one of the books selected for debate; and, 29 percent have visited the website. The data shows that readers who elect genre literature as their preferred reading choices—such as mysteries, romances, and science fiction— are less likely to participate in *Canada Reads*. For some of those readers who do participate, however, allowing the state broadcaster to evaluate the books for their literary value is problematic. For example, Jennifer from Wolfville, Nova Scotia, questions the text selection process and at the same time articulates her own level of confidence in evaluating Canadian literature (Fuller 2011). Of the selected titles, she says: "They do tend to go for more *serious* [books]—which I think is, in some ways, annoying because they decide what's literature, and I find that aggravating because often the books they cut out as *not* being literature or not being considered are an excellent read and are well-written" (emphasis in the original). The conversation with the other focus group readers continues with further questioning of the authority of *Canada Reads*:

Jenn: But they don't talk about the "best"; they talk about the one Canada *should* read.

Jean: Well, but that "should" . . .

Blanca: No, it's a conversation . . .

Jean: It's preachy. Instead of . . .

Blanca: It is. It's preachy, *and* it's also very competitive—like, this year was very competitive. (CR FG 7 P, 2006; emphasis in the original)

For some of the readers, the cultural authority of CBC and *Canada Reads* is evident and is unquestioned. For others, like Jenn, the implied authority is troublesome, and for readers such as Jean the moral imperative connoted by "should" confirms her hesitation to participate in *Canada Reads*. Blanca agrees with the moral imperative, but it is the competition format that is troublesome for her. The game show nature of the program and the celebrity reviewers' book talk often caused uneasy responses from readers. For Jenn and others in our focus groups, the attempt to make a highbrow practice into a popular culture product is disingenuous. She said, "having the celebrities instead of the academics is their only attempt at making it not snooty—because they try to sell it as, like, this more popular element of CBC" (CR FG 7 P, 2006).

The producers might choose celebrities to play into celebrity culture—that is, celebrities add entertainment value—they also demonstrate that reading can be enjoyable for all types of people. However, readers who listen to the CBC have expectations learned through years of listening to book programming. These readers have a cultural literacy that can be recognized in terms of their highbrow literary culture practices. In the following exchange, we see how the assumed cultural authority of CBC works to inform listeners-readers' response to *Canada Reads*, in particular the use of celebrity reader-champions:

Marie: . . . certain people have a certain resonance for you that other people don't have, and, and, sort of titles do, too. So you know, some years some people might be more involved than others or . . .

Donna: Some years the link between the celebrity and the book seems very tenuous and arbitrary. Some years you, you at least have the illusion that they chose that book themselves, or [that they] personally wanted to champion it. And some years it seemed like "OK, you're in *Young Canada Reads*[17] this year, here's your book!" You know? And there wasn't the real, genuine . . . actually years three and four, I, I thought a couple of the celebrities just weren't pulling their weight or really didn't seem to be genuine readers or. . . . (CR FG 1 P, 2006)

The idea that celebrities cannot be "real" or "genuine" readers seems to resonate with those listeners and readers who are comfortable with their own levels of cultural literacy. Respondents to our survey would appear to fit that profile because 91 percent of them have at least some university education, and 39 percent have finished a graduate degree. Another 7 percent are working toward one.[18] Similarly, for many of our focus group readers who reacted negatively to the panel, the question of "authority" of the person or the "authenticity" of his or her interpretation was at the heart of their criticism. Reader opposition to celebrity book reviewers also appeared in cyberspace: on the program's website (although these comments were monitored), on Twitter, and in literary weblogs (litblogs). One litblogger/radio show host created her own panel on community radio. "Here's the deal: I'm a big fan of *Canada Reads*, but I think it's unfair only celebs get to play," she wrote to introduce her idea. She continued: "Because I know lots of smart, literary types who could make great debaters, and I love to hear them talk about books . . . Turns out I can produce a radio show (hey, I didn't say a good one). And we did pick the same book (Nicolas Dickner's *Nikolski*). But the discussion was different enough to validate having bookish people talk about books [. . .]" (Knoch 2010).

   The litblog is called "Keepin' It Real Book Club" and the panel, "Civilians Read," reframes the title of *Canada Reads*, and indicates some struggle with the idea of having celebrities as reviewers or book champions. The "civilians" who are imagined as readers are presumably the "bookish people" who are "great debaters" and, by implication, more qualified and authoritative readers than the CBC's panelists. We heard similar protestations from many readers who distinguish themselves as having as much, or more cultural literacy, than the panel celebrities. In common with the readers in our study who questioned the quality of the televised book discussions for the RJBC, readers who spurned the book talk on *Canada Reads* may be expressing their desire to maintain the status of book reading as a "special" leisure pursuit. Canadian readers' discomfort with a popular format is exacerbated by the gear-change that *Canada Reads* represents in terms of the CBC's historical relationship to Canadian literature. Many such readers prioritize the cultural authority of established CBC literary personalities—such as Eleanor Wachtel—over those celebrities who are not known for their literary expertise. Take Anne, for example. She is a forty-nine-year-old reader from Prince Edward Island who chooses her books based on reviews in *The Globe & Mail* and *Kirkus Book Reviews*, both of which are well-established sources of literary authority. She also listens to the audio performances of Canadian books broadcast as *Between the Covers* on CBC Radio1. When we asked her why she did not participate in *Canada Reads*, Anne employed a humorous and vivid vernacular expression to make her point:

Anne: I get my recommendations from people I trust! [laughing]

Anouk: And you don't trust them?

Anne: I don't trust Scott Thompson as far as I could spit with my mouth shut! [general laughter] (CR FG 9 NP 2006)

Scott Thompson is a Canadian comedian and actor who starred in a very popular, if sometimes raunchy, television program called *Kids in the Hall.* Anne obviously took issue with a comedian recommending reading choices to her and was careful to distinguish herself as a serious—aka highbrow— reader who makes her reading choices with the help of others who are more qualified than the likes of a comic actor. Whereas some of our study's participants rejected or were suspicious of particular celebrities such as Thompson, other readers did not trust the format of the program. This is what Marie had to say:

I, I don't know—I like some—I trust some of those voices and others grate on me. I find it cutesy, I find it gimmicky a lot . . . A lot of CBC delivery on Radio1 is gimmicky to me. And maybe I'm just not their audience, I'm not sure, they have a strange sort of sense of humor that I don't share. I don't. It feels that they're too smart for their own good— only they're not, you know? I'd rather hear something that really felt intelligent rather than something that feels to me like they're pretending to be intelligent. (CR FG 1 P, 2006)

Marie, who is a reader in her sixties, actually highlights an interesting finding in our *Canada Reads* data. Those readers who are older and have learned to associate a certain type of traditional radio book programming that features a learned interviewer talking with an author, for example, tend to respond more negatively to *Canada Reads* than younger readers. Our survey results parallel those focus group readers who react negatively to the celebrity nature of the panel: 62 percent expect the *Canada Reads* host to have literary cultural authority. The survey data, however, also shows the division between our readers. Like the younger members of our focus group readers who participate in *Canada Reads*, 44 percent of survey respondents support the idea of celebrity panelists. The younger readers have learned the role of the CBC from their parents, but they are also comfortable with the reality-TV-type format. They appear to appreciate it more. Antonio and Avery are thirty-something readers in Vancouver. Their discussion is illustrative of the younger readers' responses to *Canada Reads*:

Antonio: Yeah, and it's not your typical people who you expect to hear talk about books. And, um, so I actually find *Canada Reads*— I'm always *really* intrigued which of the books are on *Canada Reads*. You know, and again, because of time, I don't always read them. But the *Canada Reads* [selections] influence me much more than the One Book, One Vancouver [ones].

DeNel: Could it be that it's CBC? And you trust CBC? Or is it—

Antonio: I also trust the library. I think it's a combination—I *do* trust CBC, but I think—but if the CBC just put up a poster: "Here's five books . . . "—you know, would that have much of an impact? [emphasis in the original]

Avery: Yeah, I think it's a representation from various people who are bringing their own opinion and it conflicts with other people, so it's not like it's a scripted or prescriptive thing, that, you know: "This is what we're gonna read because everyone agrees it's the best book to represent Canada"—or whatever the sort of notion behind it is. You know, "my opinion is valid even if I like it and you don't"; it's still—I mean, it's a discussion.

. . .

Antonio: Yeah, there's just—and, uh, it's fun. Like, again, I don't listen to it that *much* just because of the timing of it, but when you do, it's like, "Oh, this is cool! This is *Canada Reads*!" (OBOV FG Mixed P and NP SFU Book Club 2006; emphasis in the original)

Antonio and Avery illustrate the potential success of reaching "a younger, hipper" CBC audience, but their discussion also demonstrates that listeners already have to be readers to participate, and that they have to already trust the CBC as a cultural arbiter of literary value. The popular entertainment genre adopted by the show is acceptable to both Antonio and Avery because they find the competition "fun" and entertaining, and also because they trust the CBC to provide them with reading choices. Rather than understanding the book talk as "scripted" or "prescriptive," or, indeed as frivolous and not "serious" (as some other readers protested), Antonio and Avery frame the expression of differing opinions as the type of "discussion" that fits into what they have learned to expect from CBC Radio.

These two readers confirm, then, that to be a participant in *Canada Reads* requires a fair amount of cultural literacy. Moreover, their conversation suggests that the capacity to really enjoy the show depends upon a listener's familiarity with literary book talk *and* with popular contemporary formats from other media, as well as an open-ness to celebrity culture. The possession and display of what we might term hybrid cultural taste (and the competencies needed to acquire it) demonstrated by the shift of Antonio's narrative from "I'm always really intrigued which of the books are on *Canada Reads*" to "Oh this is cool!" can also enhance the pleasures that readers derive from "high-pop" cultural products. Readers whose taste in print genres focuses on non-fiction or genre fiction are understandably less attracted by the relatively highbrow literary tastes represented by the *Canada Reads* selections. Our survey data found that 80 percent of those readers who list Romance, History or "SciFi" as their top three genre choices were less likely to read *Canada Reads* books ($p < 0.05$). That means that not only does a reader have to have enough time to participate in the program, but also that he or she has to share the cultural tastes that are promoted by the selected titles.

As in most general readership studies, such as "Reading and Buying Books for Pleasure" (Canadian Heritage and Créatec 2005), more women (88 percent) participate in the program than men. Many of these readers are members of face-to-face or online book clubs ($p < 0.05$). When readers' cultural literacies and tastes clash with the genres generated by media convergence, the readers articulate un-ease with the production strategies employed by the program's producers. We see this in Donna's interpretation of the celebrity's abilities to critique—and defend—the merits of the selected texts:

Donna: I've never seen *Survivor*. [laughter] I don't mind it if it's genuine. Uh, if they're paying lip service to defending a book when they haven't really even read it that closely or don't really—aren't really personally engaged, then it just strikes me as disingenuous, um, but you know, if you had a panel of like, Eleanor Wachtel, and Ian Brown, and Bill Richardson, all defending a book they really, personally chose, that would be fabulous.

DeNel: Because they're literary and you know that they are?

Donna: Um, no because they, they would—they have the integrity for one thing to, to insist on choosing their own book. I mean, I found it hard a few years to believe that all the celebrity panelists really did pick their own book, uh, and really cared for it. (CR FG 1 P, 2006)

The cultural literacy Donna demonstrates extends beyond her ability to place reviewers on a hierarchical scale according to their knowledge of literature. Her words also imply an understanding of the production processes behind a literary radio program that attempts to blend genres across different media. Discerning listener-readers expect the celebrity reviewers to passionately defend their book in the competition, and in order to do that, they believe that the celebrities need to choose the books themselves. The book talk, for Donna and readers like her, needs to be authenticated by the emotional and intellectual investment of the defenders in their selection so that the on-air readers come across as "personally engaged."

The cultural literacy that readers articulated was often threaded through with notions of taste hierarchies. Similar to The Richard & Judy's Book Club focus group readers, some of our *Canada Reads* listeners-readers do a "dance of distinction"—identifying themselves against an MRE because of its popular culture game show nature. However, others accept the CBC as an established cultural authority. For other reader-listeners, still, there is a response to the selected texts as being too highbrow. In the following discussion, Jean, who is a judge and an avid reader, discusses the winner of the 2005 season, *Rockbound* (1928), in the context of the *Canada Reads* lists:

Jean: Well . . . no, I mean: if you took out some Oprah's choices and some of *Canada Reads'* choices and you put them on the table, and you let everybody (you know, just *regular* people) choose a book, they're not gonna choose the *Canada Reads* books! Because I mean, I tried to read *Rockbound* not too long ago and I just—

Chris: I liked *Rockbound*!

Jean: I know, my mother liked *Rockbound*. Maybe it's because I'm not reading seriously, I'm reading—

Blanca: But when we *do Canada Reads*, we don't—

Jean: I'm reading for fun.

Blanca: but we're also reading Canadian! You know?

Jean: Well, that's true. I mean, I *do* like reading Canadian, and I don't get my Canadian books from *Oprah*—I mean, obviously. But I don't get my Canadian books from *Canada Reads*, either, I can tell you right now! (CR FG 7 P, 2006; emphasis in the original)

The perception that the *Canada Reads* selections are "serious" and that she doesn't "read seriously right now" in itself suggests that Jean feels that she needs to qualify and account for her reading choices and practices. Her sense that she may be judged on the basis of her book selections is no doubt heavily influenced by the presence of a pair of academic reading researchers and other focus group members. But even more interesting is the conflict that Jean articulates between the pleasure of reading and the perceived nature of the *Canada Reads* lists. For Jean, if a book is on *Canada Reads*, it is a serious book and not one meant for pleasure reading. Similar to the critic's arguments against the highbrow nature of the CBC of decades past, Jean and reader-listeners like her, assume a hierarchy of cultural tastes that the producers of *Canada Reads* say that they are working against. The focus group talk that Jean was involved in also leads us to question what it means to "read Canadian." Or, to put it another way, what is the identity work that is performed by *Canada Reads*?

Identity Work

Philip Savage argues that CBC Radio has been successful in "developing new content to address dynamic notions of identity and audience reflection" (2010, 273) in comparison to other forms of media utilized by the CBC. He argues that the CBC can do this successfully by engaging audiences with local content. For their part, the producers of *Canada Reads* have worked to choose texts that are regional and panelists who hail from different parts of the country. In doing this, they provide opportunities for local CBC stations to create their own programming. Some of that programming takes place in the studio and others in the community, such as panel discussions and high school presentations. Of the readers in our online survey, 28 percent (273) note that they participate in CBC-sponsored local events. These are reading events that illustrate another layer of media convergence. Local programmers engage with the national project by hosting their own public debates, such as the Nakusp (British Columbia) Public Library's *Canada Reads* Discussion, or the now-annual *Young Canada Reads* competition in Halifax, Nova Scotia.

Readers' responses to the national and regional identity work performed by *Canada Reads* illustrate the complexity of their own identity work as readers of Canadian literature. Their interpretations of nationalism and regionalism through the literature they choose to read are also mediated by the CBC's cultural authority as a promoter of Canadian identity. Whereas some of our younger readers who listen to radio mainly for music do not identify personally with the CBC,[19] others uncritically identify as Canadian through the CBC. Donna, for example, says that its pervasiveness in her life is part of the reason the network informs how she thinks of herself and how she articulates her nationalism:

> I guess because I listen to it so much, and I don't watch television news. I read the local paper which doesn't give you much about [laughs] what's going on in the world, so, um, yeah, that's the way I know what's going on across the country, and what the weather's like across the country. I listen to a lot of Canadian music and often the first time you hear a group when it's surfacing is on CBC, you know, before they hit the mainstream? (CR FG 1 P, 2006)

For Donna, and other readers like her, not only is CBC radio a communication tool, but it is also a way to connect to and learn about Canadian cultural products. *Canada Reads* works as part of the mix of programming that she perceives to be distinctly homegrown.

The readers who place high symbolic value on the role of *Canada Reads* in promoting national literature would have taken issue with Canadian author Hugh Garner, who in 1958 criticized the efforts to create a national heritage through cultural products. In an article titled "Spoon-Fed Patriotism Won't Work in Canada" for *Saturday Night*, he wrote, "patriotism by persuasion is an attempt by misguided zealots to transfer love of country from one person to another by means of written and spoken word" (Garner, cited in Kuffert 2003, 185).[20] Readers, such as Trisha, a twenty-three-year-old from a rural area near Halifax, illustrate that the nationalist project supported by the CBC has in fact worked for some readers:

Anouk: How important do you think it is to Canada or to CBC to have a group of people who represent Canadian books?

Trisha: I think it's important for *someone* to.

DeNel: Do you?

Trisha: And, I think it's appropriate that CBC would.

DeNel: Why?

Trisha: Because of the association. You know, they're the Canadian Broadcasting Corporation, so if they're going to promote books, I think it's appropriate for them to be promoting Canadian content. (CR FG 5 NP, 2006; emphasis in the original)

Like Trisha, our survey participants identify an obligation for the national broadcaster to support national literature. Of the 347 respondents to the question "What is the best book choice for *Canada Reads*?" 11 percent (42) of the readers noted "[n]ational, regional or cultural relevance" as the most important criteria for creating a *Canada Reads* list. Even readers who do not participate in *Canada Reads* articulated nationalist expectations of the CBC.

Cultural nationalism also manifests itself in other types of mass reading events. One Book, One Community programs across Canada nearly always feature Canadian authors, for example. This focus often helps local producers create programming that can take advantage of author readings and local, place-based programming, such as organized trips to locations featured in the book. The choice for regional-based literature is a practical one, and it also illustrates the skill of librarians who recognize that the representation of region or place inspires a mode of affective belonging in readers (Fuller 2011), as we explore further in Chapter 6, Reader. As we have already noted, the *Canada Reads* producers attempt regional representation. However, their definition of regionalism does not always coincide with that of readers who search for an association with a book's place or characters.

This was particularly evident in our focus group discussions in Halifax when readers referred to *Rockbound* by Frank Parker Day, the *Canada Reads* winner for 2005. Because the book is set in rural Nova Scotia, and was defended by the popular Newfoundland writer Donna Morrisey, the book was a well-known title to our readers in the region. Almost all of them made some reference to the novel's local setting (Fuller 2007, 27–30).

But to produce a program that represents an entire nation is, as we have already noted, an idealistic task. Donna, who is a librarian, questions the role that agents within Canada's print culture field can have in creating a stronger national identity:

Donna: Well, um, I also have a professional cynicism . . . I thought when I heard *Canada Reads* the first time that librarians and readers and writers are not the power base in the country. And, for this big ambitious program to have been launched, it's almost like somebody behind the scenes in Ottawa said, "We need to forge a stronger national identity, let's do it in a real low-key way by starting a discussion about books"—ostensibly. And when you, when you look through the discussions, [you say], "Wow, this is so Canadian", like, there's so much about all of us and our lives thrown into the little snide remarks people are making about the books. So, to me, it always seemed like it was about something more than just getting everybody to read . . .

. . .

Anouk: Can I, can I pick up on the word "cynicism" that, um, do you think then that this program, that *Canada Reads*, shouldn't have a nationalistic impulse to it?

Donna: Oh I, no—I think it's fabulous. Uh, I think anything that gets more people reading Canadian books is a wonderful thing. Um, but it's just, all the, um na—natural stakeholders for Canadian literature are not the people that have the power to make something like this come to pass. (CR FG 1 P, 2006)

Donna's commentary suggests that she perceives the power brokers behind national identity are not *Canada Reads* panelists. Rather, her comment implies that these people are in fact, less likely to inform attitudes even if she thinks it's a "good thing" that more people read Canadian literature. Considering what *Canada Reads* might do, she echoes other readers in our study. Her words sound similar to our participants in The Richard & Judy Book Club focus groups who spoke about the unquestioned status of reading as a good and liberating thing, for example.

For some of the readers we spoke with, highlighting Canadian literature is problematic because they do not philosophically agree with the promotion of Canadian content. The conversation that follows took place among a group of readers in Halifax:

Caroline: One of the things I've realized during this discussion is my level of snobbishness, because I actually find Canadian content discussions totally irritating. I just find, I agree that you have to promote Canadian culture, but when you try to keep it in a box, and keep everything else out, it stifles all the creativity. And to me I just think you need to be more eclectic. And I understand the principles behind *Canada Reads*, but I think maybe that's what I find stifling about it.

Beth: But what about good Canadian books, not just because they are Canadian, do you understand what I'm saying? They're trying to promote Canadian literature, which, I think, is a great thing.

Caroline: I don't disagree, I'm just saying this is one area of my snobbishness I guess. When I'm hearing about Canadian books, I don't relate to them for the most part.

Johnny: I fully agree with that, I get squeemish, too. It's almost like everything American just comes in by default, if we don't look closer. If there is anything commercial involved, it's like the gates just open and it's American.

Karen: I guess, but back home they don't box things in, rather than, and I think that's part of the issue with me and *Canada Reads*. I don't know how to address that.

Johnny: Well, I think one way to address it would be to have more people like George Elliot Clarke, people like, Martell. I mean, people who point out Canada's—and this is going to sound horrible, it sounds like I'm working for the government, but Canada's like international flavor, or whatever. (CR FG 2 NP, 2006)

This long exchange among young Haligonians illustrates well the differing views and discussions about "Canadian content" produced by the protectionist stance of Canadian cultural policy (see Chapter 4, "Money"). These readers also debate and negotiate here their various understandings of what it means to be and to read "Canadian." As this lively exchange suggests, *Canada Reads* and the CBC might have a legislated responsibility, but that does not make their work any easier. As the public broadcaster, the government agency finds itself in a position where it is promoting the virtues of reading through a nationalist lens. With *Canada Reads*, it also recommends *what* people ought to be reading. Both of these practices—as these Haligonian readers articulate—alternatively please and irritate Canadian readers.

CONCLUSIONS: OLD MEDIUM, NEW CONUNDRUMS

As we have argued throughout this chapter, a function of the CBC is to promote the reading of Canadian writing, on the assumption that this will facilitate the production of a Canadian national identity. *Canada Reads* constructs a specific national identity that works for some readers-listeners and does not work so neatly for others. The series produces this situation by selecting Canadian literature that is championed by Canadian celebrities whose book talk highlights relatively uncomplicated notions of what it means to be Canadian (Fuller and Rehberg Sedo 2006). But this is not the only type of cultural work that *Canada Reads* performs. Through *Canada Reads*, the CBC perpetuates the long-standing debates about the elitist nature of the institution. Although the producers of *Canada Reads* deliberately moved away from the CBC's traditional book programming formats when they designed the series, the focus of the show upon literary genres, and the inclusion of books by many of Canada's most internationally acclaimed writers (including Michael Ondaatje and Margaret Atwood), maintains the CBC's association with high-status cultural artifacts. Whereas the producers attempt to engage readers through multiple media, the cultural authority and symbolic capital of the CBC cannot translate easily across media.

Canada Reads enables the corporation to continue its historical relationship with readers and the publishing industry, by dedicating a sizeable portion of its website to books (http://www.cbc.ca/books/). The annual series advances the corporation's relationship with reader-listeners even further by attempting to engage them in multiple modes of interaction. The interdependency of print, the Internet, television, and radio is evident to the producers of *Canada Reads* and they have attempted to harness it since the series began, although, as we noted above, they have to operate with limited human and economic resources. Despite these limits, the producers exploit new technologies well and have tried to build in more reader interactivity year-on-year. Whereas they tried and dropped television programming in 2004, they have successfully moved to the Internet through video streaming on YouTube and by using the social networking platforms Twitter and Facebook. Through experiments with multiple modes of engagement, *Canada Reads* illustrates the success of on-demand programming. The immediacy of social media, short videos, on-screen chat, or podcasts that can be accessed according to the user's own schedule is appealing to a generation used to online content production.

By attempting to appeal to different age demographics through different media and trading upon the coextensive nature of print, radio, the Internet, and television, *Canada Reads* works to fulfill the broadcasters' legislated mandates of facilitating national unity and promoting Canadian cultural products. The MRE can also be considered an economic success based on the number of sales of the selected texts. According to BookNet Canada, a sales tracking agency of the publishing industry, Thomas Wharton's *Icefields*

(1996), which was a 2008 selection, increased by 4,400 percent in sales "from the week before the announcement to the week following" (2007). Overall, the five titles that year enjoyed an "average sales increase of more than 4,200%" (ibid). To some extent, *Canada Reads* also illustrates the "successful" disruption of the ideological meanings of reading in English Canada, which rarely takes into account French writers and their work. As means of illustration, consider author Nicolas Dickner, the winner of the 2010 competition. In an interview, he said that his book *Nikolski* "had some attention, but not that much [when it was published in translation] . . . The book was basically invisible before *Canada Reads*—[then] it really went from nothing to being noticed" (Landau 2011). He continued: "We weren't expecting it to be so big. We hear about *Canada Reads* in Québec, but we do not know how much it reaches the audience in Canada, so we were pretty surprised to see how many readers were looking at the book."

As we have argued throughout this chapter, the popularity of *Canada Reads* serves Canadian authors and Canadian publishing in ways that are consistent with its role in previous decades. Unfortunately, the ideological tensions we observed have also been there since the CBC's beginnings. The program illustrates the impossible tightrope that the state broadcaster has to walk: to attract mass audiences, and in particular, to involve younger audiences while fulfilling the expectations of their older, established listenership. High-class status is hard to disrupt. Whereas the cultural tension produced by the RJBC upset our focus group readers in the UK, our Canadian focus group readers were mostly comforted by the cultural authority realized by the CBC. We think that the different readers' reactions lie partly in the economic structure of the network: *Canada Reads* does not pander to commercialization. It does sell books, but it is not branded commercially. Because it is produced and broadcast on a state-sponsored network, it appears to stand apart from commercial demands—for at least some readers, for some of the time.

The RJBC can be considered successful in creating new readers through the different book genres that the producers selected and via the format of the book talk that the show engendered. *Canada Reads* is less successful in these respects. The producers have adapted well in reacting to changing reading practices via technology, but to engage with *Canada Reads* demands cultural competencies that not all readers possess. Our case study illustrates that not only do readers have to be able to engage with contemporary genres of broadcast programming, they also have to have an understanding and appreciation of Canadian literature in order to participate in this mass reading event.

All readers do not have equal access to literature. The competencies, expectations, and literacies of the *Canada Reads* audiences that we studied encourage us to be cautious of Jim Collins's (2010) idealism about the availability and accessibility of literary experiences across media. Further, not all media are considered equal by readers in terms of their adaptation or re-presentation of books and the promotion of reading. Our research shows that different media are still regarded by readers as having different symbolic value, and are sometimes perceived as serving different cultural functions. The readers we studied confirm that the cultural value normally assigned to the various media—in these last two chapters, to radio and television—and the genres within those media, influence readers' perceptions and interpretations of the kinds of reading each program promotes.

Like our analysis of the format and content of the RJBC, our conclusions about *Canada Reads* illustrate that the meanings of reading change with broadcast book programming, depending on the network, the genre of the book program, and the medium itself. Nevertheless, whatever "fun," drama, and entertainment is created for listeners or spectators through the employment of new or hybrid formats in the programming, the medium is the message (McLuhan, 1964) in that radio trumps television for its traditional symbolic value (Bennett 2006). Similarly, the book itself wields significant cultural power. As we discuss further in Chapter 7, "Book," the material artifact of a book frequently symbolizes knowledge.

What then does an analysis of *Canada Reads* tell us about the meanings of reading in the contemporary moment, and what role does media convergence play in our articulations of these meanings? The definition of popular culture may shift, but the symbolic value that middle- and upper-class Canadian readers ascribe to reading books, especially those within the category of Canadian literature, does not. Moreover, in the early twenty-first century, readers who wish to exploit the full range of literary experiences that multiple media offer require both economic and cultural capital. Readers need, in fact, to possess "transliteracies"[21] that allow them to fully engage with and understand different genres across different media. And the acquisition of such skills does not in itself change readers' evaluations of formats like *Canada Reads* that disturb genre hierarchies. The readers in our study of *Canada Reads* illustrate that over time, the meanings of reading do not change quickly, especially perhaps when the pursuit of leisure reading is so overtly connected to the project of exploring and understanding national identity. As we pointed out in Chapter 1, "Reading," the reading of books has often been promoted via governmental and educational institutions in North America and the UK as a civilizing force that can help to create a better educated, and thus more economically productive, citizenry. In the next chapter, we examine how ideas of money and moral power are frequently articulated together within the planning and branding of mass reading events, especially those which adopt the One Book, One Community model. As we explore in some detail, within the context of neoliberal cultural policies, shared reading events become sites inscribed with cultural anxieties about community cohesion and overburdened by imperatives to provoke social change. Such feelings about books and reading are also, we argue, inflected by the globalized structures of English-language book publishing. Having considered two media (television and radio) that have played pivotal roles in popularizing shared reading, we therefore move on to a consideration of how and why money is dispersed across other agencies within the reading industry.

4 Money

Three smiling men in business suits gather around a gleaming new car while a fourth man seated at the wheel offers the car keys through the rolled-down window (see Figure 4.1). The man in the driving seat is Ziad Ojakli, Ford Motor Company Group Vice-President for Government and Community Relations. Receiving the keys from him is David Kipen, employee of the National Endowment for the Arts (NEA) and Director of the Big Read program, which has made grants to hundreds of OBOC shared-reading events across the United States since 2006. Looking on as the 2008 Ford Hybrid Escape is donated to the program are NEA Chair, Dana Gioia, and Ford Motor Company Washington Counsel, James W. Carroll, Jr. The customized car is brightly colored and covered in a pattern that repeats the Big Read logo. According to the caption accompanying the photograph, the Ford will "help build awareness of the Big Read" and "help inspire new readers" by transporting NEA staff as they "'criss-cross' the country to attend and speak at Big Read events." Men, cars, and a road trip across the US: these constitute a powerful appeal to a masculine American mythos of mobility and individual agency, of self-discovery and self-transformation. Partially visible in the photograph is a slogan emblazoned on the side of the car, "Escape with a book," a witty, if obvious, play on the model name for this particular Ford vehicle and a reference to the imaginative possibilities that reading books is commonly believed to inspire.

The messages constructed through the branding practices on display seem at first to cohere very neatly. However, the choice of a family-friendly model Ford car conflicts with a notion of masculinity predicated on escape and solitude, and, with the idea of the solitary reader. After all, this particular brand and model of car suggests a shared experience of escape from everyday life: a more apt image for the Big Read, certainly. The other message in play, and the one that the NEA wanted to foreground (as their requested credit line under the photograph in this book also makes clear), is the way that partnerships among corporations, arts organizations, and communities enable Americans to read "for pleasure and enlightenment." The car, meanwhile, represents a practical means by which a corporate sponsor can contribute to the marketing of the project by "building awareness" about the activities and book selections at "the heart" of this nationwide MRE.

Figure 4.1 Big Read Car and National Endowment for the Art's Staff and Sponsors
[Supplied by NEA] Ford Motor Company Group Vice President for Government
and Community Relations Ziad Ojakli (right) hands over the keys for The Big Ride
to EDA Director of The Big Read David Kipen as NEA Chairman Dana Gioia (far
right) and Ford Motor Company Washington Counsel James W. Carroll, Jr. (far
left) look on. The Big Read is a program of the National Endowment for the Arts,
designed to "restore reading to the center of American culture" (NEA 2012). The
NEA present The Big Read in partnership with Arts Midwest. The Big Read brings
together partners across the country to encourage reading for pleasure and enlightenment. To help build awareness of The Big Read, the Ford Motor Company has
donated a 2008 Ford Escape Hybrid to the program.

Source: Photo courtesy of National Endowment for the Arts. Available at http://www.nea.
gov/national/bigread/press/PhotooftheDay1.html

At first glance, a partnership between a car manufacturer and a public
institution that promotes the arts, and, in this particular case, a program promoting the reading of literary fiction, may seem a little odd. After all, you can
hardly read a book and drive at the same time, and in terms of affordable
luxuries (deemed essential purchases to some, of course), books and cars are
several expense categories apart. But the photograph of Ford and NEA representatives gathered around the branded car visualizes a significant financial
reality about shared reading events in general. The organizers of most MREs
in North America and the UK must obtain corporate sponsorship and collaborate with nonprofit agencies such as private foundations in order to deliver
their programs. In the case of OBOC events, public funds obtained via grant-
awarding bodies or through stake-holder institutions such as public libraries
are rarely sufficient to meet the costs involved. Mass-mediated reading events

such as the RJBC and *Canada Reads*, meanwhile, depend heavily on other types of business partnership such as the cooperation of the book publishers whose titles these broadcast events promote. If large quantities of the featured books are not put into circulation on time, readers cannot buy the books and will not participate in the broadcast book clubs. Put simply, there can be no large-scale shared reading events without some money on the table. Such observations about the economic transactions and power relations involved in the manufacture, marketing, and distribution of cultural products are commonly made by scholars as part of their analyses of cultural industries such as television, film, and music (e.g., Frith 2001; Kellner 1990; Straw and Sutherland 2007) or studies of the contemporary book industry in North America and the UK (e.g., Coser, Kadushin, and Powell 1982; Greco 2004; Squires 2007; Thompson 2010). Our analysis extends this type of enquiry to MREs in order to explicate and theorize how ideological imperatives and economic relations inform their material production, and how local organizers negotiate with these relations and values. For, like this chapter, the photograph tells more than one story. In addition to the representation of a public-private funding partnership, it also suggests another story about the symbolic benefits that the Ford company gains from acting as a "literacy sponsor" (Brandt 2004, 166) for a project that aims to do nothing less than "restore reading to the center of American culture" (NEA 2005).

MONEY MATTERS

The 2008 Ford Hybrid Escape retailed at around US$26,000. Because the car represents Ford's gift to the Big Read, and Ford was the only corporate sponsor in that year, this sum suggests the relatively small scale of corporate support for MREs compared to the commercial sponsorship of major sporting events or a nationwide tour by an opera company. The model was also a judicious, but not especially glamorous, choice in keeping with the modest nature of Ford's in-kind contribution. Launched in 2008, the second-generation Hybrid Escape was marketed as an affordable, small sports vehicle for families and the advertising campaign emphasized its economic consumption of fuel (at least, by SUV standards). Like the car, MREs that employ the OBOC model do not cost very much to run compared to other participatory arts projects. One of the attractions of the model to organizers is the ease with which it can be adapted in terms of types and number of program activities, size, and demographic of the intended audience, the extent of its geographic reach, and, crucially from an economic viewpoint, in terms of modest or ambitious goals with regards to participation rates (Grams 2008). The majority of OBOC programs operate at the scale of one town or city, typically encoding the desired scope of the program through the incorporation of a place-name within the title: Seattle Reads; OBOC Vancouver; OBOC San Diego; OBOC Chicago; or, Liverpool Reads. Whereas there is little variation in the brand name for citywide MREs, there is considerable variation in terms of the amount of money available up-front to organizers. OBOC Vancouver programmers, who are staff members of that city's public library system, have an annual budget of around CAN$6,000, for instance (Janice Douglas, pers. comm., 2006), compared to their librarian colleagues in Chicago, where a typical budget for OBOC is US$40,000 (Nan Alleman and Barbara Schmittle, pers. comm., 2004). In both cases more funding is made available from other budget lines within the public library system for purchasing additional copies of the selected book, for example, and to pay for or to cover some staff costs incurred through overtime, and, in the case of Chicago, with its unique twice-yearly OBOC program, to support one librarian to work full-time to coordinate both OBOC Chicago and the city's fall Book Festival.

However, even the most generous dedicated budgets are rapidly consumed by the costs of producing and distributing reading guides, bookmarks, posters, street banners, and other marketing products, such as branded buttons, book bags, and pens, maintaining web pages, paying for the travel costs of the featured book's author and/or those of other speakers, and in some locations, hiring venues outside central and branch library spaces for themed events. Because most OBOC organizers share the ethos of social inclusion and accessibility that is inferred in the MRE model's key brand name, many also attempt to keep the costs to potential participants as low as possible. For this reason, activities associated with OBOC programs such as public talks about the book, its author and related topics, book group discussions, film screenings, visual art projects, and musical performances are frequently free at the point of use. This holds true regardless of whether the core program is designed and coordinated entirely by public library staff as it is in Vancouver, Seattle, and Chicago and in many other cities in North America, or by a community-based coalition such as the volunteer committee of librarians, writers, book-sellers, literary editors, high school teachers, and local councilors who organize OBOC Kitchener-Waterloo-Cambridge (KWC) in southern Ontario, Canada. When events do incur a charge, they inevitably limit their potential outreach to those who can afford a $50 ticket for a bus tour of places and landscapes associated with the chosen book, or who have the spare cash to participate in "One Book, Three Pubs"—a type of literary pub crawl that formed part of the regular KWC activities in the early years of its programming (2002–2003).

Organizers subsidize the costs of delivering citywide MREs by brokering partnerships with other agencies that can provide some type of in-kind contribution and, ideally, share in the promotion costs for a specific event. Typical partners include local newspapers and radio stations that run features about the program and donate advertising space; institutions such as museums, theaters, cinemas, and art galleries that can offer a venue space or speaker and may take on the organization of a related activity such as a curated exhibition or film series, and educational institutions such as schools and colleges or city-run leisure facilities that may have suitable spaces, such as gyms or meeting halls, capable of accommodating several hundred people. Not all partners are directly involved in delivering public goods such as arts, culture, or education; some, like book publishers, clearly have a commercial interest in supporting a citywide reading event. Indeed, the involvement of the selected book's publisher is crucial to the economy of many OBOC programs, not least to the sharing of travel expenses for the featured author so that he or she can appear at a series of headline events, but also to the provision of free and discounted books.

Other types of in-kind contributions, such as hotel rooms, flights, stationery, printing costs, and publicity, are sometimes made by businesses who become involved in citywide reading events as sponsors. Sponsorship by large companies with national or global reach is more common in the United States, where there is a tradition of philanthropic giving by commercial enterprises and successful business people (Bremner [1960] 1988). Boeing, Target, Allstate, and Motorola are among the sponsors past and present of OBOC Chicago, for example. Meanwhile, Ford's "in-kind" support of a donated car contributes to the viability of the Big Read by offering material assistance to the transportation of the NEA's organizing team charged with visiting a selection of the OBOC projects and the local organizers who won the Big Read grants in 2008. More common, especially in the UK and Canada, is the small-scale sponsorship offered by local or regional businesses willing to donate a service such as a restaurant meal for invited speakers or gifts for door prizes at public events. Regardless of the scale of sponsorship, the size or nature of a partner agency's contribution, the organizers of citywide reading events depend on these economic collaborations. Without them and the money or services provided, it is still possible to organize an OBOC program, as our Huntsville case study below demonstrates. However, as the Huntsville librarians point out, creativity and community networks only take you so far when the goal is to reach beyond regular readers and library users.

MORAL POWER

Money and in-kind donations contribute to the delivery of MREs in practical and tangible ways. But what do commercial sponsors, companies such as Ford and Boeing, gain from their association with shared reading programs? Sponsoring performing arts events such as opera or theater, or even a city's Book Festival offer opportunities for companies to play host to staff and clients by giving away free tickets and, perhaps, by holding an exclusive reception where performers or writers may appear in person. MREs present far fewer occasions for such corporate hospitality and contact with well-known artists, and they are hardly the glamorous highlights of the cultural season. However, there is useful, symbolic capital to be accrued by companies associated with programs that promote not only the reading of "good" books, but which also aspire to building communities around the practice of sharing experiences related to or inspired by a specific book. There is actually a double payoff for any sponsor or partner: the prestige associated with books as culturally valued artifacts, and the socially conscious orientation of the OBOC model (which is more overt and visible than the outreach and education programs run by opera and ballet companies). This golden combination produces a kind of discursive moral power because of the implied idea that shared reading makes people better, more outward-looking and socially responsible citizens. Whether this belief is empirically verifiable does not matter; rather, it is the social function of this pervasive perception about what reading can do that lends it currency. Simply put, because print literacy is a highly valued skill in industrialized societies and book reading is associated with an individual's capacity to increase their knowledge, a program that facilitates (or appears to facilitate) the growth of these assets can easily become the object for the expression of desires about social uplift, and equity of access to knowledge and education. Moreover, the kinds of professionals and institutions that endorse MREs usually possess a degree of moral authority.[1] Consequently, the appeal to a notion of a common good and shared well-being wrapped up in the representation of MREs to sponsors, and indeed, to the wider public, assumes a moral force.

Moral power is ideological in its operation because it promotes certain moral concepts, such as duty, justice, and virtue as desirable, and as universal rather than as socially and historically specific ideals. Like all ideologies, it conceals the social function that it is performing. Conceptualizing moral power in this Marxist-inflected way helps to explain the normalizing and normative effects of shared-reading-event rhetoric. The rhetoric promises so much in terms of social benefits to individuals and communities, but the values shaping the expression of those benefits forestall the politically progressive potential of the MRE model. Economics and institutional politics also play their part in structuring both the meanings and the material delivery of events, of course, as the examples in this chapter and the experience of cultural workers and managers explored in the next chapter illustrate. In the context of our discussion of moral power, however, we want to underline how, within a commodity culture, money and moral power are often articulated together. Such articulations are often easier to discern when the commodity is an object that can be purchased by an individual rather than a model for delivering culture to groups of people such as an MRE. But here, once again, the synergy of the donated Ford Hybrid Escape with the NEA's Big Read program is illuminating.

The television commercial for the 2008 Hybrid Escape depicted a family driving a gleaming car through a wilderness landscape passing by animals that were unperturbed by this intrusion into their environment, with a single-line voice-over: "If an Escape Hybrid drives through the forest, does anyone hear it?" A quiet, clean inexpensive car that does not disturb nature as your family escapes their urban or suburban everyday life: the semiotics are easy to comprehend and effective in conveying a message that speaks to the consumer's economic concerns while appealing to their social conscience. There is no need for guilt about owning this particular SUV, the advert infers, because its hybrid technology will enable you to move effortlessly, silently, and pristinely through the forest. Nothing will be disturbed or changed—including your habits of consumption and motor vehicle use. The match between money and moral power, donor and recipient, could not be better. Even the contradictory nature of this appeal to a notion of social good about the environment neatly parallels the unquestioned idea that MREs are socially worthwhile enterprises.

The NEA's Big Read program claims on its home page, for instance, that it is "creating a nation of readers" (2012). The assumption operating here is that this is a socially desirable outcome. In the US of the twenty-first century, shared reading is often imagined as a collective activity capable of producing civilizing and socializing effects upon participants, ultimately resulting in a literate citizenry. The Big Read website makes clear that the project of "creating a nation of readers" is not only about increasing the cultural capital of individual Americans, but also about producing social capital by encouraging various forms of face-to-face participation. The relationship between money and this particular discourse of civility is revealed by the history of attitudes to and definitions of print literacy in the US. Deborah Brandt notes George W. Bush's echoing of Thomas Jefferson's associations of literacy with citizenship (2004, 487), for example, whereas Thomas Augst historicizes the role of the public library in promoting literacy and reading, from Benjamin Franklin's explicit and liberal use of the language of a "civilizing mission" (2003, 7) to Andrew Carnegie's more conservatively inflected language of "moral uplift and social control" (11). Brandt argues that in the US after the Second World War, "literacy was irrevocably transformed from a nineteenth-century moral imperative into a twentieth-century production imperative" (2004, 485). A "nation of readers" (NEA 2012) is thus also a nation of better-educated, better-paid, self-regulated workers earning salaries that can be spent on goods and services. Commercial sponsors of MREs may therefore feel somewhat reassured that their cash or services are contributing to both the social *and* economic well-being of the nation, region, or city targeted by a particular shared reading program. However, the moral force underwriting the NEA's aim to put "literary reading" at the center of American culture (NEA 2012) resonates with the moral values associated with pre-twentieth-century ideas about literacy and the benefits of reading books. The NEA rhetoric suggests that the generation of economically productive citizens does not have to replace older ideas about the morally uplifting effects of reading. Rather, these economic and social values become discursively connected in the marketing of the Big Read as a project of civic restoration of community, and of literary reading. How and why this occurs becomes more comprehensible via our examination of neoliberalism, cultural policy, and late-twentieth-century constructions of cultural value below.

Supporters and partners can also get behind other aspects of MREs that underscore their moral force, such as their size and immediacy. The large-scale vision suggested by a "nation of readers" is matched by the material scale of the Big Read, for example. Over one thousand community projects have been sponsored, the list of books that can be chosen as the focus for shared reading has grown from four in 2005–2006 to thirty-one in 2012–2013, and hundreds of thousands of reading guides have been downloaded or given away in print form (NEA 2012). Through these artifacts and the agencies that stage the local events, scale becomes knowable and measurable. Quantity of product, plus quantifiable data about books circulated, number of activities held, and event attendance can then be used to justify and account for any dollar donation or in-kind gift. Local organizers of MREs are usually obliged to collect such data as part of grant agreements and they are often required to document it in final reports. Such imperatives of accountability and their accompanying mechanisms of evaluation suggest the utilitarian impulse shaping a regime of cultural value within which statistics, "hard" outcomes and the "legacy" of each arts project must be "evidenced" as occurring in the present time, rather than imagined or assumed to contribute to society in a nebulous way at some undetermined future moment. Culture, especially cultural activity that involves a degree of public funding, must pay out as well as be paid for—and it must be seen to pay out quickly.

NEOLIBERALISM AND THE VALUE OF CULTURE

Money, moral power, and culture, or, more specifically, the co-construction and articulation of economic, moral, and cultural values, coalesce readily within a free-market economy. In other words, another way of framing our comments about money and moral power is to understand their articulation as a product of the cultural policy cultures shaped by late-twentieth-century neoliberalism. Neoliberal capitalism, the "revival of free-market economic policy" (McGuigan 2005, 229), has consequences for how culture is made and how it is valued. David Harvey's ([2005] 2007) incisive study, *A Brief History of Neoliberalism*, begins with a definition that usefully foregrounds the structural and ideological impact that this "doctrine" has had on national economies such as the US, Canada, and the UK, as well as on the international institutions that "regulate global finance and trade":

> Neoliberalism is in the first instance a theory of political economic practices that proposes that human well-being can best be advanced by liberating individual entrepreneurial freedoms and skills within an institutional framework characterized by strong private property rights, free markets,

and free trade. The role of the state is to create and preserve an institutional framework appropriate to such practices . . . if markets do not exist (in areas such as land, water, education, health care, social security, or environmental pollution) then they must be created, by state action if necessary. But beyond these tasks the state should not venture. (2)

Two aspects of Harvey's ([2005] 2007) definition that are especially helpful for understanding how neoliberal economics affects artistic production and cultural policy-making are, first, the existence or creation of free markets in every sector of society, and, second, the nonintervention of the state once marketization, privatization, and free trade are secured. Subsequently, state patronage of the arts is reduced, and cultural producers are expected to compete in the marketplace in order to generate profit or they must find subsidies from business or private foundations. Ideologically, culture ceases to be valued primarily as a "public good," and instead becomes subject to the rules of domestic and international marketplaces. During the first decade of the twenty-first century, increasingly integrated global financial systems and the transnational flow of cultural goods also prompted changes in the ways that cultural policy was made in the three nation-states of our study. National and supra-national legislation about trade, monopolies and mergers, copyright, and intellectual property all played their part in the commercialization of culture.

It is tempting to overgeneralize about the impact of late-twentieth-century neoliberal economics on notions of cultural value in the UK, the US, and Canada. Whereas it is impossible to provide a nuanced comparative history of arts funding and cultural policy in these three nation-states here, we can register some distinctions regarding the politics of public funding for culture and the structural delivery of that funding. Doing so reveals how different policy cultures produce different cultural forms and differently focused MREs, such as the nationalist and regional emphases in the Canadian events. One immediate contrast between the US and its northern neighbor, for example, is the relative paucity of federally funded institutions for the arts and the complex combination of private and public contributors. The NEA and the National Endowment for the Humanities are the most visible recipients of money allocated by Congress, and, subsequently, "the foci of legislative cultural politics for [more than] thirty years, prospering during periods of congressional favor and suffering during periods of controversy" (DiMaggio and Pettit 1999, 7). Some specially chartered federal museums, such as the National Gallery of Art, and the Smithsonian Institution, are also directly funded by Congress. Other public agencies that support the arts through grants and dedicated programs such as the Institute of Museum and Library Services (a partner in the NEA's Big Read program) and the Department of Education (Arts in Education Model Development program) also receive legislative allocations. But, as a study undertaken by the NEA points out, the majority share of public funding for the arts in the United States actually flows from state agencies (2007, 6–7). Six regional arts organizations enable several groups of states to collaborate in order to leverage their Arts Endowment grants and their state appropriations that "are dependent upon state tax revenues [and thus] tied to the general economic conditions in the state" (7). One such regional agency is Arts MidWest, which has been providing training and advice to OBOC event organizers since the inception of the Big Read program.

This "dizzying" infrastructure with its "hierarchy of government agencies, composed of city, county, state, regional and federal strata" is further complicated by the hybridity of public and private funding, "comprised of . . . tax policies, legislative allocations, donated bequests, restricted endowments, education mandates, and social agendas" (2). Not surprisingly, given this setup and the lack of a Ministry of Culture, "there is no single, definitive cultural policy directed toward achieving a single goal" (Wyszomirski 2008, 41–42). Bill Ivey, who was appointed Chair of the NEA by Bill Clinton (1998–2001), is not alone in his critique of this structure, the diffuse funding model, and the consequent disconnect among policy fields:

> The absence of a single agency, a policy hub, around which issues of trade, diplomacy, arts education, and heritage can be debated and resolved, has made it all too easy for the marketplace to shape the rules. (2008, 291)

Ivey's (2008) left-leaning politics inflect his commentary, of course, but his point, that commercial rules have been king, goes hand-in-hand with the fact that "the United States has the largest and most powerful set of private culture industries" in the world (Lewis and Miller 2003, 8). The increasing influence of neoliberal economics on the US economy since the first Reagan administration has made it difficult for institutional cultural advocates such as Ivey to effect any change in attitude or infrastructure, despite direct lobbying of members of Congress (2008, 252–57). Public opinion tends not to fall behind national public funding for the arts, at least, not very vocally: the traditional suspicion of "big" government in the United States helps to account for Paul DiMaggio's and Becky Pettit's (1999) finding that there is strong minority opposition to federal arts funding but weak majority support for it.

By contrast, the history of public funding for arts and culture in both Canada and the UK demonstrates a more robust ideological commitment to the notion of culture as a public good, at least, until the mid-1990s. By that juncture, the impact of neoliberal economics, free trade legislation (of the North American Free Trade agreement in Canada), the transnational power of multinational media conglomerations and a discursive emphasis within government departments on market values influenced a paradigm shift in cultural policy-making (Godard 2000; McGuigan 2009a, 129–55). Canada's geographic proximity to the United States, its most financially significant export market, is one reason for national legislation such as the "CanCon" laws, which ring-fence broadcast time for Canadian-made radio and television content, and funding practices that are ideologically protectionist in character (Druick 2006; Filion 1996b; Raboy and Taras,

2007; Tinic 2010). As the last chapter illustrated, state-funded institutions such as the Canadian Broadcasting Corporation operate within an explicitly nationalist mandate to "connect" Canadians and to "enlighten" them about each other. High-profile disputes in which the Canadian federal government invokes the "cultural clause" of the North American Free Trade Agreement against the financial might of US media companies, and the role played by Canadian delegates to UNESCO in establishing the Universal Convention on the Protection and Promotion of Diversity of Cultural Expressions (2007) has lent Canadian cultural nationalism considerable cachet, especially among scholars of international and comparative cultural policy (Belfiore and Bennett 2010, 3; Singh 2010, 11).[2] However, these protectionist maneuvers exist in ideological tension with reductions to arts funding via arms-length national agencies such as the Canada Council, and cuts to the arts at the provincial level from the 1990s onward as neoliberal politics took hold (Godard 1999, 2002; B. Jenkins 2009, 332).

The "culture must pay its own way" rhetoric of contemporary Canadian cultural policy-making is also in contrast to the legislative outcomes and the foundation of national agencies (such as the Canada Council, the Canadian Broadcasting Corporation, and the National Film Board of Canada) inspired by the Massey-Lévesque Commission's report on "National Development in the Arts, Letters and Sciences" (Royal Commission 1951). The Commission's recommendations recognized the importance of regional and cultural diversity and democratic access to the arts, but, significantly in a country where arts and education policy are controlled by provincial governments, the recommendations lent substantial power to the federal government. Zoe Druick argues that these "centralizing tendencies" should be understood in the context of Cold War politics and internationalism: "Postwar nationalism [in Canada] has been indebted to a logic of internationalism, and it inherited many of its contradictions and tensions" (2006, 178). Traces of these "contradictions" emerge when we compare the nationalist discourse framing the *Canada Reads* broadcasts, with the ways that many Canadian readers employed the show and its book selections to explore their sense of a local or regional identity.

Many of Canada's national arts institutions, museums, and performing arts companies were originally modeled on their imperial British counterparts. Both nation-states maintain a Ministry (or, in Canada, federal and provincial ministries) that has cultural activity and the arts as part of its mandate, although the relative economic importance and populist appeal of the arts as compared, for example, to tourism and sport, is reflected in the various name-changes and responsibilities covered by these Ministries that have occurred over the last twenty years.[3] Arts Council England (ACE), Creative Scotland,[4] and the Arts Council of Wales are among the national agencies that receive money, including funds from the National Lottery, from the Department for Culture, Media and Sport (DCMS) within the British parliament and, in the case of Scotland and Wales, from the two devolved National Governments. The grants and awards adjudicated by these organizations are complemented by local government funding for arts and culture. Private investment in the arts made by business, private donations, private foundations, and trusts reached an all-time high of £687 million in 2008 before the "crash" and the economic recession (Ward and Dolphin 2011, 4). Private money accounted for 15 percent of the income of arts organizations in the UK that year, in contrast to the 53 percent provided by public funding (ibid., 4). By comparison, about 13 percent of arts funding in the US is public money with just 9 percent of that amount coming from federal government (NEA 2007, v).

In the summer of 2010, the UK's Conservative/Liberal Democrat coalition government announced a series of severe cuts and mergers for the arms-length arts agencies as well as drastic cuts to local government spending. Radical restructuring of the Arts Council in the wake of a 30-percent budget reduction meant that Regularly Funded Organizations such as the Bristol Cultural Development Partnership responsible for producing the city's Great Reading Adventure, among other events, lost the financial security that accompanied that status. Booktrust, a charity focused on reader development and literacy, and one of the primary agencies through which Tony Blair's government articulated its notion of reading books as a form of social inclusion, also had its ACE funding dramatically reduced. Many arts and culture organizations suffered a double hit, as local government also reduced support for public library systems, small press publishers, book festivals, and arts centers in their regions or cities. In the wake of a recession, cultural producers and arts agencies were exposed to market forces more severely than ever before.

But neoliberal economics and neoliberal ideology had already played their part in shaping notions of cultural value in the UK, well before the financial crash of autumn 2008 or the election of a minority Conservative government in spring 2010. When New Labour came to power in 1997, "culture" was at the center of Prime Minister Tony Blair's vision for Britain, "captured in the media-friendly idea of a 'Cool Britannia'" (Böhm and Land 2009, 79), but at first it was valued in explicitly economic terms (77). When cultural activity ceases to be regarded by state and federal governments as primarily a public good, and is instead conceptualized as another market, we might expect the tenor and language of cultural policy to reflect the "marked shift of aesthetics to economics" (McGuigan 2010, 122). However, in the UK during the early 2000s, the authors of government-commissioned reports and policy documents often expressed cultural value in terms of indirect benefits such as "creativity and innovation," "employability," and "social inclusion" rather than in terms of direct economic benefits (Böhm and Land 2009, 79–80). Such language belongs to the vocabulary of neoliberalism in "social-democratic guise" that Pierre Bourdieu and Loïc Wacquant (2001) named "NewLiberal-Speak" (McGuigan 2009a, 138), of which both Tony Blair and Bill Clinton, not to mention members of their communications and public relations teams, were fluent speakers. Echoing the emphasis on creativity and innovation, and influenced by ideas about the information economy, other terminology also shifted, so that the cultural industries were referred to as "the creative industries" (Garnham 2005, 20–21; Hesmondhalgh and Pratt 2005, 4).

Such "creative economy" rhetoric barely masks the expectation that what will be "created" are jobs, tourist income, and exportable cultural artifacts. Wealth generation and the commercialization of "expressive value" (the exploitation of intellectual copyright, for example) were envisioned as the primary work of the creative and cultural industries, but social inclusion and the creation of social well-being also became their task (McGuigan 2009b, 297). Caught up within the neoliberal ideology of New Labour, the differentiation of cultural from social policy became somewhat blurred and cultural participation was frequently imagined as a substitute for social support systems. Eleonora Belfiore and Oliver Bennett argue that claims for the social impact of the arts have often been overstated in Department of Culture, Media and Sport-commissioned studies, yet evidence for their impact on poor communities is in fact "paltry" (2010, 348). Despite this empirical reality, the British version of "NewLiberalSpeak" proffered the arts as "an implausible palliative to exclusion and poverty" (McGuigan 2010, 125). Our own sense that programs promoting shared reading are frequently overburdened by their organizers' desire for and expectation of effecting social change, clearly owes much to a context of policy-making that both discursively and structurally prompts cultural agencies to perform first economically, then, as an afterthought, to deliver a kind of social service. John Holden made a related point in "Capturing Cultural Value" (2004) when he noted that cultural organizations had become very good at articulating social outcomes and measuring the economic impact of culture in grant applications: functional terms that, he argued, were a response to the cultural policy de jour. Organizations in the US responded in a similar way, as George Yúdice explains in his analysis of the "management" of culture as a "resource" for neoliberal governments: "The 'bottom line' is that cultural institutions and funders are increasingly turning to the measurement of utility because there is no other accepted legitimation for social investment" (2003, 16).

Back in the UK, Holden's (2004) influential paper, published during his tenure as Head of Culture at the think tank DEMOS, explicitly took up then Secretary of State Tessa Jowell's (2004, 8) call for "another story to tell on culture." His recasting of cultural value as "public value" was "shaped by an advocacy agenda" that sought more "holistic" evaluations of culture in order to justify public funding, and thus did not entirely escape the instrumentalist language and policy that he critiqued (Belfiore and Bennett 2010, 9–10). As this example suggests, the national government was not the only agency promoting the neoliberal agenda, nor the sole creator of cultural policy. Stevenson, McKay, and Rowe conclude in their review of UK policy-making in the 2000s:

> Cultural policy is now the province of all levels of government as well as of supra-state bodies such as the European Union (EU). It is also an arena

where the influences of consultants, quasi-private "think tanks" (such as DEMOS) and private agencies have increased in recent years with much cultural policy now being made at the junction of the public and the private, as well as of the local, national and international. (2010, 159)

In other words, despite the existence of a national ministry, the Department for Culture, Media and Sport, the process and realities of cultural policy-making in the UK during the first decade of the twenty-first century came to bear more resemblance to their US counterparts than ever before. Such "institutional and instrumental hybridity in cultural policies" makes for a tangled web of public and private interests that is increasingly common in various regions of the world (Singh 2010, 11–12). This is the case regardless of whether the state is the main funder of the arts, as it is in France, Germany, or India, for example, or in countries such as the UK where a mixed economy of state funding, private donation, and earned income is in operation, or, in the US where private sector finance and philanthropic support have long outstripped public spending. If it is subsequently sometimes difficult to identify exactly who the brokers of cultural value are within a particular national context, what is clear in the cases of the UK and the US is the discursive value invested in culture as an economically generative sector of society. Nowhere is this more apparent than in the adoption by "think tanks" and government departments alike of Richard Florida's concepts of the "creative city" and the "creative class" (2002, 2005, 2008) and Robert Putnam's ideas about social capital and civic responsibility (2000, 2003). There is, in fact, no easy marriage between their ideas. Florida's work disputes Putnam's emphasis on social capital, arguing that creative capital is more significant for wealth creation (McGuigan 2009a, 164). But then, as Stuart Hall points out in a blistering critique of "the neoliberal crisis" in the UK, "Ideology works best by suturing together contradictory lines of argument and emotional investments . . . Contradiction is its *metier*" (2012, 713). Thus, because consistent logic is not required by neoliberal governments intent on putting culture to work, the ideas of Florida and Putnam helped to shape a policy language about the social and economic benefits of the creative economy. These policies influenced the development of particular cultural forms, including shared reading events such as the OBOC model.

TALKING UP THE CREATIVE ECONOMY

Florida's (2002, 2005, 2008) theses about "the creative class" refer to an educated group of talented, liberal-minded people, often cultural producers, whose leisure-time consumption of all things artistic can transform deindustrialized urban centers into "creative cities" that attract new investors. These ideas, communicated through a combination of anecdote and statistical data, proved, unsurprisingly, to be attractive to researchers in

North America and the UK tasked with assessing the role and value of culture for government. Florida's (2005) theory about the economic impact of concentrating "technology, talent and tolerance" (6) in successful cities has been especially influential on cultural policy makers and city governments keen to regenerate downtown areas in the postindustrial cities of the "developed" world. Although his case studies are frequently drawn from the United States, Florida's (2002, 2005) work has been taken up by government researchers and government-commissioned researchers around the world, including Canada (where Florida often acted as a consultant) (e.g., FCM 2002; Gertler et al., 2002) and the UK (e.g., Work Foundation 2007). Florida's was not a lone voice. By the end of the first decade of the twenty-first century, the role of cultural production and cultural spending in boosting economic development was a lively and well-established field of investigative activity involving cultural policy makers and academics from around the globe. As a result, Florida's (2002, 2005, 2008) ideas are widely cited, but his work has also been subject to vigorous critique from reviewers and scholars concerned with, among other things, his neoliberal assumptions about economics, the validity of his statistical evidence and his oversight of relevant literature (e.g., Banks 2007, 2009; Dudley 2008; Glazer 2008; McGuigan 2009b; Peck 2005). But his concepts, books, and Creative Class Group consultancy continue to exert considerable influence on mayors and city councilors wishing to attract "innovative" people and investment to their cities.

Florida's (2002, 2005, 2008) theses tend to emphasize the relationships between cultural regeneration and economic prosperity. Moral power is inferred rather than overt in the notion that a creative city is socially preferable to one where cultural goods are not produced and circulated. A more obvious articulation of moral power with social power is evident in the influential work of sociologist Robert Putnam (2000, 2003) about the role that community groups, associations, and activities can play in producing an active citizenry. Putnam's (ibid.) lament about the decline of community associations and clubs in late-twentieth-century America, and his quest to find examples of groups and projects engaged in "restoring the American community" (the subtitle of *Better Together*, 2003) struck a chord with politicians and social commentators as well as cultural policy researchers. Whereas Florida's vision of creative cities rang with the sound of cash waiting to be made, Putnam's analyses and cases studies articulated a liberal view of a once-functioning but now fragmented society that required mending. His championing of bridging and bonding social capital appealed to a wide constituency of local and national government advisors variously concerned about disaffected youth, low voter turnouts at election time, and downtown streets through which, at night, either tumbleweed rolled or hooligans strolled (e.g., DCMS 2003; Jeanotte 2000, 2003; NEA 2004;[5] Wright 2007, 15–18). Libraries and shared reading had their part to play in producing social capital and regenerating civic engagement, according to Putnam, perhaps not surprisingly given that, like NEA Chairman Dana Gioia (NEA 2005), he suggested that Americans were spending too much time watching television (2000, 283–84). In *Better Together*, his sequel to *Bowling Alone* (2000), Putnam described the Chicago Public Library (CPL) system as "an active and responsive part of the community and an agent of change" (2003, 35). Putnam used as his example the work of employees at the Near North Branch Library, one of several new "neighborhood" branches opened in Chicago in the late 1990s and early 2000s, applauding their many efforts at "outreach" and social inclusion (35–43). Commenting specifically on OBOC Chicago, Putnam suggested that the aims of the program were "consistent with the library's role as a force for social connection and social improvement" (52). Whereas we would not dispute this claim, our own investigations into OBOC Chicago suggested that the program's organizers were equally concerned with promoting the profile of the CPL (N. Alleman, pers. comm., 2005). The picture that Putnam paints of the social impact of shared reading is too uncomplicated and highly celebratory, but usefully it foregrounds the creative agency demonstrated by CPL branch librarians.

Most significant to our discussion of the articulation of money with moral power in relation to MREs is the ideological grist that the work of these commentators provided for advocates of the creative economy. Florida's (2002, 2005, 2008) work also stokes the aspirational desires of the professional middle class to live in economically vibrant cities where a substantial section of the population is engaged in either making or consuming diverse art forms and cultural artifacts. The title and self-help style of his most overtly popular book, *Who's Your City? How the Creative Economy Is Making Where You Live the Most Important Decision of Your Life* (2008), hails the individual as the arbiter of his or her economic destiny and personal happiness. Besides lending scholarly ballast to a neoliberal discourse about culture and a somewhat instrumentalist approach to its value, Florida's (2002, 2005, ibid.) ideas about "the creative class" and Putnam's (2003) about bridging and bonding social capital, appealed to middle-class anxieties about loss of community and social degeneration. These anxieties are echoed in the air of moral panic evident in the NEA's initial press release for the Big Read program (2005), and in the linking of cultural participation to social reintegration in "A Place For Culture," a report charting the success of New Labour's "culture offer" to youth and young people, including those who "may have drifted away from formal education" (DCMS 2010, 6). Within both the American and British neoliberal visions of the creative economy, cultural production and community participation in the arts are lent a restorative as well as a regenerative power that carries with it a morally inflected message of social improvement. Within this discursive regime reading—especially shared reading—can "restore" American culture by appealing to both the hearts and minds of American citizens (NEA 2005). One reason why such an appeal is credible is that its emotive tenor and message of self-transformation are comprehensible to many keen readers who have acquired a vocabulary for describing and "achieving affective states" (Radway 1997, 13) through the books that they read and talk about in book clubs or with friends. How books reach the hands of readers, however, is a business that repays some consideration, especially because that business has changed fairly rapidly since the mid-1990s.

MAKING BOOKS, PRODUCING READERS

Books, it is important to remember, are commodities that are part of an economy of production, even if we only ever receive them as gifts or borrow them from libraries. Many readers—including many participants in our research study—would certainly regard books as "special" commodities, and many, particularly the readers we met during our focus group work around the RJBC, would like to disavow the economics involved in the making of a cultural artifact that to them variously denotes pleasure, learning, entertainment, and the possession of cultural capital. In the twenty-first century, readers living in the UK and North America have more books to choose from than ever before. In fact, in 2009, the number of new books published in the UK reached an all-time high of 157,039 (Nielsen 2011), whereas new titles in the US numbered 288,355 in 2009, half a percent less than in 2008, and a very small blip in the upward trend during the first decade of the twenty-first century (Bowker 2010).[6] A reader's hunger or thirst for books—and here we ask you to choose your metaphor of consumption—is quickly satisfied where commodity culture reigns supreme and customer expectations about choice and speed of service are high. Readers can buy or borrow books faster and more conveniently than in the previous century, thanks to digital technologies that enable public libraries to provide online access to their catalogues and reservations systems, the 24-hour availability of online bookstores, and the ability to download audiobooks to MP3 players and e-books to electronic reading devices such as the Sony e-reader and Amazon Kindle, and to mobile telephones. Changes in the ways in which books are delivered to a reader's hands and to the physical book as an artifact—the choice of codex or digital—are, perhaps, the most visible and everyday signs of some of the major shifts that have taken place in Anglo-American book publishing and retailing over the last three decades. Other signals of change, such as the radical reduction of space devoted to book reviewing in newspapers and other areas of the mass media, may—or may not—have been noticed by members of the reading class. After all, there are literary blogs a-plenty, online and offline book groups, dedicated magazines such as *newbooks*, plus—until recently—Oprah Winfrey and, in the UK, the RJBC, to provide recommendations instead. But what are the economic realities for reading industry agents who produce books and how have books retained their status as "special" commodities when they are produced on such a massive scale? Highlighting some of the key changes and challenges experienced by those working in the publishing and bookselling industries of the twenty-first century helps us to understand the relationship between money and prestige in the contemporary "field of literary production" (Bourdieu 1993). It also reveals the economic and symbolic value of MREs to the companies and cultural workers who need books to reach readers.

Company mergers, buy-outs by multinational, multimedia corporations, price wars, and electronic inventory systems: these are the headline changes that have altered how books are made, distributed, and sold. In her analysis of the "structural and far-reaching reorganization of contemporary publishing" during the last three decades of the twentieth century, Eva Hemmungs Wirtén nominates "conglomeratization, content, and convergence" as the three themes through which the "story of producers can be told" ([2007] 2009, 395). Hemmungs Wirtén's ([2007] 2009) account of how publishing became integrated into large (often transnational media) conglomerates such as Bertelsmann, Time Warner, and Viacom describes how "consolidation in two dimensions" enabled these corporations to not only acquire "content" through vertical consolidation, but also to "control" its distribution "over all possible channels" through horizontal consolidation and technological convergence (401). Consolidation is not a new phenomenon in the book industry. The executive directors of publishing houses and bookstore chains have been engaged in the acquisition of other companies since at least the 1930s (L. Miller 2006, 40–44). In the aftermath of World War II, for example, large American publishing firms responded to demographic changes, increased access to higher education and the subsequent growth of domestic and international markets for all kinds of books (including textbooks, children's books, and scientific and medical journals) by creating larger firms that enabled them to leverage more capital (Luey 2009, 29; 2010, 45–60; L. Miller 2006, 40). Since then, as Laura Miller notes, merger and acquisition activity has taken place "in successive waves . . . first in the 1960s, then again in the mid-1970s, a renewed surge in the late 1980s, and another beginning in the mid-1990s" (41). The foreign-owned media corporations, such as Bertelsmann (based in Germany) and Thomson (based in Canada), entered the fray in the late 1980s, whereas the 1990s saw integrated entertainment and information conglomerates such as Times Warner and News Corp. acquire, and often rather rapidly resell, publishing houses when the digital revolution failed to yield large profits (Luey 2009, 48–50; L. Miller 2006, 42; Hemmungs Wirtén [2007] 2009, 402).

By the turn of the twenty-first century, six publishing corporations occupied powerful positions within the field of Anglo-American trade publishing: HarperCollins (owned by News Corp.), Simon & Shuster, Penguin, Random House, Hachette, and Holtzbrinck (Thompson 2010, 128). Many of these companies house old and iconic imprints, formerly independent presses, that have acquired a good deal of symbolic capital, such as Bodley Head, Chatto & Windus (Random House UK), and Alfred A. Knopf and Pantheon (Random House USA). Symbolic capital is significant in the production and selling of books. Although readers rarely, if ever, choose books on the basis of who publishes them, the process by which books are selected for publication in the twenty-first century depends on a series of relationships among literary agents, editors, and sales and marketing personnel. These social networks and the trust between individuals that has been generated across time are mediated not only by business concerns and profit and loss calculations, but also by the prestige that particular imprints, or indeed, even individual editors such as Nan Talese (Knopf Doubleday, part of Random House) and Phyllis Bruce (HarperCollins Canada) have accumulated. Similarly, individual literary agents and their agencies possess symbolic capital. During the last twenty years, the power of literary agents has increased as they expanded their role "to incorporate editorial functions" and "rights management," thus reflecting changes in industry structures (Squires 2007, 35). In the UK, during the late 1990s, a number of experienced editors moved from "prestigious literary imprints into agenting," taking with them their editorial expertise, industry contacts, and, perhaps, the ability to offer continuity to authors during a period when company mergers prompted considerable movement of editorial personnel (ibid.). When the object that is being manufactured and sold is widely regarded as a cultural good, it is perhaps not surprising that the reputation of all parties involved should play a significant part in decision-making and in considerations of risk.

Knowing that the author has a high public profile or a good sales track-record or that his or her literary agent has a gift for spotting new talent or the next best seller helps an editor to determine not only whether to publish a specific book, but also what scale the print-run should be, what marketing dollars to allocate, and whether to pitch the book to a firm's publicity and sales personnel as a frontlist title. Given the large numbers of books published by the big publishing houses, their sales reps cannot possibly describe all forthcoming titles to wholesalers and retailers, so a handful of books are selected as a publishing house's frontlist for each seasonal sales cycle. Frontlist titles are the books that editors believe will sell well, and to help them reach their intended audience, publishers pay for display space on the ends of shelving, on book tables, on special promotional book ladders, and in the windows of bookstore chains as well as for special offers such as "Buy 3 books for the price of 2." These advertising deals are known in the book trade as "co-op" and they have a huge impact on which books a reader sees when she first walks into a branch of Barnes & Noble (in the US) or Waterstones (in the UK). Many readers in our UK focus groups mentioned their penchant for "3 for 2" offers and their propensity to try out an unfamiliar genre or author because of the discount. What few readers realized, however, was how managed these deals are and none displayed any knowledge about publishers paying for promotional space in-store.

Frontlist titles, special offers, and co-op advertising deals are just some of the responses made by publishers and retailers to a market that is very competitive, saturated and subject to regular floods of new product. The pricing of that product can vary considerably: a situation that did not exist in the UK until the end of the NET book agreement in 1995. In the US, the Robinson-Patman Act (1936) ensures that publishers must offer the same discount to all booksellers who are in the same class, such as wholesalers, for example (Thompson 2010, 300–1). However, no such regulation exists in the UK, so there is "tremendous pressure on publishers to increase the discounts they give to the largest and most powerful retailers" (301). The "most powerful retailers" are no longer the high-street bookselling chains such as WHSmith and Waterstones, which, prior to 1994, represented about 90 percent of the market share in the UK (303), but supermarkets such as Tesco and Asda and online retailers such as Amazon. These new channels for bookselling expanded their market share rapidly during the 2000s and continue to grow, whereas the "traditional" outlets are static or in decline. Even the big-box chains, or "superstores" as they are commonly known (such as Barnes & Noble in the US, Chapters-Indigo in Canada), which started appearing in the 1990s, are not as powerful, although they are still important to publishers. They also offer hands-on access to many thousands of books for readers, especially those who live outside metropolitan areas where independent and specialist bookstores are comparatively rare or nonexistent (Collins 2010, 56–67; L. Miller 2009, 100–2; Striphas 2009, 47–79). It is now possible that, after a fiendish struggle about the size of the discount, a deal between a trade publisher and one of the new retailers can put a book straight on to the best-seller list in the UK. It can also happen in the US, where the larger economies of scale within a market that is about five times larger than the UK's, combined with the selling power of a retail giant like Costco, can propel a book to best-seller status on publication. That best seller is most likely to be a nonfiction title or a work of commercial fiction such as the latest John Grisham—books that readers can instantly recognize as a reliable buy, either because the author is known to them, or because the subject of the book is instantly identifiable (as it is with a celebrity biography, for example). Generally speaking, these are not the kinds of books that are selected for MREs, although the RJBC featured a number of celebrity biographies, memoirs, and other nonfiction books during its televised years. Indeed, the Book Club, as we noted in Chapter 2, "Television," had a significant effect on book sales, famously making millionaires of several featured authors as sales of some titles rocketed toward (and past) half a million copies within two months of each list's launch (Thompson 2010, 276).

The RJBC and Oprah's Book Club are effective "recognition triggers," John Thompson's (2010) term for agents operating in the literary field that bestow visibility and credibility on books (276–77). Prizes such as the Mann Booker and movie adaptations can also achieve the same ends: rendering a book worthy of being selected by a reader and offering a recommendation from a source that does not appear to be directly involved in the production and selling of the product. In addition to selling books and generating profits for publishers, booksellers, authors, and their literary agents, the "special" status of books as commodities is preserved because the economic relations structuring the transaction are not rendered visible to the consumer. The hostility expressed by some of our British readers toward branded stickers on Oprah's Book Club's and the RJBC's selections, which we argued was motivated by the desire to reaffirm their own book knowledge and ideas of good taste, can also be understood in terms of the threat of revelation that such high-profile advertising poses. Advertising and marketing for literary best sellers, however, often plays to contemporary formations of taste by appealing to ideals of self-transformation or notions of life-style choice, thereby producing a type of "effaced consumerism" in which the acquisition of material objects for money is represented instead as an aesthetic decision (Collins 2010, 235). Examples, as noted by Jim Collins, include during the mid-2000s, the selling of books in American furniture stores such as Urban Outfitters and Restoration Hardware where the "consumer-reader" was presented with an apparently seamless narrative consisting of "a host of interdependent choices that form a total taste environment" (236–37). Implicitly, the message conveyed was "Customers who bought this sofa also purchased and enjoyed this novel." Within the book industry itself, the perpetuation of various myths has often had a similar "effacing" effect by representing the business of publishing and bookselling as if they were not about products and profits, but only about culture. Laura J. Miller demonstrates how bookselling in America has often been construed as "a moral endeavor" rather than a commercial one (2006, 219), whereas Beth Luey points out that there never was a time when publishers did not worry about money (2009, 52). In the same vein, the "disaster narrative" perpetuated in the memoirs of industry figures such as publishers André Schiffrin (2001) and Jason Epstein (2002) about quantity trumping quality as a result of the major changes in the industry that have taken place over the last thirty years (Greco [1997] 2004, 203) cannot be proven (Hesmondhalgh [2002] 2007, 293). Declension narratives about the quality of books in circulation tend to reveal more about the taste and aesthetic preferences of the writer or speaker concerned, and about the ideological tension between culture and commerce, than they do about the material and financial realities of the contemporary book trade.

Amidst the myths and misperceptions of the book trade, two important realities help to explain the benefits of MREs to the book industry. The first is the struggle for "visibility" in a marketplace awash with books and within a media environment where building any kind of "platform" for a book or its author depends as much on the creative use of micromedia (e.g., YouTube, social media, blogging, author websites) as it does on the "traditional" mass media (Thompson 2010, 203, 257). The second connected phenomenon is the shift of influence in terms of book recommendation as the space devoted to reviewing by quality broadsheet newspapers, television and radio has shrunk (see Figure 4.2). Large trade publishers now seek publicity for new books by marketing directly to book club members (Fuller, Rehberg

Figure 4.2 Newspaper Advert for *The Interpretation of Murder* by Jed Rubenfeld
Purchased space provides coverage not always provided by reviewers. This 1/4
page appeared on the back page of the *Observer* newspaper's Review Section.
Source: Beyond the Book project: Artefacts and Ephemera, available at: http://epapers.bham.
ac.uk/1469/ Image titled Newspaper Advert: The Interpretation of Murder by Jed Rubenfeld

Sedo, and Squires 2011), and by sending review copies to book bloggers
(Pederson 2008; Steiner 2008; Thompson 2010, 253), as part of a strategy
to build "word of mouth" recommendation. MREs of the OBOC variety are
therefore useful to publishers, authors, and their agents because they offer a
public platform for an author while also employing the power of groups and
"word of mouth" to build the profile of the selected book (Gladwell 2001,
171). The emphasis on face-to-face activities within most OBOC programming may at first glance seem rather old-fashioned in the age of the Internet
and new media. But it is very much of the moment in terms of providing a
"literary experience" that offers "a shared mode of consumption" coextensive with other popular ways of sharing and experiencing books, especially
literary fiction—going to book clubs, watching Oprah's Book Club or the
RJBC, and seeing an adaptation of a novel in a multiplex cinema (Collins
2010, 185). In common with these other examples, the books selected for
OBOC programs are never brand new, partly because organizers rely on the
availability of affordable paperback editions, so MREs are not helpful for
the promotion of frontlist titles, but they do operate as a means of representing books from publishers' lists.

Because OBOC programs offer a target market, publishers sometimes
produce a special "badged" edition of the selected book or are even prepared to revive an out-of-print title. The latter was the case for the 2003 edition of Stuart Dybek's (1990) short-story collection *The Coast of Chicago*
(first published by Knopf) and produced in a special edition print-run with a
sticker on the cover of 7,500 copies by Picador for OBOC Chicago in Spring
2004 (James Meader, pers. comm., 2011). As James Meader, the Executive

Director of Publicity at Picador, commented, "Th[is was] a significant first print, due in part to promotional support from Borders, which had many strong retail stores in the Chicago area at the time, and the Chicago Public Library system" (ibid.). Meader's comments suggest that partnerships among for-profit and public sector agencies can work effectively as promotional tools for a selected book, especially if key personnel within those agencies are active in backing the community-wide reading event. The return for the publisher who becomes involved in such partnerships is nearly always worth the investment, even for programs running in smaller cities and towns. If a public library system in a city of the size of Vancouver (with a metropolitan population of 2.3 million people)[7] orders between 600 and 1,000 extra copies of a OBOC Vancouver selection at a specially brokered "deep discount" price of between 50 and 70 percent, and the organizing team receives one hundred complimentary copies to give away as prizes, a publisher can still expect to sell as many as 6,000 copies in the city and adjoining areas (Janice Douglas, pers. comm., 2006). That means that as many as 7,000 copies of a Vancouver selection are put into circulation through public libraries and bookstores—far more than would normally be the case without the event. In 2002, the inaugural OBOC Vancouver selection, *The Jade Peony* by Canadian author Wayson Choy, was checked out of the Vancouver Public Library system over 7,000 times (2010). Such exposure, combined with the quantity of free publicity generated by event activities, displays in public libraries and bookstores, and media coverage (especially when the author comes to town) more than compensates for any free books that organizers may have persuaded away from the publisher's warehouse. Or, for that matter, for the contributions that publishers often make in-kind or as part-payment for the production of OBOC-branded bookmarks, posters, and a small amount of advertising in local newspapers.

As we have already noted, deep discounts and free books, publicity, and the availability of a featured author are keys to the visibility and success of most OBOC programs. The organizers of many MREs depend on collaborations with book publishers and retailers, usually favoring partnerships with larger publishing houses because of their capacity to reprint a selected title quickly, to discount beyond the trade standard of 40 percent off the cover price, and the potential availability of marketing dollars to offset some of the author expenses. Conversely, the same organizers may prioritize partnering with local, independent bookstores to promote the book and the program. This has been the case in Seattle, Vancouver, and Kitchener-Waterloo-Cambridge, where organizers perceive independently owned bookstores such as The Elliott Bay Book Company (Seattle), 32 Books (North Vancouver), and Words Worth Books (Waterloo) to be serving the local community. The team behind OBOC Vancouver, for example, has tried from the beginning to work with independent bookstores because, in Janice Douglas's (pers. comm., 2006) view, "They're the ones that provide the backlists and the really big customer—like, you know, the customer service for real readers. So . . . we have attempted to, uh, support the small independents, yes. That would be our first choice." However, the same team consistently selects books by the larger, foreign-owned publishing companies such as HarperCollins Canada because they need the financial support that those companies can provide.

No organizer whom we interviewed overtly ruled out choosing a book published by a small press, but the lists of titles featured by the MREs in our own study indicates a strong bias away from the independently owned houses. The exceptions were OBOC Kitchener-Waterloo-Cambridge's 2004 selection of Nino Ricci's novel *Lives of the Saints* published by Canadian small press Cormorant Books, and one of the five 2006 *Canada Reads* titles, *Rooms for Rent in the Outer Planets: Selected Poems 1962–1996* by Al Purdy, published by Harbour Publishing, an owner-operated company based in British Columbia. Such exceptions reflect the nationalist tendency of Canadian MRE organizers to select books by Canadian authors, but they also hint at the structure of the contemporary publishing industry in Canada. In the Canadian book market, with only a few exceptions, the largest firms are foreign-owned, whereas Canadian-owned firms are on average noticeably smaller—the majority making profits of less than $200,000 per annum (Turner-Riggs 2008, 27, 53). A research study about the book industry commissioned by the Department of Canadian Heritage and published in 2008, states that, "Despite their smaller numbers, foreign-owned firms accounted for 59% of domestic book sales [in 2004] . . . [and in the late 2000s] foreign-owned publishers produce roughly 23% of the Canadian-authored titles published each year. The majority of new, Canadian-authored titles, however—the remaining 77% of the total—are produced by Canadian-owned publishing firms" (49). However, many of these "Canadian-authored titles" are textbooks. Best sellers in Canada, regardless of genre (self-help, gardening, history, literary fiction) or category (trade, education), are generally the products of foreign-owned publishing houses. Significantly, given Canada's large landmass but (relative to the US and the UK) small population, print (and now digital) distribution in North America is also dominated by large, foreign-owned companies such as Ingram, HarperCollins, and Random House. For these firms, it is not "financially viable" to deal with companies making less than $500,000 per annum—in other words, the majority of Canadian-owned presses (5, 15, 49, 53). Distribution of books within and across Canada remains, as it always has been, a major challenge for small press operators who cannot access the geographic coverage and warehouse capacity of the big distributors. The Canadian federal government continues to offer some support to Canadian-owned publishing firms through the Canada Book Fund operated by the Department of Canadian Heritage, but such measures, whereas symbolically valuable in terms of encouraging the production and dissemination of Canadian writing, are of relatively low commercial value.[8]

These industry realities are a stark illustration of the transnational structures and power relations shaping Anglo-American publishing and the impact that the organization of the industry has on which books eventually reach the hands of readers. On the one hand, the early twenty-first century reader living in North America or the UK appears to have a huge amount of choice in terms of the number of English-language titles available for purchase or accessible through public library systems. On the other hand, which books constitute that "choice" are heavily determined by the financial aspects of cultural production, and further mediated by the agents and cultural intermediaries (Oprah, prize juries, the selection committees for MREs, among others) who attribute symbolic value to selected titles. Within the arena of shared reading, especially in terms of MREs, commercial concerns converge with the evaluations of books made by cultural authorities and intermediaries to produce imperatives about what to read. Although these imperatives are rarely overtly moral—the first press releases for *Canada Reads* did, however, refer to the book that "Canadians should read" (CBC 2003)—there is often a moral undertone to the sense of social imperative embedded in the public participatory model: we are encouraging everyone in the city to read this book, so maybe you should join in? At the same time, MREs, particularly those adapting the OBOC model, extend the promise of pleasure, learning *and* community to potential participants through their "offer." The cultural and social aspects of community-wide events are foregrounded, whereas commodity culture and the creative economy are backgrounded. Once again, the rhetoric employed to promote the reading and sharing of books plays in to the dialectic between commerce and culture that pervades the production and consumption practices associated with print cultures.

"A FEELING FOR BOOKS"

By examining aspects of the organization and economic operation of the book publishing industry above, we wanted to suggest the often subtle, but nevertheless tangible ways in which the production and circulation of books affect their reception. These material factors contribute to "a feeling for books" (Radway 1997) that is, to a culture of emotional and ideological investments in the reading of printed books as a social and moral good. *A Feeling for Books* is, of course, the title of Janice Radway's (ibid.) seminal analysis of the ways in which the Book-of-the-Month Club constructed an ideal of literary taste that satisfied the middle-class desire of its socially and economically aspirant American members during the middle decades of the twentieth century (ibid.). In an era of rampant consumer capitalism and new digital technologies, "a feeling" for printed books persists in industrialized societies such as the US and UK. It is "a structure of feeling" (Williams 1961, 1977) experienced by a relatively small group of people who maintain an active relationship with print book cultures whose artifacts are produced and circulated in ways that have changed, at least in some important respects, from those described by Janice Radway in her study of the American Book-of-the-Month Club. That structure of feeling is not only inflected by time, place, gender, and generation, but also, as in Raymond Williams's (1977) classic formulation, it is unevenly distributed through society. This is partly because access to educational institutions is uneven, but also because not all groups within American or British society privilege print culture above other forms of communication such as oral modes of expression. However, as we demonstrate in Chapters 5 and 6—"Worker" and "Reader"—in particular, the emotional and social attachment of book readers to printed books often characterizes their lived experience of the quality of life.[9]

Possessing and demonstrating a "feeling for books" (Radway 1997) is still granted a good deal of prestige within societies that have a "reading class" (Griswold 2008). Members of the reading class typically have the time, money, and education, not only to buy and acquire books, but also to pursue book-centered activities. Figure 4.3 shows the amounts of money that readers in our quantitative survey spent on books in one year, and indicates that the readers who responded to this question chose to use at least part of their disposable income purchasing books.

Meanwhile, a lack of time was the reason participants gave for not participating in an MRE regardless of their geographical location, age, or job (32 percent or 542).[10] The readers in our survey were predominantly keen

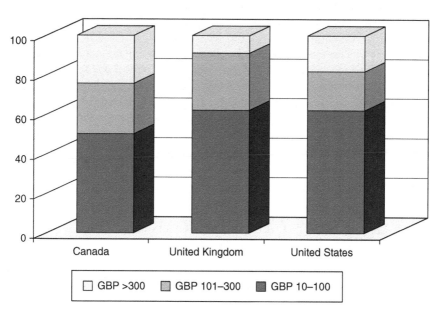

Figure 4.3 Money Spent on Books in a Year
Money Spent on Books in a Year by Nation-State

readers; 42 percent (1,471) read two to five hours per week and 53 percent (1,854) spent six or more hours a week reading. Of those who were keen readers, only 27 percent (283) had participated in an MRE, and some of them only had time to read the selected book. Such data suggests that the reading class of contemporary North America and the UK is time-poor even while they are generally well-educated and often working in fairly well-paid professional jobs. These circumstances help to explain the preponderance of retired and senior people at face-to-face shared reading events. Not only do they belong to a generation who grew up without television or who experienced its early days, but they have reached a life-stage where they have increased leisure time. They have the capacity, if they so wish, to express their "feeling for books" (Radway 1997) through social practices such as book discussions or attending author talks.

Perhaps "a feeling for books" (ibid.)—the emotional attachments in particular—is more visible or it has become easier to articulate because we live at a time when some readers perceive the printed book to be under threat from digital media and the new formats it enables. Other book readers (not necessarily those under twenty years of age!) are excited by new media and actively engage with it by creating literary blogs, contributing to fora on their favorite author's website or by cataloguing their entire libraries on LibraryThing.[11] Many see social opportunities emerging from the ways in which literary culture is repackaged as various popular cultural formations via television, radio, film adaptation, and MREs. However, others interpret popularization and the "blockbuster culture" of best sellers as a vulgarization of their "special" and "distinctive" relationship to books and literary culture. A feeling for books and feelings about books run deep among keen readers. Those who *provide* books to the reading class are sometimes, as Janice Radway (ibid.) pointed out, also those who have a "feeling for books," a formulation that connects the idea of selling books to the idea of reading them. In both cases, "feeling" something connected to books and reading is what matters. "A feeling for books" is thus an apt and multivalent phrase that underpins our key contention in this chapter. Economic capital does not overdetermine the meanings of shared reading although money shapes it in important material and symbolic ways, as the following two case studies demonstrate.

OF PARTNERSHIPS, PROJECTS, AND PUBLISHERS: BRISTOL'S GREAT READING ADVENTURE

> We were just holiday makers [in Chicago in 2001] and we said, "Why are there so many copies of *To Kill a Mockingbird* in the book shops?" and the booksellers were telling us and we went to the library just to see what it looked like there, and then we just added it to the list of things to do! (laughter) (M. Kelly, pers. comm., 2005)

The casual quality of Melanie Kelly's story about the inspiration behind Bristol's Great Reading Adventure belies the professional business infrastructure that has delivered the city's version of OBOC since 2003. The holiday-makers were Melanie and her husband, Andrew Kelly, who is the director of Bristol Creative Projects, formerly the Bristol Cultural Development Partnership (BCDP), which was, in Melanie's words, "a mixture of private sector, public sector and . . . volunteer organizations." In the early 2000s, Melanie Kelly was working part-time as a cultural researcher on "a regular salary" for a private sector company, Business West—now GWE Business West—one of the key partners in the BCDP (pers. comm., 2005). The "business" of GWE Business West is economic development, and the company offers training, advice, and networking services to businesses located in and around the city of Bristol. The other main partners in BCDP were two public sector organizations: Bristol City Council, which allocated an annual portion of its budget to the arts, and the southwest regional branch of the Arts Council. Until 2010, when Arts Council England restructured its delivery of funding in the wake of UK government cut-backs, the BCDP was a Regularly Funded Organization that guaranteed continued support in three-year cycles for the delivery of a combination of arts programs. All three partner agencies thus contributed funds to support arts and culture projects in the city of Bristol under the aegis of the BCDP with Andrew Kelly, its director since 1993, brokering additional partnerships for individual programs. Some of these collaborations were in the form of in-kind arrangements, for instance, media partners such as the *Bristol Evening Post* newspaper for the Great Reading Adventure (GRA), which has featured many stories about the annual citywide read. The newspaper, which is the most widely read local daily in the city, has also made a significant contribution to increasing access to the shared reading event. During the first GRA in 2003, the paper ran a serialization of *Treasure Island* (1883), and, in recent years, the *Post* has published tokens that can be exchanged at participating book shops and libraries for a free copy of the selected book.

Cultural managers such as Melanie and Andrew Kelly play a crucial role in sustaining and expanding the economic web of funding and partnerships for cultural projects in an era when the arts in the UK have been supported through a mixed economy of state and private money. In addition to carrying out research and producing evaluations for programs such as the GRA, Melanie Kelly made a series of successful applications for additional public sector funds from, for example, the Heritage Lottery Fund. As the name implies, the Fund consists of monies raised by the National Lottery, and these are administered by the National Heritage Memorial Fund, a non-departmental public body accountable to the UK parliament via the Department of Culture, Media and Sport. The sums awarded, such as the £50,000 for the Small Island Read in 2007 (M. Kelly 2007, 5), can make a significant contribution to the overall budget for a program like the GRA, but the application process is laborious and time-consuming, and organizations are required to obtain funding from other agencies, with private sector funding deemed to be a most desirable, if not essential, element of the package. As mentioned above, accountability is part of the regime of mixed economy funding and this means not only clear and transparent budgeting at all stages of a project, but also detailed evaluation of "outcomes," "legacy," and "lessons learned." All of these terms feature in the reports on the annual GRA prepared by Melanie Kelly, and they are typical of the language used to express a neoliberal conceptualization of cultural value.[12] Recipients of state funds for artistic and cultural projects must demonstrate that the "investment" has been worthwhile and that the "anticipated return" has been achieved (A. Ross 2009, 25). The documentation of the GRA in the fifty-plus pages of the glossy evaluation reports is elaborate (e.g., M. Kelly 2007): analysis of the demographics of participation, quotations from participants about the educational and transformative value of the GRA, commentary from librarians and on-site event organizers about the success of the program, many photographs of children and adults of various ages and cultural backgrounds clustered around copies of the selected book, quantitative data about the number of books given away, library circulation figures, the value of in-kind media support, and, of course, the budget. Such detail is employed as evidence that "public goods like diversity, access, relevance, civic pride, community innovation, and social inclusion" have been furthered (A. Ross 2009, 25). As Melanie Kelly pointed out, these reports also become advertising brochures that can be used in Andrew Kelly's ongoing search for more corporate sponsors and public sector partners.

The way that the GRA is organized, funded, and delivered thus offers a vivid illustration of the business model promoted through New Labour's cultural policy, which was, in turn, inspired by ideas about and research focusing on the creative economy. In an interview with blogger Chris Thurling for the online marketing, media, and PR website *Brand Republic*, Andrew Kelly's own engagement with the functional ideology informing the creative economy was explicit:

> We have had different goals in the fifteen years we have been in operation . . . Now we are about ideas—especially arts and sciences—and our projects are geared towards celebrating and developing Bristol's position as a city of ideas. There's been lots of work—by people like Richard Florida and organisations like the Work Foundation—on the role of creative people in cities and we seek to use and build on this. (Thurling 2009)

As Andrew Kelly (ibid.) goes on to explain, the BCDP has tried to boost the creative economy through involvement in capital projects such as the renovation of the Arnolfini art gallery and Harbourside area of the city, as well as organizing Bristol's bid to become European Capital of Culture 2008. Although the bid failed, and the honor went to Liverpool, the BCDP proceeded to ensure the delivery of the majority of events and programs, including the now annual Festival of Ideas. The inclusion of Birmingham, Oxford, and Newcastle-Gateshead as the other finalists for the Capital of Culture 2008 bid was significant because, as Jim McGuigan points out, "culture" has been key to government plans and policy for transforming Britain's former manufacturing and industrial strong-holds: "from the point of view of cultural policy, neoliberalism sets the regeneration agenda in once great cities that have fallen on hard times" (2010, 117). Creative Britain was supposed to arise from the wreckage of post-industrial urban landscapes, and indeed, a few brown-field sites in cities such as Bristol and Liverpool were redeveloped during the early 2000s to house artistic and creative businesses.[13]

The Great Reading Adventure was part of Bristol's Capital of Culture bid slate, but Melanie Kelly indicated the more minor role of literary culture relative to other creative and cultural industries in Bristol when she told us:

> Bristol Cultural Development Partnership [had] the idea of using culture in its broadest sense but obviously including literature as part of the regeneration of the city. So, so that's why [that] sort of literature is important for Bristol not for its own sake, but also [for] the fact that it gives this sense of being sort of a buzzy creative city, which is actually very good . . . The real strength in Bristol is probably more to do with . . . animation and computer and sort of digital technology. (pers. comm., 2005)

Melanie Kelly's commentary goes some way to explain the relatively low profile of the GRA—at least, in terms of its visibility downtown and public awareness about it—compared to other nationally famous Bristol cultural products such as Aardman animation studio's much-loved creations Wallace and Gromit. Attempting to turn Wallace and Gromit's brand recognition to their advantage, the Kellys brokered a partnership with Aardman that resulted in the popular characters appearing on publicity for the GRA in 2003, 2004, and 2006. Book choices for each year were also tied to a theme that the BCDP used as a unifying idea for a series of different creative projects. Thus, in 2006, the selection of Jules Verne's novel *Around the World in Eighty Days* was billed as part of Brunel 200, a series of events celebrating the bicentenary of the birth of Isambard Kingdom Brunel and the contributions made by the "versatile and audacious" engineer to technology and industry (BCDP 2006).[14] The public rationale given for the book choice was its "theme of opening up the world through transport and technology as well as the fact that Jules Verne, its author, travelled on Brunel's ship, the SS Great Eastern" (BCDP 2006). Meanwhile, thanks to another partnership brokered by the Kellys, Oxford University Press produced a special edition of their Oxford World's Classics translation of *Around the World in Eighty Days* featuring Wallace and Gromit on the cover. Via a combination of branch libraries and commercial bookstores, the BCDP distributed 52,000 free copies of the novel throughout the southwest region of England—the first time the MRE had been extended beyond the city (Melanie Kelly, pers. comm., 2006).

Additionally, 50,000 free copies of a specially commissioned illustrated version for children were given away to schools and community groups, along with 40,000 copies of a full-color, fifty-two-page reading guide (ibid).

Prior to 2006, the BCDP had a three-year deal with Penguin books that enabled them to buy as many as 30,000 copies of a book for as little as 72 pence each (M. Kelly, pers. comm., 2005). Perhaps due to their confidence in their business model and their emphasis on delivering arts and culture as part of building a "creative city," the Kellys are the only MRE organizers in our study who were prepared to be frank and open about these costs and the influence that a relationship with a publisher might have on their choice of books. As Melanie Kelly noted, the reading guides and free books are "why the project is really expensive to do. We plan to do it annually but it's a struggle each year to get the money." The struggle was exacerbated when they decided to expand the geographic reach of the GRA even further in 2007, selecting Andrea Levy's novel *Small Island* (2004) and collaborating with agencies in three other cities—Liverpool, Hull, and Glasgow—all of which have historical links to the Transatlantic Slave Trade and long histories of immigration. The Small Island Read 2007 also incorporated the southwest region and extended beyond the city of Liverpool to the northwest region, chiefly via the public library system in those areas. Levy's (2004) novel was chosen because "it describes the arrival in post-war Britain of black Jamaican immigrants, the descendants of enslaved Africans" and the UK's biggest ever MRE was thus tied in with the commemorations of the 200th anniversary of the passing of the Slave Trade Abolition Bill (M. Kelly 2007, 5).

The challenge of paying for and distributing sufficient quantities of free books and reading guides to a much larger constituency of potential readers was significant in itself, but the BCDP ran into a new problem: they had chosen not only a book that was still in copyright, but an award-winning international best seller. The economic realities of the contemporary book industry and the power relations among its actors suddenly loomed large. Whereas Levy quickly agreed to participate in the launch events in Liverpool, her literary agent baulked at the idea that 50,000 copies of *Small Island* were going to be given away for free (Bea Colley, pers. comm., 2006), thereby denying her client (and herself) their cut of profits (usually 10 percent for each party per book sold). In the summer of 2006, the fate of Small Island Read 2007 hung in the balance as negotiations among Andrew Kelly, Levy's agent, and her publisher took place. Ultimately, Levy was paid a special fee as compensation for the lost income and the different key agencies involved in the multiple-city read—Glasgow's "Aye Write" festival, Liverpool Reads, Hull City Council—were each asked to contribute toward it (B. Colley, pers. comm., 2006). Hodder Headline (Levy's publisher) produced a special promotional pocket book edition of the novel, smaller in size than the commercially available trade paperback and thus distinctive from it in shape, although not in terms of the shared cover image. The special edition also featured references to Small Island Read 2007 on the back cover and inside front page.[15] The Kellys funded the cost of buying the special edition books from their grant income and then offered these books to event organizers at discount. A total of 13,000 copies went to Liverpool, including 1,000 copies to the Reader offices (the organizational base for Liverpool Reads) and 6,250 each to the Bluecoat Arts Centre and the Lister Drive Community Library (M. Kelly 2007, 9). Such a quantity far outstripped the number of free copies of previous Liverpool Reads' selections made available as giveaways. Bea Colley, who managed Liverpool Reads for three years, remarked, "You don't need thousands of pounds to do a citywide read. I mean, obviously it helps a lot, but you need your community of readers, and you need people to spread the word of reading, rather than just lots of money to throw at different projects" (pers. comm., 2006).

Colley's (ibid.) emphasis on community and social networks suggests a contrasting organizational model to the BCDP's financial brokering. As we explore further in the next chapter, the "grassroots," ground-up mode of working with community partners such as Asylum Link, various local schools, the Caribbean Community Centre and the Kuumba Imani Millennium Centre is influenced by the beliefs and activist experiences of The Reader's director, Jane Davis. The Reader Organisation quite literally accommodates the project manager for Liverpool Reads through the provision of office space. Bea Colley and her successors have thus been able to benefit directly from Davis's management expertise, as well as gain access to her extensive network of community contacts. Nevertheless, the necessity of raising money to pay for reading guides and free books, workshops, and other events has meant that Davis has formed a number of financially beneficial partnerships to support Liverpool Reads since the city's version of OBOC began in 2003. These alliances have included the Liverpool branch of Arts and Business, a UK organization that brokers partnerships between arts agencies and for-profit companies as well as offering funds to support projects. Arts and Business was listed as one of the "major local funders" of Small Island Read 2007 (M. Kelly 2007, 59), having previously supported Liverpool Reads in 2004 by matching the funding that Bloomsbury (the UK publisher of Louis Sachar's novel, *Holes*) provided.

For the majority of citywide or region-wide reading events, books and reading guides represent a considerable portion of project expenditure. According to Melanie Kelly (2007, 8), for Small Island Read 2007, the BCDP distributed 80,000 copies of the reading guide and 50,000 books at a cost of £76,888 from a total expenditure and income of £215, 438 (the figure includes both cash and in-kind support by the BCDP and its partners) (49). To put the costs into perspective, in 2006 the GRA cost £100, 015, whereas Liverpool Reads cost £30, 966 (ibid.). In 2007, books and guides were the second largest expense after workshops (£81,750). What emerges from the Kellys' experiences at securing the special print-run of *Small Island* is the crucial role that the affordability of the selected book can play within an economically driven organizational model of MREs. Deals made with the other agents within the reading industry, specifically those involved with the production of books, can make a book affordable, as can securing more corporate partners if they are willing to donate cash or buy a quantity of discounted books. In 2007, for example, Rolls Royce Engines based at Filton, near Bristol, bought a thousand copies for its factory workers (9). If the creative city is to be developed and the public goods of "developing the standards of literacy," "stimulat[ing] new forms of creativity inspired by reading," "learning about the past," and "bring[ing] diverse communities together . . . and foster[ing] a sense of shared identity" are to be furthered, then the right economic partnerships have to be brokered (5). These outcomes of the GRA, listed and "evidenced" in the annual report, deploy the language produced by a cultural policy culture in the UK that has blurred the distinctions between profit, the production of cultural artifacts and services, and a social improvement agenda.

If this sounds too cynical an assessment of the BCDP's work and achievements, it is mitigated, or at least complicated, by Cynthia Martin's (pers. comm., 2005) point that two significant measures of the value for GRA from the viewpoint of Bristol's public library system are: first, the positive media coverage for the library service that it has generated, and, second, the professional development opportunities that it has helped to create for assistant librarians in the city, because "it's helped to inspire and develop our staff." Martin, a Reader Advisory librarian and manager of fourteen branch libraries in north Bristol, has been involved in GRA from the outset and is, in fact, a crucial partner for BCDP. Her role in the GRA as an advocate for the program within the library system is a potent reminder that partnerships based on expertise and influence are as crucial to the success of MREs as economic collaborations with businesses such as publishers or commercial service industries. Nowhere is this more evident than in the partnership model of institutional collaboration with national, regional, and municipal organizations adopted for the NEA's Big Read program. Within the NEA model, The Institute for Museums and Library Services plays a significant part, not only in terms of supporting staff within the public library system so that they can assist in the delivery of OBOC activities, but also, through their representatives on the Big Read team in Washington, D.C., in terms of influencing how shared reading is sold to the general public.

THE QUICK-FIX AND THE HARD-SELL: THE BIG READ FROM WASHINGTON, D.C., TO HUNTSVILLE, ALABAMA

How do you *sell* reading and how do you—you know? It's difficult for a group of lifelong readers, passionate readers, to think about, how do you talk about this? (M. Flanigan, pers. comm., 2006; emphasis in the original)

Maryrose Flanigan made this astute, self-reflexive assessment during a lively discussion we had with her and her colleagues from the NEA and the Institute of Museums and Library Services (IMLS) about the challenge of promoting the Big Read program to libraries, communities, and the media across the US.[16] Like Flanigan, the other members of the group had also been engaging with different ways of valuing, understanding, and representing reading as part of their work organizing the public relations campaign, writing and designing the reading guides, and preparing other materials such as the special CDs and teacher's guides produced for each featured book. Photographic representations of reading were sifted—"We rejected the one with the guy just sitting alone reading; you don't want people to see it as too escapist, too solitary" (ibid.); the purpose of the CDs and reading guide was analyzed—"When you listen to the CD and you read the reader's guide, it's kind of like—even if you were doing it on your own—it's kind of like the novel hasn't ended. You're still going back into it. And it also ties into the reading for pleasure idea, which we're really pushing" (ibid.), and assumptions made during preparations for the pilot year of 2005 were trumped by the experience of visiting community sites as David Kipen revealed: "It never occurred to us until I actually *sat* in the back of this combination general store/bookstore in Sioux Falls, South Dakota, that the discussion questions [in the reading guide] that we had thought, uh, might be primarily for classroom use or people asking each other, um, people were sort of using this as a script with which to conduct a book group" (pers. comm., 2006; emphasis in the original).

As a tried-and-tested formula, the OBOC model may have offered the NEA a quick-fix response to the "decline of literary reading" headlined in the "Reading at Risk" report (NEA 2004), but designing and delivering the Big Read program involved these NEA and IMLS employees confronting, not only the inevitable logistical problems involved in producing large quantities of support materials, and delivering grants to communities through third-party agencies such as Arts MidWest, but also ideological struggles. The NEA workers adopted a language of promotion that belongs to late-twentieth-century commodity culture: "How do you *sell* reading?" But for some of them, the sales pitch approach stood in contrast to (and in tension) with their investment in the notion that literary reading could be individually transformative. Whereas they all spoke respectfully, indeed admiringly, of NEA Chairman Dana Gioia, not everyone shared his Oprah-like conviction that reading could save your life. Maryrose Flanigan offered a more moderate version of this discourse of transformation when she said, "We're not telling people, like, 'If you read *To Kill a Mockingbird*, you're going to be smarter.' That's not what we're saying; what we're saying is, you know, 'If you read *To Kill a Mockingbird*, it might change your life in some way and how you experience things in that type of way'" (pers. comm., 2006). Other committee members were more cautious. Karen Motylewski, the Evaluation Officer from the IMLS, found the discussion about the special role of "literary reading" rather enlightening: "I think that—the oddity for *me* is that—and now I begin to understand where *literary* reading comes out of the mission of the National Endowment for the Arts, because for me *all* reading has the capacity to transform. And I have not gotten, until just now, why [the Big Read program] has been focused on literary reading" (pers. comm., 2006; emphasis in the original). Motylewski's professional affiliation with the public library service inflects her view that "*all* reading," that is, all genres of books and, perhaps, other forms of print culture, too, can provide a transformative experience for a reader. The focus of the Big Read on "literary reading" lends a special force to the genre of fiction and its "capacity" to "transform" the reader, as indicated by the proscribed list of books that feature many "classics" of modern American Literature. There may also be a structural and institutional rationale at play here. By defining the Big Read as a project that highlights "literary reading," the NEA employees align the reading of books with participation in "the arts," rather than emphasizing the notion of reading for education and edification (more the purview of the National Endowment for the Humanities).

David Kipen differentiated himself from his boss, Dana Gioia, more directly, when he told us with reference to our own upcoming meeting with the Chairman:

> You *will* get it ["the transformative power of literature"] at 3:30 from a guy who, you know, who came from fairly humble beginnings and if books hadn't picked him up by the scruff of the neck and, you know, then the Chairman would be in jail or dead by now. Um, whereas, you know, somebody like me, from comparatively more comfortable circumstances, all books saved me from was medical school, probably! (pers. comm., 2006; emphasis in the original)

As David Kipen implies, literacy and books had played different roles in the committee member's own private and professional lives in ways that were shaped by specifics of class, gender, and ethnicity. For Kipen, the "transformative power" of literary reading is a useful shorthand for marketing the Big Read to program partners, but not a message to communicate to readers because:

> People don't necessarily *want* their lives transformed. Um, you know, it's not the way to sell it to, you know, the readers *themselves*, but as a way to remind people who already read of what there is to it and of, you know, a way of talking amongst ourselves and to publishers and to, you know, libraries and our partners, um, that *there*, I think, is where that sort of language comes in handy. (pers. comm., 2006; emphasis in the original)

What is interesting about these particular negotiations around the meanings of reading is the snapshot they offer of institutional employees actively engaging with the issues of money and moral power up-front. Implicitly aware of the symbolic power that the NEA can wield, despite the agency's relatively low levels of federal government funding, the organizers thought hard about the messages that their actions, materials, and press statements might send to the general public. Charged with the task of delivering the agenda of a political appointee (Gioia) chosen by a Republican President, these NEA employees and their IMLS colleagues had to balance meeting the Chairman's goals and ideals with empowering the communities who won the grants. As Hope O'Keefe, who worked in the National Initiatives Office of the NEA noted, the "quick fix" approach—adopting and replicating an extant shared reading model—could easily take on the appearance and feel of a top-down, homogenizing maneuver (pers. comm., 2006). She added, "We don't want to understate the good job that's been done in the 250-so communities that have done One Book, One Community [prior to 2005], but there *is* that kind of an 'economy of scale' for developing materials and things like that at a national level. We don't want this to be a top-down program. It's grown organically, and we want to continue building that" (ibid.; emphasis in the original). Set against this image of organic growth and local creativity, however, is the reality of the federal government requirements shaping the NEA's granting policies:

> All of our grants require partnerships, so that was the marketing component, to help the cities out with that and to require them to work with their businesses, school districts, libraries, military bases—whoever is there. (ibid.)

The NEA itself depends on partners such as the IMLS and Arts Midwest, both long-term collaborators in the Big Read, as well as one-off partnerships with organizations such as the Poetry Foundation (in 2007). These collaborations are necessary, in part, because the NEA receives a relatively small amount of state funding and these partners bring additional economic resources along with staff expertise. In 1998, for example, the United States government spent $0.38 per capita to support the NEA, compared to equivalent agencies in Canada and France, where per capita support of the arts was $32 (J. Ryan 1998, 3). Just over a decade later, the NEA was in receipt of $155 million from the US government, a figure that the incoming Chair, Rocco Landesman, publically derided in the *New York Times* as "'pathetic' and 'embarrassing'" (cited in Pogrebin 2009), not least because this figure represented a considerable decrease in real terms from a 1992 budget of $172 million (Pogrebin 2009). By 2011 the budget had still not caught up, and President Obama's request to Congress included $161.3 million to fund the NEA (2012). Congress ultimately allotted $167.5 million, which was just sufficient to maintain the key areas of support and major programs like the Big Read (NEA 2012). However, only $1 million was awarded for 75 OBOCs to run between September 2010 and June 2011 (the budget and number of awards for 2011–2012 and 2012–2013 were almost identical), compared to $3,719,265 in awards to 267 nonprofits for 2009–2010 (NEA 2012). Grants from the program have typically ranged from $5,000-$25,000 each year (ibid), since the pilot year ended in 2006 and the national launch took place in 2007. Given that, by July 2012, the NEA had awarded Big Read grants to over a thousand nonprofit organizations (ibid.), the necessity of securing partnership funding at both the national and local levels in order to continue the program becomes clear.

In Huntsville, Alabama, a long way south of Washington, D.C., the organizers of One Book, One Madison County were extremely content with the trade-off between receiving a $25,000 grant from the Big Read for their 2006 event, and the labor and time required to fulfill the obligations of the award (David Lilly, Judy Purinton, Mary Wallace, pers. comm., 2007). These included securing match-funding, two of them attending formal training in another state as well as a briefing session in Washington, D.C., brokering local partnerships, and stoking the publicity machine that would bring in participants to their program of events. For Mary Wallace, Judy Purinton, and David Lilly, the main organizers of the Huntsville program, the tangible benefits of a cash injection combined with the supply of ready-made Big-Read branded reading guides, CDs, bookmarks, and posters outweighed any concerns about the bureaucracy of accountability imposed by the NEA. Prior to the Big Read, Wallace and Purinton had been creating programming for OBOC with no budget outside of regular library funds, which meant that they were confined to a read-the-book/screen-a-film/discuss-the-book model. They had plenty of creative ideas, but lack of funds prevented them from inviting guest speakers, for example. The grants that they have received since 2006 have enabled the team to focus on programming and publicity—the latter having increased substantially, due to the marketing requirements bound up in the award of Big Read money. As Mary Wallace explained, one of her colleagues had to take on special responsibility for putting the "hard sell" into action because:

> There was *so* much publicity involved in this. Um, it was comprehensive; it wasn't just flyers and bookmarks and stuff. We had Internet postcards, radio, T.V., newspaper ads, you know—what else out? We had speakers go out; I mean, it was just *endless*, the amount of publicity. (pers. comm., 2007; emphasis in the original)

Constraints placed upon book choice by the NEA's list of proscribed titles were also dealt with in a matter-of-fact manner by the Huntsville team. They were not especially worried about the type of literary fiction represented by the first four books that had been selected for the program by a committee of "experts" convened in Washington, D.C., nor by the fact that the Big Read limited them to a choice from one of these "classic" titles. They did, however, pick novels with Southern US associations: *The Great Gatsby* for 2006 (Zelda Fitzgerald was a Southerner) and *To Kill a Mockingbird* for

2007 (Harper Lee is an Alabama native and the novel is set in the southern part of the state). Or, perhaps Purinton and Wallace were especially canny when applying for their first two years of NEA support, because these books were the two highlighted in Dana Gioia's press release announcing the pilot for the Big Read:

> . . . if cities nationally unite to adopt The Big Read, our community-wide reading program, together we can restore reading to its essential place in American culture. Call me naïve, but I can actually envision an America in which average people talk about *To Kill a Mockingbird* and *The Great Gatsby* with the same enthusiasm as they bring to *Lost* or *Desperate Housewives*. (NEA 2005)

Regardless of whether Gioia's press release directly influenced the Huntsville team, Mary Wallace was quick to admonish NEA representatives whom she met during a 2005 briefing session in Washington, D.C., about the economic impact of book selection:

> I said, "Look: two of the books you've picked, they're $14 a copy, you know, the trade paperback copies in print. The mass-market paperback that usually costs $6 isn't in print anymore for two of the books that you have on this list. So you might want to think about that when you add new books to this thing, to get cooperation from the publishers to get those $6 copies back into circulation before you select another book." Because, you know, that's a big factor if somebody's gonna buy their own copy: $6 vs. $14? (pers. comm., 2006)

In practice, participants do not need to spend any money on books if they can borrow the selected title from their local library, but Wallace knew from the previous Huntsville iterations of OBOC that library wait-lists for the selected book can grow very long, very quickly. And, although Huntsville is home to many middle-class professionals because of the NASA Space Center, the US Army Aviation and Missile Command base at the Redstone Arsenal, and the high-tech industries that service them, the areas around the town are not as prosperous. The possession of economic capital—as well as print literacy—impacts very directly on who can take part, especially in activities that depend on getting access to the text—such as a book discussion, for example. In Arkansas, organizers addressed these challenges by using $10,000 of their NEA grant to buy the serial rights for *The Great Gatsby* so that they could run it in the local paper (NEA committee, pers. comm., 2006). The panel evaluating their Big Read grant application accepted their rationale that, as Maryrose Flanigan explained, it "is such a rural state, and they made the point that a lot of the citizens couldn't get to libraries *or* bookstores or maybe couldn't afford, even if they couldn't get to a bookstore, to do the Amazon thing" (pers. comm., 2006; emphasis in the original). Other grant recipients have, like the Kellys in Bristol, negotiated directly with publishers to obtain up to 700 free copies of a book so that they could be given away.

The formation of partnerships similar to this, which respond to local social and economic conditions, suggests the creative agency of OBOC organizers in receipt of NEA's Big Read grants. Book choice may be limited, partnerships compulsory, and match-funding obligatory, but, as the Huntsville, Alabama, team testified, the grant money can be the difference between being able to deliver an OBOC program or giving up on the model (J. Purinton and M. Wallace, pers. comm., 2006). Furthermore, in states such as Alabama and Arkansas, the provision of mass-produced NEA materials such as CDs, teachers' guides, bookmarks, and funds to buy books are also crucial resources that facilitate outreach to readers who are not committed library patrons or book buyers. For many local organizers, the goals of increasing the accessibility of print culture through creative programming and the wider distribution of books within their city or region are connected to the values that motivate them to complete their funding applications and to build partnerships with publishers and for-profit organizations outside the cultural and creative industries. In other words, their feeling for reading books is ideological, emotional, *and* connected to the material forms and economic structures that shape the circulation of print cultures in the twenty-first century.

CONCLUSIONS: GOOD VALUES

Money matters for MREs: whether it comes in the form of cash from the national coffers via a state-funded institution such as the NEA, or from a publishing house in the form of discounted books, or from a corporate sponsor such as Ford in the form of a car. Beyond the material necessities that money can provide for staging cultural events such as OBOC, the mere receipt of in-kind contributions and corporate donations confers symbolic value on an event or program. By lending their logos as well as their resources, partner organizations "badge" MREs both literally and figuratively, signaling approval for shared reading and community-building, while also advertising their commitment to corporate social responsibility (not to mention their commercially available products and services). A degree of symbolic value is thus returned to the sponsor associated with an MRE. The apparent circularity of this process highlights how the idea of reading books, especially the sharing of reading with others, is readily accepted, not just as a culturally highbrow activity, but also as a social good by members of well-financed and/or well-educated groups. But in the case of for-profit sponsors of MREs, the circularity of symbolic capital is also driven by the donation of money or products in return for the social legitimacy that comes with having a stake in a cultural program. The economic investment is worthwhile precisely because this exchange of "goods" takes place within market economies organized according to neoliberal ideology that translates aesthetic and cultural value primarily into economic terms, but secondarily into social value. In the late twentieth and early twenty-first century, cultural policy in the UK articulated and legitimated this translation, whereas in the US, the "new" norm of neoliberal economics and its accompanying vocabulary left the imbalance between public and private funding for arts and culture undisturbed. Ideologically, there is more common ground than difference among the three nation-states of our study when it comes to constructions of cultural value, although the cultural nationalism detectable in Canadian policy-making offers some resistance to the marketization of culture and of the so-called creative and cultural industries. Even so, it is more accurate to describe the resistance as a type of cultural protectionism in which the market for "homemade" products is maintained and supplied by local products in an era of free trade, rather than as a form of resistance to a market economy per se.

We could, in fact, think of the OBOC model as a perfect articulation of the temporal, spatial, and economic contexts within which it was first formulated. As a typical cultural artifact of its time, the model traveled transnationally in the form of an idea, thanks in part to new technologies that enabled the rapid flow and sharing of information. Whereas its first iteration was in the politically liberal city of Seattle in 1998 using funds from a private foundation, the model was quickly adopted, adapted, and reproduced all over the United States before being taken up and "mass produced" by a federal institution. Cultural managers and workers from other nation-states, primarily those from advanced market economies with print-centric cultures, were eager to seize upon this idea for large-scale shared reading that they heard about through their virtual and actual social and professional networks, and the model proliferated, particularly, although not exclusively, in regions of the world where English-language publishing has an economic foothold. Equally important as an explanation for the transnational journey of the OBOC model through various advanced capitalist economies, is the fact that it is a good "fit" with neoliberal notions of cultural value. It is therefore attractive to potential partners, whether the partner is a corporate sponsor with a social responsibility charter to fulfill, or a municipal government with a "creative community" agenda informed by the regeneration of a postindustrial downtown core. The ideological "fit" is one reason why OBOC is, in our view, a conservative contemporary cultural formation of shared reading. Another is the ease with which money and moral power can be articulated together, discursively and textually in funding applications and in the rhetoric of event promotion, and materially in terms of partnerships that are brokered between event organizers and for-profit agencies. Moreover, the OBOC model is much less threatening to traditional "highbrow" notions of literary culture than mass-mediated MREs such as the RJBC, which, as we explored in Chapter 2, "Television," explicitly employ elements of popular culture, in particular, celebrity culture, in order to appeal to potential participants. Whereas the RJBC contests the privileged place of literary reading within contemporary culture, OBOC often confirms or reaffirms it. Finally, the ideas vaunted in grant applications, project evaluations, and OBOC event publicity of bringing people together to share reading, of building bridges among communities in a city, and of citizen engagement and responsibility are not radical or disruptive of the prevailing neoliberal ideology.

Nevertheless, in an era of the quick fix and the hard sell, when cultural events must prove their economic and social worth, it would be too easy to argue that money overdetermines the meanings of shared reading. Cultural workers and readers actively engage with the ideals informing shared reading events and, whereas there is often complicity with normative notions of cultural value, it is also possible that the events themselves may produce unforeseen and unsanctioned consequences. Cynthia Martin, the Reader Advisory Librarian involved with Bristol's Great Reading Adventure, had this to say about the social benefits that exist beyond the time frame and spatial borders of each GRA:

> Quite a lot of libraries actually manage to place their stock [of books] [. . .] at local schools. Say, oh, you know, we'd like thirty copies, that's enough for a class, um, and then what we've got left at the end certainly for the first two projects (2003 and 2004), they've gone to Book Aid to go to Africa. So they, they keep on working. They're not, at the end of our project, they are not thrown away. They go to—sort of—to be of use to people in lots of places. (pers. comm., 2005)

Martin's comments resonate with our earlier discussion about the social change that keen readers—and neoliberal governments—believe that books and shared reading can effect. There is even a moral force to Martin's (ibid.) image of recycling the GRA books within local and far-flung communities of need, where the books "keep on working," presumably making life better for those who receive them. The neocolonial and racialized power relations involved in sending (secondhand) printed books to Africa from one of the erstwhile centers of imperialism are clearly problematic. What we cannot account for here is *how* the books may or may not "work" for those who receive them. They may be read, treasured, used for fuel, thrown away, or simply ignored. What we can say is that this image of librarians (most of whom are women) sending books to Africa relates to the visual image that opened our chapter in some fascinating ways. The men surrounding the gleaming Ford car signify continuity with a history of corporate and philanthropic giving that is more common in the US than it is in the UK. That image also represents an ideal of masculinity predicated on a certain degree of wealth, and associated with ideas of personal agency and mobility. By contrast, the image of low-paid library assistants packing up books for a charity to distribute overseas resonates with the history of volunteerism and charitable "good works" performed away from the public gaze. The books will move across continents, but the women may not. Both images, however, suggest that these groups of people believe that books—and the sharing of books—have the capacity to transform individuals and communities.

Martin's reflections on the afterlife of the Bristol GRA books also serve to remind us that whereas money and moral power may structure many of the formal relationships required to fund MREs, cultural workers such as librarians and fund-raisers, as well as the participants in OBOC programs, actively "use" books and programmed events in ways that cannot be predicted or entirely contained by the conditions of funding or the notion of value promoted in cultural policy documents. Furthermore, government-supported arts institutions such as the NEA in the US deliver programs, not only thanks to public and private funds, but also because of the skill and enthusiasm of employees who are usually passionate about arts and culture. These workers actively negotiate with economic imperatives, the marketization of culture, political directives, a public service mandate, and their own emotional attachment to a "structure of feeling" (Williams 1961, 1977) for reading books. But these negotiations exact a cost, as we explore in the next chapter.

5 Worker

I guess I'm just so passionate about books that all I think about is how can I get people to read more books? That's all I think about, all the time. How can I get people to read more books? And so, I guess that's just my mantra, you know what I mean?

—M. Wallace, pers. comm., 2006

Adrenaline highs, job satisfaction, community gratitude, local fame, cultural capital, and social authority are among the rewards garnered by the organizers of shared reading events. But what is involved in the performance of this type of cultural labor—ideologically, materially, and emotionally? And how does the "passion for reading" and for books articulated by cultural workers such as librarian Mary Wallace inflect their role as shared reading event organizers? Wallace's "mantra"—"How can I get people to read more books?"—expresses passionate feelings about her work inspired by her identity as a book-lover, while also articulating an ethical goal appropriate to her professional role. Because book reading is still regarded as a worthwhile leisure pursuit in North America and the UK, expressing passion about it in public is socially permissible, even de rigueur, if you happen to be a Reader Advisory librarian, literature teacher, or Book Festival organizer. The desire to encourage people to read, or to read more books, coincides neatly with the professional objectives of these jobs in the reading industry. Cultural workers are not, however, supposed to reveal the personal costs involved in the translation of these aspirations into shared reading events. It is fine for them to acknowledge some of the pleasures and perks, such as the thrill of introducing a best-selling author, for example, because excitement signals the glamour associated with literary celebrity, thereby enhancing the spectacle effect of a staged event. But the cultural worker cannot articulate in public the negative or toxic effects of overwork, or rather, she cannot verbalize it, although the lines on her face or a slow gait might register emotional and bodily fatigue to the observant audience member. Yet, the body of the worker is as crucial to the successful performance of cultural work as her sense of social mission, her "passion for reading," and the creative skills and specialist knowledge that she employs in the programming and staging of events.

The organizers of citywide and community reading events are actively involved in promoting print texts, shaping audiences, and producing specific meanings of literary reading in the early twenty-first century. As cultural mediators, they mediate between books and readers.[1] Often, the cultural mediators (in common with the majority of MRE participants) are women performing creative and cultural work that has become socially inscribed as "feminine," gendered labor, for reasons that we discussed in Chapter 1, "Reading," and which we reconsider at the end of this chapter. Sometimes these workers mediate between books and readers in a very literal sense through physical, face-to-face encounters in book group discussions, for example. When organizers make formal introductions at larger reading events, such as the film screenings and author talks that are typical of many OBOC programs, the ideological "framing" work of cultural mediation assumes a more explicit form and public function. The practical and ideological labor of organizers is therefore absolutely vital to the material production of MREs and to the ways in which shared reading is widely understood today. And yet, critics have not examined in detail the roles that event organizers play, how they feel about their work, and how their work influences contemporary formations and meanings of shared reading.

CULTURAL WORKERS AND CULTURAL WORK IN THE READING INDUSTRY

During our interviews with MRE organizers, we heard many of them express their "passion for reading," frequently using that exact phrase, but we were also given unprompted accounts of overwork and fatigue mixed in with stories of glittering successes. Cultural workers involved in the reading industry are far from alone in their articulations of work narratives similar to these, ones that interweave experiences of intense emotional engagement and a sense of social purpose with anxieties about time-pressure, financial constraints, and exhaustion. Recent scholarship about labor in the creative and cultural industries has begun to explore the complex mix of costs and benefits involved in work that is creatively self-fulfilling but often irregular in terms of work patterns and financial reward. Taking up sociologist Arlie Hochschild's (1983, 1997) conceptualizations of "emotional labor," "emotion work," and "the time bind," David Hesmondhalgh's ([2002] 2007, 2008; and Baker 2011) notion of "emotional work" has been developed through his studies of cultural workers in the television, music, and magazine industries. Also influenced by Hochschild, Angela McRobbie's (2002, 2006, 2013) conceptualization of "passionate work" emerges from her studies of labor in microenterprises such as fashion design, art-making, curating, and multimedia. There are, of course, some material differences across these sectors of the cultural industries, not only in terms of the everyday working environment, but also with regard to job security, and employees' access to trade unions and professional associations. There is also an important structural difference between the arena of reading activities and reading event promotion that are part of what we term the reading industry, and the sectors scholars usually recognize as "cultural industries." Unlike those working in television production, for example, MRE organizers do not all work within the same sector. Some of the organizers of MREs work within the media industry; some are self-employed arts administrators, whereas others are employed full-time as professionally trained specialists within state-funded institutions, usually public library systems. Despite these differences among and between work sectors, case studies about reading event organizers can offer new insights into the rewards and costs of pursuing creative labor.

In the context of MREs, the term "cultural worker" could refer not only to the main organizers of events, but also to their partners and sponsors, such as publishers or local government "expert" contributors such as university professors who sometimes write supporting material for websites or printed reading guides, and performers, not the least of whom are the authors of selected books who actively participate in many OBOC programs. All of these agents are diversely invested in attracting readers to book-centered events: some, such as publishers, are motivated primarily by commercial profit, whereas others are investing their time, money, or energy in what they perceive to be the symbolic capital produced by reading events. All creative labor that produces cultural events focused on the sharing of reading brings with it some influence on public opinion about the value of book reading and literary taste. Similarly, all cultural workers situated within what we characterize in this book as the reading industry benefit from the social prestige that is attached to the relatively "high culture" practice of book reading, and to their own "artistry and knowledge" as professional and/or expert readers (Hesmondhalgh and Baker 2008, 102). Feeling and enacting "a passion for reading" is, as we noted above, a legitimate emotion for workers in this arena, who frequently seek to reproduce that "passion" via a face-to-face event so that other readers may experience a similar sensation.

If an organizer's knowledge, passion, and social conviction are in evidence as part of her self-presentation—or performance—in public, what is obscured? When a worker in the reading industry represents a public institution such as a library or a nonprofit arts organization, her material body is usually rendered invisible: at the very least, it becomes a substitute for the larger, noncorporeal body of the agency that employs her to mediate between institutions, the public, and commercial markets (in an era of late capitalist consumption, books are commodities; shared reading events are just one leisure option among many). In less public circumstances, such as an interview or conversation with coworkers, vocational rhetoric may also efface the worker's body and the materiality of her labor. The worker's expression of emotional commitment (the "passion for reading") can easily sweep aside the detail of her work; the rhetoric of service (the love of the job) often masks the day-to-day pragmatic challenges involved, and altruism (e.g., "It's important work, so it's worth it") glosses over any ideological tensions that may be bound up in the mediating role. If, however, we understand the expression of "a passion for reading" as an embodied belief that inspires and motivates many event organizers, then it becomes important to analyze cultural labor as a set of material practices, not just as a set of values about shared reading.

Before examining the costs of those practices, we introduce three key cultural workers whose labor is especially significant to our study of the contemporary formations of shared reading. It would, in fact, be more accurate to describe these three women as cultural *managers* who lead teams of workers. Unlike many of their work colleagues, whose creative labor is rarely publicly acknowledged, Nancy Pearl, Chris Higashi, and Jane Davis have all received local, national, or international recognition for their work within the reading industry. However, as we shall see, they are differently positioned within that industry because they have acquired different amounts of social and cultural capital. As we related in Chapter 1, "Reading," Nancy Pearl and Chris Higashi are the initiators of Seattle Reads, the first OBOC program in the world, which was begun in 1998, whereas Jane Davis is the founder of Get Into Reading (GIR), a grassroots group reading program that she initiated in Liverpool, UK, in 2001. The cultural and creative labor of these women impacted the contemporary meanings of reading in North America and the UK because they have developed innovative and adaptable models for shared reading that have been successful well beyond their original and local contexts. Indeed, they have all actively encouraged the "creative reinvention" of their models by others (Grams 2008, 194).

SOCIAL MISSION: READING FOR CHANGE

Although their life stories and experiences of creative work are not identical, Pearl, Higashi and Davis all believe that reading—and sharing—books enables learning, social bonding, and, potentially, some kind of transformation. Their own passion for books combined with a sense of social mission to inform the models they created. Jane Davis's original goal was to take literature "out of the academy" and into communities where books and reading were rarely identified as a useful primary resource for recovery, well-being, or pleasure (pers. comm., 2005). In order to achieve this type of social change, the GIR model brings people from socially marginalized groups together with a trained facilitator. The GIR team defines socially marginalized groups as people who are from low-income backgrounds or who are subject to racism, ageism, or homophobia, or who have been rendered mentally and/or physically vulnerable due to ill-health, age, or addiction. From the perspective of the GIR team, such groups cannot access educational opportunities or cultural activities as readily as, for example, middle-class British people whose greater economic and cultural capital lend them a greater degree of social agency within contemporary UK society. Moreover, the people who join GIR groups are often experiencing social isolation and low self-confidence, as a result of their social, physical, and economic circumstances. Reading and talking about literature is perceived by Davis as "a kind of social glue" that can help to overcome these challenges (pers. comm., 2005). The GIR facilitator reads selected texts aloud as a departure for group discussion, self-exploration, and emotional, empathetic connection among group members. GIR groups generally operate weekly and last from a few months to several years, depending on the circumstances and needs of the group. During the life of the group, the membership may alter and a range of texts—poems, stories, plays, and novels—may be chosen.

By contrast, as we described in our brief history of the OBOC model in Chapter 1, "Reading," the programs pioneered by Nancy Pearl and Chris Higashi usually run annually for a period of between two to four months, with just one selected text as the focus of attention. Pearl and Higashi's model operates on a citywide scale, and their version of it, Seattle Reads, involves a series of high-profile public events as well as smaller group-based book discussions. The format holds a strong appeal for keen readers, many of whom belong to the city's vibrant network of book clubs. Despite the differences in scale and constituency from the GIR model, Pearl and Higashi's program is informed by ideals that resonate with Davis's: the belief that the sharing of reading, especially when this involves literary fiction, can promote not only self-understanding for the individual reader, but also improve social cohesion within and across communities.

This ideal of social change, then, is part of the ideological or symbolic cultural work that these shared reading models are expected to perform, although these ideals are inevitably inflected, not only by the sense of social mission of each model's creators, but also by local circumstances. Even the cofounders of Seattle Reads articulate the values of their program differently. For Nancy Pearl, bringing people together to share reading helps to overcome social isolation and the individual's experience of fragmentation by promoting what she describes as a "shared humanity" (pers. comm., 2006). For her colleague, Chris Higashi, the OBOC model has come to adopt a more explicit sociopolitical goal to engage with Seattle's Asian- and African-heritage communities and to encourage cross-cultural understanding (pers. comm., 2006). Both these images of social bonding are informed by a liberal humanist politics that combines the "liberating" and "civilizing" projects that have historically been attached to reading. We discussed several such historical examples of shared reading in Chapter 1, "Reading." Here it is important to note that the discourses of reading as "liberating" or "civilizing" are not mutually exclusive, nor are they inherently conservative or inherently radical in ideological terms. Deborah Brandt suggests that, in the post–World War II United States, an emphasis on the "civilizing" effects of book reading on the individual was underwritten by a functionalist notion of literacy that equated it with economic productivity (2004, 494–99). Her analysis of the relationship between the ideology and economics of literacy goes some way to explain the appeal of the Higashi-Pearl OBOC model for the NEA's Big Read program that we examined in the previous chapter. As Wendy Griswold and her colleagues have highlighted, cities and government agencies support book programs because of the "extraordinary value" that society places on reading (2008, 59) and the "almost unquestioned assumption that reading and talking about reading is a social good" (Griswold, McDonnell, and Wright 2005, 135). Examining the cultural labor and beliefs of the organizers who deliver these programs is one way of interrogating that assumption.

ROCK STARS AND RENEGADES: GLAMOUR AND CELEBRITY IN THE READING INDUSTRY

In order to deliver successful events, managers like Higashi, Pearl, and Davis have to mediate between their own ideals and the goals of the institutions and funding agencies that finance their shared reading programs. Part of the skill involved in this type of cultural work lies in the ability of the organizer to align various social and ethical objectives and yet allow her team to retain some creative agency in terms of testing out new kinds of activities, venues, or partnerships, for example. Operating in the cultural arena of books and readers presents other challenges to mediation, however, that may threaten to obscure the social mission element of cultural work through instantiating a process of commodification. There is a degree of glamour attached to working in this area, thanks to the rise of blockbuster publishing that involves spotlighting a handful of books and authors in the hope of producing a best-seller and a literary celebrity (Fuller 2008; Godard 2000; MacSkimming 2003; Squires 2007). A brush with celebrity culture can certainly offer some compensation for hours of mundane hard work. Several reading event organizers mentioned wining and dining famous authors whose books they admire and enjoy as an exciting and pleasurable aspect of their job. Higashi, the organizer of Seattle Reads, was especially exhilarated by Isabel Allende's 2004 visit to her citywide reading program (pers. comm., 2006). Similarly, the organizers in Kitchener-Waterloo-Cambridge were deeply impressed by the charm, stamina, and sincerity of Impac-winning Canadian author Alistair MacLeod whose novel, *No Great Mischief*, was selected for their first OBOC event held in 2002 (pers. comm., 2003).

The celebrity quotient of reading events and the attendant glamour factor have increased with the involvement of the media industry in the publication and promotion of literary fiction through carefully marketed broadcast events such as the RJBC and *Canada Reads*, which we examined in Chapters 2 and 3, "Television," and "Radio." Amanda Ross, the cultural manager who produced the UK's *Richard & Judy* television show and the "inventor" of their Book Club, is certainly at the higher end of the glamour spectrum, not least because of her association with Britain's most famous television couple. Aside from the film industry, television is still the most powerful (and celebrity-studded) of the media and creative industries, and Ross herself became something of a celebrity because of the economic influence that the increased sales generated by the RJBC had on British book publishing as we noted in Chapter 4, "Money" (Dugdale 2006; Hattersley 2006; Langley 2007; Tivnan 2008). Unlike Higashi, Pearl, and Davis, however, Ross has never claimed that the Book Club was intended to create social change. Her capacity to turn the authors of selected books into millionaires was thus not at odds with her goal of making entertaining television that helped viewers to choose a book that they might enjoy reading and, perhaps, talking about with friends. In fact, as we argued in Chapter 2, "Television," from a production point of view, the commodification of the Book Club selections through marketing and advertising played a crucial role in the TV Book Club's success.

Ross's celebrity status highlights how different cultural workers and managers possess differing amounts of symbolic and cultural capital, social influence, institutional power, and public visibility. Even those working within the same organization are differently positioned in relation to celebrity and commodity culture. Whereas Pearl has won transnational fame and fortune as a "rock star" librarian, Higashi's role as a co-creator of the OBOC model is not well-known and is rarely recognized outside of Seattle. Higashi's narratives about her labor articulate emotional satisfaction and her ethical commitment to the program, but her stories also express the toxic effects of overwork. Her mixed vocabulary of love and fatigue was echoed by many organizers whom we interviewed when talking about their work. Their commentaries underline how exhaustion and low morale are also part of vocationally driven creative work, and their words describe the physical and psychological toll exacted upon their bodies. These narratives trouble the idealized notion of "a labor of love," and suggest ways in which passionate work is demanding even (perhaps especially) for those with deep ideological convictions and in possession of charismatic personalities.

Jane Davis, the subject of our second main case study, for example, is an inspired cultural manager and an inspiring team leader. Her ability to articulate her "passion for reading" and social mission is central to the recruitment of new GIR facilitators and project funders. Davis aims to produce nothing less than what she terms a "Reading Revolution" (pers. comm., 2006). Her community-centered work resembles social activism in its desire to effect structural change and in terms of both the skills and practices evolved within the organization of GIR. In the early days of GIR, Jane Davis could be characterized as a "renegade" working at a distance from the ruling relations of power.[2] Now that the GIR model has received awards and national media coverage and has been replicated in several different regions of the UK, often with the institutional and financial support of the National Health Service (NHS), Davis has a more complicated set of mediations to perform in order to keep her "revolution" on its ideological track.

PASSIONATE WORK AS EMBODIED WORK

Whether, like Jane Davis, cultural managers can be categorized as "renegades" or, like Nancy Pearl, as "rock stars" benefiting more directly from celebrity commodity culture, it is crucial not to allow the ideological force of cultural managers' labor and the symbolic power of the products they help to create and disseminate, to overdetermine the analysis of their cultural work. The material conditions within which that labor is carried out are significant, especially if cultural work is understood as embodied work. Recent analyses of cultural work within the creative and cultural industries have, for instance, highlighted issues of precarity and casualization (see, e.g., Banks 2007, 2009; Beck 2003, 4), overwork and "bulimic time patterns" (Gill and Pratt, 2008; McRobbie, 2006, 2007), and the handling of "emotional labor" (Hesmondhalgh and Baker 2008, 105) as aspects of "cultural labor in altered times" (Murdock 2003, 15). These "altered times" and working conditions have been produced by, among other factors, economic pressures, including cuts in public funding to the arts and culture industries as we discussed in Chapter 4, "Money." Other alterations include the organizational restructuring that was often prompted by transnational company mergers and buyouts, and the vertical integration that often accompanied these within particular industries such as media and publishing (Hemmungs Wirtén [2007] 2009) as we explored in the last chapter. Technological innovations, especially digital technologies, have also had an impact on the physical working environments and the temporal demands experienced by workers in the creative industries.

Taking our cue from contemporary cultural studies scholarship, we make sense of cultural labor in a way that honors the workers' own experience and knowledge (Gill and Pratt 2008, 19, 21), while attending to the specificity of the cultural sector within which they work (Hesmondhalgh and Baker 2008, 99, 101) and the material conditions within which reading events are organized. We believe that thinking about the cultural work of MRE organizers involves recognizing how some aspects of their labor reproduce normative values about reading and books. At the same time, we respect their commitment to social change, their professional achievements, and their willingness to help us in our own labor as researchers of shared reading events. We take their "passion for reading" seriously, and understand this expression as a heartfelt emotion that motivates and is in excess of the material and ideological labor undertaken in its name. Analyzing the labor and beliefs of cultural workers enables us to understand the relationship between institutional ideological imperatives and an individual worker's commitment to a politics of social change. It also allows us to examine the tension between discourses of "reading as liberating" and "reading as civilizing" that inflects the organization, rhetoric, and ideology of MREs. We conceptualize their type of cultural labor as an act of nonromantic love lived out in public. But such an act of love, a performance, or iteration of "a passion for reading," exacts cost from the worker's body and well-being, and frequently involves an emotional effort on her part that may be as great as or in excess of the performance of physical and ideological work. Such materialities and complications are, however, often obscured by contemporary commodity culture. A striking example is provided by the plastic reproduction of Nancy Pearl's body as an action-figure that can be purchased online.

"SECOND ONLY TO JESUS": THE CULTURAL WORKER AS ROCK STAR

Nancy Pearl is probably "the world's most famous librarian."[3] Her celebrity profile is "second only to Jesus" (pers. comm., 2006). Or, to be more accurate, worldwide sales of the plastic action figure made in her image are "second only" to those of the Jesus action-figure from the same series. Pearl's disciples, her colleagues, and readers who purchase the figure presumably have a sense of humor about the cultural stereotyping of librarians: dressed in a rather shapeless, dowdy suit, the mini-Nancy's right arm can be moved by pressing a button on her back, bringing her index finger to her lips in "an amazing 'shushing action'."[4] Ironically, it is difficult to imagine the real-life Nancy Pearl asking anyone to be quiet in a library: she is much more likely to engage a library patron in a conversation about his or her current mood and the type of pleasure that he or she takes in reading books of various kinds. That, at least, is what she counsels her colleagues to do when she is involved in professional development events with Reader Advisory librarians (Pearl 2008).

Whether the appeal of the action figure lays in its ironic reference to mainstream stereotypes of librarians or not, the original icon proved to be so popular that the manufacturers exploited its success by releasing a second, "deluxe" model. In common with special editions of Barbie and Action Man/GI Joe, this "Nancy" comes with accessories: a computer monitor, several stacks of tiny plastic books, and a shelving trolley. These items bear little relationship to the daily realities of work for the majority of professionally trained graduate librarians, who are more likely to be applying specialist skills within particular fields such as digital assets management, Youth or Children's programming, or Reader Advisory with adults. However, reshelving is part of the repetitive labor performed by library assistants in public and private libraries around the world. Even for library workers who are unfamiliar with Pearl's creed and products, the action figure offers a potential means of identification with this fantasy image of a "star" librarian.

Pearl is in fact a "rock star librarian" with a self-confessed addiction (to books), one who is involved in global travel and well-attended performances, has a transnational fan-base and inspires "wannabes"—at least one of whom writes a blog, *Nancy Pearl Wannabe*. Retired from her role as Executive Director of the Washington Center for the Book in Seattle, Pearl's current work aligns her more closely with the writers involved with OBOC programs than their organizers or her fellow-librarians. Having left a public-service organization, Pearl's freelance portfolio resembles that of many workers within the contemporary cultural industries whose experience of working outside of institutions and large organizations is "less secure, more responsible and more autonomous" (Hesmondhalgh [2002] 2007, 199). Unlike the majority of cultural industry workers, however, Pearl has achieved fame not only within her professional realm in North America and the UK, but her books, broadcasts, and online recommendations are also familiar to many readers who belong to book groups in the US and Canada. She is the best-selling author of three books that recommend "good reads," and her public advocacy of pleasure reading "for every mood, moment, and reason" extends beyond print into other media, including a Twitter account (Pearl 2005, cover). As a regular contributor to National Public Radio's *Morning Edition* and its affiliate stations in Seattle and Tulsa, Pearl is able to promote her ideology about reading as "pure pleasure" (as well as her star persona) via her commentary and selections. Her website, maintained by Pearl and her publisher, Sasquatch Books, includes biographical and "tour" information as well as "The Book Lust Shop." Fans can buy customized products, such as calendars and reading journals, via the website, but there is also the opportunity to enter into a more dialogic and noncommercial form of exchange with an "expert" reader via "Nancy Pearl's Book Lust Wiki," billed as a "community for book lovers." Here, then, is another example of the ways in which the commercial, social, and creative-interpretive practices associated with books and reading can coexist within a twenty-first-century media environment without any explicit acknowledgment of conflicting value systems. Jim Collins suggests that there is no conflict in a converged media environment because Pearl is a "national librarian," that is, one of the "new reading authorities [who] had to emerge from within the mass media in order to reach a mass audience of readers in hot pursuit of the right book" (2010, 81). However, as we discuss below, Pearl's transformation of her specialized book knowledge from cultural to economic capital, and her criss-crossing of both professional-public sector and commercial fields, have met with some criticism from professionals within library science. Pearl's entrepreneurial profile as both a manager and maker of symbolic products for the reading industry also differentiates her position from that of her former colleague, Chris Higashi. Pearl's various work roles—as teacher, author, radio host, consultant, and librarian—have increased her cultural capital. Her expertise as a reader's guide has been legitimated by university institutions and professional associations, whereas Higashi's has not.

Pearl's deployment of multiple media and social networking technologies may well be inspired by her original profession and its involvement in the management of knowledge and information, but it also responds to the market economy of twenty-first-century celebrity. In the digital age of information-overload, celebrity is entwined with and sustained by cross-media visibility. Stardom is produced by and depends on not only the proliferation of images and branded products, but also the ability of the personality and her publicity agents to adapt to and mobilize across new media platforms as they rise and fade in popularity. Historically, this has been a challenge faced by public relations professionals and the cultural industries since the early twentieth century, but it is complicated in the contemporary moment by digital technologies with applications that alter quickly, and which blur and alter the roles of consumer and producer (Breakenridge 2008; Gamson [1992] 2007, 152). Within this challenging environment, Pearl, her literary agent, and her publishers have successfully aligned her brand, products, and public persona. In addition to maintaining a direct means of communication with her wider public via the Wiki, Pearl's messages about reading are consistently "reader-centric" and privilege an individualized reader identity that is likely to appeal to many enthusiastic readers. Her publications and presentations focus on the reader's mood, the interpretative "doorways" that individuals take into books, and an advocacy of eclectic reading (Pearl 2008). Publicly declaring her own identity as a "promiscuous reader" and a "readeraholic" as a way of connecting with nonprofessional readers (2005, ix), Pearl is often photographed hugging books to her chest (and who would dare wrest them away from her?!), while offering the camera a broad and satisfied smile. Even the titles of her books, *Book Lust*, *More Book Lust*, and *Book Crush*, equate the desire for reading with sexual appetite, as well as referring to the appropriative aspects of our consumer-oriented culture.

Clearly, Pearl has, through a mixture of talent, hard work, and the right contacts, managed to market her own "passion for reading" very effectively. Professionally, her expertise in Reader Advisory is sought after, and in addition to teaching occasional courses within the Library Science program at the University of Washington, Pearl is a popular speaker and workshop leader for professional development activities within North America. She is also accredited with cultural authority by major state US institutions such as the NEA for whom she acted as a consultant on the Big Read program. More controversially, and in another cross-over between the public and commercial functions of her cultural labor, Pearl's brand of literary taste in the form of Pearl's Picks™ was sold to the publisher EBSCO as content for its NoveList database. One of several commercially produced reading recommendation tools used by public libraries within North America, NoveList is also available to UK libraries.[5] Canadian library scholars Juris Dilveko and Candice Magowan are highly critical of these electronic databases that, in their opinion, turn "library staff members [into] little more than low-paid, deskilled, and devalorized check-out clerks" (2007, 171). Whereas the prospect of the branch library becoming akin to a supermarket is likely to put fear into the hearts of most book-loving patrons and library professionals, Dilveko and McGowen's (ibid., 185) own empirical research demonstrates that trainee graduate librarians found NoveList to be a useful tool for their Reader Advisory work and one that expanded their book knowledge rather than replacing it. What is informative about their critique for our examination of cultural work and the meanings of reading is the anxiety it exhibits about the status and future of professional knowledge in a commercial, digital environment, and the threat posed to the promotion of reading as the pursuit of "meaningful education through serious and purposeful literature" (172). If electronic resources can produce reading recommendations tailor-made to an individual library patron's personal "entertainment" needs, who will promote "analytical reading," they ask (185)? The tension between "pleasure" and "critical" reading, or books for education versus books for entertainment, is a historical and enduring tension within the discourse and practices of the library profession in the English-speaking northern hemisphere (Lamonde et al. 2005, 265; Pawley 2003, 100; Radway 2007, 232; Wiegand 2009, 432–33). It is also symptomatic of a more widely articulated early-twenty-first-century unease with the resignification of books and reading as a popular pursuit that can be easily accessed and consumed via mass and digital media. As we argued in Chapters 2 and 3, "Television" and "Radio," the remediation of both material object (book) and practice (emphasizing the sharing of reading and its pleasures) via television shows such as *The Oprah Winfrey Show* and *Richard & Judy*, has been met with anxiety by many keen readers in our study. Their association of television with "low culture" and their suspicion of the media conglomerates that stand to profit from the high-level sales generated by successful television book clubs suggest a perceived threat to the acquisition of cultural capital. Whereas these anxieties may echo responses to new technologies and shifts in patterns of consumption that occurred in both the nineteenth and early twentieth centuries, they are nonetheless concerns that have particular significance for constituencies such as lower-middle-class women, whose relationship to esteemed cultural practices may be experienced as fragile and insecure.

Significantly, given our own interrogation of the contemporary literary field in this book, Dilevko and McGowen (2007) are particularly piqued by the widespread dissemination of Pearl's reading tastes via commercially produced byte-sized data. They critique both medium and message in strong terms. Drawing on Bourdieu's (1993) analysis of "the logic of commercial production," Dilevko and McGowen conceptualize Pearl's collaboration with NoveList as symptomatic of the ever-increasing circulation and market-dominance of "entertainment-oriented bestselling books . . . chosen by and filtered through distance and organization" (2007, 172). It is not only the loss of specialist knowledge provided by direct contact between library patron and library professional that is being lamented here, but an anxiety about the "dumbing down" of the meanings of reading.

With close reference to Pearl's best-selling books of reading recommendations, Dilevko and McGowen convincingly argue that Pearl is biased, unbalanced, and ideologically naïve in her book selections (188–92). Nancy Pearl is thus an unsettling figure for some of her colleagues, and perhaps for other readers who share the belief that reading is not only about leisure and learning, but also about complicating and problematizing one's world-view. But her success also troubles the old-style, clear-cut divisions between producers and consumers that are disappearing in an age of media convergence and increased online activity. Nancy Pearl is a type of "double-agent" within the reading industry: she is both an intermediary and a celebrity producer, both a consecrator of other people's texts and of her own.

It's a Library Thing™

The commodification of Pearl's "professional" image via the plastic action-figure, of her knowledge via NoveList, and the perpetuation of her brand values via objects such as a calendar and the *Book Lust* journal shape and perpetuate her celebrity. As products of a commodity culture, these items necessarily obscure the labor that made them as well as the labor of Pearl's former colleague and cofounder of the OBOC model, Chris Higashi. Nancy Pearl has become the "poster girl" of OBOC programming. By contrast, its co-creator, Chris Higashi, rarely receives any public recognition for initiating a mode of shared reading that has been widely replicated not only in the US and Canada, but also in Europe, Singapore, and Australia. What started out for Higashi and Pearl as a project sponsored by the Wallace Foundation, which they hoped would connect up the numerous book groups proliferating within the Seattle public library system, has now become more prescriptively applied as the NEA seek a remedy for the "decline" in "literary reading in the US" (NEA 2005), as we discussed in Chapter 4, "Money."

The Seattle Reads program, which began in 1998 as "If All of Seattle Read the Same Book . . .", is still a library-driven operation that is deeply entwined with the city's many book clubs. According to Chris Higashi, by 2006 there were four hundred book groups registered with the Seattle Public Library, with one hundred and fifty groups borrowing materials every month (pers. comm., 2006). In a city with a population of 594,210 people,[6] this is an impressive figure, especially because they are likely to be many more book groups that are not registered at the library (pers. comm., 2006). In order to "maximize their book group money," Higashi and her colleagues operate an "honor system" for their book-club book bundles (ibid.). This saves on cataloguing costs that run at upward of $25 US per book (ibid.) or twice the cover price of many mass-market trade paperbacks, and enables groups who do not meet at the library to benefit from the collection. The public library system's extensive support for shared reading exists in the context of a city that offers strong infrastructural support for its "reading class." Wendy Griswold's (2008) analysis of the ways that places and regions inhabited by groups of affluent and literate people produce and reproduce reading cultures is also applicable to Seattle. Certainly, Seattle's well-educated citizens perceive it to be a cultured and politically liberal city. Readers in our focus groups were quick to inform us that their city was the most literate in the US, an accolade first achieved and reported in *USA Today* in November 2005 (Marklein 2005). Leah's (Seattle Reads FG 3 NP, 2007) perception of her city was based, in part, on media coverage of this study and also on her observation that, "There are definitely tons of book shops." During another focus group, Diane and Emily offered images of Seattle as a "reading town" and suggested some humorous, but credible, local incentives for reading as well as some of the more unusual spaces in which reading is observable:

Diane: Seattle's a reading town. Like, per capita, just like David indicated about the libraries, they have more library support per capita than any other city. There are more book stores per capita, more books sold per capita. I think it's because of the weather. [group laughter]

Diane: Well, I mean, it rains ten months of the bloody year. And video, all anybody wants to do is go out and rent a video. Now, that's a phenomenon I never experienced until I moved to Seattle.

Anouk: So, rent videos rather than read, or rent videos and read?

Diane: In other words, all they want to do is rent videos and read here. There's nothing else to do.

[. . .]

Emily: I always see people on the bus reading.

Diane: They walk down the street reading!

Emily: Yeah, I do that. I'm like, "I can't put this book down." (Seattle Reads FG 5 P, 2007)

Not all of these readers, who were in their twenties and thirties and who identified themselves as belonging to a variety of ethnic groups, had heard about Seattle Reads, although most of them were library patrons. Nevertheless, in their opinion, the public library system is well used, and this belief was derived from their experiences of being on long library "wait lists" for new books, which led David to comment: "I was number 75 for *The Hot Sun* when it first came out," whereas Melissa noted that "the holds last, like a year or something, and some of them expire before you get them" (ibid.).

These readers' perceptions, as the "America's Most Literate Cities" studies evidence, are well-founded. In a series of annual research studies, the city has either placed first (2006), second (2007), or joint first (with Minneapolis, 2008).[7] Seattle also ranks particularly highly for its large number of bookstores (used and new), and in 2008, placed fifth in terms of library support (number of branch libraries per 10,000 of population), holdings, and utilization (J. W. Miller 2008). When Seattle's citizens visit their library, they can either go to one of the many upgraded neighborhood branches or the impressive showpiece downtown library building that was designed by

Rem Koolhaas and completed in 2004. Like its funky and popular Canadian counterpart across the border in Vancouver, Canada, the Seattle main library is spacious, with plenty of places for friends to meet: this is library as destination, not just a waypoint to finding a book to read or free Internet time. Other aspects of Seattle's book culture reflect not only the city's technology industry, but also relatively recent changes in book retailing. Amazon, founded by Jeff Bezos in 1994, has its home base in the city, and Costco, an important supermarket retail outlet for books in the United States, has its headquarters there. Even the man who decides which book will be featured in seven thousand US branches of Starbucks is a native of Seattle, although the Starbucks Entertainment content team exchanged the city for Los Angeles in 2006. Seattle, as Jim Collins has also noted, has become a city where "literary taste making" for the whole of the United States occurs (2010, 81).

It was within this print-culture-friendly context that Higashi and Pearl decided to make a grant application to the Wallace Foundation in 1997, and their project idea, "which was really about sort of making a big, giant book group" was grounded by the existence of "this network of book groups that we already had contact with, that we had a way to reach, who would potentially and very likely be interested in this project" (C. Higashi, pers. comm., 2006). The basic model has altered very little since 1998, except for a title change to "Seattle Reads" and a once-only deviation from the selection of one book to the oeuvre of a selected author (Isabel Allende) in 2004. Seattle Reads originally reached its peak in March each year, with a series of events featuring the author of the selected book. However, bureaucratic difficulties with Marjane Satrapi's travel visa delayed the 2006 author events by several months, extending the "build up" time well into spring of that year. As Higashi explained, various logistics of OBOC have to be organized so that the public visibility of the program does not dissipate across time. The unexpected delay of an author visit adds pressure to the organizer's workload, especially in terms of keeping interest in the events alive. Seattle's program requires the circulation of extra copies throughout the library system (in the case of Satrapi's *Persepolis*, about 1,100 books) while "preliminary and related programming that's about the book, that's about the topic of the book" occurs, all in time for the author's visit in May of the same year (ibid.). Subsequent Seattle Reads schedules have kept to this Spring timing with book selections announced (and library copies in place) as early as the previous November. The program's website makes a direct appeal to book groups by offering a means to reserve the Seattle Reads title, and a downloadable version of the *Reading Group Toolbox*, a printed reader's guide for the selected book, which typically includes an interview with the author, contextual information, further reading suggestions, and advice about how to organize a book group discussion. The reading guide, author events, and book group discussions in branch libraries are recognizable as the core materials for most OBOC programs and, more significantly, of the OBOC model adopted by the NEA for their Big Read program.

For Chris Higashi and Nancy Pearl, the Seattle program was—and remains—an attempt to expand the already-popular phenomenon of the book group to a citywide experience, while keeping the Seattle Public Library as the organizational locus and book groups as its key constituency. These features guarantee an audience at main events and loans of the books, but, as some of the readers we met pointed out, they can also exclude new immigrants; busy, time-pressured professionals; and people who are not sufficiently confident in their literacy to visit their local library. Emily's reflections during a focus group on the books that were chosen for Seattle Reads led her to question the aims and library-focus of the program:

> I would just kind of wonder, like, yeah, who does attend these things, and who do they want to bring in? And is it bringing in the people that they want to? Because if it's only bringing in people who already do use the library a lot, then I would wonder if that's really accomplishing what you know, the purpose of a library . . . you know, they talk about making books and resources accessible to all sorts of people. . . . (Seattle Reads FG 5 P, 2007)

There are other types of limits. As Chris Higashi pointed out, there are many potential partners who would like to be involved in Seattle Reads, particularly schools and agencies focused on encouraging print literacy among young people (pers. comm., 2006). In 2006, Higashi received numerous phone calls requesting a visit from Marjane Satrapi, author of the already-popular, two-volume graphic memoir, *Persepolis*, but constraints of time, energy, and money meant turning down practically all the requests. For some community workers, this situation was perceived as resulting from the library-centric nature of Seattle Reads. Bruce Burgett, a Professor at the University of Washington, who is involved in the Seattle chapter of the writing and publishing initiative 826, which is aimed at young people aged six to eighteen, commented: "Seattle Reads do their stuff at the library, so we were asking, 'Could Satrapi do something at 826?' And it didn't work out, she was difficult to schedule, and Seattle Reads is more a library thing. I'm more interested in creating networks" (pers. comm., 2006). Burgett's commentary about both the program and the library implies that the library is not networked into the Seattle arts and culture scene, at least not in the ways that he understands community networks to operate. Book groups in Seattle do, in fact, form a large network that is created and supported to a significant extent by the library, but this would be practically invisible to people who do not belong to the library or a book group.

Seattle Reads is indeed, a "library thing" (ibid.) that grew from the proliferation of book groups. These tend to operate as intimate, private communities rather than as open and public groups, even if their meeting spaces are libraries and bookstores rather than member's homes (Rehberg Sedo 2007). Through their work on Seattle Reads, Pearl and Higashi have created a series of public spaces and events within which existing book groups are more visible, at least to each other. Just as significant, perhaps, is the way that Seattle Reads lends institutional legitimacy to reading in groups: a leisure activity that is popular among women in the United States, and which, by association, is often viewed within the media as a gendered, even feminized activity (Elliot 2002; Robbins 2007). Many of the readers who we saw attending the main events in 2007 had come along with their book group. Nancy Pearl even acknowledged their presence from the stage and praised their participation, while she was interviewing Jhumpa Lahiri, the author of the 2007 Seattle Reads' selection *The Namesake* (2003). Glancing first at Lahiri and then out at the audience, the overwhelming majority of whom were women, Pearl exclaimed: "These are such good questions because you can see that book clubs have read these books and these are questions which have no resolved answers!"

Pearl's validation of the questions operates as approval of book-club discussion practices that explore different interpretations of and ideas about texts, rather than seeking consensus. These are, of course, practices that Pearl also advocates in her own publications, but this does not detract from the symbolic value conferred by her upon Seattle's book groups, especially given the highly mediated format of this particular "question and answer" session. During most author events, the usual practice is to take questions directly from the floor, but on this occasion, Higashi collected written questions on cards from the audience that she then handed to Pearl, who in turn addressed them to Lahiri. Readers were thus placed at a double-remove from the Pulitzer prize-winning author, Lahiri, and were also ventriloquized by "the world's most famous librarian," whose cultural authority was underlined by her physical proximity to Lahiri and the equal amount of introductory "hype," which preceded their joint arrival on-stage.

Such framing devices foreground some of the structures and contradictions of performing the author-function within contemporary literary star culture. The interview between Pearl and Lahiri took place at the Seattle Town Hall, formerly the property of the Church of Christ Scientist. A high ceiling, former pews ranged in semi-circles, and a stage lit for filming, created an atmosphere that was austere rather than intimate, despite the friendly tone established by Pearl in her opening conversational gambits. Yet, as the site for a meeting between an internationally recognized writer and a famous Reader Advisory librarian, the building was ironically appropriate in its referencing of religious ritual, community, and reverence. The layout of the space and the technical exigencies of recording the interview for local television and the library's archives, which included controlling the sound levels in an echoing room by having participants submit their "Q&A" questions on cards, positioned the audience as the witnesses to the discourse of special individuals who could not be directly approached or even vocally addressed. As Chris Rojek has commented about the agents, minders, and intermediaries who work for contemporary celebrities, the "retinue's management of contact between the celebrity and fans . . . enhances the aura of magic that surrounds the celebrity" (2007, 177). However, although Lahiri was poised, eloquent and intellectually astute throughout the one-and-a-half-hour event, her body language indicated that she was not entirely comfortable in a situation where contact with the audience was doubly mediated. Whereas Lahiri turned her gaze and opened her seated body to face the audience during the "question and answer" sections during two previous events, at the Town Hall she rarely did so, instead directing most of her answers at Pearl who, looking far more relaxed, was sitting on a comfortable chair angled toward her.

In contrast to the star turns performed on-stage by Pearl and Lahiri was the silent off-stage work of Higashi, who took the question cards that had been collected by other library staff from the audience and then passed them on to her former colleague. The symbolism of this public enactment of a work-place hierarchy is instructive because it foregrounds the power inequalities among team members who cooperate behind the scenes to deliver cultural events. From our viewpoint as researchers, there was a poignant aspect to this event during which Higashi's contribution as a cofounder of Seattle Reads was literally and publicly side-lined. As we examine below, both Higashi and Pearl have brought their ideas about "good books," book discussion, and their understanding of what shared reading can achieve to the program.

"What a Good Book Can Do"

We have highlighted the "Nancy and Chris" story, not just as an exemplar of celebrity culture in the arena of the reading industry, or the ways that "grassroots" programs can get co-opted by state-run institutions such as the NEA, but also because, underneath the glitz, their cultural labor involves ideological, material, and emotional effort that echoes that of other OBOC organizers such as the Huntsville librarians (Chapter 4, "Money") or the Kitchener-Waterloo-Cambridge committee (Chapter 6, "Reader"). Pearl and Higashi may, however, understand their position within the literary-cultural field more clearly than some of their colleagues. Each woman is conscious of her cultural capital and the values around literacy inflected by her professional training, university education, and current class position. Higashi's and Pearl's extensive knowledge of twentieth-century and contemporary writing, combined with their professional experience of facilitating book discussions and their advocacy of book groups, clearly informs their selections for Seattle Reads.

Pearl, for example, nominates a "good" OBOC choice as a "well-written" work that raises "deeper issues" (pers. comm., 2006). In her interview with us, she continues, "I think that literature has to be more than the felicitous use of language. I mean, I think it has—to be a book that you want to talk about, I think there has to be a moral dimension to it." Among the early selections that Pearl and Higashi made were Russell Banks's novel *The Sweet Hereafter* (1993), which was chosen for Seattle Reads in 1998;

Ernest J Gaines's *A Lesson Before Dying* (1997), selected in 1999; *A Gesture Life* (1999) by Chang-rae Lee, which was selected in 2003; and seven works by Isabel Allende (2004). These are critically acclaimed works of late-twentieth-century literary fiction that are neither formally experimental nor avant-garde. Most of the Seattle Reads selections are also recommended or referenced by Pearl in *Book Lust* or *More Book Lust*, which suggests that they are judicious and relatively accessible choices for an OBOC event that makes an explicit and prominent pitch to book groups on its website and in its publicity materials.

Chris Higashi's (pers. comm., 2006) analysis of a "good book discussion" foregrounds her belief in the emotional power of mimetic reading practices. Her experience as a book group leader who values this mode of reader engagement inflects her definition of the affective, but also self-reflective response, which a "good book" prompts in the reader:

> One of the things, I think, about a good novel is that the author does such a good job of, uh, painting that picture of that character that people start to think of those characters as real people. So, you know, people kept asking him things [about *The Sweet Hereafter*, the first "Seattle Reads" selection] like, "so, what happened to Billy? Did he go into counseling?" You know? They wanted to know what happened to that dad who was so furious and, you know, in pain and stuff like that. So, you know, it's that kind of thing that when people start to do that—I mean, you know, that's what a good book does, right? I mean, it really puts people into this world which is—another world—which is also theirs. I think that what makes for such a good book discussion is where there *are* these kinds of life issues and choices and decisions that characters make, that a reader can speculate about and kind of apply to their own life. (ibid.; emphasis in the original)

Interviewed separately, Pearl (pers. comm., 2006) echoed Higashi's (pers. comm., 2006) convictions about the type of individual identity work described above. Not surprisingly, Pearl also expressed her commitment to facilitated book talk: "moderated discussion is a really good—a *really* good way of getting people both to read more deeply into the book—[. . .] but also, to develop this sense of *shared humanity . . .*" (pers. comm., 2006; emphasis in the original).

As these comments suggest, Higashi's and Pearl's views are underpinned by a liberal humanist notion of subjectivity that posits the individual subject as cohesive, but capable of change. They not only understand shared reading as having a therapeutic value for the individual reader, but they also believe that it can have a more collective, socially transformative effect. How the instigators of the OBOC model conceptualize social transformation appears to differ, however. Pearl's (ibid.) idea that directed book talk develops a reader's "sense of shared humanity" infers that there are pedagogical processes and moral benefits to be gained by the individual within a group setting. Such ideals coincide with long-standing American notions about the value of reading as part of "self-cultivation" (Rubin 1992) and as a "social good," values that, as Wendy Griswold has suggested, frequently go unquestioned within contemporary US society (2008, 59). Further, whereas Pearl (pers. comm., 2006) is referring to a secular set of practices and scenes of reading, groups that are part of faith communities might well attribute the same goals (and combined pleasures) of edification, moral contemplation, and sociability to shared reading.[8]

Chris Higashi's (pers. comm., 2006) version of "transformation" is more sociopolitically nuanced than her colleague's, particularly when she describes her memories of the consciousness-raising effect that she believes some of the Seattle Reads programs have had on readers and event audiences. Higashi's commentary on the 2005 program centered on Julie Otsuka's (2003) novel *When the Emperor Was Divine* (see Figure 5.1) is particularly indicative of the OBOC event organizer's ethically motivated approach to her work. It also suggests that the OBOC model can effect social change by setting the scene for readers and participants to examine issues and histories that receive relatively little mainstream representation in other American media. Described by Random House Inc. on their American website as a novel that "reveals the dark underside of a period in American history," the events organized around Otsuka's book became, in Higashi's (pers. comm., 2006) words, "a celebration" of the many Japanese-American internment survivors living in Seattle when, on at least two occasions, they were asked by the person chairing the discussion to identify themselves by standing up. The recognition of the survivors' experience within a public setting was not a planned aspect of any 2005 event, but, when it occurred, Higashi understood its social significance, in part because of her personal and professional involvement with Seattle's Japanese-American community. As Higashi herself (ibid.) points out in her commentary, she facilitates a book group for older members of that community and her aunts are members of the generation who were involved in the internment. Her compelling narrative about the 2005 events expresses both her local knowledge of Seattle's history and her awareness of how the politics of recognition operates when shared histories of trauma and oppression are finally articulated and heard in a public setting. According to Higashi's interpretation of the events she witnessed, a public recognition of a racist act from the past occurred against the backdrop of contemporary urban regeneration—the latter symbolized for her by the establishment of a new neighborhood library:

> What happened was um, first of all, we were in a fairly newly opened branch library, um, a 10,000–square-foot library. They had been in this little horrid—and I mean, this *horrid* storefront for years, broken down, leaks, just a crappy thing. And this big new library and, you know, we had been talking it up a lot and doing a lot of book discussions there because it's a—there's a very strong Japanese-American community in

SEATTLE READS

WHEN THE EMPEROR WAS DIVINE

by Julie Otsuka

Meet the Author

Bainbridge Joins Seattle Reads

Thursday, May 5
7 p.m.

IslandWood
4450 Blakely Ave. N.E.
Bainbridge Island

For more information, call
Bainbridge Branch Library (206) 842-4162

This program is free and everyone is welcome. Tickets and reservations are not required.
Seating is limited; first come first seated. Books will be available for purchase and signing,
courtesy of Eagle Harbor Book Company.

"Seattle Reads *When the Emperor Was Divine*" is presented by the Washington Center for the Book at The Seattle Public Library. It is part of
"Reading Across the Map," a multi-year project to foster reading and discussion of works by authors of diverse cultures and ethnicities, made
possible by The Wallace Foundation, with additional support from KUOW 94.9 Northwest Public Radio and Anchor Books. "Bainbridge Joins
Seattle Reads" is made possible with support from IslandWood.

Figure 5.1 Seattle Reads 2005 Julie Otsuka Poster

Author Julie Otsuka's *When the Emperor was Divine* was the 2005 Seattle Reads
selection

Source: Authors' collection.

this neighborhood. And so, there were all these—and then, my aunts are in this book group that I facilitate, eighty-year-old aunts. And so, when—so Tommy Keda was moderating the discussion with Julie Otsuka, and at one point he—well, there's one more side, sorry—but he said, "You know, I notice that there are quite a few, um, Japanese-American seniors in the room tonight." So we had one hundred and thirty people squished into the room, and they were everywhere! But he said, "Um, can I ask those of you who were interned to please stand?" And you know, these people are not people who are used to calling attention to themselves, and so they rose very slowly: thirty of them from around the room. And the room—oh, you could just hear the sigh! And then, people applauded and cried. I mean, it was *unbelievable*; it was so moving. Yeah, I mean, every time I tell this story, you'd think a year later I could do it without weeping. (ibid.; emphasis in the original)

Higashi's (ibid.) account operates as testimony on two levels: her own witnessing of Japanese-American seniors, including her own aunts, having their experiences acknowledged and thus being "honored" by all those present, and the public, community recognition or witnessing of the internment experience. There is no guarantee of any kind of long-lasting transformation arising from this act of recognition, nor does Higashi make such a claim. Yet her narrative indicates the radical potential of the OBOC model when it brings people together to discuss issues that some participants might find emotionally upsetting or to explore ideas and experiences that unsettle normative social relations, official histories, and institutional structures. In such circumstances, shared reading becomes a social practice that is not only ideologically dynamic and disruptive, but also potentially creative and even politically empowering in terms of permitting citizens the agency to speak out loud about subjects that were tacit knowledge.

Significantly for our analysis of cultural work, Higashi's narrative about the "celebration" of Seattle's Japanese-American community also illustrates and enacts her role as a worker and a manager inspired by an ethical project. She reports her own response of being deeply moved, but she does not assume that others present felt the same way, although her comments that "you could just hear the *sigh*! And then, people applauded and *cried*" (our emphasis) suggest that some audience members did express an affective reaction. She continues:

And then, it happened again two nights later at another branch. And in the north-end of Seattle, not a very ethnically mixed neighborhood or anything, the same thing happened. You know? And again—I don't know: twenty, thirty people. You know, from the people who were children or born in the camps to the eighty-something year-olds, you know. And again, you know, they stood up and the same thing happened *but* the most interesting—*one* of the most interesting things to me was that also in the room at every event were the people who had been left behind, who saw their neighbors pack up and leave; the children who were in school one day and the next day, their classmates were all gone. So *those* people were all there, too. So, you know, oh my God! It was *so* moving because, you know, it wasn't our intent but I know what we did was we honored those people. (ibid.; emphasis in the original)

Higashi's foregrounding of the audience demographic at the second event and her interest in the presence of "the people who had been left behind, who saw the neighbors pack up and leave," indicates her comprehension of how a racist and traumatic act aimed at one cultural group can also fragment families and neighborhoods who may not be directly subject to the brutality of what was, in the case of the Japanese-American internment, a form of state-sanctioned violence. If, as Sara Ahmed has argued, an ethics of pain involves "being open to being affected by that which one cannot know or feel" (2004, 30), then Higashi's (pers. comm., 2006) emotional response to the cross-cultural effects of internment can be understood as an ethical act. Significantly, Higashi (ibid.) does not claim that she is seeking to reproduce her own emotive experience via her programming decisions, but her efforts to promote activities within specific branch libraries, the choice of text for the 2005 Seattle Reads, and her selection of an appropriate facilitator and venue seem to have contributed to these spontaneous moments of public recognition.

The ethical intention within Higashi's organizational work is also evidenced by her staging of a series of historical contexts for Otsuka's novel and in her promotion of a variety of narratives about the internment, presented through different media. She achieved this by partnering the Seattle Library with other cultural institutions. The experience of the internment was consequently represented in films by local filmmakers, an exhibit about one hundred years of Japanese-American history in Washington State was displayed at the main downtown Seattle Library and organized by the Wing Luke Asian Museum, and explored in a Fifth Avenue Theatre production of a play for children. Such a project corresponded to Higashi's institutionally authorized goal outlined in 2002 to the Wallace Foundation, who are key funders for the Center and thus for Seattle Reads, of "extending the reach of the Washington Center for the Book's programs to Seattle's Asian American, African American and Latino communities" (ibid.). The program's website publicity, which is also authored by Higashi, expands this outreach objective to incorporate the promotion of cross-cultural awareness: "Seattle Reads is designed to foster reading and discussion of works by authors of diverse cultures and ethnicities."

Such claims are easily made but less readily realized, of course, but the explicitly sociopolitical shift registered by these outreach goals and program aims has been supported by a series of book selections pertinent to particular cultural groups within the city. Because Higashi assumed the directorship of the Washington Center for the Book after Pearl's retirement in August 2004, she has overseen Seattle Reads programs focused on a novel examining the Japanese-American internment (2005); Marjane Satrapi's *Persepolis 1: The Story of a Childhood* (2003), a graphic memoir dealing with recent Iranian history and the experience of growing up within an Islamic state (2006); Jhumpa Lahiri's *The Namesake* (2003), which portrays the multigenerational experience of a Bengali family who emigrate to the United States (2007); *The Beautiful Things that Heaven Bears* (2007), a debut novel by Dinaw Mengestu that tells an even more tension-ridden story of immigration from the perspective of three African immigrants (2008); and, in 2009, the first year of Barack Obama's presidency, *My Jim* (2005) by Nancy Rawles, a Seattle-based writer, whose novel reimagines Mark Twain's *The Adventures of Huckleberry Finn* (1884) from the perspective of Jim's enslaved family. Like *Persepolis*, the 2010 selection, Laila Lalami's novel *Secret Son* (2009), is not set in the US and deals with issues of family, identity, and Islamic fundamentalism, this time in Morocco. Meanwhile, *Little Bee* (2009) by British author Chris Cleave was the focus of Seattle Reads in 2011 and *The Submission* (2011) by American writer Amy Waldman was the selection for 2012. Both novels deal with the personal or public legacies of traumatic events, and with conflicts between people that arise from the misunderstanding of ethnic and cultural differences. With the exception of *Persepolis*, these choices are all realist novels. Apart from Satrapi and Cleave, they are all books by writers living and working in the United States, and all the books were first published in the twenty-first century. In terms of their themes and the histories that they explore through fiction, these books speak to Higashi's desire to appeal to readers and potential readers from cultural groups who frequently experience social and economic exclusion. The cultural and political topicality of Higashi's choices also make sense in the Democratic left-leaning city of Seattle, whereas the concentration on contemporary American authors from different areas of the country frames Seattle Reads as an outward-looking program and prevents it (and the library) from appearing to be too parochial. The earlier Seattle Reads selections, by contrast, are more varied in terms of genre and subject, and, taken together, suggest that Pearl and Higashi were experimenting with what a "good book" can do within their still-evolving OBOC model.

Adding to the variety of Seattle Reads events and situating the selected book within its social, local, and historical contexts through other media was a further departure from the program's original focus on book group discussion and author events. The cultural work that Higashi performs through book choice and programming can thus be understood as an ethical act that is shaped by a coincidence of her professional experience; by institutional agenda, including the outreach function of the public library system; and Higashi's committed belief, inflected by her training as a librarian as well as by her own life experiences, in the capacity of books to teach people about events and communities that may not be given much mainstream representation. Higashi's motivation to educate the general public through the programming around the book selection is illustrated by her narration of an incident that occurred in her workplace during the 2005 Seattle Reads, when a younger colleague announced, "'What a great thing that you're doing this! I'm sure glad we didn't do—you know, I'm from Canada. I'm sure glad we didn't do that [intern Japanese Canadians].'" Higashi continued:

> And I said, "Uh...A—, you did." She said, "What?!" I said, "Canada not only interned the Japanese-Canadians; they took them to ghost towns. They took their property and sold it and kept the money! They did not permit them to return to the west coast after the war!" I mean, she was just flabbergasted. She came up several days later and she said, "I am so embarrassed." I said, "Well, don't be embarrassed, A—. You're"—first of all, she's younger; she's like a whole generation younger than I am. And, you know, it's the kind of thing that is not widely taught, so it's not that surprising. (pers. comm., 2006)

Recalling this exchange, Chris Higashi represents herself as assuming a mentoring role toward her colleague: dispelling her ignorance by teaching her the facts, and also reassuring her that embarrassment is neither a necessary nor (implicitly) an appropriate emotional response. Higashi's programming for *When the Emperor Was Divine* could be understood as extending the ethos of this intercollegial dialogue into a large and more heterogeneous community, where there are no guarantees that people will recognize their ignorance or reflect on their possible complicity in this or other racist acts.

"Sleepless in Seattle": Overwork and Its Affect

Higashi's experiences of the *When the Emperor Was Divine* author events at various branch libraries around Seattle underlines the potential for social change to occur at both an individual and at the collective, community level as a result of book selections that are pertinent to particular groups of city residents. Remembering a year later how moving it was for her and for others to see so many elders stand up to be recognized at this series of events, still made Higashi, who also identifies as a member of that community, cry. Higashi's articulation of her experience suggests, however, that the tears of the cultural worker be understood, not only as an expression of her conviction that Seattle Reads has a sociopolitical role to play in the cultural life of the city, but also an indicator of the emotional involvement she is prepared to expend over and over again. In other words, Higashi acknowledges the political, ethical, and emotional effect that may result from her own labor, and this operates as payback, a type of profit, for her efforts.

The type of work required to organize and run an OBOC event is, nevertheless, stressful as well as exhausting, both physically and emotionally. As David Hesmondhalgh and Sarah Baker have argued, "Cultural workers might be thought of as the pampered children of the bourgeoisie, and they may be relatively privileged compared with other kinds of worker, but the human costs of their working conditions are real enough" (2008, 103). Higashi expressed those "human costs" particularly vividly:

> I *am* the Center for the Book. I don't have anybody else . . . I nearly killed myself; I mean, I worked so—I just worked day and night. There were some months when I just did so many programs, it was insane! But I really—I mean, I found it hard to say no because these were all opportunities to bring—I think—to bring a lot of new people into the library who were not normally library users. (pers. comm., 2006; emphasis in the original)

Higashi's understanding of excessive work registers its disruption of liberal notions of temporality—what we have come to think of as "work/life balance." Such disruptions are commonly experienced by workers within the creative and cultural industries of this century (e.g., Banks 2007; Hesmondhalgh and Baker 2008; McRobbie 2002, 2006). Even more striking is Higashi's vision of herself as not only representing the Seattle Public Library's Center for the Book as its sole worker, "I *am* the Center for the Book" (pers. comm., 2006), but also her sense of becoming and embodying that institutional site. She is aware of the toxic effects on the body and mind, and her expression of her motivation for overwork ("to bring a lot of new people into the library . . .") is aligned with her professional commitment as a librarian to a public service ethic.

If the meanings that Higashi gives to her own labor are ignored, her actions could be interpreted simply as a form of complicity with structural-institutional pressures for cultural workers and managers to meet "performance indicators" that will help to secure public and private sector funding for future projects. Certainly, as several scholars have highlighted, the effects of creative labor can be "normative and disciplinary" for the cultural worker and can also contribute to forms of self-regulation that include the repetition of exhausting and bulimic work patterns (Banks 2007, 81–84; McRobbie 2002; Gill and Pratt 2008, 17). By attending to Higashi's understanding of her overwork, however, the coexistence of the pleasant and unpleasant aspects of high-intensity creative labor become visible. The adrenalin rush, feelings of inspiration, and the pleasure of sociability derived from Higashi's sense of direct engagement with the readers of Seattle are interwoven with the burden of responsibility for the organization and delivery of reading events, and the physical and mental stress endured. These feelings and experiences are embodied by the individual subject—"I *am* the Center for the Book" (pers. comm., 2006; emphasis in the original), but they are also structurally produced by the organization of the workplace. Institutions such as universities and public libraries, with their long histories of promoting liberal humanist understandings of edification for the "good" of the civilized subject and public, have, in these neoliberal times, come to rely increasingly on the "entrepreneurial" skills of their workers. For a creative library professional such as Chris Higashi, this translates into having to pitch projects to senior management in order to secure some internal resources, while also seeking external funding and partnerships with other organizations. Higashi's passion for books and for the OBOC model of shared reading can therefore be understood as both an affective and an effective driver of her committed approach to her work. Not only does this conflicted model of passionate work disrupt the social prestige and legitimacy lent to the notion of professional vocation, but emotional labor also becomes part of the librarian's required skill-set—yet not necessarily one that is rewarded by her employer.

Narratives of fatigue, overwork, and overtime labor (which is frequently not financially recompensed), motivated by a passionate commitment to promoting reading, books, and literacy, recurred in our interviews with cultural workers and managers. Before receiving their first NEA grant, the Huntsville, Alabama, team was on the verge of abandoning their OBOC program. Mary Wallace and Judy Purinton, two of the founding organizers, described their experience of several years of no-budget trial and error with the model using a mixture of self-deprecating good humor and exasperation at the energy they expended. Their mistakes included unsuccessful book selections, such as overpriced hardback books and genre fiction that failed to provoke discussion: "It's a thriller; there's a serial killer; you know, he cuts up a whole bunch of people; the end. You know what I mean? It was terrible! A terrible choice!" (Wallace, pers. comm., 2006). Fortunately, their 2006 NEA-supported program, which focused on F. Scott Fitzgerald's *The Great Gatsby* (1925), saw a greater number and cross-section of their community get involved. Wallace and Purinton told us, with great feeling, how this delayed payback for their efforts came just in time to inspire them to continue:

> Mary: I mean, it was exhausting, but I think if we hadn't had the response we had, we—well, *I* would've been crushed just because we spent so much of our time and our energy and our love into this project. You know, we wouldn't do it next year if it hadn't have been a success; at least *I* wouldn't have been a part of next year if it hadn't been a success.
>
> Judy: Yeah, it does just take too much time away from other stuff. (pers. comm., 2006; emphasis in the original)

Wallace and Purinton employ a vocabulary of love that is common among contemporary cultural workers (Gill and Pratt 2008, 15) but, like Chris Higashi, their discourse of love and passion is entangled with narratives of overwork and images of bodily and mental exhaustion. Judy Purinton's (pers. comm., 2006) observation about how working on OBOC diverted them away from other aspects of their regular jobs, also usefully forestalls any idealization of this "labor of love": the regular, perhaps more mundane, aspects of a worker's job do not disappear. Purinton's comment also indicates a difference in working environment between cultural workers like public librarians involved in creative programming, and workers located in small-scale or project-based market-driven cultural industries such as television production companies. Cultural workers in areas such as the music industry and television production may have less job security than the people whom we might term "institutional creatives" working within or very close to the public sector. However, they might also work within organizations with more flexible and project-responsive structures in terms of less institutional bureaucracy and more fluid team membership, for example. Notable among the cultural workers in our study are the original CBC *Canada Reads* production team featured in Chapter 3, "Radio," who cut through the traditional structures of working at the Toronto headquarters of Canada's national broadcaster to form a new interdisciplinary team especially for their MRE project (Fuller 2007, 14–15).

Whereas workers articulate the emotional, political, social, imaginative, and creative rewards of being involved in OBOC labor, they also nominate the deficits. Their narratives indicate that cultural labor within the arena of book programming is not only about knowledge and creativity, value-laden decisions, and budget constraints, it also demands an excess of energy, time, and imagination that may well be underpaid and unrecognized by the workers' organizations and institutions. However, because MREs are a "high-pop" product of the reading industry (Collins 2002), this particular type of cultural work can be understood as rich in symbolic capital even when its product or output reaches a relatively small or "niche" mass of readers. As the Seattle and Huntsville organizers demonstrate, their "passion for reading" not only informs their willingness to perform "passionate work" (McRobbie 2013), but it also inflects the symbolic meanings that the different OBOC adaptations produce and promote. A belief in the power of reading to initiate self-transformation in individuals and even to effect social change within Seattle shapes Chris Higashi's aspiration to create cross-cultural communities of liberal, civilized readers. Meanwhile Mary Wallace's and Judy Purinton's enthusiastic efforts "to be regional" informs their book choice and programming decisions so that the Huntsville-Madison County version of OBOC is in part an opportunity for readers to reexamine and reenact regional identities (as we demonstrate in Chapter 6, "Reader").

The second case study in this chapter focuses on a cultural manager who believes in shared reading as an experience that can radically transform individuals' lives by offering them a face-to-face community, a form of psychological healing and a quasi-spiritual environment. In Jane Davis's experience, the type of social change achievable via collective reading involves nothing less than making specialized book knowledge available to the most socioeconomically marginalized groups within contemporary British society: a project that is both underwritten by notions of reading as individually liberating and also by a community-activist ideology of tackling structural inequalities from the "grassroots."

READING AS "SOCIAL GLUE": THE
PHILOSOPHY OF A RENEGADE

Get Into Reading (GIR) is a not-for-profit organization and a registered charity running reading programs that was initiated by Jane Davis in the Wirral, near Liverpool, UK, in 2001.[9] Under Davis's direction, the GIR team has developed a model of small-group shared reading that involves people reading stories, poems, and novels aloud in the company and under the guidance of a trained facilitator. GIR deliberately selects what the facilitators define as socially and economically marginalized groups living in and around the Wirral, an area situated on a peninsula between the rivers Mersey and Dee due east and in sight of the city of Liverpool in the Northwest of England. People who have participated in GIR's eighty-strong network of reading groups include: elderly people in care-homes; people who have experienced drug and alcohol addiction; gay, lesbian, and transgendered people; vulnerable teens; asylum seekers; care givers; people with mental health issues; single parents; and patients recovering from major physical trauma to the spine who attend the neurological unit at the Walton Centre. Jane Davis has described shared reading as "social glue" (pers. comm., 2005), an image that suggests a fragmented society that requires piecing back together (Fuller and Procter 2009, 27). After several years of outreach work, Davis and her team began to employ slightly different imagery as part of their public mission statement on their website: "The groups aim to improve wellbeing, build community and extend reading pleasure . . . For us, reading is a force for social good that can build community and enhance lives" (The Reader Organisation, 2009). The subtle shift in meaning from restoring broken connections to a greater emphasis on the social agency and generative capacity of shared reading is indicative of the GIR team's profound belief in the transformative capabilities of their model. As our analysis of the team's practices and ideals indicate, these cultural workers posit the success of GIR as reaching beyond the provision of social connection among (damaged) human beings. The team understands the experience that GIR offers its reader-members as a hybrid of social opportunity, therapeutic support, educational process, and affective pleasure.

Alongside Liverpool Reads, a version of OBOC launched in Liverpool in September 2004, GIR represents one of the "outreach" strands of four programs coordinated by The Reader Organisation, of which Davis is Director. She began the organization as a literary print journal aimed at general readers, *The Reader*, first published in 1997, and edited, since 2008, by Phil Davis, Jane's life partner and a Professor of English at the University of Liverpool. Jane Davis is herself a doctoral graduate of the School of English at the University of Liverpool and a specialist in Victorian literature, whereas Phil Davis's research and teaching record demonstrate a long-standing commitment to understanding the social, cognitive, and psychological processes of reading.[10] These biographical details and the fact that the Reader

Organisation offices were located within a building belonging to University of Liverpool for several years suggest a close relationship with an educational institution and the possession of significant cultural capital by the Organisation's Director. Nonetheless, the situation of the GIR program within the ruling relations of power is complicated by its reliance on a combination of contract-based workers and volunteers and a mixture of private and public sector funding. A significant aspect of Jane Davis's workload during the first seven years of running the GIR program was the constant search and application for project-based funding derived from both the public sector (e.g., Britain's National Health Service and the Arts Council of England) and private foundations (most notably, the Paul Hamlyn Foundation and Esmée Fairburn Foundation). As we demonstrated in Chapter 4, "Money," accessing funds from agencies across both public and private sectors has become a feature of cultural funding in the UK, and we demonstrated there how Bristol, the first UK location for an OBOC program operates as a commercial organization. What distinguishes the GIR team from Bristol's Great Reading Adventure organizers and Bristol Cultural Development Partnership is their original and continuing philosophy as a community outreach project and their organizational practices, especially with regards to Davis's leadership. The Reader Organisation has, from its beginnings, undertaken partnership and alliance building with "grassroots" groups supporting, for example, asylum seekers and recent immigrants to Liverpool, and with formal institutions such as the University of Liverpool, the city government, and local for-profit companies.

There is some resemblance between these activities and the early days of community-based activism and social movement organizations. Further, as scholars of social movement theory have suggested, the transfer of skills, biographical availability (that is, reaching a life-phase where a person can commit time to social action), and informal networks, are key resources for those who form and manage organizations aiming to effect some form of social change (McAdam, McCarthy, and Zald 1988, 707–9, cited in Staggenborg, [2007] 2008, 31). Davis's (pers. comm., 2005) involvement in second-wave feminist activities and groups in Liverpool is one important influence on the ways in which she translates her politics into action. Davis, Angela MacMillan, and Sarah Coley, two colleagues with whom Davis originally taught literature within the Department of Continuing Education at the University of Liverpool began *The Reader* journal as a voluntary extension of their paid teaching work. Even when project funding provides wages for some GIR facilitators, the program and the Reader Organisation continue to rely heavily on volunteer and underpaid labor, from cofounders Macmillan and Coley, and from undergraduate interns. A significant factor enabling the Reader Organisation to thrive and develop is that its key workers, including Jane Davis, do not need nor do they expect to make a living wage from their labor. By devoting large amounts of time, effort, and knowledge to the organization in a consistent way over a period of years, these workers are responsible for producing a secure working environment for all of their colleagues in the face of financial precariousness. Their enthusiasm, ideological commitment, combined skills, and Davis's capacity as a manager, are thus crucial aspects of their work effort that sustain their project.

A further significant difference between most OBOC programs and GIR involves the sites in which GIR operates. Rather than bringing existing, returning, or potential readers into public libraries, town halls, and school gymnasia, as the majority of the OBOC projects in this study aim to do, GIR is a program that takes books, a facilitator, and the practice of shared reading into spaces that are not usually associated with reading books and engaging with literature. The GIR project very deliberately seeks out people who may never have identified themselves as readers, and whereas some members of their groups possess high-level reading skills and an existing relationship with books, there are others whose print literacy skills are not sufficient to enable them to read a poem or a book on their own. GIR workers therefore have to undertake considerable "legwork" in order to build relationships with vulnerable groups of people. They must turn up repeatedly and on a regular basis at a community center, homeless shelter, transition house, prison, primary school, or health clinic with no guarantee that potential group members will attend, participate, or stay for the full two-hour session. There is thus a precariousness of participation involved with GIR that is more extreme than the search for audience experienced by OBOC program organizers who can depend on a core constituency of regular library patrons, existing book groups, and voracious readers. Nevertheless, for all the cultural managers and workers whose labor is explored in this chapter, levels of participation are often the most obvious measure of their program's success, or, at least, information that can be clearly communicated to funders as indicative of their program's value. The difficulties of evaluating shared reading programs, which organizers know and experience as qualitative in their effects, impact, and legacy, are shared by GIR and OBOC workers alike.

Another parallel between GIR and community activism is Jane Davis's charismatic leadership. The model for GIR has evolved collaboratively through the practice of its core team of facilitators. However, the success of GIR as an organization that has expanded its reach within and outside the Wirral, won prizes, obtained funding, and attracted the interest and involvement of health professionals, businessmen, and support workers, is largely due to Davis's belief in the GIR's mission and her ability to persuade others to join it as a sponsor, volunteer, or community partner. Like Nancy Pearl, she has become the spokesperson for a model that, escalated by a feature article in the *Guardian* newspaper in January 2008, has increasingly attracted attention from both broadcast and print media (see Figure 5.2). The GIR project featured in a short BBC television documentary series about books and reading broadcast in 2009, and, in May 2010, Jane Davis was invited to take part in the UK's largest and most prestigious book festival,

Figure 5.2 Jane Davis and Karen Thompson

Jane Davis (left) of Liverpool's Get Into Reading and Karen Thompson (right) of Chicago's Literature for All of Us share ideals and ideas in a transatlantic exchange

Source: Jane Davis's photo. Permission granted.

the Hay Literary Festival, which is sponsored by the *Guardian* newspaper. Unlike Pearl, however, Davis is less a celebrity with a brand to maintain, and more akin to the leader of a social movement, in particular, a "movement entrepreneur" who possesses the ability to appeal to public sentiment and to engage the support of different kinds of constituents (Staggenborg [2007] 2008, 16). Moreover, in contrast to the replication of the OBOC model, which is no longer formally connected to Pearl, Higashi, or Seattle Reads, the GIR model is being reproduced largely under Davis's control and guidance through, for example, formal workshops (for which participants can receive accreditation as a GIR facilitator) and residential training sessions within different regions of the UK and overseas in Australia and Denmark. Indeed, in 2008, Jane Davis resigned as editor of *The Reader* journal so that she could devote more of her time to GIR. During the year that her native city of Liverpool served its turn as European Capital of Culture, Davis traveled extensively throughout the UK "meeting people who have become interested in the 'Get Into Reading' project largely through reading Blake Morrison's article in *The Guardian*" (J. Davis 2009, 101). To deliberately mix metaphors, Jane Davis is a leader on an evangelizing mission to create social change via nothing less than a "Reading Revolution." By 2009, this term had become the explicit aim and tagline for the Reader Organisation, as the website states: "Our Reading Revolution aims to put reading at the heart of life, and, sentence by sentence, line by line, to build shared meanings between people."

If the organization and material practices of GIR resemble grassroots community work and Davis's leadership is reminiscent of a movement leader, then how does the ideological work that GIR performs compare to that of Seattle Reads and the other OBOC programs in our study? A striking point of comparison lies in the politics and practices of text selection. Jane Davis is unapologetic about reproducing her own literary tastes or making explicit value judgments about literature. She is a passionate advocate of "quality" literature that offers "mental stillness and useful imagination work" (pers. comm., 2006), an experience that she believes is not possible to obtain from reading popular texts such as "a football magazine or *Grazia*" (2009, 102). In contrast to the focus on contemporary fiction within the majority of OBOC program selections, however, Jane Davis's preference for GIR texts is clearly shaped by her own knowledge and experience of reading "classic" British literature, especially Shakespeare, Dickens, and poetry. She feels strongly that there are "life lessons in the British canon that shouldn't be locked up in universities" and which all people "need" (pers. comm., 2006). Davis also believes that the British education system has failed many people by "forc[ing them] to read great books," thereby producing associations of "anxiety," "boredom," and even "terror" at the perceived difficulty of reading poetry or a canonical novel (2009, 101–2). Because Davis is an activist communicator with contacts across the broad spectrum of professionals, volunteers, and participant readers within the arena of reading advocacy, she is well aware that her impassioned stance is not shared by all such colleagues:

> I feel rather embattled about that because I feel as if, in the university, literature's been boxed off into a little corner, where only specialists can do it, and out in the wide world, librarians are, are not saying "I can't read Shakespeare with people," they're saying "I can't even read Booker Prize winners, 'cos they're too difficult." (pers. comm., 2006)

The experience of reading that Jane Davis intends for GIR participants is about making the reading of consecrated texts accessible, enjoyable, and potentially life-changing in terms of the identification work and knowledge that literature can offer the reader (the "life lessons") and the potential for psychological healing and other forms of emotional work that shared reading enhances. These aims are different in their degree of ambition rather than radically divergent in ideological terms from the goals of the OBOC organizers discussed in this chapter. After all, Pearl and Higashi perceive learning and cross-cultural communication as possible and productive aspects of shared reading. Higashi's narratives of her affective experiences also indicate the potential for both emotional and political engagement, even for moments that register social change, inspired by the careful contextualization of a selected text. However, Davis (ibid.) conceives of the GIR model of shared reading as having a more thoroughly holistic effect on the individual: physiological and emotional, cognitive and therapeutic, social, and spiritual. Further, as Davis's (ibid.) dramatic rhetoric of war and uprising implies, feelings of "embattlement" and "terror" inspire her instigation of a "Reading Revolution" as a form of public intervention: an attack on popular perceptions of literature and contemporary educational structures in the UK. Whereas Davis's (ibid.) own notion of literary value combines with a sense of social change in ways that parallel the "passion for reading" and desire to bring people together shared by many OBOC organizers, the GIR project—and Davis's mission—seeks a more radical transformation at both the individual and structural levels.

If the degree of transformation envisaged by the GIR founders is different from that envisioned by OBOC organizers, then the writing and reading that facilitate the GIR group member's journey represents another variant between shared reading models. Whereas OBOC programs often opt for literary fiction and, more occasionally, for topical nonfiction titles or graphic books, GIR group leaders employ a wider range of texts. When we questioned Jane Davis and the other founder-facilitators of GIR about the selections chosen for shared reading, they were self-reflexive about their choices and their own genre hierarchies. Although Davis (ibid.) would rather GIR groups did not spend too much time on Dan Brown and other popular writers, she accepts that some readers in the GIR groups might elect to read popular titles together. Mary Weston, another founder-facilitator, indicated that the levels of negotiation about text selections that occur within different GIR groups depends in part on the identity and interests of the membership, the context in which the group meets, and the lack of consistent membership in particular groups (pers. comm., 2006). Because the GIR model also involves reading aloud as well as discussion of poems and other genres of text, and, sometimes, the sharing of an entire novel or play over a period of several months, the selection criteria inevitably differ from those shaping OBOC choices. These circumstances, specific to the sites and acts of reading promoted by GIR, combine with the literary knowledge and taste preferences of the facilitator:

> Mary: . . . [the texts are] just sort of picked for the particular groups that I go into, so one of them is, is *The Five People You Meet In Heaven* (2003), and I needed it last week because there was one group where only one person was there, so there was no point in starting a new one, so we just did a bit of that. Um, and I have some scripts from plays now, [one of] which is a television script set in Liverpool, about kids, so that's, that's a sort of fall-back position for most groups with working-class young people, it's gonna go—gonna be OK. [. . .] Scripts are good when you've got like, um, a slightly rowdy group, com—comedy scripts, it, it just gets the energy on your side rather than against you, sort of thing. And, and because there's usually like a small part that someone who's unconfident at reading, it gets somebody who wouldn't really read to read. (ibid.)

Weston's responsive approach to group reading selections is echoed by another founder-facilitator, Kate McDonnell, who suggests how GIR sets out to challenge peoples' perceptions about genres other than the classics:

> Kate: Well 'cos I do a different kind of group, I dunno, I tend not to have—'cos we've usually, you know, it, it's more—'cos I do more health-based groups really, they're more stable, Mary's got to cope with changing memberships and all sorts of issues, but mine are stable so we'll just start with short stories that we've got, I don't know we've probably got twenty, twenty-five short stories to choose from. Um, but different groups want different things. One group is, really hooked on classics [. . .] we're having a break just now 'cos we're reading a children's book—*Skellig*, by David Almond [. . . and] that's been a revelation to some people, 'cos some people said, "What's chil—what have children's books got to do with me?" (pers. comm., 2006)

McDonnell's and Weston's commentaries suggest the well-developed relationships of trust that they have with their groups as well as their own flexibility about reading practices and choices. As experienced facilitators and graduates with degrees in English literature, they possess literary and practical knowledge that not only inflects the ways that their groups run, but also empowers them to dissent from Davis's creed about the canon. Nevertheless there appears to be some consensus about writing that is suitable for the GIR model and, not surprisingly, this is derived from practice. Angela Macmillan, another founder-facilitator of GIR, compiled an anthology of extracts that was published in 2010 by a "quality" London publisher (Chatto & Windus, an imprint of Random House UK). *A Little, Aloud: An Anthology of Prose and Poetry for Reading Aloud to Someone You Care For* (2010) runs the gamut of GIR's conception of "quality" literature, from the nineteenth-century novels loved by Davis, to "classic" poems and contemporary short stories. All of the texts take about twenty minutes to read aloud and are followed by reading notes informed by the kinds of discussions and questions that occur in GIR groups. In a preview published in *The Reader*, Macmillan indicates the collaborative aspects of anthologizing, referring to her "exceptional colleagues" who assisted with the presentation of the book proposal, to Phil Davis's provision of the title, and to Jane Davis's introduction (2009, 74). The anthology is thus symbolic in several senses: it materializes the collective practices and combined knowledge of the GIR founders; it consecrates their negotiated idea of "literature" and their notion of "value" as it pertains to their model of shared reading, and it disseminates (and commodifies) their ideals about the caring and transformative power of reading aloud to the general reading public. It is, perhaps, a sign that the "Reading Revolution" has moved one step closer to becoming a social movement organization capable of effecting structural social change.

"Loving the Book in Public"

The GIR project is an MRE operating on a rather different scale and employing shared reading practices that diverge from the OBOC and mass-mediated programs that we examine elsewhere in this book. In common with all the cultural managers and workers who contribute to MREs, however, GIR involves a great deal of time, emotional, and cognitive labor on the part of the facilitators who organize and run the different groups. Because what happens in a GIR group ranges across several different types of experience (group therapy, religious communion, education), facilitators not only require a good knowledge of literature and excellent listening skills, but also an ability to deal sensitively with people who may be socially and emotionally vulnerable. The founding facilitators understand their work as a "creative process" not a "class," during which they work collectively with GIR group members for several months to "build" a very particular type of environment within which participants can feel at ease with each other (G. Mair, pers. comm., 2006). During a discussion about the parallels between the meditative practices of diverse religious communities and the shared focus and calmness that happens in their groups when reading aloud occurs, Geraldine Mair observed:

> I think that analogy [with the] Quakers [is apt], and, to be in that situation there's got to be a lot of trust, you've got to feel properly relaxed and trusting other people that you are with. And, that's one of the things that comes over in all the book groups, nobody is intimidated by saying something, they don't feel that they're going to be challenged—or sometimes they say things, and they all challenge, but they all go and [make sense] of that situation where, "Oh it didn't really matter," you know, and it's sort of diametric opinions. But then there's still a sort of

a group . . . it's cohesive and they feel relaxed and trusting, you know, they can speak, which is a freeing experience for them. (ibid.)

As Mary Weston commented, the social and/or therapeutic aspects of group experience can be difficult for the GIR team to explain to new agencies and organizations: "No matter how much you tell people . . . the penny often doesn't drop until they actually are involved in that concentrated act" (pers. comm., 2006). The GIR dynamic is shaped over time among group members and the embodied experience of that meditative state, "it is a forgetting of the self and a remembering of the self at the same time," in Kate McDonnell's words, is not instantly reproducible through a "taster" session for professionals or gatekeepers. Weston suggests a further factor that can make their mission of setting up new GIR groups tricky: "people are quite embarrassed as well I think, aren't they? [. . .] it—it's an emotional thing" (ibid.). Part of the group leader's role is to mediate the social and emotional unease that can arise from a sense of self-exposure, so that all the participants feel less self-conscious about expressing their feelings, ideas, and responses to the selected poems and stories.

Jane Davis's articulation of what GIR work requires of facilitators, "Partly what we're doing is, is modeling to people loving a book" (pers. comm., 2005), represents a conceptual frame within which to comprehend the "emotional" openness involved in the shared interpretative practices of reading, which they encourage. For Davis (ibid.), this model of developing an emotional "reverence" for the text suggests a form of nonromantic love, and a secular devotion to the book that echoes the practices and purposes involved in the shared reading of religious texts. Davis's (ibid.) notion of "loving a book" is explicitly set against what she describes as the dominant practice in academic literary studies of "pulling it apart" and reading for themes and "political, cultural issues." "Loving a book" also operates for Davis as a rejection of the "sneering" critical distance of academia toward texts, in favor of a subjective psychological engagement of identification with the ideas, aesthetics, and stories. Alongside her concerns about the "discussability" of a book and the quality of writing, then, is her belief that reading together should involve "lov[ing] the book *in public*" (our emphasis). In this redolent phrase, Davis articulates her passion for and about reading and her belief that an emotional engagement with a book is also—at least in the context of GIR—a social expression of connection that leads toward both personal and collective transformation. Although many participants speak of the self-esteem they have acquired through taking part in a GIR group, transformation is not necessarily confined to individual recuperation and change, because of the relationships it inspires among members.[11]

As the examples above suggest, cultural workers involved with GIR require a skill-set that includes literary knowledge, emotional maturity, attentive listening abilities, and cultural sensitivity. Their labor as facilitators demands determination and a caring commitment to the communities and groups they approach because it frequently takes time to convince gatekeepers as well as potential participants of the model's value. Like the organizers of Seattle Reads, the GIR facilitators are passionate about reading and about the potential that shared reading has to produce social change. Unlike the OBOC model, GIR is underpinned by a holistic rather than a purely ideological notion of individual transformation: a change that combines aspects of a therapeutic experience with the aural, oral, and cognitive processes involved in reading aloud. The ideal for GIR thus involves the worker in the embodied performance of "loving the book in public," a process that engages her in a dynamic relationship between self, text, and reader-listener.

CONCLUSIONS: PASSIONATE WORK RECONSIDERED

All the cultural managers and workers described in this chapter reenact their own "passion for reading" through their cultural labor, but the script, choreography, and audience differ within our case studies. Institutional rules (both implicit and explicit), financial structures, national cultural policies, and local politics inflect the symbolic meanings of reading mediated through the performance of cultural work. Professional training and the degree of confidence that a worker possesses in her position within the reading industry emerge as particularly important factors shaping the work practices and decisions made and pursued within this type of book programming. Cultural managers are usually well-informed about their locality's print-literate cultures and municipal politics, and this knowledge also informs their agenda as well as their actions. Managers who are event organizers often possess—simultaneously and uncomfortably—varying degrees of agency as event producers, disseminators, and reader-consumers. The tensions produced by these multiple roles within the circuit of cultural production are also compounded by their identifications as passionate leisure readers who are, at the same time, also professionally trained readers.

Further, event organizers are usually proximate to the ruling relations of power represented by institutions such as libraries, schools, and government agencies, but they also exhibit nonformal agency through informal social networks, temporary partnerships, and ephemeral communities, which are associated with the nonruling relations of power. They often form alliances with groups such as schoolchildren, retired seniors, and, in the case of Liverpool's GIR program, with politically disempowered groups of people, including asylum seekers, refugees, and people with mental health issues. These various types of partnerships, which public libraries tend to regard as "outreach" work, enable the reading and interpretation of books to occur within spaces and communities where the dominant meanings of reading are not usually negotiated. Among the OBOC programs that we investigated, for example, instead of discussing books in libraries or classrooms, young participants in Liverpool Reads have made drama in community centers and children in Kitchener-Waterloo-Cambridge, Ontario, have made visual art in local parks. Such activities are inspired by issues and themes from the selected texts, but do not depend on print literacy, or being able to afford to buy or know how to borrow the book. Reading aloud in leisure spaces such as pubs (e.g., K-W-C), cultural and community centers (e.g., The BlueCoat Arts center in Liverpool), in therapeutic spaces such as halfway houses, and hospitals (e.g., GIR groups) lends a contemporary formation to the sharing of reading that has strong historical precedents within the various traditions of oral performance and collective study practiced by women's and African-American literary societies and working-people's educational organizations of the North Atlantic region (Lyons 1999; McHenry 2002; H. Murray 2002; Rehberg Sedo 2007; Rose 2001; Ruggles Gere 1997; Sicherman 2007).

Whereas many of the cultural managers and workers involved in MREs cherish liberal democratic ideals about improving access to books, financial constraints, and institutional imperatives can obstruct creative and radical projects. Restricted quantities of free books to give away and overburdened work schedules are just two of the material factors that managers and workers nominate as limiting their ability to engage with constituencies within their cities who have yet to participate in any aspect of their programs. An organizer's own cultural background can also obstruct or alternatively facilitate her engagement with specific cultural groups, as Chris Higashi's experiences suggest. Knowledge and skills learnt in other arenas, such as social activism, equips some cultural managers with strategies for cross-cultural work and grassroots engagement as Jane Davis's practice demonstrates. Even the more ideologically radical managers are complicit with the dominant meanings of reading to some extent, at least in terms of their investment in the benefits that "good," that is, "literary," "classic," or "informative" books can potentially bring to readers. However, the unpredictability of the reader-text encounter, and of the social dynamic that can occur within MRE events, is equally recognized and treasured by the majority of cultural workers in our study. In their openness to the potential disruption of event frames or explicit program aims that dissenting readers and event participants may produce, these cultural workers happily surrender some of their own agency as inscribers of the meanings of reading. Although none of them employed the term, their actions, and attitudes position them closer to the histories of reading as liberating: in the twenty-first century, reading can engage people's imaginations, move them, heal them, open up a dialogue with friends and with strangers, or equip them with new knowledge.

Drawing on the commentaries of a handful of cultural managers and their colleagues, we have posited a conceptualization of their labor as a nonromantic act of love lived out in public. However, this notion requires further refinement in the light of the physical, emotional, and time "costs" that it exacts from its practitioners, and in terms of its gendered and generationally specific aspects. The type of cultural work detailed in this chapter is gendered, not because it is often undertaken by women, but because it involves a combination of professional skills, emotional work, and underpaid over-work associated with the caring professions and vocational creative jobs such as librarianship that have become inscribed as "feminine" pursuits (Buschmann 2003, 9; Eddy 2003, 159; Pawley 2007, 271). In the three nation-states of our study, teaching children to read within and outside the home, and regulating reading materials has also often been the work of women, at least since the late nineteenth century, and this is a role that differently "raced" women have taken up for a range of reasons, including social aspirations of class, gender, and "race" mobility; moral and/or religious education; and as a form of political resistance.

If this type of cultural work is gendered, it may also be shaped in purpose and deed by the generation-specific experiences of second-wave feminism (Davis), civil rights (Higashi and Pearl), the expansion of access to post-graduate education in both the UK and North America, and the advancement of substantial numbers of female professionals to managerial positions achieved only as an exception by women of the previous generation. Women outnumber men on most organizing committees and work teams for MREs, and they are usually professionally trained, university-educated women aged over forty-five. Those of a younger generation, such as OBOC Chicago's Nan Alleman, who was in her mid-thirties when we first interviewed her in 2004, and Bea Colley, who was only in her mid-twenties when she assumed the organization of Liverpool Reads for two years (2006–2007), are often supported in their work by institutionally powerful, older women. Colley had Jane Davis as her line manager, and the support and experience of the original GIR team whose office she shared, quite literally behind her. Alleman's work came under the direction of Commissioner Mary Dempsey, a woman described by Alleman, OBOC Chicago author Stuart Dybek, and other cultural workers we met in Chicago as a "dynamo" who has "the ear of the Mayor" (pers. comm., 2004). Social power and cultural capital, gender and generation, all shape the performance of "emotional" and "passionate" work and can impact on its economic and noneconomic costs and rewards. Despite their various cultural situations, different organizational models, aims, and ideological emphases, what all of the reading programs and MREs that we investigated have in common is the commitment, enthusiasm, and "beyond the call of duty" labor of cultural workers. Many of the OBOC reading initiatives were begun as underpaid "off the corner of my desk" projects, or as unpaid, volunteer activities. Their creative labor can thus be thought of as an embodied act played out in an economically precarious environment.

Cultural managers and their teams of workers are crucial to the success or failure of MREs, and to the reproduction and generation of established and new meanings of reading. They often act as scene setters for shared reading through their roles as book selectors, and program designers. Their role as cultural mediators between texts and readers becomes more overt through their authorship of website copy, printed program, and reading guides. Their mediation of the meanings of shared reading is socially enacted when they introduce events or promote their programs and models at public and professional meetings. As our case studies have demonstrated in some detail, reading event organizers are active agents in the reading industry that focuses on English-language texts. Their complicated and conflicted position within that industry only serves to highlight how dynamic and fluid it has become as newer agents play a part in promoting and disseminating texts. In twenty-first-century North America and the UK, these cultural workers can be understood as "feeling" individuals whose embodied knowledge of books, reading, and social relations is iterated in public spaces. The passionate work of MRE organizers also demonstrates how gender, generation, and geography shape the reproduction of traditional values about book reading as a socially and morally transformative activity, as well as influencing more holistic, therapeutic, and creative ideals of the social change, pleasure, and relationships that shared reading can inspire. How *readers* who participate in MREs experience pleasure, and how they use these shared reading activities to articulate notions of belonging, is the subject of the next chapter.

6 Reader

. . . it's so nice to be with other people who are appreciating the same thing. And then we went to the brewery. [laughs]

—Anna, Kitchener-Waterloo-Cambridge, FG 2 P, 2004

At face value, Anna's comment appears to have nothing whatsoever to do with reading. What is clear is that she went on an outing with a group of people, enjoyed the company and the sharing of some kind of experience or object, and then rounded off a fun day with a brewery tour and (presumably) a beer. Anna, a white woman in her early sixties who lives in southern Ontario, Canada, is actually reflecting on her participation in a literary bus tour around sites associated with Jane Urquhart's novel *The Stone-Carvers* (2001), the 2003 selection for OBOC in the three neighboring towns of Kitchener, Waterloo, and Cambridge. Taking Anna's words out of context— as we have done here—underlines what we believe to be a crucial factor that helps to explain the popularity of contemporary MREs: they are a form of entertainment, well suited to the time-pressured environment of twenty-first-century everyday life. A selection of encounters with books is offered that does not involve the long-term time commitment of a private book group, nor does it necessarily depend on having read the selected book. Within each MRE, a variety of events stage different kinds of engagement with elements of a book's content and its extratextual aspects, such as topical issues, local or national connections, or the writer's biography. Anna chose an aspect of her local OBOC program that appealed to her, and she clearly enjoyed both the content of the day and the experience of sharing it.

The most successful MREs—from Oprah's Book Club to *Canada Reads* to long-running OBOC programs in Chicago and Kitchener-Waterloo-Cambridge—exploit the opportunities offered by the coextensive relationships among media to produce multiple encounters with books. Equally significant to their success as entertainments, MREs extend the possibility for multiple encounters with other people. They provide opportunities for human interaction via a socially networked event that can be engaged on- and offline, either once or repeatedly. These encounters may well be ephemeral, but, as our case studies of the Kitchener-Waterloo-Cambridge area and

Liverpool Reads below demonstrate, they are capable of producing significant moments of identification or affective connection among participants.

Like Anna, many people who choose to take part in an MRE activity enjoy the mediation of their experience through the presence and pleasures of other people. In this chapter we argue that readers who participate in OBOC programs are seeking a series of reading pleasures that the "live" activities of MREs provide. Reexperiencing a book through other readers, the author, other media, and through visits to physical places enables reading to be both a social and shared, intellectual, and even a somatic activity. Additionally, readers who take part in MREs are able to draw on various aspects of their other media experiences as listeners, viewers, spectators, and online user-creators in ways that complement and reshape their identities as readers of books. Readers involved in the events enjoy sharing, acquiring, and exchanging knowledge; different types of relationships and social interaction; and the identity-work that OBOC programs can facilitate. Occasionally, MREs even offer people a location and opportunity from which to articulate affective notions of citizenship—opportunities that are infrequent in the three nation-states of our study where the public sphere has been shrunk by decades of privatization and cuts to cultural and social programming. However, focusing on participants' experience and assessments of the face-to-face and performance-oriented OBOC activities also highlights the exclusionary aspects of the model. These include the preeminence of English-language texts, a tendency to privilege place-based history, and the choice of institutional and "high-culture" spaces (e.g., libraries, city halls, theaters) as key locations for programming. Although OBOC is in principle a public form of entertainment that usually incorporates a number of free activities, it is, therefore, neither accessible nor appealing to everyone. Indeed, many people would not even perceive MREs such as OBOC events to be a form of entertainment at all, and would rather spend their leisure time going to a movie, playing sport, or watching TV (Bennett et al. 2009). Participants' experiences of and perceptions about MREs suggest why and how this particular form of shared reading is meaningful to some people. Understanding reading events as a form of entertainment not only foregrounds their location within the contemporary media environment, but also suggests that participants are attracted to events by the combination of emotional, intellectual, and aesthetic pleasures that are available to them.

READING EVENTS AS ENTERTAINMENT

Reading events can be conceptualized as entertainments in several respects. In terms of their production, MREs emerged from the reading industry, which, as we detailed in Chapters 1 and 4, "Reading" and "Money," is driven, in part, by the commercial concerns of the media and entertainment industries: audiences must be attracted to maintain ratings for TV and radio networks (for *Richard & Judy* via their Book Club, for example), and books must be sold to keep both publishers and booksellers in business. The reading industry has to work across different formats and on various platforms in order to keep books and reading in the limelight—on the screens and in the physical places where potential audiences lurk. A second sense in which reading events are entertainments lies in the type of experience that they offer. The OBOC model combines locality, sociability, and spectacle. Such a combination reveals the way that the model combines aspects of shared reading that have historical antecedents with elements of contemporary culture. The places and spaces within which people access books and share their reading bears critical examination, as Christine Pawley (2010) emphasizes in her fine-grained study of the relationship between public libraries and Cold War ideology. Pawley "stresses the importance of locality and sociability in understanding the reading practices of ordinary Americans, particularly in the context of public policies designed to shape that reading" (28). The organizers of OBOC programs, many of whom are public librarians of course, appear to understand the importance of place and of creating a social occasion. As we argued in Chapter 4, "Money," public policy in the US, Canada, and the UK has increasingly emphasized the role that arts and cultural activities must play in creating a sense of community and social well-being. Meanwhile, the spectacle of OBOC may be modest compared to, for example, that of a rock concert, but it is often achieved, as we have already noted in earlier chapters, by drawing on other well-developed aspects of contemporary entertainment culture. Celebrity, Hollywood, and the cult of the expert are all visible in OBOC. For example, many adaptations involve the appearance of a living author in a community, or they associate the screening of a film with the selected book. The screening can be preceded by a talk given by a professor of film studies or the arts correspondent for the local newspaper.

As Graeme Turner has noted, in our "entertainment age," a period that roughly corresponds to the first decade of the twenty-first century, "Information is simply not enough. Instead, entertainment has become the most pervasive discursive domain in twenty-first-century popular culture" ([2009] 2010, 160). Turner's (ibid.) analysis is developed from an area of communication that is differently focused to ours, but his observations about the evolution of "infotainment" into entertainment remind us of the media culture within which MREs have proliferated. It is, as he suggests, "an extraordinarily rich media environment" (162), but it is also one in which the mode and contents of cultural products frequently promote "individualisation, dramatization [and] simplification" (Fenton 2009, 56 cited in Turner 2010, 174). MREs, however, can provide participants with experiences that counter the trends of individualization and simplification. They can offer scenes and sites of reading in which readers can enact collectivity, however briefly, and, where the complication of ideas and of identities becomes possible in ways that are at once not only intellectual but also affective and somatic.

As our case studies below illustrate, readers' desires for these processes of connection, learning, identification, and affect are all significant factors in determining their participation.

In an entertainment age, many readers seek pleasure beyond the book and the book group because organized events incorporate some of the visual spectacle and emotional thrills more usually associated with consuming nonprint media. The sense of occasion produced by the way a room or other kind of space is decorated and physically organized for an event, for instance, and the presence of an audience, whether it consists of ten or five hundred people, frames participants' expectations, preparing them for a performance. For readers in our study, the "liveness" of events was often a factor in producing emotional effects: "Everything becomes alive!" as several people whom we met described the feelings inspired in them by an OBOC activity. They were usually referring to events such as author appearances, themed talks led by specialists or panel discussions, dramatizations (whether full productions or selected scenes from the book), and film screenings. The animation and mediation of a book through various kinds of performance is, then, the third sense in which MREs can be conceptualized as entertainments. In common with most types of popular culture, "a logic of emotional intensification" shapes "live" reading events (H. Jenkins 2007, 3). Readers are invited into the world of the book—not only through discussions about its narrative, themes, and characters, or debate about its historical and geographical contexts or contemporary relevance, but also through the presentation of aspects of its production, such as the ideas that inspired the author, or examinations of the processes of adaptation for film or stage. Even commerce can have a place in that "world" through the book sales and author signings that might feature as the end point of the event. In this regard, MREs are very much of our era, a time in which instant gratification, or, at least the promise of more entertainment soon (if we are buying a printed book or other material artifact), can be purchased and/or downloaded at the click of a mouse.

Sometimes music and food are also included as part of an MRE, in an attempt to create a more intensely felt atmosphere or mood by engaging more of the audience's senses (see Figure 6.1). The same elements also help to foreground the sociability that is integral to the OBOC model in particular—the possibilities for social connection and the chance to "see" what would otherwise remain an imagined community of readers. Interaction among event attendees, the cultural workers who organized the event and the featured performer/s also contributes to sociability, as we explore in more detail below. Para-social relations between audience and performer, and temporary associations between audience members mediate the world of the book. The "live" events thus beckon readers into a multisensory and multimediated experience, one that, thanks to digital technologies as well as the "old" technology of the codex, can be extended beyond the temporal and spatial frame of a specific event.

Figure 6.1 Huntsville, Alabama, Jig Band

A local jig band kicks off Huntsville-Madison County Public Library's Big Read for the 2007 season featuring *To Kill a Mockingbird*

Source: Authors' photo.

Readers whom we met and observed at OBOC activities also derived pleasure from the ways in which oral cultures are revivified and remade during events. Aspects of oral culture that frequently occur during events include the sharing of memories, opinions, and interpretations—also common activities in face-to-face book groups—combined with more formalized oral performances, such as introductions, professional presentations, readings from the selected book, panel debates, and votes of thanks—elements that are not so common in private book groups. The mixing of oral forms, plus the opportunity to listen to others without any pressure to make a verbal contribution, thus indicates another difference between participating in a book club and taking part in an MRE. When the site of shared reading is a public space and the scene that is set for shared reading is one of entertainment, a reader is not required to be a reader in the straightforward sense of having read or having some knowledge of the print-text. Other identities, including what we might think of in some instances as other reading selves, can be performed. To paraphrase Janice Radway, it is important to remember that readers are more than just that: they have other selves and other practices, including other practices of media consumption (1996). Examining readers' stories and performances at MREs offers glimpses of readers and audience members as intersubjective beings in a community context who are also consumers of entertainment, inhabitants of specific places, and, usually, in possession of a certain amount of cultural capital. As our case studies in this chapter reveal, readers who took part in OBOC programs in southern Ontario, Liverpool (UK), and Huntsville (Alabama) frequently demonstrated well-developed skills in relation to critical reading and book talk. These competencies derived partly from their experiences in formal education and their professional working lives as well as from their membership of book groups or their participation in other informal groups interested in film or the visual arts, for example. Participating in OBOC programs enabled these readers to employ intellectual and social skills, while displaying their cultural capital in relation to their knowledge of print and media cultures. Demonstrating knowledge and skill, however, was only one aspect of the pleasure sought and won from taking part in activities.

Readers' commentaries about their experiences and perceptions of events indicate that they can provide occasions and locations for expressions of belonging, or, alternatively, of dislocation from place, community, or a cultural group. Readers' narratives and our own observations of OBOC activities suggest that events can inspire in participants a passionate engagement with textual worlds or curiosity about the material realities of the "real" world past and present, near and far. There is nothing inherently radical or subversive about these practices, of course, and, as we explore through our case studies, readers may use events to express or confirm prejudices, to affirm their affiliation with the mainstream or to display their identity as a reader with good taste. For us, as researchers, readers' stories and performances sometimes surprised us, but, at times, they disappointed us, perhaps because of our own desires for social transformation and our investment in the notion that reading and sharing books can—sometimes—make people more aware of inequalities of power. Silence about or avoidance of issues that might threaten to disturb a pleasant and congenial atmosphere is perhaps an inevitable outcome when events are intended to be both entertaining and informative. Other aspects of the event dynamic also shape what can happen. Just as the performers "on stage" are constrained by the event-frames, so too are the audience members who may not be permitted much time for discussion during the event, and who may feel silenced or intimidated by the spectacle and formalities that thrill other participants, or by the presence of strangers. Nevertheless, as public entertainments, these MRE activities offer some people a chance to articulate and enact selves in public fora in the physical presence of others: opportunities that are rare in the three nation-states of our study. Part of the allure for readers who participate in shared reading events is connoted by the name of the most widely adapted MRE model—One Book, One Community—a name that extends a promise of belonging.

CITIZEN READER: MASS READING EVENTS
AND THE PROMISE OF BELONGING

The promise is seductive and the inference is clear: if you form some kind of attachment to this book selection (either through reading the book or by participating in an activity related to it), you will share common ground with other people, you will experience a connection with others, known and unknown. When participants take up the opportunity offered by a "live" event to make public their feelings, thoughts, or ideas, they take another step toward the fulfillment of that promise—however ungrounded, apolitical, or imaginary that promise of belonging may be. As we demonstrate below, readers only sometimes use these moments to reaffirm their sense of belonging to a nation. Most readers tend to articulate the sense of belonging that they derive from their reading in terms of other forms of affective attachment—to place, to region, to a cultural community, for example. Because OBOC events often focus on the representation, or the connection, of a chosen text to a specific region or place, these are more likely to be the direct inspirations for modes of affective belonging. The expression of belonging, or the articulation of the desire to belong to a place, locale, or to the history of a particular community might be preferable for many readers in the US, UK, and Canada because defining an identity as attached to an idea of the state is too problematic. For some people, experience has shown them that rights are not bestowed equally on citizens. Or, it might be because it is hard for many citizens to "see" the nation-state when they live in the midst of a neoliberal democracy that conceptualizes the state as having a minimalist role to play in social services and also, as we elaborated in Chapter 4, "Money," in the cultural sector. As an expression of a different kind of belonging, one forged through reading, we think that people who find such MREs meaningful can, for this reason, be called "citizen readers." These are people who read to belong just as they feel that they themselves belong to reading as an activity located in a place, along with others who share the same interests.

In coining the term "citizen reader," we want to underline the social and public dimension that a shared reading event can bring to experiences of and possibilities for belonging. Or, to put it another way, an MRE may provide public or semi-public moments when the expression or enactment of affective modes of citizenship appears more possible than it does in everyday life, because other people are present to hear or witness its articulation. The fantasy of connection between people who are at once private and public persons, can, however fleetingly, become realized as a book becomes subject to a rereading or the point of departure for the sharing of emotional knowledge. One of the great surprises of the research for us, for instance, was how many readers were satisfied by ephemeral experiences of community. The brief encounter is socially and emotionally meaningful, of course, but does not necessarily transform anyone or anything, least of all formal political structures. MREs may provide moments of social connection, but these moments are mediated via their function as entertainment and relations with the book business. Thus, the citizen reader, as we have described her here, is acting within what Lauren Berlant has termed "the intimate public sphere" (2008, viii). She participates in a public that is produced by the consumption of "common texts and things," which appear to articulate a shared emotional knowledge, and thus proffer the fantasy of "emotional contact" with others (viii).

Berlant's "intimate public" is more of an imagined entity than a physically experienced social reality, with "women's culture" representing "one of many flourishing intimate publics" and the "first . . . mass-marketed intimate public in the United States of significant scale" (5). In its late twentieth-century and twenty-first-century American manifestation, this culture is marketed and circulated via popular textual genres such as "chick lit" and cinematic melodrama, for example. What these texts "cultivate," Berlant proposes, are "fantasies of vague belonging as an alleviation of what is hard to manage in the lived real—social antagonisms, exploitation, compromised intimacies, the attrition of life" (ibid.). The fantasies that the middlebrow popular texts of women's culture may endorse thus include the desire for conventionality and normativity, a longing for everyday life to be less complicated, as if the historical effects of imperialism, colonialism, and nationalism on race, class, and gender politics could be suspended. But, of course, they cannot be, at least not in the lived world, although some relief from this reality is provided by the sense that similar desires and longings are shared by others. The circulation and branding of popular cultural texts employing sentimental genres to a mass audience promotes this sense that there is some kind of "collective sociality" (10). Similarly, MREs, whether mass-mediated to the many via television and a series of high-street marketing campaigns such as the RJBC, or when produced and circulated on a more local scale as with versions of OBOC, proffer the fantasy of collective belonging. The texts that are the focus of MREs differ generically from those that Berlant (2008) claims for "women's culture," and are often works of realist literary fiction or, more rarely, topical nonfiction, that deal with historical and social inequalities more overtly than say, popular romance novels. But when these texts become shared by readers, they are often employed for similar ends. Through conversations about the book with other readers or through their shared participation in other types of OBOC activities, readers come to recognize their personal story as a common one. The social interactions and intimacies produced by events also help readers to validate the realm of feeling. Being moved, expressing feelings, and emotional knowledge become possible and legitimate actions. At times, the sharing of books in OBOC contexts enables readers to articulate a feeling of belonging to a locally situated intimate public.

In Berlant's analysis, "a public is intimate when it foregrounds affective and emotional attachments located in fantasies of the common, the everyday, and a sense of ordinariness, a space where the social world is rich with anonymity and local recognitions, and where challenging and banal conditions of life take place not only in proximity to the attentions of power, but also squarely in the radar of a recognition that can be provided by other humans" (10). MREs provide participants with opportunities to dwell in these contradictions, to experience moments of intense recognition in a room of strangers, to step into a textual world and to step back out into the lived one, to be moved emotionally by stories, performances, and new knowledge, and yet be returned to an everyday self. Sharing reading in MREs can enable participants to glimpse alternative ways of being, including ways of being in community, but the work of social change requires a different kind of collectivity that can directly challenge the ruling relations of power. An intimate public, by contrast, is a location where "what is personal is threaded through mediating institutions and social hierarchy" (ibid.). Intimate publics are "juxtapolitical" (ibid.). In other words, it is a sphere that is at once outside the public domain of politics, yet shaped and engendered by it. As Julie Rak observes, Berlant's (2008) work is helpful for thinking about the cultural and affective dimensions of citizenship because she explores "the citizen as a state of being rather than a sense of being in relation to the state" (2010, 10–11).

Expressions and enactments of affective modes of citizenship are important because they are the part of being a citizen that we attempt to claim for ourselves within our everyday lives. When readers choose to participate in MREs by going to an event to share an experience inspired by the book, they are sometimes able to access a more embodied version of an intimate public. We could also make sense of readers' attraction to affective modes of belonging in terms of a desire for agency in the face of neoliberal democracies in which "people's actual power over their material conditions has declined" (Peck 2010, 12). Some cultural commentators certainly make that argument to explain the symbolic and emotional power of contemporary popular cultural texts. For example, Janice Peck (2010) partly attributes the appeal and success of Oprah Winfrey's self-transformation narratives to the sense of material and political disempowerment experienced by her audience in their daily lives. Readers' articulations and experiences of belonging offer us provocative clues about the desires of citizen readers, especially women, to find "something to hold on to" aside from institutionally sanctioned ideas of national citizenship. For readers who enjoy MREs, the pleasure of connection that they experience combines with other kinds of pleasure, including the enjoyment of knowledge acquisition or an aesthetic engagement with the selected text. These latter pleasures coincide with the reasons why readers who engage in "recreational reading" do so. As Vivien Howard points out, various contemporary studies of adult readers in the UK and North America nominate "escapism, relaxation, practical knowledge, self-development, self-knowledge, and aesthetic pleasure" as reasons for reading (2011, 48). Readers who participate in MREs can redouble these pleasures while also deriving further enjoyment from the framing of an event and the way that a text is performed or represented. Such complex pleasures depend on the successful staging of a series of mediations between cultural workers, readers, authors, and texts that may lead to the production of intimacies that meet the desires of keen readers to "know" about and beyond the book both cognitively and emotionally.

"THE 'WHY' BEHIND THE BOOK": THE PLEASURE OF AUTHOR-READER MEDIATIONS

Author events bring writers literally face-to-face with readers' various desires, including a desire for intimacy with the person behind the text. Such encounters offer readers an "embodied" version of the para-social relationship that can arise from a reader's engagement with the author's books and, perhaps, from following media coverage of their careers. As one reader from the Kitchener-Waterloo-Cambridge area eloquently stated in a survey response, "The event puts me in touch with the real person behind the book. I like to know more about the author and the 'why' behind the book." As this comment indicates, a desire to connect with an author in person may be coupled with an urge to authenticate the text via knowledge of the writer's life, or to authorize and recontextualize the text as a culturally valuable object either for themselves, for a particular cultural group or, for their local community. Readers may achieve this through the types of questions they ask of the writer about his or her life or about the content of the book, especially its themes and settings. As our analysis of Canadian writer Nino Ricci's participation in OBOC Kitchener-Waterloo-Cambridge below suggests, the physical appearance of the author at various venues makes a significant contribution to some readers' urge to reinvest both the book (the commodity-text) and the author (the celebrity-text) with local-cultural meaning. These processes are at once psychological and material.

The psychological projection of the text onto the author and the identification of the author as a text is a process that Wenche Ommundsen, following Foucault, posits as a common way in which readers handle print texts in contemporary western cultural contexts (2007, 249). Our survey suggests that many keen readers seek out opportunities for encounters with authors, perhaps as a way of mediating or enhancing these projections and identifications. When we asked all of the readers (N = 3,067) about the types of book events that people attended in the course of a year, over a third (38 percent) of those who responded across the different sites nominated author readings, whereas library events (29 percent) and book festivals (17 percent) ranked as the second and third most popular options. Because many events held in libraries or featured as part of book festivals also include talks, readings, and appearances by writers, it seems that author events are popular with readers who have the time, money, cultural literacy, and information to locate and attend book-related leisure activities. Conversely, 14 percent (142) of the respondents to our survey listed as the top reason that they did not participate in events associated with OBOC programs was the fact that they had not heard about them. The second top reason for not participating was a lack of time (4 percent).

Our observations of OBOC author-events suggest that these occasions offer readers the opportunity to visually align the material book with the actual bodily presence of its original producer or their representative (such as a biographer), and, in turn, with their own bodies. In many sites, but especially in Kitchener-Waterloo-Cambridge and Huntsville, Alabama, we observed that up to half the members of an audience would listen to the author while touching, clutching, flicking through, or following along in their own copy of the book. Of course, many readers bring along their copies of the featured book so that they can obtain the author's signature in it, which is one way of authenticating the link between the material text and its originator, while also creating a material trace or evidence of a meeting between writer and reader. Readers' handling of their copies during a live event also reminds us that, for many keen readers, the physical form of the codex is extremely familiar: it is an everyday object, albeit a cultural artifact that may hold all kinds of social and emotional associations for an individual reader. The physiological aspects of reading a printed book (the smell of paper, the feel of the spine, turning the pages by hand) can be an especially pleasurable part of the reading experience for some readers, as we explore briefly in the final chapter. When readers take along their copies of a book to an author event, they may be deriving a sense of security from taking a familiar object into a public place, or displaying an identity as an owner or collector of books, exhibiting good taste in choosing a book that has been legitimated by the organizers, or subconsciously wishing to show that they are part of a community who is sharing the same book. Whatever motivations are involved, it appears that for some readers who attend author events, holding and handling their copy of the text is one means of participating in the entertainment that does not depend on having the confidence to speak in public. The sense of being both physically and psychologically connected to the material book and its author may also enhance the physical and emotional pleasure of taking part in a "live" event.

Other kinds of enjoyment inflect the complex pleasures that readers experience at events. Respondents to our survey question asking about the main reason that they participated in an OBOC-type MRE (192) nominated "provides intellectual enrichment" (10 percent), followed by "enriches the private reading experience" (10 percent). These responses indicate that, for some readers, attending public events enhances or deepens their individual cognitive and intellectual engagements with a book. The temporal span of the OBOC model is partly responsible for this opportunity to undertake a type of intensive reading, because it enables readers to develop their knowledge of the text across several months through a series of different activities that engage and reengage with the book and its contexts. Not surprisingly, participants in OBOC programs tend to be information-seekers who enjoy learning about the writer's inspirations, and his or her research and writing process. They also enjoy hearing other readers' interpretations of and ideas about the text, and the author's own explanations of characters, imagery, and stylistic features. Sylvia, a Chinese-Canadian woman in her mid-twenties, who works as a financial adviser and piano teacher in Vancouver, vividly expressed the effect—and affect—of gaining a "deeper understanding" when she talked about taking part in an event featuring the writer Joy Kogawa, author of the 2005 OBOV selection, *Obasan* (1981):

> I think it's—I think it gave me a greater understanding, like, you know, with seeing her presence and then to hear—she—you know, the way she talked? You can sort of kind of imagine what it's really like—you know, kind of her personality into the book. You probably read it once, but you just don't know—you don't quite get it? It's a story. But with some people actually . . . there and then they tell you the story—like, people asked about the background—you know, what does that, you know, the house and trees and stuff symbolize, and you realize you get deeper, you gain a deeper understanding of the book. There's more *feeling* to it. [. . .] Well, just seeing that interaction between the people, like, you know, the readers and the author: it's actually quite interesting. Like, everything becomes alive! That's what I felt. (Vancouver FG P 6, 2006; emphasis in the original)

Sylvia believes that her comprehension of the novel's meaning became "deeper" through a combination of factors: Kogawa's self-presentation and vocal performance that enhanced her ability to "imagine" the setting and world of the book; the clarification of the plot that audience members articulated and the decoding of imagery that was elucidated via the questions that people posed to Kogawa. In common with other readers whose responses to events we analyze in this chapter, Sylvia values the intensification of emotion that the author event produces, as much as the intellectual knowledge that she gains about the text. For her, the "live" dynamic of the event created by the mediation of the book among readers and author is both informative ("interesting") and thrilling in the way that it animates and dramatizes the novel ("Everything becomes alive!").

The pleasure experienced by an enthusiastic reader when he or she sees an author in person was perhaps predictable. More unexpected for us, as researchers, was the fact that the writers whom we interviewed also enjoyed readers' extended pursuit of "the 'why' behind the book," in spite of the fatigue induced by multiple appearances and media interviews. Authors such as Stuart Dybek, Nino Ricci, Jhumpa Lahiri, and Patrick Lane are no strangers to public appearances and critical acclaim. Yet they all spoke eloquently and emotively to us about their OBOC experiences, none more so than Nino

Ricci, whose novel *Lives of the Saints* (1990) was selected for the 2004 iteration of OBOC Kitchener-Waterloo-Cambridge in southern Ontario, Canada. Ricci's commentary, and our analysis of his event appearances, illustrates how the relationship between reader and author can become an active and two-way process within the context of an MRE, but also how pleasure—for both parties—is shaped by the demands of the entertainment format.

Up Close and Personal in Southern Ontario: Ricci and His Readers

One of the longest-running Canadian versions of the OBOC program, OBOC Kitchener-Waterloo-Cambridge encompasses three small cities in southern Ontario and the rural communities that surround them. Waterloo, with a population of 97,475 in 2006, is home to two universities and is part of "Canada's Technology Triangle" (Statistics Canada 2009). In addition to the presence of strong financial and insurance services, the city has a thriving research-based communications technology industry thanks to companies such as Research In Motion (RIM), inventors of the BlackBerry™, and sponsors of the RIM Institute. Cambridge, with a population of 120,371 in 2006, and Kitchener, with a population of 451,235 in the same year (ibid.), were less prosperous cities during the first decade of the twenty-first century and, unlike Waterloo, their populations were declining. There were also lower levels of education and literacy among the residents of Cambridge than among those living in Waterloo (Statistics Canada 2008). Not surprisingly, then, the presence of a "reading class" was more marked in Waterloo where there were, for example, thirteen bookstores (compared to Cambridge's six) and Kitchener (which had ten bookstores). In Kitchener, the main public library was well known locally for its dynamic events program led by Readers' Advisory librarian Sharron Smith. Angela Caretta, the librarian representing Cambridge on the organizing committee, noted that, unlike the public library resources in the neighboring cities, those for Cambridge were focused primarily on programming for children, not adults, prior to the launch of the citywide read (pers. comm., 2003).

The population demographic in and around the three small cities is heterogeneous, but not as multiracial as larger urban centers such as Toronto and Vancouver: descendants of German, Scots, British, Portuguese, and Italian settlers live alongside Mennonite communities. Of the three cities, Kitchener continues to receive a larger amount of immigrants each year than the other two, and, in 2006, just over 10 percent of the population was categorized by Statistics Canada as members of visible minority groups (2009). In an attempt to engage as wide a cross-section of this local population as possible, the organizers of the area's OBOC program have selected a range of titles since the program began in 2002, from literary fiction to genre fiction and, less frequently, nonfiction. Where possible, and in common with the programs in Chicago, Huntsville, Seattle, and Vancouver, copies of books in languages other than English have been acquired by the public library system (OBOC committee, pers. comm., 2003). However, since the focus of the OBOC Kitchener-Waterloo-Cambridge program is on books by Canadian authors, translations in languages other than French are not always available. The organizers' ongoing goal has been to achieve a modest annual participation rate of 1 percent of the population (about 4,000 people), but that goal is usually exceeded. In the first year, for example, according to the Kitchener Public Library website, "more than 6,800 readers were counted and an additional 3,000 people attended author events" (2011). By 2010, on the basis of tracking book sales, library loans, event attendance, and web-hits, the organizers estimated that over 100,000 people had participated in the program (ibid.).

The organizing committee, an overwhelming majority of whom are women, consists of several public librarians, an independent bookseller, the editors of *The New Quarterly* (a literary journal), a representative of the city of Waterloo, and occasional coopted members, including school teachers, and high school students. The committee list among their criteria for OBOC book selection the necessity of choosing a Canadian book by an author willing to spend three days, usually in September, in the community at the end of the five-month program (OBOC committee, pers. comm., 2003). For their third iteration of the program in 2004, they chose Nino Ricci's first novel, a book that was initially published in 1990, and which forms the first part of a trilogy. Ricci won several major literary prizes for *Lives of the Saints* in his native Canada, in the UK, and the US, and the novel was published in seventeen countries (Ricci 2012).[1] Not only was Ricci a well-established author in Canada by 2004, but he also had family ties to the area because he grew up in Leamington, Ontario, not far away from the three cities. Although the featured book was well known and was far from being Ricci's most recent publication, his social and cultural capital and the book's Italian setting attracted readers to the OBOC activities. These ranged from a talk about Italian wine that took place in a branch library, to a literary bus tour around Leamington and the Ricci family's tomato-growing business. Whereas the small-scale events such as the wine talk and book discussions had audiences of between ten to thirty people, and the bus tour was at capacity with fifty participants, the author events each drew an audience of two to three hundred attendees.

The sense of occasion and spectacle at these latter events was marked, partly because the author visit is the culmination of this version of the OBOC model, unlike the programs in Seattle, Liverpool, and Vancouver, which tend to feature the book's author at launch activities right at the start of the program. If the excitement and suspense created by the gradual buildup of publicity and preceding themed activities was almost tangible at author events, so was the welcoming and friendly atmosphere, as Ricci himself noted:

> Here, after the first couple of events, you sort of let loose, you feel like
> you know these people and it just feels, it feels more personal, more

intimate . . . I feel very special to be picked out in this way and to be made the center of attention and have a large number of people specifically there for this book, and over a three-day period, that's very rare . . . to have that sense that people are paying that much attention to the book and thinking about it and meeting over it and discussing it, ah, it really makes you feel that there's a point, I guess, to writing the book, 'cause as a writer you have little sense of that. (pers. comm., 2004)

Nino Ricci's reflexive description of his experience as an OBOC author indicates how self-affirming and professionally validating it can be for a writer to become a temporary, (albeit "special" and celebrated) member of a large reading community. Notably, Ricci analyzes his experience by talking about affect, which is also the way that many readers in our own study articulated their response to book events. The sensation of intimacy that he experienced in K-W-C was partly produced by the material conditions of the events: the warm introductions offered to the audience and to Ricci by committee members; the "Q & A" opportunities and book signings that facilitated interactive audience-author communications; the choice of community venues associated with family life, education, and leisure (schools, libraries, a sports center), and the fact that there was no admission charge to the readings. Although the two author events held in the evening attracted a demographic that was predominantly white, female, and middle-aged, the age range was always wide, and the mixed gender audience at the daytime author event at Elmira High School was (understandably) dominated by teenaged students.

Public author readings are always a type of performance in which the author's cultural authority and, sometimes also their celebrity status, is underlined by the conceptual and physical framing of the event. In K-W-C, publicity posters featured a large head-shot of Ricci as the background to a reproduction of his book's cover, the tagline, and details of the OBOC program events. The semiotics of the poster suggested the importance of the author and his book but also drew significant attention to the reader via the tagline, "Open Up the Book, Open Up Yourself" (see Figure 6.2). Thus, conceptually at least, the events were framed in terms of an active reciprocal relationship between writer-performer and reader-spectator facilitated by a shared text (the book), although the organization of physical space within the venues reinstalled the primacy of the author as the originator of meaning and the director of spectator response. The Elmira High School author event, for example, took place in the informal atmosphere of the school gym, but benches and chairs had been arranged to create a temporary "theater space" with lines of seating directly facing a lectern intended for Ricci's use. Current pupils and members of the public (some of them alumni of the school) made up a varied and multiethnic demographic. Two other event spaces, the Kitchener library theater and the lecture room attached to the Clemens Mills library (and high school) in Cambridge, were more formal in appearance and the physical layout of the large rooms created a notable spatial distance

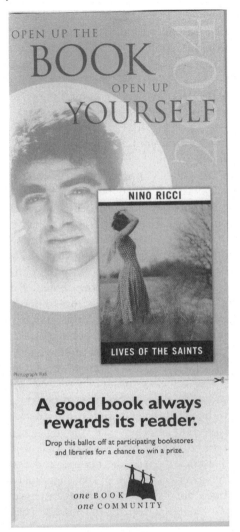

Figure 6.2 Open up the Book, Open up Yourself Placard

Local organizers ultimately concluded that "Open up Yourself" is not an effective way to promote reading programs to male readers

Source: Beyond the Book project: Artefacts and Ephemera, available at: http://epapers.bham. ac.uk/1469/ Image titled Flyer Open up the Book Open up Yourself Nino Ricci

between Ricci (standing at a podium on a raised platform) and the audience (seated in fixed raked seating). These arrangements created a clear division between performer and spectators, enhancing Ricci's "special guest" and "celebrity" status, as well as creating a potentially intimidating environ-ment. However, even levels of lighting between stage and auditoria offset the formal dynamic of these theatrical spaces, and Ricci, a well-practiced public speaker, used gentle humor and frequent eye contact to disrupt the division between himself and his listeners created by physical framing. He also spoke fluently about his life as a writer and his writing process, adopting a friendly, conversational tone as he told anecdotes about himself, his family, and the publishing history of *Lives of the Saints*. By sharing professional information, Ricci temporarily made the audience privy to a world that few of them would know about.

Whereas Ricci's public persona is neither flamboyant nor extravert, his quiet confidence, gentle manner, and an engaging reading style constituted a successful performance that held the attention of the audiences. Spectators responded with laughter and lively questions that Ricci answered thoughtfully, respectfully, and with quick-witted humor. At Elmira High School, he adjusted his performance to suit his younger audience, emphasizing the comic elements within *Lives of the Saints*, recalling and telling jokes about his youthful attempts at writing, and sharing tips with pupils who sought his advice during the discussion period. These context-sensitive and dialogic elements enabled the audience to become more active participants not only in the performance, but also in the interpretation of Ricci's novel. The writer clearly had the opportunity to authorize his text by selecting what and how he read, and Ricci used emphasis, tone of voice, and alterations in pace to enhance the humor or pathos—and thus his interpretations—of the extracts he read aloud. But questions from the audience offered other interpretative frames, along with queries about the practicalities of the writing process: (metaphorical/allegorical) "Why did you choose the last name 'Innocente' for your main character (wasn't this a bit obvious!)?"; "Were you using the title of the book ironically?"; (biographical/mimetic) "Did you base the character of the boy on your personal experience?" or "Did you base the mother on anyone you knew in real life"; or, (intertextual) "What writers have inspired and influenced you?" Whereas these questions are fairly typical of the types of enquiry raised at any author-reading event, the details of the novel that were frequently referred to by readers as the preamble to their question, indicated a particularly careful (and perhaps a repeated) engagement with the text. Audience members also felt sufficiently enthused by the events and encouraged by Ricci's personable and friendly manner to ask follow-up questions, so that a collective, conversational dynamic developed.

Both the discursive and physical frames of the events involving Ricci emphasized the local and community aspects of the program over and above the "star" status of the author. At the "gala finale" held in the Waterloo sports center, for instance, an Italian-Canadian choir began the evening section of the program by singing traditional folk songs, and folk dancers performed (see Figure 6.3). A competition focused on stories of immigration and aimed at young creative writers from local schools also featured as part of the afternoon's events. On all these occasions, Ricci's connection to the area (his family still live in nearby Leamington) was always mentioned either

Figure 6.3 Italian Dancers in Southern Ontario

Local Italian dancers grace Waterloo's sports center to celebrate Nino Ricci's *Lives of the Saints* for the 2004 season of One Book, One Community (Waterloo, ON, Canada region)

Source: Authors' photo.

during introductions or question periods. The author himself was happy to publicly acknowledge his association with the region then and in media interviews. He was also aware that, for some audience members, a more personal sense of connection with him had developed, because they had met his father and other family members during the literary bus tour sponsored by *The New Quarterly* magazine. A visit to the greenhouses run by Ricci's family formed part of the tour that took up an entire day in August and, at CAN $50 per ticket, restricted participation to those with sufficient disposable income to afford the fee and time away from paid work. For those who were able to participate, the tour offered opportunities to gain more intimate knowledge of the author's life and thus a greater sense of affiliation with him. Although the agricultural and business sites visited on the tour of Leamington relate more directly to the second novel in the trilogy, *In a Glass House* (1993), Ricci senior first charmed, and then fascinated some of the participants because of his resemblance to the protagonist Vittorio's father. After describing the bus tours as "phenomenal" events that, in common with other OBOC activities, add a "whole extra dimension" to the selected book, Anna and Liz, both white, university-educated retirees from Kitchener, made a series of astute observations about the way that Nino Ricci's father had presented himself in relation to the visitors and then to his immediate family members (FG 2 P, 2004). Anna recalled a similar incident in *The Glass House* that led her to conclude:

> I thought, he's [Nino Ricci] writing from his heart. And that . . . really as [Liz] said when he [Ricci's father] first came on the bus, he was delight-ful and he just would do anything for us, answer any questions, but as a father I think he was different. (ibid.)

Anna mentioned that she had already discussed her reflections with her book group, some of whom had been on the bus tour with her, and a few of whom had also been alert to possible parallels between what they had read and what they had witnessed. Not only does this circumstance demonstrate a tendency among these readers to interpret fiction biographically, but it also illustrates a thoughtful interest in characterization and personal relation-ships whether they occur intra- or extratextually. Interpretative strategies that highlight characterization and make connections to the lives of authors and reader's own lives are typical within the context of contemporary wom-en's book groups as we noted in Chapter 1, "Reading" (E. Long 2003, 151–56; Rehberg Sedo 2004, 214–20).

What is pertinent to our exploration of the pleasures that readers derive from MREs is the way that Anna and Liz (FG 2 P, 2004) mediate their under-standings of Ricci's novels and the book activities through *multiple* social situations and relations: the other people on the tour, a book group, the audience at the author event, and each other and the researchers in the con-text of our focus group conversation—a conversation that they explicitly acknowledged as enjoyable. Anna and Liz represented themselves to us as highly social readers: they actively seek out opportunities for "organized sociability" (Pawley 2010, 13) and they value the opportunity to reencoun-ter a book through the opinions of other readers. They are also consumers of "live" and interactive entertainments: it is Anna's humorous comment about the brewery visit during the bus tour for *The Stone Carvers* (2001) that opens this chapter. Through their participation in a series of different book-related activities, Anna and Liz are drawn into what Ian Collinson, in his study of readers and "the social economy of everyday reading," has termed "webs of sociality" (2009, 88). Within these webs, activities such as book exchanges "become a way of embedding social relationships through the shared con-sumption of cultural commodities." For readers like Anna and Liz who, like many of our focus group interviewees, are committed to sharing their read-ing, the OBOC model offers the opportunity to do so in ways that are at once public but also productive of intimacy and intensely felt emotional responses. A reader can thus move back and forth through what we might conceptualize as a series of performances of reader selves: the contemplative, silent reader who buys or borrows the selected book and reads it, the embodied seeker of knowledge clutching her book at a "live" event, the socially connected reader sharing her reflections with others in a discussion or during a bus tour, and the feeling reader, who has been touched emotionally by aspects of the events or indeed by the narrative and aesthetics of the text. None of these selves are mutually exclusive and, like all forms of self-presentation, their performance is inflected by material contexts and social codes of behavior that are in turn shaped by relations of race, class, and gender. As middle-class white women with university-level education, Anna and Liz have the financial resources, social confidence, and cultural capital to "be a reader" in complex and varied ways that bring them pleasure.

Talking with readers in the Kitchener region alerted us to an important aspect of pleasure for readers who are recently retired from busy careers, something that we were to hear many times in subsequent research sites: the opportunity that MREs provide to stimulate their intellectual lives and continue with education in an informal but emotionally meaningful way. The author events, for example, presented opportunities for readers to animate their understanding of the novel through learning new knowledge about the author and his life. Mary, a retired professional from Galt, Ontario, who had participated in the Kitchener-Waterloo-Cambridge events since the area's first OBOC program, enjoyed those featuring the author "because I'm always curious about the person behind those words" (KWC 4 P, 2004). Already familiar with Ricci's novel, Mary was, like the survey respondent from her community, motivated to find out about "the 'why' behind the book" rather than by the prospect of a vocal performance of the novel: "The reading I didn't enjoy as much 'cause I'd read it twice, I just wanted to hear him talk. I wanted to hear him talk about how you decided, how you got the characters, I thought some of the stories he had to tell were interesting, I liked that aspect better." When we asked Mary and her friend co-retiree, Betty, to reflect further on the pleasures of events featuring the OBOC author, Mary commented, "The personal touch really is, it really is important . . . Like I really got a feel of the man. You know, I was sitting close enough to him, I feel I really got a feel of this author and now that I'm reading the third book I really feel like I know the author." Mary's use of affective language, especially her repetition of the phrase "I feel . . . I really feel," constructs semantic connections between knowing and feeling, or, more particularly, between cognitive and emotional (or intuitive) ways of knowing. Her narrative also draws a parallel between her physical proximity to the author's body and her capacity to gain a sense ("a feel") of who "the man" might be. Mary then appears to take this knowledge and the intimacy of the para-social experience into her reading of the third novel in Ricci's trilogy suggesting through her emphasis ("now . . . I really feel like I know the author") that the opportunity to hear and be near the author deepens her intellectual reading experience of the text.

Betty took up Mary's emphasis on establishing a sense of intimacy with the author and the subsequent enhanced reading experience, but with a mimetic inflection that indicated a belief in creative writing as an autobiographically informed craft: "There's a connection there. There's a fact that [the author event] makes it more human, it makes it more real and more human. That this person, um, created these characters and, perhaps, I always think perhaps there's some personal stuff in there" (KWC 4 P, 2004). Betty's interest in "personal stuff" was echoed by several other readers whom we met, not all of whom, however, use this biographical knowledge to inform their reading or reinterpretation of the text. Catherine, for example, is a member of the Moody Blues Book Club, a mixed-gender group, the majority of whom are currently teachers or retired from teaching. We met the book club one evening in the café, which lends its name to their group. An enthusiastic supporter of book culture in the Kitchener-Waterloo-Cambridge area, Catherine had also attended one of the Nino Ricci author events. We asked her if doing so had made any impact on her interpretation of Ricci's novel, she replied, "I found it all interesting. I found his father really interesting, his sister, his nephews, ah, just to understand the family dynamics, and say 'I wonder how much the father, not so much in this story but the follow-up story, is his father' and, um, so it was interesting, but it did not change my opinion of the book" (KWC FG Mixed Moody Blues Book Club, 2004). For readers, author events can reanimate the book and its contexts in different ways that alternatively entertain, inform, and move them, but what they learn or experience does not necessarily alter their textual hermeneutics. For some readers, like Betty and Mary, however, achieving a sense of connection to the author does involve revisiting their interpretation of his text.

Pleasure Interrupted: When Media Clash Rather Than Converge

Ricci adeptly handled the different types of reader-identification with him and his work at the headline events, but some tensions emerged between the desire of readers and the program organizers to claim and to know him as a "local" hero, and the necessity of recognizing him as a celebrated nationally "consecrated" writer of literary fiction. The latter was partly driven by the economics of the events, but also demanded by the involvement of the local media—radio, television, and newspapers. Awkward shifts in mood, pace, and activity within the gala event foregrounded these competing demands. The choir and a City of Waterloo politician opened the evening, and the ideological project of increasing literacy, particularly among younger people, was made explicit by the politician and via the awards made to winners of the writing competition. An abrupt transition into a filmed interview with Ricci by journalist Robert Reid transferred the action from the floor-space level with and immediately proximate to the semicircles of chairs put out for the audience, to a simple but static "set" (two chairs angled toward each other and framed by leafy plants) on a raised platform. Simultaneously, the atmosphere shifted from a "folksy" celebration of the Kitchener-Waterloo-Cambridge community to an overtly mass-mediated spotlight on an individual "celebrity." After being encouraged to participate by singing along with the choir, while drinking wine and eating "Italian" foods, and applauding the competition winners, the audience was required to become quiet and physically still and relatively passive for forty-five minutes until Reid introduced a twenty-minute "Q & A" session. Although spectators complied with the changes in tempo and mood in terms of their physical behavior, the attention of many individuals waned visibly during the filmed conversation.

Whereas the interview was professionally performed by Reid and Ricci, the loss of a dynamic energy between spectators and author not only marked the shift from one form of mediation to another, but also a change in the format and pitch of entertainment on offer. The Reid-Ricci interview was not primarily produced for or aimed at the "live" audience but at a future one who would watch the exchange on television at a later date. The physically narrow frame of the "set" and the communicative strategies employed by Reid and Ricci might well have contributed to a television viewer's sense of intimacy with the author of *Lives of the Saints*, but the same production requirements stalled the emotional intensity of the "live" gala event. Moments of media "clash" such as this one suggest that some aspects of contemporary entertainment culture threaten rather than enhance certain kinds of pleasure, by obstructing rather than facilitating the intimate relationships desired by writer and readers. In the case of the Ricci gala, and, similarly at Jhumpa Lahiri's Town Hall appearance in Seattle analyzed in Chapter 5, "Worker," the media of "live" and broadcast event did not converge with ease, but interfered with the sociability of the occasion. The economies of event production and the technologies required to produce a degree of spectacle (however modest in scale and effect), not to mention the economy of celebrity culture, demand that the featured writer appear publicly in various media. MREs require the publicity and, to some extent, the cultural legitimation lent by broadcast media, in order to both attract corporate sponsors and to convince the gatekeepers of state-financed grants to maintain funds for these and similar arts ventures. But these elements—money, multiple media, celebrity, and the public event—do not always add up to a sociable and entertaining night out for readers. Whereas we would not dispute the interdependence of media in the production of contemporary "literary experiences" (Collins 2010), we do want to complicate the somewhat celebratory tone of Jim Collins' account by emphasizing that, for readers, the results are not always pleasurable.

In Waterloo and Seattle, switches in communicative strategies, plus the technical exigencies of filming or recording disrupted the types of pleasures that readers seek from "live" OBOC events. Intermediaries such as professional interviewers and production equipment enhance rather than collapse the sense of distance between reader and author, thereby reducing the emotional intensification associated with feelings of intimacy. Although the invitation to the audience to step into the world of the book is maintained, the sociability that accompanies, and for some readers, enhances this immersive opportunity, is threatened by the inevitable reduction in interactivity between attendees and the writer. In other words, the sharing of reading is made into a more rigid ritual, one that leaves little room for the vocalization of reader experience that can establish common ground among audience members. Whereas mass media contribute to the circulation of books and, for that matter, to the circulation of an OBOC program beyond its immediate geographical community, they can also disrupt the participants' relation to an intimate public sphere of shared reading in which social connection and locality are key constituents. OBOC programs hook together the local with the social. The promise of belonging that the OBOC model extends to a physically present community, however ephemerally, is often realized or grounded by the representation of a regional or local community through the book selected for MREs or via the activities themselves, as we saw with the Ricci bus tour and author events. For the reader's part, making the local social, as we term it, involves various modes of identification, including an embodied connection with place as an actual and textual environment, learning about the local area in terms of its human geography, and expressing an affiliation with place- or group-based histories.

MAKING THE LOCAL SOCIAL

Canadians in our study were especially motivated by the local and regional aspects of programming to participate in MREs. Of those who participate in *Canada Reads*, 14 percent (267) nominate "highlights local or regional author" as the fourth top reason why people participate. In the Vancouver survey, it was the top reason for participating in the city's OBOC program (19 percent; 43). This response may be underscored by the fact that several Canadian adaptations of the program deliberately focus on the connections between the selected book and the local area. In common with the Ontario focus of the early years of the Kitchener-Waterloo-Cambridge program, for example, OBOC Vancouver featured writers with a connection to the city or the province of British Columbia for nine consecutive years, beginning with Wayson Choy's memoir *The Jade Peony* (1995), which was the selection in 2002, and followed by Timothy Taylor's novel *Stanley Park* (2001) in 2003. Both writers have strong Vancouver connections—Taylor lives in the city and Choy grew up there—and both books depict areas of the city in realistic and, thus, recognizable, ways. These mimetic textual features lent themselves to some creative place-specific programming such as a cook-out in the actual Stanley Park. Other events like walking-tours of Chinatown and a dim sum hosted by Wayson Choy resonated with his book's examination of growing up as a bilingual and bicultural person within Vancouver's large Chinese-Canadian community.

Although these "hands-on" and site-specific activities are consistently popular when organizers arrange them, they can risk reproducing the racialized (and classed) geography of a city. The risk is exacerbated if the participants are predominantly white, middle-class people who are invited to undertake a style of cultural tourism in order to "discover" an area that they may not visit often, let alone inhabit. Even if groups are more diverse, many large urban cities in North America and the UK have been subject to urban planning decisions that signify cultural difference very clearly in order to attract visitor dollars and pounds. In Vancouver, for instance, Chinatown is visually coded as a distinct cultural space thanks to special bilingual street signs and street furniture. Whereas the signage draws attention to the size of Chinatown (it is the second biggest in the world after San Francisco) and infers its historical importance in the city's history (although not the long and infamous history of state-sponsored racist discrimination endured by generations of Chinese-Canadians), there is no escaping the demarcation of the area from surrounding neighborhoods. However, the direct involvement of community leaders in the organization of the program for *The Jade Peony* meant that the risk of inviting readers to adopt the "tourist gaze" (Urry 1990) and to exoticize an unfamiliar part of town was recognized and mediated. Todd Wong, a writer and member of the organizing committee, suggested how partnerships between the public library and community organizations can support communities "beyond the border of the library" and even facilitate cross-cultural dialogue in material ways. Wong observed, for instance, that "having Wayson [Choy] read at the Dr. Sun Yat-Sen Gardens [in Chinatown]—you get a double hit from the [Chinese-Canadian] community because you're supporting the community activities" (pers. comm., 2006). One way in which OBOC programs might help readers to make the local social, then, is by taking events outside of institutional spaces such as libraries to specific locations associated with histories and communities that require wider and more complex representations.

Readers themselves make local places meaningful in various ways. Trudy, a professional administrator from the Kitchener-Waterloo-Cambridge area, who is in her late fifties, offered a provocative and enthusiastic account of her participation in the literary bus tour around sites depicted in Jane Urquhart's novel *The Stone Carvers*:

> I really enjoyed [*The Stone Carvers*] and the bus tour really bought that book alive . . . because you went to places that were described that were part of the book and somehow it seems real, you know—I know it was a novel, but just, you know you could see the characters, you see the places . . . you felt that what was described could have happened and you were where it—, you were where these places were. (KWC FG 5 P, 2004)

For Trudy, the tour offered a pleasurable opportunity to construct a mimetic identification between textual representation and the physical environment. Her sense of having stepped into the world of the book in both an imaginative and physical way, moves her from an abstract textual world (a bookish space familiar to professional literary critics but not comfortable for all readers) to a more material, in the sense of visceral, relationship with the text. Trudy's embodied and sensory experience prompts a form of identity work in which she "feels" (and by implication comes to know) the events of the novel both emotionally and physiologically. Although Trudy's experience is profoundly personal in one sense, her switch between first person and second person pronouns recalls the presence and participation of her friends and bus-mates ("you were where these places were") as well as her desire to convince us as her listeners ("you know") that "the bus tour really bought that book alive." The shared aspect of the experience is, she infers, partly constitutive of the almost magical sensation of being in a place that is at once materially present and inscribed by a fictional narrative. That magical aspect, and Trudy's self-conscious account of it—"I know it was a novel, but . . . you could see the characters"—breathes life into Rita Felski's conceptualization of contemporary aesthetic experiences of reading and film viewing as enchantments: "Modern enchantments are those in which we are immersed but not submerged, bewitched but not beguiled, suspensions of disbelief that do not lose sight of the fictiveness of those fictions that enthrall us" (2008, 75). Immersed, but not alone, Trudy can, it seems, be at once profoundly within herself and yet outside her everyday self during this state of enchantment. The bus tour dramatizes the text for her, but it certainly does not simplify its meaning, its effects, or its affects.

Trudy's pleasure in reading *The Stone Carvers* was clearly deepened by the experience of the bus tour, but this redoubled pleasure was not the case for her with *Lives of the Saints*. Like Lynn, a fifty-eight-year-old teacher and self-described "obsessive-compulsive reader" who "really struggled through the first thirty pages," Trudy "struggled through that book" but claimed that "the road trip brought it . . . along for me a little bit," and also provided motivation for finishing it: "I forced myself to read it because I was going on a trip and I just felt I had to." Trudy seems to have felt that reading the book was an essential precursor to the road trip, although she was fully aware that text and place would not coincide as straightforwardly as they had the previous year, because "there was a disconnect between the book and the trip." Perhaps Trudy is also hinting at a sense of peer pressure when she says "I felt I had to" read the novel. Reading in the social context of a community of other readers can create imperatives to be prepared in advance of a group meeting (Bessman Taylor 2007, 132; Dunbar-Odom [2006] 2007, 118; E. Long 2003, 160, 178; Rehberg Sedo 2004, 183–85, 206). In any case, she found a practical but creative way to enjoy and identify with the places visited on the tour for Ricci's novel:

I found now I learned a lot on that bus tour, not related to the book particularly, but I mean the whole concept of greenhouse gardening. I mean I thought I'd do a [. . .], a greenhouse with a few tomato plants. I never had any idea of how it was done. But I found that absolutely fascinating. So, the—, the trip was—, was very enjoyable.

Knowledge gained from an extratextual context surrounding a writer's work was ultimately a sufficiently satisfying outcome for the trip, bolstered, as Lynn suggested, by their shared interest in "the insight into people" demonstrated by Ricci and provided in "real" life by the memories and stories his family chose to share with them.

Learning about local places can also promote expressions of cultural and familial affiliation. In the same focus group, Jill, a librarian in her late forties, who grew up in Leamington, talked about how she went on the tour, because: "I just wanted to see how others saw my community." Jill curated her home-place and recreated part of the tour for us within the focus group when she explained, "It's a very small community, but it's one of the most multicultural for communities that size and when you went on the tour you [. . .] saw the Lebanese Club, and we did see, um, the German Club as well, there's a German Club there . . . " Reencountering her local place and its histories through the eyes and comments of the other participants and the Ricci family lent a different tenor to the notion of making the local social. For Jill, her "place" became new: "I must admit I learned a lot of things on the trip that I didn't think of," she told us.

Jill's and Trudy's comments hint at one of the limits of OBOC programming that promotes connections between the selected text and the local landscape or built environment. For people who are recent immigrants or new arrivals to a city or town, the connections may seem less attractive and engaging, and the modes of belonging and identification on offer irrelevant or even alienating. After all, to be what Wendy Griswold has termed a "cowbird," that is, a reader who uses regional literature to put down roots in a new place, and to develop some sense of cultural identity (2008, 70–100), requires education, the resources to be mobile by choice and cultural capital. Many new Canadians who arrive in the Kitchener-Waterloo-Cambridge area are not in possession of these resources and may not feel comfortable about entering the spaces associated with OBOC programming. Libraries, in particular, are symbolically and organizationally linked to the racialized histories of literacy, as Megan Sweeney eloquently analyzes in relation to the United States (2010, 21–27, 40–46). These histories are differently inflected by national specificities in Canada where, for example, Aboriginal people frequently had English-language print literacy forced on them in the residential school system (Edwards 2005), and in the United Kingdom where the complex legacies of imperialism are still being played out in respect of print literacy. Public libraries in all three nation-states are among the sites where the meanings of reading have been traditionally made. Offering the OBOC selection in a series of languages is a small step toward countering the English-language focus of the model in these countries. Taking events into community centers and public parks (Vancouver), into workplaces such as offices (Kitchener-Waterloo-Cambridge), into children's playgroups, seniors' homes, and centers for asylum seekers (Liverpool, UK) creates alternative sites of and for reading. Who can be a reader and what reading means starts to alter and become less attached to a set of print literacy skills if events deemphasize textual interpretation and promote other pathways of comprehension into and out of the selected book's themes and ideas. Listening, storytelling, painting, photography, music-making, doing various handicrafts, and cooking are all examples of activities that organizers in Huntsville, Kitchener, and Liverpool have employed to encourage and enable people to make the local social regardless of whether they have read the book.

In spite of these initiatives, localized OBOC selections can run the risk of appealing mainly to a particular niche group of readers, whom one Waterloo focus-group member described as, "A really quite female, middle-aged and older crowd, who can afford to spend for the most part the thirty bucks to get a ticket to get someplace" (Betty, KWC FG 4P). Attempts on the parts of the organizers in Kitchener-Waterloo-Cambridge to reach a more diverse constituency than this, especially more men and younger readers in their twenties and thirties, were reflected in a shift away from the focus on contemporary literary realist fiction to a more varied selection of texts once the program had run for a few years, including genre fiction (a sci-fi novel was chosen for 2005, and mystery writer Louise Penney's *Bury Your Dead* [2010] for 2011), topical nonfiction (*100-Mile Diet* in 2008 [Smith and MacKinnon 2007]), and a Canadian political satire in 2010. For OBOC Vancouver, the local/regional connection was only severed in 2011 when the selection was *The Hitchhiker's Guide to the Galaxy* (1979) by the late British author Douglas Adams. The choice, and the change from highlighting regionally connected writing, was deemed controversial by some local media commentators who felt that the tie to local and regional realities was crucial to the aims of the program as a citywide read designed to bring Vancouverites together (Lavender 2010).

For some participants, however, the pleasure of making the local social is less about how the setting, themes, and content of the book connects to their immediate physical environment or cultural group, and more about the idea or reality of people coming together to share reading as a community. Readers articulated different notions of community ranging from the imagined to small-scale face-to-face communities. As a fifteen-year-old member of the predominantly African-American Kenwood Academy High School Teen Book Club in Chicago remarked, "It makes me feel good to be part of a city that is all reading the same book" (pers. comm., 2005). She speaks for many other reader-participants whom we met in various geographic locations and who enjoyed being part of an imagined community of readers as well as being able to share thoughts about the book face-to-face with a regular book club or as part of one of the many stand-alone book discussions that pepper the programs of virtually all iterations of the OBOC model. There were also more informal examples of book talk inspired by citywide reading programs. Joyce, a forty-two-year old part-time corporate writer and mother of young children, enthusiastically described her pleasure in taking part in a "big conversation" with her family and neighbors:

> I think [OBOC Vancouver] is so cool! It's very cool. And . . . like, I don't know if we would've had the discussion in my neighbourhood

about *Stanley Park* if it wasn't—because I think the woman that had brought it up in that conversation [among our neighbors] was reading it because of One Book, One Vancouver, and was so excited about it, and then my husband and I were excited about it, so we started this big conversation. I really don't think that would've happened otherwise. (OBOV FG 4 P, 2006)

Joyce appears to derive as much enjoyment from the sharing of excitement about the book and the program as she does from the "big conversation" that she was able to participate in with the intimate community that the book inspired. Both the excitement and the dialogue, it seems, can forge social connections among people, however temporary these may be.

Many readers described ephemeral experiences of community as sufficient to their social and creative needs. "Just seeing someone on the bus holding the book made me smile" was a phrase we heard several times, for instance. After reading an OBOC selection, several readers in different cities found themselves noticing what other people were reading while they were commuting to work on public transit. Amy, a twenty-nine-year-old hospitality professional who described herself as "Hispanic mixed race," did not feel the need to strike up a conversation with other readers in Seattle, but she explained that "it was kind of neat. I mean interesting just to notice that, you know [. . .] And after a while it made me happy" (Seattle Reads FG 4 P, 2007). Even encounters over books that are not as brief as the ones that Amy describes can produce a pleasurable sense of ephemeral community that is meaningful while it lasts, but does not necessarily translate into a more sustained set of relationships. Referring to our focus group as one in a series of OBOC-related experiences, Mary Lynn, a fifty-eight-year-old high school teacher from Waterloo, put it this way:

Like here I am on a Saturday afternoon, all kinds of things I should be doing, but I mean, to me, this is what it's all about. Here's, you know, four people I've never met before and we're all part of this community. We're on the bus trip, you know, and we've experienced together, we've experienced the book together, we've experienced other books [from OBOCs] together, um, but I wouldn't recognize them if I passed them on the street. (KWC FG 5 P, 2004)

Mary Lynn's comments suggest that her desire to be part of this textual community of readers motivates her to put aside "all kinds of things" that she "should be doing" during her weekend to come and share reflections about literary experiences with people she does not really know but with whom she nevertheless shares a common ground of texts, and OBOC activities. Connecting with strangers or acquaintances (and scholars of print culture) validates Mary Lynn's "feelings for books" (Radway 1997) and, in particular, her sense that sharing reading experiences with a loosely connected community of readers "is what it's all about." To return to Lauren Berlant's (2008) formulation, Mary Lynn (KWC FG 5 P, 2004) recognizes that she is part of an intimate public sphere, but unlike Berlant's (ibid.) conceptualization, this intimate public is actualized so that "emotional contact" and shared emotional knowledge is not only an imagined "fantasy" but also, however briefly, a lived experience of connection (viii).

The sense of belonging that Mary Lynn articulates might appear to be rather superficial in terms of her relationship to other community members, but it is clearly fulfilling some kind of personal need. As a working person with a family, Mary Lynn, in common with other men and women in similar situations, has limited leisure time and the "pick and mix" aspect of OBOC programming can suit a busy schedule in the way that a regular book group may not. Different modes of belonging to the different communities that constitute a person's everyday life can also satisfy a desire for a range of relationships to people, places, and creative texts. Lynn, the "obsessive-compulsive reader" who was part of a Waterloo focus group that we discussed above (KWC FG 5 P, 2004), eloquently described and contrasted the different experiences of community that she encountered through her membership in a series of arts-centered groups:

Lynn: I think some communities are intimate and I consider my book club to be intimate and I consider the small group that I go to the movies with to be intimate. And I reveal myself to them. But this One Book, One Community gives me a whole other social network that is part of the warp and the woof of holding a community together. I can carry that book with me into a restaurant or to have a cup of coffee and somebody will stop and say, "I've read that book."

DeNel: Has that happened to you?

Lynn: Yes. So I think that that's the important part is the casual . . . I've read that book oh, so were you part of the program? What program? Oh, One Book, One— . . . and then you can do the little sort of casual . . . I may not recognize that person two weeks from now, but it's certainly happened to me twice. (KWC FG 5 P, 2004)

Lynn's commentary articulates the added social and public dimension that a shared reading event can bring to the experiences of and possibilities for belonging. What Lynn appears to enjoy is the contrast between her "intimate" communities, where she is prepared to "reveal" her private self, and the sensation of a more public self that is moving through the "whole other social network" that constitutes her wider community. For Lynn, OBOC enables her not only to imagine herself as a part of a larger community, but also to render it fleetingly visible as she conducts a casual conversation with a stranger. In that brief moment of mutual recognition, Lynn and her interlocutor are citizen readers, articulating a common ground and a mode of belonging constituted by (geographic) place, the program, the text, and their shared sense that reading is valuable within their daily lives. Whereas they are part of an intimate public sphere that legitimates the realm of feelings and affective engagements with books, they are more than "consumers of common texts and things" (Berlant 2008, viii)—they are also recognizing each other as situated in time and as connected to a specific place. A casual connection in this case is one that allows for an encounter that illuminates Lynn's sense or states of being (a consumer, a reader, a local, a stranger, among others) as well as her modes of belonging. Of course, Lynn's keen interest in the arts and self-awareness about her membership in various kinds of community may inform and deepen what she comprehends to be the symbolic meaning of a brief chat about a book. An experienced member of various groups, Lynn is most likely alert to relational ways of knowing and being.

There is some evidence from our study that suggests that people who are likely to participate in OBOC either by reading the book or attending an event are predisposed to join groups focused around a common interest, especially those focused on the arts. Among the relatively small number of survey respondents who answered an open-ended question about the types of groups to which they belonged, 41 percent (133) nominated book groups, 12 percent referred to theater and/or musical groups, and 5 percent were members of writing groups. Athletic clubs and university or school clubs were also mentioned by 11 percent and 12 percent of respondents, respectively, and religious groups by 8 percent. Although the quantitative data is not conclusive, it prompts us to reflect further on the desires and affiliations of the citizen reader. Perhaps the citizen reader is a person who, like Lynn, is an active member of several kinds of communities, or, to recall Robert Putnam's (2000) work on the cultural and social significance of associations and clubs, someone who already possesses social capital (as well as cultural capital). So, do readers use MRE activities to enhance their social capital?

When we asked survey respondents who had attended an OBOC event whether they had gone alone or with other people, just over half of those who responded (55%; 202) reported that they had participated with companions. During our participant-observation of public events, we noticed that the majority of audience members were attending with at least one friend or family member. Larger groups of, for example, five or six people (frequently all women), when approached directly by one of us, generally turned out to belong to the same book group. Meanwhile, among the respondents answering a survey question about meeting someone new at an OBOC event (208), only 18 percent stated that they had done so and would stay in touch with that person. Taken together, then, these findings suggest that OBOC events, whereas they may render visible a formerly imagined social network of readers, do not necessarily enable a participant to expand her friendship circle or develop bonding social capital in the way that her book club might. Meanwhile, it seems that book groups engage with OBOC activities not only to experience the various pleasures that we have been delineating above, but also as a way of enhancing their group bonds. Appearing as a book group in public at an event, as opposed to gathering together in a more private space such as a member's home or a meeting room in a library, may also enable members to garner cultural legitimacy for their hobby. Occasionally, cultural intermediaries or authorities refer overtly to the presence of book clubs as part of their introductions to or commentaries on events, as Nancy Pearl did during the Seattle Reads event with Jhumpa Lahiri when she praised the quality of questions being posed to the author (see Chapter 5, "Worker").

Readers engage with citywide reading programs because they can pursue a variety of behaviors and enact a range of, what we have called above, reader selves. Whether she is alone or with others, whether she has read the book or not, a participant can engage with social practices of reading. Groups of attendees may use an evening out at a film screening or an author talk to reaffirm their social bonds as book clubs, family members, or friends. Other readers enjoy the fleeting physical encounters with fellow readers in their community or catching a glimpse of the "wider social network" to which they belong. Readers also articulate a range of feelings of intimacy and connection that they derive from their participation in OBOC events. As we have illustrated, these experiences vary from their para-social relationships with the author of the selected book to embodied (and enchanted) engagements with the "imagined" landscape of the selected text during a literary bus tour. Lynne Pearce has noted "how reader-text and reader-audience intimacy reproduce one another" (1997, 236) within small groups of readers, and we demonstrated how, on a larger scale, this combines with readers' intellectual and emotional curiosity about "the 'why' behind the book" to shape the performance dynamic at author talks. That dynamic is successful for readers when their desire to know and their need to act as feeling individuals is catered for by a thoughtful or energetic performance, a flexible event format that is not too rule-bound nor too orchestrated by cultural intermediaries, and a space that is organized so that participants can see and hear each other. The pleasure of being part of the entertainment can be disrupted or stalled by the intrusion of other media if the effect is to distance the audience from the action, as the events in Seattle and Waterloo demonstrated. However, some aspects of contemporary media and popular culture enhance the enjoyment of participants, adding glamour and a sense of occasion that help to dramatize the world of the book, not only its contents and its contexts, but also its production history and status as a cultural object. As we have demonstrated, locality, sociability, and a degree of spectacle combine to produce successful shared reading events. Celebrity authors, experts, local journalists, and even stars from film or television are among those employed by citywide reading programs to talk about, act out scenes from, or read aloud from the selected book. The importance for readers of bringing the book and its world "alive" is underlined by the pleasure inspired by the opportunities that OBOC events offer to reanimate and share older cultural forms like storytelling. In this regard, OBOC programs represent an interesting variety of forms and practices that relate to print and nonprint media. As readers of books negotiate with "the late age of print" culture, this variety appears to provide some (at times nostalgically inflected) reassurance as well as some strategies for making sense of books in a digital era.

"EVERYTHING BECOMES ALIVE!": REACTIVATING ORAL CULTURES

Not surprisingly, the more loosely structured activities for smaller groups of participants such as book discussions, and hands-on craft and visual art workshops (painting, scrap-booking, making collages) often prompted the sharing of memories, as well as interpretations of the book and the issues that it raised. But even at some of the larger, more formal events, readers felt sufficiently relaxed and inspired to share personal stories. Julie, a white woman in her thirties from Liverpool in the UK, articulated her pleasure in hearing a culturally diverse group of readers compare their own lived experiences about immigration to those portrayed in Andrea Levy's novel *Small Island* (2004). This public sharing of personal histories occurred in a large downtown public library during a headline author event as part of 2007's Liverpool Reads, which formed part of the four-city Small Island Read discussed in Chapter 4, "Money":

> Some people talked about when they were growing up in Ireland . . . people talked about growing up as a black person in Liverpool [. . .]—it was just lovely to see that, that people with different experiences were all bringing them to this book event, this reading, and then sharing in the enjoyment and being able to relate to this book in their own ways, everyone obviously related to it in different ways. (FG 5 P, 2007)

In common with readers in other locations, Julie enjoys the sense of being part of a community of readers and seeing her local community temporarily transformed from an imagined into an actual physical formation. Like many contemporary readers, Julie is clearly also interested in hearing about other people's interpretations of texts. However, her comment that "it was just lovely to see that" suggests how unusual it might be even in a port city with a long history of immigration and an ethnically diverse population for people to share their personal and familial histories with each other. Whereas Julie's enjoyment in hearing about "different experiences" could be understood and dismissed as the glib consumption of cultural difference or simplistically relativist ("everyone obviously related to it in different ways"), her description of the OBOC event infers the deeper cultural and historical significance of the "different experiences" that she heard. "Growing up in

Ireland . . . growing up as a black person in Liverpool" recalls the infamous "No Blacks, No Dogs, No Irish" signs that were posted by landlords in most British cities from the late 1940s through to the late '60s, a racist trend that is represented through the actions of landlords and shopkeepers in several scenes of Levy's 2004 novel.

The memories articulated by Liverpudlians at the Small Island Read launch event authenticate Levy's work because they draw direct parallels with "real life," but their discursive power extends beyond a reading of the book. Reexperiencing a book through the medium of other people's narratives can begin to alter or complicate the ways that inhabitants of a city understand the history and contemporary realities of the places they occupy and the spaces that they move through. What "becomes alive" during an author event can thus refer to more than just a convincing performance of the text by the writer. For these Liverpudlians, sharing memories about the difficulties and pleasures of immigration constructed a complex narrative about their city that identified Liverpool as a significant node within a series of global diasporas, not the least of which is the African diaspora. The audience thus de-emphasized the London location, which is central to the novel's plot, so that the local relevance of the historical, cultural, and social impacts of imperial relations that Levy explores became more visible. As we have explored elsewhere, the politics of this collective "reading" of *Small Island* are significant because the city of Liverpool is often represented nationally and internationally through images that foreground white, working-class masculinity (Fuller and Procter 2009, 27).

An accomplished and entertaining performance can certainly help to foreground the serious issues raised by a book by animating characters and interpreting the world of the text. Levy's ability to represent her novel orally by modulating her voice and referring to her own family history was highly praised by several readers whom we met. The Liverpool Reads event that Julie and others attended incorporated Caribbean food and music as well as a high level of interaction between the author and the four-hundred-strong audience. Such a multisensory experience combined with Andrea Levy's skill at reading aloud to bring the book "to life again" (Suzanne, Liverpool Reads FG 6 Mixed, 2007). Suzanne, an African-Caribbean woman in her early forties, went on to note that "the music set an atmosphere . . . It was quite evocative." Hearing Levy's voice and the information that the author shared about her family history brought *Small Island* "alive" in a multidimensional way for Liverpudlians. As Tracey, another African-Caribbean woman in her early forties in the same focus group put it, "[Levy's] experiences came through and you can see how she [. . .] kind of portrayed the personalities and that came out in the way she spoke and their [. . .] personalities came out through her, the way she was speaking and I thought that was, uh, that was really good." Anne, a white woman in her fifties who was also part of the discussion about the launch event, explained how Levy's performance "made me want to read [the novel] again for the third time. Because when she did her bit, and she, you know, she can do the accents. When we read . . . you don't say it out loud, do you? I don't read out loud, not any more, anyway." Anne's comment was met by murmurs of agreement from the other members of this particular focus group, because only two of the younger people in the group had small children at home with whom they read aloud.

Anne's narrative about the Levy event suggests that OBOC activities that engage with or which inspire oral practices such as storytelling remind many adults of their earlier reading or listening pleasures as children. In another UK city, Viv, a retired teacher from Birmingham, recalled:

> I can remember very, very distinctly reading with my mother early on, or at least being read to by my mother and it was the wonderful Grimm's fairy stories and all of the Hans Anderson stories, and I still have, I can feel the magic of being read to and later on taking those books and getting under the covers with the torch and reading them. (R & J FG 2 P, 2007)

Viv's memories about the "magic" of reading that she went on to reproduce when she could read print on her own were echoed by many other readers in our study who had grown up with books in their homes. For readers whose parents could not afford books or who were not inclined or able to read for pleasure, the public library or primary school were usually the sites where the "magic" of being read to and access to books was realized. Readers' first memories of print culture were often visceral and delightful, but there were also indications that formal education can stifle the pleasure associated with these early practices of reading that were immersive in both an imaginative and somatic way. For another Birmingham reader, Sibyl, a white woman in her late forties whose professional life includes writing, listening to audiobooks with her stepchildren during long car journeys, rekindled a love of canonical literature, after the "desire" to read the classics had been "quite successfully killed" by university study (R & J FG 1 Non-P, 2007). Sibyl's comment highlights the gap between the purpose and function that literary reading can have in a reader's everyday life and the institutional versions advanced in the academy. Not only is reading, in Sibyl's terms, suffused with longing, desire, and love, but it is associated with listening and sharing. Reading, in this definition, is less about the form and technology of the artifact (that is, codex versus audio recording) and more dependent on intense emotions and a social context that bring the desire for "the classics" back to life. Sibyl's experience serves as a reminder that, as the artifacts of print culture become remediated through current and yet-to-be-imagined digital technologies, the possibilities with regard to the social practices and processes of reading are expanding.

One of the significant social dynamics at play in many face-to-face OBOC events is the restoration and reanimation of oral cultures of storytelling and reading aloud. Some of these practices, like being read to, may trigger nostalgic memories of early encounters with books, whereas others are more culturally specific to particular times and places, perhaps, as in the Liverpool example, inspiring storytelling by readers themselves. Another site where this practice occurred was in Huntsville, Alabama, during events that formed part of the program for the 2007 iteration of OBOC Madison County. When we attended book discussions and formal talks about the film adaptation of *To Kill a Mockingbird* and the author Harper Lee's life, we repeatedly observed senior participants articulating their initial encounters with both the book (published in 1960) and the film (released in 1962). Such memory work frequently involved speakers locating themselves geographically, sometimes citing familial connections to Lee's family, offering commentary on aspects of the social context such as race relations, describing their enjoyment of the text, and then reflecting on how a recent rereading had differed from earlier readings. A senior at the last presentation and discussion of the film recalled for the audience the omnipresence of heat in the book. He said he felt the hot, Southern sun as he read. Yet, as a young person growing up in the South, he did not remember feeling the intensity of the heat that Lee was able to evoke in the book and that, he felt, the film also represented effectively.

Other participants explored what had and had not changed about small-town life in Alabama in the intervening years since their first encounter with the novel. The organizers of the Huntsville events created an interactive format, allowing plenty of time for questions and discussion. In common with the organizers of the Andrea Levy event in Liverpool, they served refreshments, and provided a space for the audience to meet and talk together before and after the formal segments of the events, whether that was a talk by Harper Lee's biographer or a presentation by a professor of film studies about the Oscar-winning film adaptation. The combination of a hospitable atmosphere, a much-loved "modern classic" book choice, and an Alabama setting and author were all factors that encouraged readers to engage in personal storytelling that sought to make sense of the tellers' lives (past and present).

"Not That Much Has Changed": Storytelling and Silences

In Huntsville, the social dynamics of one type of shared reading practice became vividly visible. Readers articulated various forms of individual and place-based identification, and these articulations were validated and made collective through the exchange of stories. Some narratives were conservatively nostalgic or even sentimental in tenor and content. For example, readers talked about being able to play outside safely when they were children, or about the simplicity of life in the 1930s and '40s. Other readers hinted at painful experiences such as racial segregation, poverty, and the isolation of rural living. Most reminiscences, whether they were personal histories or whether they related to a first reading of the novel, tended to prompt reflection on how economic and social circumstances in Alabama had changed for the better. However, several participants in our focus groups lamented the fact that the public discussions had not led to any real debate about contemporary racism. One middle-aged white man felt the book afforded a real opportunity for such a discussion, given how effectively, in his words, "Harper Lee really captures something about the South: the way that kindness sits alongside violence" (FG 2 P, 2007). Huntsville librarian Cleareaser Bone, who runs an African-American book club, reflected on the reasons why the events attracted a predominantly white audience.

> So . . . as far as the blacks go, like I said, "what's in it for me?" It's not a great ending. And I think the attitude is, "well, not that much has changed." And I think the take on [*To Kill a Mockingbird*] is a bit different than whites, who feel that, "yes, it [civil rights issues and racial equality] is better." And I'm not saying it's not, but it's not where it could be, or not where it should be. And even in Huntsville, it's not where it could be. So I think that was why there was a little less involvement I think, on the part of blacks participating in this [program]. (pers. comm., 2007)

Bone's comment complicates the notion that a book with local relevance will inevitably generate reader engagement and pleasure: it might result in a lack of engagement and feelings of social marginalization. Her reflections also foreground how programming and book selection may exclude some groups of people while satisfying the needs and pleasures of other cultural groups.

As the Huntsville example suggests, there may well be silence rather than dialogue when it comes to the present-day realities of "race" relations in a city or region. The entertainment format of events and social mores about behaving politely in public can prevent the exploration of troubling topics. At the events that we attended, the performance of southern hospitality often reinforced the tacit rules of polite social interaction: the offering and sharing of food and drink was a sincerely felt ritual, but one that also reaffirmed the status quo by denoting traditional ways of understanding social etiquette. The careful display of a silver punch bowl (containing fruit punch) surrounded by fresh-cut flowers at a talk and book discussion at a branch library, for example, represented the apotheosis of old-fashioned, elegant, and deeply gendered hospitality. As visitors, it was remarkably difficult for us not to comply with the rules and consume that extra cookie or accept a slice of cake, whereas as researchers, we felt compelled to increase the standard and quantity of treats and beverages that we brought to focus groups. Social ritual can be charming and seductive even when it is entwined with histories of inequality. Many of our focus group participants from different cultural backgrounds were keen to remind us that Huntsville is not "typical" of Alabama or the American South, yet the practices of hospitality that they were all keen to demonstrate suggested otherwise.

The modern-day, well-educated population of Huntsville may not be "typical" of Alabama or the American South in respect of literacy levels and income,[2] yet the city's geography remains, as it has been for decades, racialized along a north-south axis marked by the major arterial road. Participation at OBOC events tended to reproduce this polarity so that the only large event held in the north of the city at Alabama A&M (Agricultural and Mechanical) University (a historically black university) had a majority African-American audience. Meanwhile, book discussions held in various branch libraries south of the highway and music evenings, film screenings, and a talk by Lee's biographer Charles Shields, all of which were staged in the main library in the small downtown area, drew a predominantly white, predominantly middle-aged and older, audience. The only exception was an amateur production of the theatrical adaptation of *To Kill a Mockingbird*, which had a short run at a downtown theater. Perhaps reflecting the cross-racial and cross-generational constituency of the cast, the play attracted a more diverse crowd in terms of age, gender, and ethnicity than any other event that we attended.

Thousands of miles away in Liverpool, the legacies of the transatlantic slave trade were being discussed more openly at reading events. The framing of the novel for the Small Island Read 2007 partly accounted for this because the official materials contextualized Levy's text in terms of the history of British slavery and postwar immigration (see Chapter 4, "Money"; Fuller and Procter 2009, 30–33). However, as we have explored in detail elsewhere, some readers who took part in book discussions demonstrated only a gestural empathy with the everyday racism encountered by two of Levy's character-narrators, Hortense and Gilbert, acknowledging that it "was awful" but failing to make any connections with instances of discrimination in contemporary Britain (34).[3] Other readers, like Tracey, Anne, and Suzanne, whom we quoted above, whose personal and professional lives had generated a nuanced knowledge of their city's interracial relations and class dynamics, were quick to reinterpret the novel's representations of racism in terms of current issues. These included the ways that British tabloid newspapers portray asylum seekers. During the focus group, these readers also identified class and race as covectors that shaped their city's geography and they offered a thoughtful analysis of urban space in Liverpool (34–36).

As the lead organizer of activities for the 2007 iteration of Liverpool Reads, Bea Colley had paid attention to this geography (pers. comm., 2006). Building on the "grassroots" work of partnering with community organizations begun by Jane Davis which we discussed in Chapter 5, "Worker," Colley ensured that book discussions, visual arts, and other creative events related to the themes of *Small Island* or the partner books selected for younger readers (*Refugee Boy* by Benjamin Zephaniah, first published in 2001, and a picture book, *Amazing Grace* [2007] by Mary Hoffman), took place across the city in locations like schools, community centers, and hospitals. Specific projects included working with the Asylum Link (book discussion group), the Yemeni Arabic community (youth drama project), young Somalis (creative writing), and primary schools (art project run by refugee artists). Whereas this approach did not create many opportunities for cross-racial or mixed-age groups of people to come together, it did continue the long-term work of The Reader Organisation to create better access to books and reading for Liverpudlians, especially groups whom Davis and her colleagues define as socially marginalized or socially vulnerable. At the community- and location-specific events that we attended, it became clear that the safety of being able to talk about painful experiences within a known group of people was important to, for example, young men who were asylum seekers.

Citywide reading events may, as they did in Liverpool, facilitate the sharing of experiences and personal stories that articulate the troubled histories of cities and its inhabitants. As the examples from both Huntsville and Liverpool suggest, however, there are no guarantees that these stories or the interpretations shared during book discussions or "live" staged events will lead to cross-racial empathy or the construction of what Elizabeth Long, in her longitudinal study of book groups, terms an "intersubjective bridge" (2003, 186). Superficially, it would seem that established reading groups are more likely than OBOC events to offer an environment in which readers might explore experiences outside their own lives in depth, even if doing so brings up unsettling issues and emotions. Unlike book groups that meet regularly, and which over time establish trust among members, protocols about behavior and shared preferences in terms of book selection and reading practices, OBOC programs can be relatively undemanding of participants. A panel discussion, a talk by an expert, or a dramatization can be enjoyed without any prior knowledge of the selected book and there is no expectation that each audience member will ask a question or offer an interpretation of the text unless they wish to do so. Even the book discussions held as part of OBOC programs, while aimed at smaller groups of people than the more formal staged events, can be attended as a "one-off" activity without any obligation that a participant return for subsequent meetings. For time-pressured individuals who are interested in ideas, books, and reading, the OBOC format represents a viable option among many leisure and entertainment activities.

Despite the limitations of the various event formats, however, OBOC can, as Liverpool Reads and OBOC Madison County did in 2007, bring attention to issues of racism, cultural difference, and social injustice. By approaching these topics through a series of different activities, the organizers of both programs staged a series of public opportunities for discussion, debate, and storytelling. As we have shown, these mass-reading initiatives appealed to and proved meaningful for some participants, who took up the chance to share their memories, personal histories, and opinions. In neoliberal democracies, public forums for discussion are increasingly rare, and people's agency over their material realities has declined, so that popular cultural formations and texts assume greater symbolic and emotional power (Peck 2010). Therefore, OBOC events are among those formations that can enable participants to explore various modes of being and belonging, many of which are experienced and articulated in terms of affect.

CONCLUSIONS: STATES OF BEING, MODES OF BELONGING

Analyzing the practices and narratives of readers who participate in OBOC activities demonstrates two important things about the nature of shared reading that occurs in MREs. First, the pleasure of this type of shared reading is more about social relations and the experience of moving within the social network produced by the OBOC model than it is about textual hermeneutics. The multiple mediation of the text through various kinds of formal performance by authors and experts, theatrical, cinematic and visual art adaptations, visits to the built or natural environment, and other participants may, of course, add to or alter an individual reader's interpretation of the selected book. But it is the emotional connections and social intimacies that these multiple mediations make possible that intensifies the pleasures of learning about the world of text. Some readers are able to perform or display different aspects of their subjectivity, including various reader identities that range from an internalized and reflective persona to a highly social reader actively seeking out opportunities to reencounter the text and connect with other people. Who can be this type of reader, however, is circumscribed by the need to possess cultural capital in relation to literary culture, and a degree of social confidence that enables access to the sites and spaces of OBOC events. As we briefly explore in our final chapter, sometimes that confidence derives in part from intensely somatic and physiological relationships with the book as a material object. For some readers, displaying their love of books is a literal and physical action that can be replayed in the company of others in order to display their identity as an experienced and passionate reader.

Second, what the model offers are modes of belonging that include what we have termed ephemeral community (Fuller 2011; Rehberg Sedo 2010). In other words, participants can make connections with other people, but, unlike book group membership, for example, there is no firm requirement to read the book, or to speak about it. Not much maintenance work is needed in order to be part of a temporary community, and a sense of belonging can come just from seeing another reader holding a book. But, as we have also explored, citywide reading events offer participants other opportunities for expressions and experiences of affective belonging that involve more emotional effort and social engagement on their part. The extended time that readers are encouraged to spend with the selected text over the course of several months activates an immersive experience of reading. This kind of immersive reading involves both inner reflection and an emotional and intellectual movement beyond everyday life and a person's idea of their subjectivity or self, as our analysis of reader activities in Kitchener-Waterloo-Cambridge illustrated. When participants articulate their emotional knowledge about this kind of experience in public, the fantasy of connection between people who are at once private and public persons can, however fleetingly, become realized. The citizen reader, as we have conceived of her, is not necessarily a person who volunteers her time and gives back to her community in material ways; rather, she is a reader who engages with shared reading events in order to feel part of a social network that is visible in a public domain.

Articulations of belonging and community offer provocative clues about the desires of citizen readers, especially women who form the majority among participants, to find "something to hold on to" aside from institutionally sanctioned ideas of citizenship. Even if what is being offered is imbricated with conservative fantasies, such as a nostalgic yearning for small-town community, what is felt is no less "real" to the citizen reader, as Trish, a public relations assistant from Nova Scotia in her early twenties, who is a regular participant in *Canada Reads*, explains:

> I often find myself reading books that take place in small towns, regardless if it's Canadian or American . . . being from a small town . . . it . . . makes me . . . really appreciate what I have, because it's something to hold on to. (CR FG 5 NP, 2006)

MREs engage with and play in to these readers' desires to "hold on" to something familiar. The books and related events key in to readers' place-based identifications or familial histories or their appetite for knowledge about the wider social and political relations in which their local community is situated. In these various ways, shared reading programs hold out the promise of belonging, offering an occasion for, and even the location of, affective community.

7   Book

I go into other people's houses and like they have two books or not many of them, and I'm like, "What do you do with all your time?"

—Anna, Big Read FG 5 P, 2007

I like the feeling of a new book. I like opening it for the first time. But I do like the old books, too. I like the musty smell, and I love going into libraries, but there's something that feels so good when you take it out of the Chapters' bag and the receipt is still inside the cover, hopefully the spine breaks for the first time. I don't know what it is!

—Jacqueline, CR FG 2 NP, 2006

I love that old image of the wingback smoking chair, with the ladder up to the, like I want one of those libraries one of these days, and the smell of books, I love that, to me it's very important. So, yeah, I go to a used store but I don't tend to take books out of a library 'cause I know I want to own the book. And I want it to be nice, like I like hard copies a lot of times over paperback, because I really want to own it for a long time.

—Sarah, KWC FG 3 NP, 2004

I like to buy books. I love books (laugh) so we've built shelves and shelves and shelves in our basement to house all our books and then when we run out of room, we have to start giving some away. So, then we go through and we pick out our least or the least favorite (laugh) and get rid of them. Or I'll give them to my mother, or they'll cycle through friends or something like that. But we tend to hold onto books that we really enjoy, I don't know, they're kind of like a piece of art, you might go back and look at it again or, you know, reappreciate it in some way.

—Judy, KWC FG 1 NP, 2004

What does reading look like in the contemporary moment? This question still intrigues us as the research project we began in late 2004 draws to a close. During the intervening years, we have witnessed the proliferation of digital alternatives to the codex format of the book and the introduction of mobile devices upon which to read them. These technological innovations have engendered new ways of promoting reading and changed the experience of reading itself. In previous chapters, we considered the ideological, symbolic, and cultural foundations of contemporary shared reading practice. However, we have left our discussion about the aesthetic aspects of the book and readers' relationships with books as material objects as a fitting way to conclude our exploration of MREs in the twenty-first century.

In the last chapter, we touched on the emotional response triggered in some people when they talk about growing up with or without books and reading, and how this suggests that a broader discussion could take place concerning relationships that readers have with their books. We introduced the notion of the book as a physical object when we illustrated how readers touch and caress their books while listening to an author speaking at an event. This physical response to the materiality of the book can have various meanings, ranging from an unconscious display of the emotional comfort that a book provides, to a conscious exhibition of "good taste." Similar to the readers we highlighted in previous chapters, the readers we quote at the beginning of this one reveal a profound physical and emotional attachment when describing their books and the place of reading in their lives. These articulations of readers' feelings about the smell, size, and texture of books express their somatic relationship to their book collections. The physical presence of books brings these readers pleasure and comfort, makes them feel at home, and allows some of them to share their passion for reading with friends and family. For others, books are "art" objects to collect, treasure, and review across time: commodities to be owned, certainly, but also aesthetic artifacts that reward repeated acts of contemplation. Our readers demonstrate that the codex evokes a powerful response in its devotees, and that the book as an object remains both emotionally meaningful and culturally significant for many keen readers. Taken together, the quotations adeptly point toward the special place that reading occupies—and that the codex book maintains—in an era of media digitization that is evolving from one week to the next.

Some scholars have argued from a humanist perspective that the nature of the book as a written communication technology leads to its community— and intellect—building potential (Birkets 1996; Reinking 2009, 488–89). As our readers attest at the opening of this chapter, the codex book is an ideological "sociocultural artifact" (Reinking 2009, 491). Whereas the cultural and intellectual values ascribed to the codex book have always been debated, David Reinking suggests that they have consistently been perceived as authoritative and informative (ibid.). As a written genre, books encourage "linear, serious and abstract arguments" (496). Further, Sven Birkets (1994, cited in Reinking 2009, 489) argues that the contemplation that a printed book demands serves a sociocultural function because it encourages reflection and the discussion of ideas. But, as the readers quoted above make clear, and as Reinking himself notes, "Books are [also] a valued form of aesthetic expression and pleasure" (2009, 493).

One of the reasons why reading books remains a popular leisure activity and why there has been a "resurgence" in shared reading practices—or, at least, widespread recognition that shared reading serves individual needs as well as the public good—is because the book in its codex form still has a special status. The act of reading, commonly viewed as credible and significant, imbues the codex with symbolic power in the contemporary culture of the nation-states that we investigated. Consider book collecting as an illustration. Those who collect books, we might assume, are doing so to create new knowledge or perhaps, a new kind of knowledge evident in the collection itself (DeMaria, Jr. 2009). The book as a physical artifact is invoked when we consider what books can teach us, and how they might facilitate and encourage a productive and enlightening exchange of ideas. As we see in the opening quotations, the ownership of books, too, carries with it not only physical emotions and reactions, but also real and symbolic capital. This is true especially for collectors as well as within the portion of society that values reading. Manjit, a thirty-three-year-old woman from Bristol, illustrates the symbolic relationships that readers have with books as objects, even if they do not always read the books they possess or purchase: "My father-in-law . . . buys books like mad and doesn't always read them but just likes to see them" (FG 1, Bristol, 2006). The physical act of buying and owning books also evokes strong emotional responses from readers, such as that from Kate, a thirty-five-year-old student and nurse in Bristol. When she told us about her mother's response to the many books that she owns, she said: "[my mum asked] 'Are you sure you need all these books?' [and] 'How many of them have you actually read?' And I don't think she grasps that I just love them" (FG 2 Feb 17 2006). For Kate and almost every other reader with whom we spoke, the emotional relationships that one has with books are linked as much to the physical book as to what is inside the covers. Readers encode the physical artifact with a conception of what reading is, and with what books can offer. Their reactions are often tied to memories of pleasurable experiences that they have had, as is illustrated vividly by Blanca, a sixty-one-year-old poet and writer in Nova Scotia:

> I have a vast collection of children's literature. Um, I think when we moved, I stopped counting at a thousand books. My friends said they were never going to help me move again. And three of the bookcases in our downstairs is all children's books, especially, um, sort of . . . the middle—the beginning of young adults readers. I love that genre; I've always really, really loved it. And we have *tons* of picture books, too, but I have a whole bookcase filled with, um, Nancy Drew and *Anne of Green Gables* and *Little Women* and things like that. (CR FG 7 P, 2006; emphasis in the original)

Blanca and other readers were often clear in identifying themselves as readers first, and then, second, but just as crucially, as readers who have very specific taste preferences. In this way, the memory work that our focus groups facilitated helped to identify readers' "feelings for books" (Radway 1997). Readers, and the cultural workers who produce OBOC programs, may find pleasure in reading as both a solo and a shared activity, but they also suggest ways in which the materiality of books reinforces an experience of distinction upheld by many contemporary readers.

We began our analysis in *Reading Beyond the Book* by emphasizing our interest in the uses that readers make of books and reading. The experiences described by readers above—the physical sensations inspired by paper, binding and covers, the physiological relationships with the codex, the pleasures and distinction associated with collecting books—are, of course, significant uses. However, in an era when reading experiences are available in different media and formats, and the future of the codex form of the book is in question, we suggest that reading be considered as a "media experience" (Ytre-Arne 2011). Rather than limiting our ideas to "media use" or "media consumption," understanding reading as a "media experience" (ibid.) provides a richer picture of the perceptual and aesthetic notions of reading as it occurs on various media platforms and through different types of technologies and devices. Dimensions of "media experience" (ibid.) include economics, technologies, perceptions, aesthetics of technologies and texts, and cognitive, emotional, communicative, and social experiences (Gentikow 2005a, 2005b). Many of these dynamics have preoccupied us in this study. Our examination of MREs in *Reading Beyond the Book* can thus be understood as a demonstration of how printed books contribute to media experiences during a period when the codex still occupies a special place in keen readers' lives. Our study illustrates that, as in the past, books enjoy a relatively high cultural status that is not shared by magazines, movies, television, games, and other media forms.

As book historians and researchers into contemporary reading practices, we have naturally been curious about the growth of MREs in the period surveyed. Why has there been a proliferation of MREs when there are so many other ways to spend one's leisure time, including opportunities for engaging in popular culture? And why reading events, when there are so many alternatives available to the person who wishes to experience storytelling? The answer lies, at least in part, in the special status that the book has retained within the three nation-states highlighted in this volume. Traveling storytellers in various parts of Europe, family salons of the nineteenth century, and feminist literary societies of the 1960s demonstrate how shared reading has evolved over many centuries. Regardless of the form they take, these opportunities to read together maintain their strong attraction, and the MREs of both the late twentieth century and early twenty-first century illustrate the most recent resurgence in shared reading. However, contemporary iterations of shared reading involve more agents and are delivered and remediated through more channels than in the past. Digital technologies and innovations in communication allow contemporary readers to experience the story and share their impressions in ways that go far beyond words on a page. People who participate in MREs are offered an immersive opportunity, through multiple media, to not only share a book, but also to connect with other people through a series of "live" events as well as via online forums. Our analysis of these events demonstrates, too, that traditional meanings of reading persist. Reading books, and, in particular, reading literary fiction, is socially inscribed as a worthwhile pursuit in Western cultures, whether the goal is knowledge or pleasure. Finally, there are agents within the reading industry (publishers, agents, television producers, publicists) who recognize the financial potential of MREs and work to keep reading in the popular public consciousness.

In part, the popularity of MREs is indicated by the steady growth of programs in North America and the UK, and by the number of readers who participate in them. The perception that book reading is equally available and accessible to everyone (Collins 2010) lies in the growing middle-class populations in each of the nation-states that we studied. This observation, alongside an increase in levels of education, further explains the "Why now?" aspect of shared reading events. Particularly relevant to contemporary reading culture is the fact that more women are accessing higher education than even forty years ago. Meanwhile, the graduates of forty years ago, a time when book clubs in their current form became popular, are reaching retirement age. These women are more likely to have attained senior positions in their chosen field, and often seek new ways to use their skills when they retire and have more leisure time. For this demographic of women, the community-focused aspects of MREs, alongside the opportunity to share reading in creative and intellectual ways, are very appealing. The shared reading model that has traveled from Seattle to Halifax, and across oceans to London and Brisbane is a gendered model of reading that adapts aspects of contemporary book groups, such as relationality, sociability, and personalized ways of reading. Not surprisingly, women readers, cultural workers, and managers have also been integral to the model's success.

Throughout this book, we have conceptualized events that are organized around the cultural product of printed books as social formations and processes. We are interested in "why people come together to share reading" and, in conceiving our original project, we were much less focused on individual interpretive practices. "Beyond the Book," the title of our research project, illustrates our early observation that MREs are more than an individual book and its reader. As our case studies have illustrated, MREs are social and cultural phenomena that form, inform, and reproduce contemporary meanings of reading.

Those meanings include an idea of fun: an expectation that entertainment and spectacle, social connection, intimacy, and, perhaps, a sense of belonging to a community, are part of the reading experience. Contemporary readers, after all, are always involved in more than one set of media practices. Readers are also moviegoers, online game players, and television comedy show watchers. These practices interrelate and reconfigure the meanings of each media experience. Our study of contemporary *reading* practices, however, tells us much about what it means to live in an era of neoliberalism. As we have argued throughout the book, reading is often promoted by institutions or event organizers as a way for individuals to better themselves and (by extension) society. But it is problematic to conclude that the act of reading a book is always a potential tool for social change (see Sweeney 2010). Reading along with shared reading, in particular, illustrates the contradictions and inconsistencies that result from readers distinguishing themselves from others, while at the same time seeking human connection through pleasurable leisure-time activities. In *Reading Beyond the Book*, we have analyzed the various structures and agents that inform cultural policy discourse, as well as the organization of media corporations and the interlocking "fields of cultural production" (Bourdieu 1993) that exist within the reading industry. In doing so, we have created a more complete picture of how a specific aspect of contemporary reading culture is modeled as an entertainment, and then transferred and taken up by different media in an era of global media networks.

BOOKS, READING, AND MRES: THE POTENTIAL FOR SOCIAL CHANGE

As our chapters have illustrated, MREs are produced by cultural workers who, and funded by government and private organizations that, often idealize the potential for social change through shared reading programming. Our analyses have also led us to question how we might conceptualize social change: What scale should be considered? What is the relationship between individual transformation and wider social change? Is change only change when it is structural, or can change be ideological, philosophical, and symbolic? Elsewhere we recognize that writing groups and book groups do have a social dynamic that can produce some type of group agency (Fuller 2004; Rehberg Sedo 2004). However, that agency does not necessarily connect with or inspire individual or group involvement in social activism or social movements. The same largely holds true for MREs. However, we do not dismiss the change as insignificant because it is small-scale and social in its effect. We argue that instead of disregarding what happens in shared-reading contexts—whether in book groups or in MREs, and, indeed, those that take place over the digitized airwaves—analyzing them can tell us much about contemporary cultural and social values.

Whereas their goals are laudable, MREs do not create new readers or effect fundamental social change. However—turning once again to Raymond Williams's (1977) work—change always includes some aspects of continuity. Williams allows us to think about contemporary reading events as social phenomena and relationship-building opportunities that are not simply ends in themselves. Rather, each MRE is a dynamic process that impacts in some manner, positive or negative, the dominant, residual, and emerging culture of reading in the sites where it takes place.

We observed, for example, a reproduction of social values in the MREs that we studied. Members of sponsoring organizations and individuals who participate usually come from similar social demographic backgrounds: middle- to upper-middle-class, white, professional women in their mid-forties and older. In many instances, the readers articulated the same idealized goals of the events, and indeed, of reading, as did the event organizers. This is, in part, a result of the production and reproduction of the value of reading as it is represented in the mass media. The shared values among organizers and participants also illustrate the consistent, symbolic, and cultural values that educated women bring to the public arena.

On a small scale, however, social change can happen. In Chapter 5, "Worker," we introduced Liverpool's "Get into Reading" (GIR) program (Figure 7.1). Reading programs similar to this and Chicago's "Literature for All of Us" do not necessarily fit our definition of MREs, but we recognize

Figure 7.1 Jane Davis, LaCoya Kote, and Rebecca Brown

Jane Davis (center) of Get into Reading spends time in Chicago with book club leaders LaCoya Katoe (left) and Rebbeca Brown (right) of Literature for All of Us after meeting at the 2007 Beyond the Book conference

Source: Jane Davis's photo. Permission granted.

the influence that their producers have had on the literary print culture networks in their respective cities and, in fact, on each other.[1] Quite apart from the number of people who have been involved in reading groups as these programs have expanded, the collaboration between their producers demonstrates the importance of the social and collegial networks within the reading industry. Similar success at attracting new readers and promoting social change can be seen in branch libraries of Vancouver Library Downtown Eastside and in cities where the programming included primary and secondary schools, and immigrant and newcomer organizations in Chicago, Vancouver, Kitchener-Waterloo-Cambridge, Liverpool, and Bristol. The social change that we witnessed takes the form of nonelite groups gaining access to various forms of literature. When a young pregnant woman is permitted to choose the book for her book club, or a group leader is given the flexibility to choose a poem or prose work for a GIR group, the empowering nature of these acts encourages social change at an individual level.

The GIR project and "Literature for All of Us" were perhaps the most "radical" of the reading programs we studied. They are equalizing forces and can be considered change agents because they attempt to bring print culture and knowledge to the masses in a capitalist society where print literacy is a necessary prerequisite for economic survival. The GIR program is unusual because participants do not need reading literacy skills in order to participate. In effect, the GIR model attempts to shift what we mean by reading when we refer to the operation of reading printed texts, even as it democratizes the notion of who can be a reader.

We also encountered moments when, through reading, people became empowered to challenge oppressive systems and attitudes and open up possibilities for change in their own lives and the lives of others. In addition to the examples that we considered in Chapters 5, "Worker," and 6, "Reader," for instance, we heard about a woman confronting her parents' racism when discussing Andrea Levy's *Small Island* with her mother, and a young woman in Chicago articulately addressing sexism in her high school. These disruptive moments do not necessarily alter social structures, but they may "puncture" how people perceive their everyday world (Fuller and Procter 2009). It is also important to consider *where* these moments occur. In virtually every research site at the large events such as panel discussions and theater productions, we noted the marked absence of opportunities for confrontation and communication that could work to enable social change. As we noted in Chapter 6, "Reader," this limitation is due, in part, to the public nature of the spectacle and the emphasis on entertainment. In order to have any social impact, the act of articulating that which is tacitly held to be true, or exposing hidden knowledge to wider scrutiny must take place within the presence of others. These public moments can be made available through the MREs, but as we saw in Huntsville, and, to a large extent, in Liverpool, the potential of challenging contemporary race relations can be lost because of cultural attitudes surrounding public literary events that encourage safe and polite topics of conversation. Much of the failure to generate meaningful conversations about race and gender inequities (which are frequent themes of literary works selected for OBOC events) can be traced to participants' expectations of being entertained. Because the success of many OBOC events lies in their entertainment value, the possibilities for structural social change can be minimal.

Racialized cultural attitudes that regard leisure reading as being a white, middle-class activity can sometimes be successfully disrupted by moving the event outside the library. Although librarians may work hard to make it accessible, the public space of the library remains uninviting to some new citizens. While visiting Bristol, we spoke with Tammi Redmond, a librarian whose branch serves a large African-Caribbean immigrant population. She was frustrated by a prevailing attitude among parents who viewed the library both as a useful place and a valuable learning resource for their children, but not as a space that could offer them anything. Her experience reminds us that book culture is not part of the social history of some immigrant groups in the nation-states of our study. MREs that include nonprint-centered activities, other art forms and aspects of oral cultures, may, however, appeal to a wider constituency of participants if the organizers can actively engage community leaders and community spaces, as they did, to some extent, in Liverpool and Chicago.

Whereas policy makers and some producers regard shared reading as a way to create communities that cut across racial and social lines, the limited nature of the OBOC model means that these communities are not socially inclusive. However, the social formations that are enabled will be important to those who participate. In Chapter 4, "Money," we concluded that the ideological "work" that the promotion of reading is being made to perform in North America and the UK reflects the utilitarian notion that the MRE model—a cultural project—can result in the improvement of society. That is, governmental agencies believe it is less expensive to fund cultural events as social activities than to invest in the systematic reformation of social welfare structures. And whereas minor improvements may, in fact, occur because of these programs, it is unrealistic to expect books and shared reading programs to carry such a burden.

ENHANCED ENGAGEMENT: ENTERTAINING THE CONTEMPORARY READER

If social change is desired by the sponsors and producers as an ideal outcome of MREs, then providing a form of entertainment is viewed as a pragmatic aim. The reading industry as we have conceptualized it throughout this book pays special attention to the spectacle nature of contemporary book programming. At the core, we identify entertainment as a consistent element in the producers' motivations and readers' expectations of MREs.

Indeed, MREs produce serious entertainment, or what we might call *smart entertainment*. Successful OBOC events provide readers with an opportunity to engage in the "modern enchantments" of conscious participation in storytelling (Felski 2008, 75), but in a way that makes the readers feel as if they are also involved in learning. OBOC events produce smart entertainment that allows readers to participate in the book in a myriad of ways that can at once be individually pleasurable while also performing identity work. In this way, then, we would assume that the most powerful agents in the reading industry are those who have the economic backing to create the largest spectacle. Instead, we think the most powerful agents remain those who possess the dominant cultural and symbolic power: publishers and celebrity authors. And, in the era of large publishing houses with large marketing departments, publicists are those who have the ability to get their books into the event producer's hands so they, too, have considerable power—albeit, economic power. As we discussed in Chapter 5, "Worker," interacting with an author can be a job perk for OBOC organizers who work long hours with little or no expectation of financial gain for all the effort it takes to stage these events. These interactions are viewed as rewarding because of the cultural and symbolic value that Western societies place on most codex books as receptacles of information, knowledge, and wisdom. The authors of books selected for MREs are thus also often perceived by producers and readers as knowledgeable individuals. In addition, celebrity culture creates an expectation of intimacy with a public figure, as well as an aura of glamour. Alongside these very contemporary configurations and understandings of what might be involved when authors, books, and readers congregate, the events provide readers with opportunities to engage in the centuries-long tradition of writer-performer and reader-spectator interactions. Our research also revealed that authors who participate in OBOC events are rewarded financially and, more importantly, derive sincere pleasure from connecting with their readers, as we explored in Chapter 6, "Reader."

All MRE producers want to show that reading can be an enjoyable part of life, and that it is not always about edification. They know that the term "popular culture" implies something that is fun whereas many people regard leisure reading as a serious activity. To carry out the necessary spectacle in any successful program, producers recognize that some books are more "discussable" than others. This does not always coincide well with the other material limitations that producers face, such as the requirement that the book is readily available in paperback format or that the topic and theme appeal to a local audience. Consider, too, that the producers of *Canada Reads*—as an overt example—need to attract a wide audience, while honoring the historical culture of the CBC "to inform and educate" Canadians. As our case studies in Chapters 3 to 6 suggest, contemporary fiction most often leads to successful book talk not only on radio, but also in face-to-face book programming.

The readers we investigated illustrated the social value of cultural engagement. For many, the significance of shared reading to identity formation was palpable. But whereas feelings of affective belonging are easily detectable among members of book clubs, the same cannot be said of MRE participants because of the ephemeral nature of these events. And yet, readers who found pleasure in participating readily articulated feelings of affinity and community. As we argued in Chapter 6, "Reader," whereas producers and readers express a shared ideological conception of the OBOC model in their articulations of the social bridging potential of MREs, the readers we investigated derive from their reading a sense of belonging, not only to a collective of like-minded people, but to a place, a region, or a cultural community. However, members of socially marginalized groups find that access to these communities is unattainable, either by choice or by economic and cultural circumstances.

Our analyses demonstrate that the collective interpretation or reinterpretation of stories through reading events and other readers' narratives adds a layer of pleasure to the experience of reading that, on the one hand, might be interpreted as superficial, but, on the other hand, can sometimes be profound in emotional, intellectual, and social ways. Attending public or semipublic events provides readers with opportunities to perform notions of belonging, for instance. Readers can also identify as intellectuals who participate in a perceived high-culture activity. The "intimate public sphere" (Berlant 2008) presents readers with a space in which to confirm, enact, and enhance distinct identity and affiliation. In an era of diminishing opportunities for agency, readers—especially the women readers with whom we spoke—seek an affiliation that satisfies their desire to belong to something beyond institutionally sanctioned ideas of national citizenship. Participating in OBOC events and in radio and television programs offers women a chance to step away from the burdens of paid and unpaid labor, however briefly. Like Janice Radway's (1984) romance readers, readers who participate in MREs may be pursuing an escape or engaging with a fantasy outside their everyday lives, but, unlike the romance genre, which can also fulfill these needs, MREs also extend to readers opportunities for learning, and for being with other people who enjoy the same leisure activities.

In Chapter 6, "Reader," we argued that MREs are successful, in part, because they are a suitable form of entertainment for a certain segment of the population: keen readers who, in the company of other like-minded readers, wish to experience a book in ways that go beyond simply discussing its content. These readers are well educated and can participate because they have at their disposal discretionary time and income. Whereas some readers seek the often ephemeral pleasures offered through the various entertaining events that successful MRE producers stage, other keen readers may refuse to participate because of their resistance to the popular cultural format of the event, or to the selected book, or because they prefer to read alone. So, whereas there are more ways to be a reader and to share reading at the beginning of the twenty-first century, who actually reads and participates in shared reading has not necessarily changed. Readers' education level, gender, age, class, and race do not appear to have shifted radically from previous modern eras. But just as important to this contention are those readers who cannot, or make the choice not to, participate in MREs.

One of the goals of *Reading Beyond the Book* was to provide a transnational analysis of contemporary reading practices through selected case studies investigated via multimethod research. What we have found to be common across the three nation-states of our study are the organizing principles of the programs. Another similarity is the ideals that producers and funders articulate about what shared reading can achieve. In Chapters 1 and 4, "Reading" and "Money," we described how the OBOC model traveled across the nation-states largely because of individual producers from the UK traveling to the US, and via professional librarian networks in North America. The similarities in the model extend from the structure of the events and the texts themselves to the motivations of organizers for producing the programs in the first instance.

While neither numerous nor particularly important or profound, the differences across nation-states seem limited to the emphasis and inflections of the "self-transformation" narratives evident in book programming (see Rubin 2009, 423). Political transformation, or social transformation, is particularly evident in discourse around books and shared reading in the US, as we illustrated with regard to the NEA's Big Read program in Chapter 4, "Money." In the US, the ideology of individualism has arguably been more central to conceptualizations of the citizen than it has in Canada and the United Kingdom. However, as we have argued throughout this book, the politics and economics of neoliberal governments place further emphasis on the notion of the citizen as an independent, yet socially and civically engaged, person. This neoliberal ideology extends across the regions and nation-states that we examined. There are also no notable differences in the cultural assessment of books across the sites. Readers separated by oceans and national boundaries use books in similar ways: not least as a means to articulate a cultural identity, and as a way of displaying their cultural capital to other readers. As we move into a new age where innovations in modes of access will lead inevitably to new definitions and understandings of books and reading, we expect that the ways in which readers engage with books in their various manifestations will provide even more nuanced ways to distinguish oneself from others.

BEYOND *BEYOND THE BOOK*

In a recent class of undergraduate students studying "Reading and Popular Culture," one of Fuller's students asked her classmates, "How many of you would give up all of your codex books if I gave you a Kindle?" Surprisingly, only two of sixteen students raised their hands. Although anecdotal, this experiment illustrates the emotional attachments readers have to their books as material objects. As readers become more familiar with new reading technologies, however, the role of the codex will alter. And on the day when print is no longer *the primary* way for the majority of people to access books, that is when the meanings we attach to reading will change. But to judge by the deeply personal feelings that readers have expressed regarding the codex—not only older readers, or those quoted at the beginning of this chapter, but also readers who are the same age as those undergraduate students at the University of Birmingham—we anticipate that the meanings of reading will change slowly.

We foresee exciting opportunities for future research, some of which emerge from the glimpses that *Reading Beyond the Book* offers into the changing media experience of both reading and shared reading. For example, we were not able to conduct an in-depth investigation into how readers might prefer to read on screen and engage with literature and book talk in a virtual environment. Eventually, readers will be using and combining the new technologies and formats in ways that are unimaginable to us right now. As well, as the number of books produced in electronic formats multiplies, we suspect that books in codex form will become more coveted. Because of the special status of reading and the relationships many readers have with their books, we predict that the codex format will retain its symbolic significance for some time to come. Perhaps the codex will even gain in terms of symbolic status as material books become rarer rather like the collecting culture that has reemerged around long-playing records on vinyl. For the same reason that it is impossible to predict what the next remediation of "a book" will look like (Reinking 2009, 488), future definitions of "a reader" remain beyond the scope of the present study. With *Reading Beyond the Book*, our intention has been to provide an impression of what it means to be a twenty-first century leisure reader *at the present moment*. What we can be sure of with regard to the future, however, is that sharing the experiences of reading is an activity that will survive because readers, as well as the reading industry, are likely to adapt—possibly even to thrive—in the face of changes and innovations in media formats and delivery platforms.

Readers' articulations about reading as a way to reexperience, reenact, or reform the meanings of reading suggest how we might better understand the motivations for and benefits derived from participation in an activity that produces cultural capital while attracting a degree of popular and critical derision. What we have offered in *Reading Beyond the Book* are a series of critical insights into a popular cultural formation that until very recently has not been understood as fashionable within mainstream culture or the scholarship of cultural studies. Our study pays attention to readers and contemporary book cultures in ways that have never been undertaken before. By examining how and why people come together to share reading through publicly staged activities—at the local community level, through broadcast media and online—we have provided a nuanced analysis of a particular product of the reading industry. We encourage cultural studies scholars to approach contemporary book reading practices, as we have done, as part of popular culture that exists across media. At the same time, we recognize how the transnational model of the MRE illustrates the pervasiveness of privilege accorded to book reading as a leisure activity in a neoliberal era. However, as we have demonstrated in this book, interrogating the paradox of promoting a prestige-laden activity on a large scale and via mass media opens up a productive critical pathway for thinking about the ways that cultural value is brokered within "creative" economies.

We ask reading researchers to acknowledge that, whereas we struggle to define future meanings of reading, we must be cognizant that issues arising from incongruent levels of both literacy and access have not disappeared. These inequities are not exclusive to developing nation-states; they are also evident in the countries that we investigated. We invite other researchers interested in reading practices to explore interregional commonalities or differences because the formations of shared reading could look very different in other parts of the world. For the readers in our study who take part in MREs, reading and book talk add structure to their lives. A reader's involvement might satisfy a desire to continue learning, or to discover new ideas and authors. It might help them reaffirm their national, regional, or community identity. Participation in MREs serves various cultural and social needs. Readers read for more than one reason, and many read widely and across genres. Reading for pleasure, as we learned early in our research, is a diversely practiced activity. What is less diverse is that most readers in the nation-states that we examined are quite clear that they classify book reading as a prestigious, high-status activity. Another study in other regions might reveal different values and uses for shared reading.

We do not know what shared reading will look like in another twenty years. But history suggests that many people feel compelled to share their experiences of reading with others. The textual forms that readers will share will undoubtedly change from those in use today. The process of sharing reading experiences might be mediated in a different way. New social formations of shared reading will certainly emerge. But groups of people will continue to read and talk with one another about what they read. Meanwhile, at the beginning of the second decade of the twenty-first century, the OBOC movement remains vibrant and new adaptations of the model continue to appear. Broadcast book programs are also evolving on-air, on-screen, and online. Reading beyond the book is a social practice with a future.

Methods Appendix

The research we employ in this book is a result of a three-year, international project, funded by the Arts and Humanities Research Council, in which we conducted context-specific comparative case studies of reading events. In addition to textual analysis of *Canada Reads* and the RJBC broadcasts, the books selected for the programs, and the media reports and promotional materials of the MREs, our project utilized four empirical investigative measures to better understand contemporary reading practices. In ten research sites across the UK, the US, and Canada, we held focus group discussions, conducted online surveys, carried out individual in-depth interviews, and acted as participant observers during event activities.

The fieldwork locations were chosen based on our familiarity with the local print culture, or because of their significance to the OBOC event model. We also wanted to establish a range in the scale of events and communities we studied (see Chapter 1, "Reading"). Our analysis also includes the qualitative data collected during a British Academy–funded pilot study conducted in Waterloo, Ontario, and interviews in Chicago undertaken in September 2004.

FOCUS GROUPS

Across the three nation-states, a total of sixty-two focus groups were held. In each location, at least four focus groups were conducted with readers who were screened as participants in the MRE, whether it was the broadcast version, such as viewers of the RJBC, or attendees at an author reading for OBOC Vancouver. There were a minimum of two groups with readers who were not participants, and in some instances, groups consisted of both participants and nonparticipants in the events. See Table A1 for demographic information about the readers and the type of focus group they participated in. In a few instances, only one person attended for the discussion.

The focus groups were held between 2004 and 2007 while a particular MRE took place. The date of the focus group is evident in Figure A1. In most locations, we held the focus groups within a two-week period.

Table A1 Focus Group Participants

Key

Responses are noted verbatim, unless identifying information was evident.

X = Reader did not provide information.

Gender

M = Male

F = Female

T = Transgendered

P = Prefer not to say

N = None of the above

Ethnicity

As noted by reader, except when he or she noted Caucasian. In this case, we have entered a 'C.'

Education Level (to accommodate UK and North American systems)

N = No secondary education

S = Some secondary education

O = O levels, GCSEs, CSEs, or equivalent

A = A levels, NVQs, GNVQs, further education, tertiary education, or equivalent

U = University or college degree

H = Some postgraduate or higher education

P = Postgraduate degree

V = Some university/college

D = High school diploma

Class/Social Status

W = Working class

LM = Lower middle class

M = Middle class

UM = Upper middle class

U = Upper class

O = Participant has given an answer outside of the list of choices.

Focus Group (FG) Details

P = Participants in MRE

NP = Nonparticipants in MRE

M = Mixed group of MRE participants and nonparticipants

Name/Pseudonym	Residence	Gender	Ethnicity	Age	Occupation	Education	Household Size	Children under 18	Class/Social Status	FG Details/Date
Judy	Guelph	F	X[1]	X	Teacher	U	2	0	X	KWC FG 1 NP/ 19 September 2004
Liz	Kitchener	F	X	X	Retired	P	2	0	X	KWC FG 2 P/ 20 September 2004
Anna	Kitchener	F	X	X	Retired	X	X	X	X	"
Gayle	Kitchener	F	X	X	Engineer	X	X	X	X	"
Megan	Cambridge	F	X	19	Student intern	V	2	0	X	KWC FG 3 NP/ 20 September 2004
Dot	Cambridge	F	X	X	Union admin	X	2	0	X	"
Sarah	Cambridge	F	X	X	Student admin worker	V	X	X	X	"
Betty	Cambridge	F	X	65	Retired	H	2	0	M	KWC 4 P/ 25 September 2004
Mary	Cambridge	F	X	58	Retired	U	1	0	M	"

(Continued)

Table A1 (Continued)

Name/Pseudonym	Residence	Gender	Ethnicity	Age	Occupation	Education	Household Size	Children under 18	Class/Social Status	FG Details/Date
Lois	Waterloo	F	X	69	Retired librarian	P	1	0	X	KWC FG 5 P/ 25 September 2004
Mary Lynn	Waterloo	F	X	58	Teacher	H	1	0	UM	"
Jill	Kitchener	F	X	47	Librarian	P	1	0	UM	"
Lynne	Waterloo	F	X	60	Consultant	P	2	0	M	"
Trudy	Waterloo	F	X	58	Library administrator	P	2	0	UM	"
Elizabeth	Kitchener-Waterloo	F	X	52	Teacher	H	3	1	M	KWC FG 6 P/ 25 September 2004
Laurie	Kitchener	F	X	55	Retired teacher, bookseller	U	1	0	UM	"
Barbara	Guelph	F	X	X	Teacher	H	3	0	M	KWC FG 7 P/ 27 September 2004
Sue	X	F	X	X	Teacher	X	X	X	X	KWC FG Mixed Moody Blues Book Club (BC)/

Name	Location	Gender	Class	Age	Occupation					Date
Michelle	X	F	X	X	X	X	X	X	X	27 September 2004
Jean	X	F	X	X	X	X	X	X	X	"
Lois	X	F	X	X	X	X	X	X	X	"
Murray	Waterloo	M	X	35	Teacher	U	3	1	LM	"
Liz	Waterloo	F	X	52	Teacher	U	4	0	M	"
Catherine	Waterloo	F	X	62	Retired teacher	P	1	0	M	"
Evelyn	Waterloo	F	X	61	Retired educator	P	1	0	M	"
Mary	Kitchener	F	X	61	Retired teacher	U	2	0	M	"
Linda	Kitchener-Waterloo	F	X	55	Retired teacher	U	3	0	M	"
Carolyn	Waterloo	F	X	53	Physiotherapist	U	2	0	X	"
Elaine	Kitchener	F	X	61	Retired teacher	U	3	0	M	"
Barry	Bristol	M	Poor White Working Class	53	Between jobs	A	2	1	W	Bristol Great Reading Adventure (GRA) FG 1 P/ 17 February 2006

(Continued)

Table A1 (Continued)

Name/Pseudonym	Residence	Gender	Ethnicity	Age	Occupation	Education	Household Size	Children under 18	Class/Social Status	FG Details/Date
Liz	Bristol	F	X	65	Retired	O	1	0	M	"
Manjit	Bristol	F	Indian	33	Human resources manager	H	2	0	LM	"
Judith	Bristol	F	British/White	35	Freelance	U	2	0	M	"
Jill	Bristol	F	C	34	Art Conservation	P	1	0	M	"
Caroline	Bristol	F	C	58	Support work and receptionist	U	2	0	M	
Jane	South Filton–Gloucestershire	F	X	69	Retired	P	1	X	UM	"
Glynis	Bristol	F	White English	53	Audit Commission inspector	P	1	0	X	Bristol GRA FG 2 P/ 17 February 2006
Kate	Bristol (Hotwells)	F	White British	35	Student nurse	U	1	0	M	"
Laura	Bedminster	F	White	31	Volunteer coordinator	P	2	0	M	"

Name	Location	Gender	Ethnicity	Age	Occupation					Group
Denise	Bristol	F	British	32	None	U	4	2	M	"
Neil	Bristol	M	X	50	Self-employed recruitment consultant	A	1	0	W	Bristol GRA FG 3 NP/ 18 February 2006
Ruth	Bristol	F	Black Caribbean	45	Community development manager	U	1	0	W	"
Mary-Jane	Bristol	F	English	55	X	O	3	0	M	"
Sarah	X	F	X	20	Student	A	6	0	M	"
Sarah	Bristol, Avon	F	White	48	Unemployed / novelist (unpublished)	P	2	1	O – Upper middle class in education otherwise classless/ Bohemian	"
Elise	Bristol	F	White British	66	Retired	H	1	0	M	Bristol GRA FG 4 P/ 18 February 2006
Cathy	Bristol	F	British	64	Part-time yoga teacher, retired library assistant	P	2	0	M	"

(Continued)

Table A1 (Continued)

Name/ Pseudonym	Residence	Gender	Ethnicity	Age	Occupation	Education	Household Size	Children under 18	Class/ Social Status	FG Details/ Date
Alex	North Somerset	F	British	26	Teacher	P	3	0	M	Bristol GRA FG 5 NP/ 19 February 2006
Eleanor	Bristol	F	White	26	Painter	U	4	X	M	"
Mike	Bristol	M	White British	49	Café/ secondhand bookshop owner/ manager	H	2	0	M	"
David	Bristol	M	English	43	Driving instructor	A	1	0	LM	"
Lancelot	Bristol	M	British National (White)	18	Student	A	3	0	M	Bristol GRA FG 6 NP Bristol Grammar School/ 20 February 2006
Sonja	Bristol	F	White	18	6th form college student	A	4	1	M	"

Name	Location	Gender	Ethnicity	Age	Occupation					Source
Bethan	Bristol	F	White British	18	Student	A	4	1	M	"
Selina	South Gloucestershire	F	Chinese	17	Student	A	4	2	W	"
John Smith	Bristol	M	British-Asian	17	Student	A	4	1	X	"
Suzanne	Bristol	F	White	17	Student	A	2	1	W	"
Kate	Bristol	F	C	19	Student	A	3	0	UM	"
Katherine	Bristol	F	White	18	Student	A	2	0	M	"
Sarah	Avon	F	White British	17	Student	A	3	1	M	"
Axeworthy	Avon – City of Bristol	F	British	17	Student	A	5	3	LM	"
The Whistler	Bristol	F	White	18	Student	O	3	1	M	"
Tom	North Somerset	M	White C	18	Student	A	3	0	M	"
Gary	Halifax	M	No ethnicity Q on the form	24	student	V	2	0	M	CR Student Focus Group NP/28 February 2006
Laura	Halifax	F	No ethnicity	23	Student, part-time	V	2	0	M	"

(Continued)

Name/Pseudonym	Residence	Gender	Ethnicity	Age	Occupation	Education	Household Size	Children under 18	Class/Social Status	FG Details/Date
			Q on the form		salesperson					
Lauren	Halifax	F	No ethnicity Q on the form	18	Student	V	2	0	M	"
Ashley	X	F	No ethnicity Q on the form	21	Student	V	5	0	M	"
Carrie	Halifax	F	No ethnicity Q on the form	35	Arts-theatre	U	1	0	LM	"
Lourdes	Hammonds Plains	F	C	40	Webmaster	U	2	0	M	Canada Reads (CR) FG Mixed Peggy's Book Club[2] / 23 April 2006
Jane	Bedford	F	Canadian	55	Health executive	P	0	0	UM	"
Peggy	Halifax	F	Canadian	50+	Administrator	P	1	0	M	"

Bab	Dartmouth	F	Anglo-Saxon	56	Pryenuk	P	2	0	UM	"
Zoey	Halifax	F	Canadian	49	Nurse	P	1	0	M	"
Donna	Halifax	F	Vanilla Canadian	43	Librarian	P	2	0	M	CR FG 1 P/ 25 April 2006
Kim	Spryfield	F	C-European	39	Volunteer Amnesty International and part-time pilot project-activism coordinator	U	4	2	LM	"
Marie	Halifax	F	C	60	Professor	P	1	0	UM	"
Cathy	Halifax	F	C	20	Student	V	X	X	X	"
Cathy	Halifax	F	White	48	Artist/teacher (prof)/ researcher	P	2	0	M	CR FG 2 NP/ 25 April 2006
Evelyn	Dartmouth	F	C	43	Teacher	U	2	0	M	"
Beth	Halifax	F	Eastern European/ Jewish	25	Work at ecology action centre on marine issues	P	3	0	UM	"
Jacqueline	Halifax	F	C	25	Graduating student–public relations	U	2	0	M	"

(Continued)

Table A1 (Continued)

Name/Pseudonym	Residence	Gender	Ethnicity	Age	Occupation	Education	Household Size	Children under 18	Class/Social Status	FG Details/Date
Cory	Halifax	M	Mixed	29	Student/labourer	U	3	0	LM	"
Johnny	X	M	Trickster-Divinity	36	English teacher	P	4	0	M	"
Janis	Halifax	F	British	50	Research associate/registered nurse	P	4	2	M	"
Eleanor	Halifax	F	C	42	Nurse	H	1	0	M	"
Caroline	Dartmouth	F	Canadian	26	Graduating student–public relations	U	2	0	M	"
Allen	Halifax	M	Anglo-Norwegian–C	59	Professor	P	4	0	M	CR FG 3 P/ 26 April 2006
Peggy	Halifax	F	Overprivileged white girl—kidding—White	43	Art gallery worker, freelance writing	U	4	1	UM	"
Irene	Halifax	F	C	26	Masters student HUCD-SLP at Dalhousie	H	2	0	LM	"

Name	Location	Sex	Ethnicity	Age	Occupation				Class	Focus group/Date
Claire	Dartmouth	F	French-Canadian	58	Clerk	V	1	0	LM	"
Wayne	Dartmouth	M	Canadian	59	Retired	U	2	0	LM	"
Vicki	Eastern Passage	F	WASP	41	Director, nonprofit organization	U	5	2	UM	"
Ellen	Halifax	F	American (of Irish descent)	37	Professor	P	1	0	M	CR FG 4 NP/ 26 April 2006
Marji	Dartmouth	F	C / English	57	Day care worker/stay at home mother	V	4	0	M	"
Emma	Halifax	F	C	23	X	U	3	0	LM	"
Ray	Halifax	M	Some what white	Gone fifty	TV writer/ producer	P	3	0	O-I don't	"
Cathleen	Dartmouth	F	Irish	40s	Lawyer	P	1	0	M	"
Laurel	X	F	C	27	PR/student	U	3	0	M	"
Judy	Halifax	F	C	58	Public relations	H	3	0	M	"
Cheryl	Halifax	F	Scottish	59	Homemaker	U	3	0	UM	"
Trisha	Hubbards	F	C	23	Communications	U	4	0	LM	CR FG 5 NP/ 27 April 2006

(Continued)

Table A1 (Continued)

Name/Pseudonym	Residence	Gender	Ethnicity	Age	Occupation	Education	Household Size	Children under 18	Class/Social Status	FG Details/Date
Chris	Halifax	F	C	32	Career counsellor	P	3	1	M	"
Martha	X	F	White/C/Canadian	47	At home, full-time mother	V	5	3	M	CR FG 6 P/ 28 April 2006
Karen	Wolfville	F	C	50s	Policy analyst/ pharmacist	H	3	0	M	"
Beth	X	X	X	X	X	X	X	X	X	"
Mary	Wolfville	F	British/ Scottish/ Irish	52	teacher/ homemaker/ mother	U	3	1	M	"
Ellen	X	X	X	X	X	X	X	X	X	"
Jean	Wolfville	F	C	44	Lawyer	P	4	1	M	CR FG 7 P/ 29 April 2006
Blanca	Canning	F	Spanish/ French	61	Poet, writer	V	2	X	X	"
Jenn	Wolfville	F	C	30	Instructor, business communications	H	3	2	M	"
Chris	Wolfville	F	C	54	Secretary	U	1	0	O n/a	"
Toni	Charlottetown	F	Canadian – Anglo background	44	Writer	U	4	2	LM	CR FG 8 P/ 30 April 2006

Name	Location	Sex	Ethnicity	Age	Occupation					
Anne	Charlottetown	F	Canadian—parentage: Irish Newfoundland	49	Professor (English, linguistics)	P	2	0	UM	CR FG 9 NP/ 30 April 2006
Nora	Charlottetown	F	Canadian	47	Teacher	U	4	2	UM	"
Jeff	Charlottetown PE	M	Canadian	43	Editor	U	1	0	M	"
Karin	Chicago (Hyde Park)	F	No question on ethnicity	25	Textbook publisher image coordinator	U	2	0	M	One Book One Chicago (OBOC) FG 1 NP[3]/ 18 October 2005
Bea	Chicago	F	"	26	Student	H	1	0	UM	"
Eugene	Chicago	M	"	28	Student	H	0	0	M	"
Carlos	Chicago	M	"	28	Recent graduate	P	2	0	M	"
LaDonna	Chicago	F	"	36	Prophet, poet, public minister (Rev'd)	P	2	X	LM	"
Bob	Matteson, IL	M	Euro-American	39	Special education teacher	P	1	0	LM	OBOC FG 3 NP/ 22 October 2005
Michael	Forest Park IL	M	White	39	Software development team	U	1	0	M	"

(*Continued*)

Table A1 (Continued)

Name/Pseudonym	Residence	Gender	Ethnicity	Age	Occupation	Education	Household Size	Children under 18	Class/Social Status	FG Details/Date
Greg	Chicago	M	White, American, European descent (Lithuanian/Croatian)	49	X	P	2	0	M	OBOC FG 4 P O'Hare Airport Book Club / 26 October 2005
Barb	Chicago	F	Irish American	X	Executive secretary	V	1	0	M	"
Kate consent form only										"
Nessa	X	F	No question on ethnicity	50	Clerk	V	6	2	M	"
Debby	Chicago	F	"	43	Public relations	U	2	0	UM	"
Nadine	Chicago	F	C	41	Principle revenue analyst	U	2	0	M	"
Mary Jane	Chicago	F	C	48	Financial analyst/accountant	P	1	0	M	"

Marva	Chicago	F	No question on ethnicity	54	n.d.m.n. assistance	V	3	0	M	"
Gino	Chicago	M	"	60	White collar	H	Occasional overnight guests	0	M	"
R. Holloway	X	F	"	49	Clerk	V	7	3	M	"
Barbara	New Westminster	F	White	54	Homemaker	D	2	0	M	OBOV FG 1 P/ 8 June 2006
Elly	North Vancouver	F	Canadian C	46	Administrative	X	1	0	M	"
Crissy	Vancouver	F	South Asian	62	Retired social worker	P	1	0	M	"
Tracey	Vancouver	F	Asian	41	Clerical/administrative	U	1	0	M	"
Barb T	Vancouver	F	X	54	Library technician (unemployed)	U	2	0	M	"
VG	Vancouver	M	White, black, yellow, red, other	24	Construction	V	2	0	M	"
Amanda	Vancouver	F	C	31	Lawyer	P	1	0	UM	OBOV FG 2 NP

(Continued)

Table A1 (Continued)

Name/Pseudonym	Residence	Gender	Ethnicity	Age	Occupation	Education	Household Size	Children under 18	Class/Social Status	FG Details/Date
Katherine	Vancouver	F	White	58	Administrator	P	2	0	M	"
Sharon	Vancouver	F	Canadian—Ukranian-British heritage	63	Therapist, teacher	P	1	0	M	"
Abigail	Vancouver	F	White C	67	Librarian	P	1	0	M	"
Crystal	Vancouver	F	Canadian/C	23	Student	P	2	0	M	"
Reta	Port Coquitlam	F	C	55	Professional	U	1	0	M	"
Jennifer	North Burnaby	F	C (Euro-Canadian)	27	Graduate student	P	2	0	M	"
Margaret	Kitsilano	F	C	mature	Public speaking instructor	U	2	0	UM	OBOV FG 3 P/ 11 June 2006
Doug	Vancouver—Hastings Sunrise	M	Canadian	35	Physicist	P	2	0	M	"
Lori	Vancouver—Hastings/Sunrise	F	White	39	Professional student/?	U	2	0	LM	"

Name	Location	Gender	Ethnicity	Age	Occupation					Source
Carol	Vancouver/ Mount Pleasant	F	Canadian (ancestors from the UK)	59	Tutor	P	1	0	LM	"
Joyce	New Westminster	F	Western European	42	Part-time corporate writer, part-time university student, stay-at-home mum	V	4	2	M	OBOV FG 4 P/ 11 June 2006
David	Vancouver	M	Canadian	77	Retired	P	2	0	M	OBOV FG 5 NP/ 12 June 2006
Andrea	BC	F	Latin	33	Writer	H	2	0	LM	"
Margaret	Vancouver	F	C	53	Contract specialist	H	1	0	M	"
Bob	Vancouver	M	Free Thinker	70 some	X	U	3	1	pensioner/ aspiring writer	"
Tracy	Vancouver	F	C	42	writer/ teacher	P	2	0	M	"
Nora	Vancouver	F	White	52	ESL Teacher	H	2	0	M	"
Elva	Pt. Grey	F	Canadian	70+	Retired	U	2	X	M-UM	"
Sylvia	Vancouver	F	Chinese/ English	26	Financial advisor/ piano tutor	V	2	0	M	OBOV FG 6 P/ 12 June 2006

(Continued)

Table A1 (Continued)

Name/Pseudonym	Residence	Gender	Ethnicity	Age	Occupation	Education	Household Size	Children under 18	Class/Social Status	FG Details/Date
Bonnie	Vancouver	F	?Irish?/German/English	46	Computer geek	V	1	0	O- I see myself as upper middle class – my cash flow is not always there	"
Harriet	Surrey	F	Canadian	44	Co-op coordinator	U	3	2	UM	OBOV FG Mixed P and NP SFU Book Club/ 16 June 2006
Marcia	New West	F	White through & through	37	Coordinator	U	2	0	M	"
Antonio	Vancouver	M	Portuguese Canadian	39	Educational Services (Post. Sec)	U	4	2	M	"

Name	Location	Sex	Ethnicity	Age	Occupation	H		X	LM/M	Focus group
Avery	North Vancouver	F	Scandinavian	29	student advisor co-op education		2	X	LM (in Vancouver!), M	"
Clare	X	F	British	28	Administrator for a network of international research-led universities	U	2	0	LM	R & J FG 1 NP/ 23 January 2007
Sonal	X	F	British Asian	31	Researcher	P	1	0	O- I don't know	"
Sarah	X	F	White British	33	Researcher	P	2	0	O- unsure	"
Sibyl	X	F	White Other	47	Freelance literature worker/writer	U	4	2	M	"
Ben	X	M	White British	27	Arts Administrator	U	2	0	M	"
Allison	Birmingham	F	Welsh	55	Teacher	P	2	0	LM	R & J FG 2 P/ 30 January 2007
Lauren	Birmingham	F	British	24	Sales and information assistant	U	2	0	LM	"

(Continued)

Table A1 (Continued)

Name/ Pseudonym	Residence	Gender	Ethnicity	Age	Occupation	Education	Household Size	Children under 18	Class/ Social Status	FG Details/ Date
Harvey	Birmingham, West Midlands	F	British Asian	30	Administrator	U	4	0	M	"
Helen	Warwickshire	F	White British	43	Marketing executive	U	1	0	M	"
Viv	Redditch Worcs.	F	English	63	Retired teacher	U	2	0	M	"
Sarah	Smethwick	F	White	31	NVQ assessor	U	1	0	LM	R & J FG 3 P/ 3 February 2007
Frances	Staffordshire	F	English	64	Semi-retired	A	2	0	M	"
Deborah	Rubery / Worcestershire	F	White	48	Health and safety for a university	U	4	1	LM	"
Sue	Warwickshire	F	White British	58	Librarian	U	2	0	LM	R & J FG 4 P/ 6 February 2007
Sam	Birmingham	F	White British	32	Full-time mum, business writer, dancer	U	3	1	M	"
Ann	West Midlands	F	British	59	Housewife	U	2	0	LM	"
Laura	West Midlands	F	British	21	Sexual health worker/	U	3	0	LM	"

Name	Location	Sex	Ethnicity	Age	Occupation					Notes
Rachel	West Midlands	F	White British	56	receptionist–charity for young people	P	1	0	M	"
Philippa	Birmingham	F	White British	71	Retired speech and language therapist/lecturer	H	2	0	M	R & J FG 5 NP/ 27 March 2007
Natalie	Birmingham	F	British	28	Librarian	P	2	0	LM	"
Carol	South Staffs	F	White British	62	Retired teacher	H	2	0	W	"
Una	Birmingham	F	Irish	54	Project coordinator People's Bank	O	1	0	M	R & J FG 6 P/ 31 March 2007
Lesley	Birmingham	F	British	50	Librarian	H	3	1	X	"
Miriam	West Midlands	F	British Jewish	60	X	P	1	0	M	"
No name	Birmingham	F	British	60	Retired	O	2	0	LM	"
Janet	Bournville, Birmingham	F	White	63	Retired	A	4	0	LM	"
Winifred	X	F	White	77	Retired	U	2	0	M	R & J FG 7 Mixed/ 2 April 2007
Jerry	X	F	Irish	81	Retired	O	0	0	W	"

(Continued)

Table A1 (Continued)

Name/Pseudonym	Residence	Gender	Ethnicity	Age	Occupation	Education	Household Size	Children under 18	Class/Social Status	FG Details/Date
Judy	B'ham	F	X	68	Retired	H	1	X	M	"
Mair	X	F	Is this relevant?	69	Retired	H	1	0	M?	"
Frances	Northfield	F	X	63	Retired teacher	V	2	0	O- I worked, therefore, I guess, I'm working class	"
Kim	Wallasey, Wirral	F	European	47	Customer services assistant	O	3	1	W	Liverpool Reads FG 1 P4/ 17 February 2007
Barbara	Warrington	F	White	50	Student	V	4	0	W	"
Robin	Waterloo	M	White	48	Student	X	2	0	W	"
Sarah	Liverpool	F	Half Scottish Half Welsh	40	Part-time arts administrator, part-time lecturer	P	4	2	M	Liverpool Reads FG 2/ 17 February 2007
Laraine	Walton	F	White British	59	Housewife	O	2	0	M	Liverpool Reads FG 3 P/

Name	Area	Sex	Ethnicity	Age	Occupation					Session
Lara	Walton	F	White British	34	Student	A	2	0	M	19 February 2007
Brenda	L12	F	British	57	Librarian	U	1	0	LM	"
Chris	X	X	X	X	X	X	X	X	X	"
Linda	X	X	X	X	X	X	X	X	X	"
Sophie	Wavertree	F	White	20	Student	U	3	0	M	Liverpool Reads FG 4 NP/ 19 February 2007
Siobhan	L7	F	White British	20	Student	V	9	0	M	"
Lucy	Grove Street	F	White British	20	Student	V	7	0	M	"
Sophie	Wavertree	F	British	19	Student	V	3	0	LM	"
Ada	City Centre	F	White	26	Student	P	2	0	M	"
Joanna	City Centre	F	White	24	Project worker	P	4	0	W	"
Julie	X	X	X	X	X	X	X	X	X	Liverpool Reads FG 5 P/ 21February 2007
Margaret	Old Swan	F	Irish	53	Project coordinator	U	2	1	W	Liverpool Reads FG 6 Mixed/ 22 February 2007

(Continued)

Table A1 (Continued)

Name/Pseudonym	Residence	Gender	Ethnicity	Age	Occupation	Education	Household Size	Children under 18	Class/Social Status	FG Details/Date
Martin	Old Swan	M	White C	55	Learning technologist	P	2	0	LM	"
Anne	Aigburth	F	White	59	NHS radiographer	P	1	0	M	"
Sue	Allerton	F	White	52	Library assistant	P	3	0	W	"
Kerry	L15	F	Black	42	Refuge manager	V	3	0	W	"
Tracey	Liverpool 8	F	Black British	45	Director	H	4	2	W	"
Claire	Wavertree	F	White	31	Sales manager at university	U	3	1	LM	"
Suzanne	L8	F	African	Over 21	Carer	U	2	X	W	"
Mike	Huntsville	M	White	X	Ex-navy, work in electrical manufacturing	U	X	X	X	Big Read (Huntsville) FG 1 NP/ 3 May 2007
Jarod	South	M	White	26	Plant engineering manager	H	2	0	M	"

Candace	Huntsville	F	White	mid/late 20s	Part-time administrator at Virginia Tech	U	4	1	X	"
Nell	North West	F	Black American	46	Secretary	U	2	0	LM	"
Marquise	X	M	African-American	late 20s	X	U	X	X	X	"
RJ	Madison	M	White	35	Military	H	4	2	M	"
Joe	SE	M	White	46	N/A	H	4	2	M	"
Patrick	SE	M	Scottish-American	25	Test engineer	U	0	0	W	"
Kimberley	X	F	African-American	late 20s	Admin	U	X	1	X	"
Florence	Madison, AL	F	Black	56	Logistician	H	2	0	M	"
Rita	NW	F	X	51	Civil service	U	1	0	M	"
Scott	Madion	M	White	45	Foreign military sales	H	1	X	M	"
Sylvia	NE	F	African American	38	Test engineer	H	1	0	UM	"
Robert	South	M	White	36	Reliability engineer	H	2	0	M	"
Leslye	SE	F	C	35	Student	H	X	X	UM	"
Doris	East (Madison County)	F	African American	40	Manager	U	2	1	M	"

(Continued)

Table A1 (Continued)

Name/Pseudonym	Residence	Gender	Ethnicity	Age	Occupation	Education	Household Size	Children under 18	Class/Social Status	FG Details/Date
Ken	NE	M	C	48	HW/SW technician/	U	3	1	M	"
Marshall	X	M	White	40s	Ex-military	U	2	X	X	"
Paige	X	F	African-American	Late 20s	X	U	X	X	X	"
Sam	NE	M	X	65	Retired custom service representative	V	2	0	O-World Class	Big Read FG 2/ 5 May 2006
Sarah	South	F	White-European descent	X	Marketing/graphic design	H	3	1	M	"
Tim	SW	M	White or C	53	Database administrator for a defense contractor working on a government site	P	3	1	UM	"
Sandra	Decatur	F	C	34	Program administrator	H	1	0	M	Big Read FG 3 NP/ 7 May 2007
Martha	South	F	Mixed	50+	Teacher	U	2	0	M	Big Read FG 4 P/ 8 May 2007

Name	Neighborhood			Age	Occupation	V				Big Read
Anna	South	F	White	39	Bookkeeper		2	1	LM	Big Read FG 5 P/ 9 May 2007
Judy	Madison	F	Irish/ Ukranian	59	Banking cashier	U	1	0	LM	"
Susan	Hampton Cove	F	C	over 60	Civic volunteer	P	2	0	UM, U	"
Allie	Southeast	F	White	16	Phone personnel	S	2	1	M	Big Read FG 6 NP/ 10 May 2007
Caitlyn	Balley Cove Estates Southeast	F	White/ Spanish	16	Student	S	4	2	M	"
Amy 1	Southeast	F	White	16	Cashier/ student	S	5	2	M	"
Briana	Southeast	F	White/C	16	Hostess	S	5 or 6	3	M	"
Victoria	Southside	F	Black	16	Cashier	S	3	1	UM	"
Robert	Southeast	M	White	16	Student	S	4	3	UM	"
Naomi	Southside	F	African American	16	0	S	5	1	M	"
Courtney	Southeast	F	White	16	0	S	4	2	UM	"
Amy 2	Southeast	F	White	16	Cashier	S	6	3	UM	"
Luke	South	M	White	16	Student	S	5	1	UM	"
Garrett	SE	M	White	17	X	S	3	1	M	"

(Continued)

Table A1 (Continued)

Name/Pseudonym	Residence	Gender	Ethnicity	Age	Occupation	Education	Household Size	Children under 18	Class/Social Status	FG Details/Date
Michael	SE	M	White	15	X	S	2	1	M	"
Steve	South	M	White	16	Lifeguard	S	3	1	M	"
Kassidy	South	F	White	X	Lifeguard	S	5	3	M	"
Caleb	Southeast	M	White	16	X	S	4	2	M	"
Bethany	Southeast	F	White	16	Student	S	3	1	UM	"
Amber	X	F	X	15	X	S	5	3	X	"
Sam	Southeast	M	Asian/Oriental	16	Student	S	3	1	M	"
Robyn	Southeast	F	White	16	Student	S	3	1	M	"
Genie	WE	F	C	over 50	Concierge/tour guide	V	2	0	M	Seattle Reads FG 1 Mixed/16 May 2007
Megin	Magnolia	F	White	38	Homemaker	U	3	1	UM	"
Lindsay	Seattle	F	African American	56	Buyer	U	1	0	M	Seattle Reads FG 2 Mixed
Padma	Redmond	F	East Indian	31	N/A	U	2	0	M	"
Tara	Lynnwood	F	C, Jewish	60	Sales, marketing, author, teacher	S	1	0	W	"

Don	Bothell	M	African migrant	27	Management trainee (lending)	P	1	0	M	"
Meg	Capitol Hill	F	White	27	Community organizer	U	2	0	M	Seattle Reads FG 3 NP/ 17 May 2007
Leah	Laurelhurst	F	Non-Hisp/ Asian		Data/ information systems coordinator	U	2	0	LM	"
Edith	Capitol Hill	F	White	70	Retired teacher	H	2	0	M	Seattle Reads FG 4 P/ 17 May 2007
Charly Buch	X	F	X	X	Temp worker	P	2	1	LM	"
Bryce	Capitol Hill	M	C	31	Counselor at community college	P	2	0	M	"
Amy	Capitol Hill	F	Hispanic/ Mixed White	29	Hospitality	U	2	0	W	"
Ed	Capitol Hill	M	define	80	Retired, inter alia archivist	H	2	0	LM	"
Rachel	Wallingford	F	White	29	Student	P	1	0	UM	Seattle Reads FG 5 P/ 18 May 2007

(Continued)

Table A1 (Continued)

Name/ Pseudonym Residence	Gender	Ethnicity	Age	Occupation	Education	Household Size	Children under 18	Class/ Social Status	FG Details/ Date
Lee S Bellevue	F	Black	58	HR consultant	U	1	0	UM	"
Emily Downtown	F	White	26	Office administrator	U	2	X	W	"
Erica Green Lake	F	American/ British/ German	23	Teacher and legal administrative assistant	H	3	0	M	"
Dave N.E.	M	White	43	Student	H	3	1	W	"
Melissa Ravenna	F	Asian-American	25	Freelance Web developer	U	6	0	M	"

[1] In the pretest site of Kitchener-Waterloo-Cambridge, Ontario, readers were not asked their ethnicity. The demographic information presented here is verbatim from information sheets collected along with the informed consent documents provided to each reader.

[2] Canada Reads focus groups 1 through 5, CR Student Focus Group NP, and Peggy's Book Club discussion took place in Halifax, Nova Scotia; groups 6 and 7 were in Wolfville, Nova Scotia; and groups 8 and 9 were conducted in Charlottetown, Prince Edward Island.

[3] OBOC FG 2 P took place in a master's English course at DePaul University on 19 October 2005. There were twenty-five students in a room who were taking a module built around the One Book, One Chicago selection; age range: 18–22 years old; equal number of men and women; and, various ethnicities.

[4] In Liverpool, we spoke with members of a student support group of sixteen girls at Belevedere Girls' High School. Demographic information was not collected.

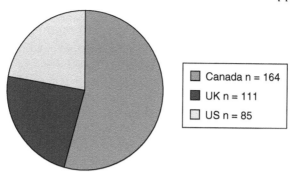

Figure A1 Focus Group Participation in Each Nation-State
A total of 360 readers participated in our focus groups

In each location, we hired a local graduate student or part-time worker as a fieldwork assistant who helped us to better understand the local culture and to facilitate recruitment of both focus group and online survey participation. This person also helped in securing accessible facilities, ordering refreshments, and acted as a liaison between us, the event organizers, and the readers.

Our aim was to recruit age-, class-, ethnic-, education-, and gender-diverse groups of readers in each location. We promoted the groups through posters, flyers, and bookmarks, which were distributed to public spaces in different parts of each city. We also purchased advertising space in weekly arts or alternative newspapers. The local research assistant was encouraged to use professional and personal networks to recruit readers and to use snowballing and key gatekeepers (such as librarians and community leaders) to generate our samples. The assistant screened the readers for nonparticipation and participation in the OBOC program, which included attending an event in the past or current year and/or reading the selected book. As a token of our appreciation, readers were given a portable reading light. While it was sometimes difficult to recruit focus group members because there was no monetary inducement for their time (as is the case with market research), readers seemed pleased with the gift gesture. In almost every group, the readers expressed their pleasure in hearing each others' ideas about books and reading. The talk sometimes mimicked book talk that is often found in face-to-face book groups.

As is illustrative in Table A1, the readers who participated in our groups were quite homogeneous, although we made many attempts to recruit from marginalized communities. Nearly half (40 percent; 102) of those readers who reported their ages were between the ages of forty and fifty-nine. Like the survey respondents that we discuss below, the focus group readers were also well educated. Most (48 percent; 128) have a university or college degree and some postgraduate or higher education. Twenty-four percent (65) of the focus group readers have a postgraduate degree. The snowball sampling procedure we used to recruit focus group participants may account for the large proportion of older, well-educated readers in our groups. We advertised for focus group participation in local newspapers and through posters in public spaces such as community centers. The adverts were published in English (all three nation-states), French, and Spanish (US and Canada). Additionally, we also made concerted efforts to hire research field assistants who were from a range of ethnic and social backgrounds, and occasionally hired two assistants from different cultural groups within one research site. In each city, the field assistant was asked to recruit from inside and outside their own social networks in addition to the paid advertisements. However, generally, the results of their (and our own) efforts illustrate quite vividly that reading, and talking about reading, remains a privileged leisure activity determined by how much free time a person has, his or her income, and his or her level of formal education. Access to these assets is skewed in each nation-state of our study by social inequalities, the legacies of colonialism, and ongoing racism. Focus group discussants were representative of the readers who attended the reading events. Eighty-one percent of the readers were women, 88 percent identified as Caucasian, and 61 percent as middle class. In almost every city, we were fortunate to visit high school or university classrooms to discuss reading with young people. These group discussions were treated as focus group data in our analysis when the discussions were recorded.

Each of the focus groups was facilitated by one or both of the authors, and sometimes by Dr. Anouk Lang, who was the postdoctoral research fellow on our project. While one person was facilitating the conversation, the other was taking notes: these roles were usually reversed halfway through the focus groups, which ran for ninety minutes. The discussion guidelines changed very little over the course of the project, and usually only to address the specificities of local print culture. A pilot project in Ontario, focused on OBOC Kitchener-Waterloo-Cambridge (September 2004) offered vital insights into how readers participate in MREs. The preliminary work helped to shape the direction of the larger project and informed the qualitative and quantitative research instruments (Fuller and Rehberg Sedo 2012, 243–44). Through that study, we also began to recognize who does not participate and why. A copy of the guidelines we used in Seattle, which was our final field study site, can be found on our website (www.beyondthebookproject.org). The overall goal of the focus group discussions with readers was to investigate reading practices, attitudes to literary culture, and the uses of events. In some categories, we quickly reached what is often referred to as *theoretical saturation* (Charmaz 2006, 113–15). That is, we were hearing the same things from readers in each research site. We were cognizant, however, that we were doing a comparative study and continued to discuss the same issues in each location, and in some cases, we attempted to test our theories from previous sites in subsequent conversations. The pleasures readers get from discussing books with others who have also read the same book, for example, was evident early in the project. As a way of testing our evolving theory of shared pleasure reading (see Chapter 6,

"Reader"), we asked questions that would make evident identity work and distinction in readers' articulations of why they attend events.

The focus groups were audio recorded, and in some instances, we took photographs of the readers. Participants were provided with an information sheet and signed informed consent forms that included permission to be photographed. Each group discussion was transcribed, and coded using close textual analysis aided by qualitative analysis software (NVivo). The coding categories evolved over the course of the project, providing valuable opportunities for the research team to engage in intellectually rigorous discussions, which in part, resulted in the contents of this book (Fuller 2012, 93–95).

While we found the focus groups to be excellent opportunities to effectively communicate with a large number of readers, we do recognize that this method has limits as well as benefits.[1] As others have identified, focus groups can enable agency in participants (Bennett et al. 2009, 261). However, while focus groups in which readers participate illustrate how they "co-const[ruct] a social order of reading and of texts," the focus group always occurs within a contrived setting (Benwell 2009, 301). A discussion group convened for the purposes of research can create talk that would not normally occur without the presence of researchers. For example, the flow of conversation in a focus group discussion is guided by the moderator's questions and occasional direct invitations to participants to speak, even when there are parts of the discussion in which the moderator does not intervene verbally. Group dynamics can also perpetuate power inequities between group members and the researchers, and among group members themselves (Krueger and Casey 2009, 85–91; Stewart, Shamdasani, and Rook 2007, 20–28; 70–78). As we observe in Chapter 2, "Television," however, some participants actively negotiated inequities of knowledge, power, and cultural capital within the focus group setting. Finally, we recognize that the readers' articulations and our interpretations illustrate what Janice Radway (1988) identified as the "ever-shifting nature of subjectivity produced through the articulation of discourses and their fragments" (368, cited in Benwell 2009, 305). That is, readers are not fixed subjects. Instead, through sharing their experiences, offering their opinions, and talking about their media practices, readers demonstrate how their subjectivities are "fluid, destabilised, [and] ever-shifting." In a focus group setting, "the accounts" (Benwell 2009) that participants offer about themselves emerge from a performance of their subjectivity undertaken in a semipublic situation. Participants' performances were mediated by social codes of behavior, the desire to please us as researchers, and the presence of other people who were usually strangers. In this book, we therefore treat our focus group data as interpretations of reality, not reports on reality. At the same time, in our analyses of readers' accounts of their everyday lives and reading practices, we have tried to honor the knowledge articulated by focus group participants as they make sense of their values and habits. When the co-construction of meaning with other participants was particularly striking, especially through the moderation of an opinion, we have sought to render that conversational dynamic visible on the page through quotation and/or our critical commentary on it. Given our interest in readers' perceptions about reading cultures and MREs, their expectations and evaluation of print culture, and other arts activities in their areas, focus groups afforded us the opportunity to investigate social practices and social values within a social setting that, like the events we were examining, was time-limited and involved meeting strangers (as well as friends).

INDIVIDUAL INTERVIEWS

Table A2 illustrates our sample of in-depth individual interviews. Our aim early in the project was to get a sense of the new phenomenon of MREs from insiders, including cultural critics, policy makers, publishers, and the innovative producers. We wanted to determine both the explicit aims and implicit cultural meanings of events and as the project progressed, we adapted our discussion guides to include opportunities for the producers, in particular, to be co-creators in our analytical process. We began our analysis of the MREs from the producers' and supporters' standpoints, and their own understandings of their actions and values, but our critical commentaries in this book move beyond their evaluations to consider how other agents (including invited authors), institutions, and policies inflect their labor and the discourses they employ to describe events.

THE ONLINE SURVEY AND ITS ANALYSIS

As part of our investigative methods, we hosted an online survey on our website. The first version was influenced by readership surveys conducted by Statistics Canada (1998), Duxbury (1995), and James Lorimer (1981), and pretested in our pilot study in Ontario. Because the pilot study was conducted in Canada, we began the project using readership surveys that were respected by both the academy and publishing industry. The survey was then adapted to fit our research questions and agenda. In each subsequent site, we pretested with—at minimum—six readers to capture the nuances of each site's specific print culture. That means that although the surveys were nearly the same in every site, we did make changes to questions about local book programming events, media outlets, currency, language, and education. We made changes only to reflect local contexts. For example, we sought information on book festival participation, which had to be specific to each city, region, or country. The final version in each city was largely quantitative; five of the fifty-six questions asked participants to write responses. Because of the size of the survey, we have not reproduced it in this book. It can be accessed via the electronic holdings of the University of Birmingham library (http://epapers.bham.ac.uk/64/). A complete database of the anonymized survey responses, data notes, codebooks, and the metadata information sheet are also available.

Table A2 Interviewees

Name	Job Title or Role	Industry or organization	Location	Date of Interview
Canada Reads; Canadian MREs Generally				
Jean Baird	Creative director of Canada Book Week	Writers' Trust of Canada	Toronto	3 July 2003
Talin Vartanian and David Bernard	Program producers	CBC Canada Reads	Toronto	7 July 2003
Rob Firing and Micheala Cornell	Marketing executives	HarperCollins Canada	Toronto	7 July 2003
Mona Kiame	Program officer	Canada Council for the Arts	Via telephone	9 July 2003
Krys Ross	Vice president and general manager	McClelland and Stewart	Toronto	9 July 2003
Trisha Walker	Producer, Western Reads	University of Western Ontario	London, ON, via telephone	23 July 2003
Laurie Brinklow	Publisher of Acorn Books; past president; panelist for local Canada Reads events	Atlantic Publishers Marketing Association	Charlottetown, PEI	6 May 2006
Kimberly Walsh	Associate producer, social media and online community	CBC Books	Halifax, NS	30 May 2007

(*Continued*)

Table A2 (Continued)

Name	Job Title or Role	Industry or organization	Location	Date of Interview
Richard and Judy's Book Club; UK MREs Generally				
Mike Poole	Senior executive producer, documentaries and contemporary factual programs; executive producer, The Big Read	The BBC	Bristol	19 April 2005
Mark Williams	Reader and literature development officer; producer of "One Book for Coventry"	Coventry Central Library	Coventry	26 April 2005
Ciara Eastell	Project worker	The Reading Agency	Taunton, Somerset	25 September 2005
Amanda Ross	Producer	*Richard & Judy*	London	29 June 2006
Birmingham Book Festival				
Jonathan Davidson	Director/organizer	Birmingham Book Festival	Birmingham	28 April 2005
Bristol's Great Reading Adventure				
Cynthia Martin	Assistant libraries manager; Great	Bristol Libraries	Bristol	20 April 2005

	Reading Adventure coproducer		
Melanie Kelly	Great Reading Adventure producer	Research director and project manager, BCDP at GWE Business West	20 April 2005
Tom Sperlinger	Educator; involved in reader and lit activities; town/gown initiatives; has set up reading group for medics	University of Bristol	20 April 205
Christine Clark	Teacher; supporter of the Great Reading Adventure	Bristol Schools	20 April 2005
Lucy Shepherd	Teacher; supporter of the Great Reading Adventure	Bristol Grammar	20 April 2005
Tammi Redmond	Librarian	St. Paul's Library	20 April 2005
One Book, One Chicago and Chicago reading programs			
Nanette Alleman	Public librarian; coordinator Chicago Book Festival; creator of OBOC	CPL	? January 2004 ; 1 October 2004; 24 October 2005

(*Continued*)

Table A2 (Continued)

Name	Job Title or Role	Industry or organization	Location	Date of Interview
Barbara Schmittle	Staff member; resource guide writer for OBOC	CPL	Chicago	1 October 2004
Debby Rabeor	Department of Aviation; Book Club leader; OBOC supporter	O'Hare Airport	Chicago	28 September 2004
Daniel Born	Editor *The Common Review*; OBOC advisory member and supporter	The Great Books Foundation	Chicago	28 September 2004; 17 October 2005
Karen Kakiernan-Burke	Coordinator of literacy	Chicago Public Schools	Chicago	28 September 2004; 19 October 2005
Bonnie Oberman	Director; OBOC advisory member and supporter	Facing History and Ourselves	Chicago	29 September 2004
Stuart Dybek	Author of *The Coast of Chicago*, which was chosen for the program in spring 2004	X	Chicago via telephone	5 October 2004
Roz Anderson and Denise Knox[1]	Educators; hosts of Teen Book Clubs	Kenwood Academy High School	Hyde Park	30 September 2004; 18 October 2005
Eileen Seifert	College teacher; OBOC supporter	DePaul University	Lincoln Park	30 September 2004

Name	Role	Location	Venue	Date
Katey Schwartz	Community Relations Manager; OBOC advisory member and supporter	Barnes & Noble	Chicago	1 October 2004
Joyce Miller-Bean	Actress; college teacher; OBOC supporter	DePaul University	Lincoln Park	19 October 2005
Karen Thompson	Founder and director	Literature for All of Us	Chicago	25 October 2005
Taishiya Nix Bull	Participant	Literature for All of Us via a reading group called Book Sistas	Chicago via telephone	8 December 2005
Janet Vega	Participant	As above	Chicago via telephone	9 December 2005
Huntsville's Big Read				
Mary Wallace and Judy Purinton	Librarians and organizers of the One Book, One Madison County (received Big Read grants)	Huntsville-Madison County Public Library	Huntsville	23 May 2006
Al Elmore	Professor of English and law in Huntsville, Alabama	Athens State University	Huntsville	23 May 2006
Bob Middleton	Retired from the NASA space program; local historian; Big Reads presenter	Huntsville-Madison County Public Library	Huntsville	24 May 2006

(Continued)

Table A2 (Continued)

Name	Job Title or Role	Industry or organization	Location	Date of Interview
Karen Motylewski, Kate Kaiser, Marcia Semmel, Maryrose Flanigan, Tom Bradshaw, Hope O'Keeffe, David Kipen, Dana Goia	The Big Read work team and director of the NEA	National Endowment for the Arts/ Institute of Museum and Library Services	Washington, DC	25 May 2006
Cleareaser Bone	Librarian; leader of Sister to Sister, Brother to Brother, African American authors book club	Huntsville-Madison County Public Library	Huntsville	9 May 2007
Diana LaChance	Community volunteer; new resident to Huntsville	n/a	Huntsville	9 May 2007
Mary Wallace, Judy Purinton, and David Lilly	Librarians and organizers of the Big Read	Huntsville-Madison County Public Library	Huntsville	10 May 2007
Kitchener/Waterloo/Cambridge One Book, One Community				
Kim Jennigan and Rossalyn Worth	Members of Producing Committee	*The New Quarterly*	Waterloo	2 July 2003
Trisha Siemens, Katherine Seredynska,	Members of Producing Committee	Words Worth Books, Kitchener and Waterloo	Waterloo	3 July 2003

Name	Role	Organization	Location	Date
Sharon Smith, Angela Caretta		Public Libraries		
Doug Gibson	President	McClelland and Stewart	Toronto	15 July 2003
Nino Ricci	Author of *Lives of the Saints*, which was chosen for the K/W/C program in 2004		Waterloo	23 September 2004

Liverpool Reads and Liverpool reading programs

Name	Role	Organization	Location	Date
Jane Davis	Editor of *The Reader* and primary producer of Liverpool Reads, Founder and director of Get Into Reading	*The Reader* Magazine	Liverpool	21, 22 April 2005; 22 February 2006
Bea Colley	Producer	Liverpool Reads	Liverpool	27 June 2006
Jane Davis, Kate McDonnell, Geraldine Mair and Mary Weston	Reading group facilitators	Get Into Reading	Liverpool	27 June 2006
Adam, Kayla, Emma, and Gemma	Young participants in a read along group with Get Into Reading	Rocket Training Centre	The Wirral	20 February 2007
Beccy Jones	Participation manager; member of Liverpool Reads committee	Bluecoat Arts Centre	Liverpool	21 February 2007

(*Continued*)

Table A2 (Continued)

Name	Job Title or Role	Industry or organization	Location	Date of Interview
David Melia and Jane Findley	Facilitators of Get Into Reading program at institution that serves people with neurology, neurosurgical, and pain management issues	Walton Neurological Centre	Liverpool	21 February 2007
Steve Padgett	Freelance education practitioner; producer of educational material to accompany Liverpool Reads books	n/a	Aigburth	22 February 2007
Seattle Reads				
Chris Higashi	Producer	Seattle Reads, SPL	Seattle	7 June 2006
Nancy Pearl	Former producer	Seattle Reads	Seattle	7 June 2006
Bruce Burgett and Gray Kochar-Lindren	Professors; supporters of Seattle Reads	University of Washington	Seattle	7 June 2006
Diane Douglas	Staff member; supporter of Seattle Reads	Bellevue Community College	Bellevue	21 June 2006
One Book, One Vancouver				
Janice Douglas	Youth services coordinator; producer of OBOC	VPL	Vancouver, 1st via telephone	23 July 2003; 19 June 2006

Name	Role	Organization	Location	Date
Carmen Munoz	Youth leadership program for immigrants and refugees; ESL Book Club leader; OBOV supporter	Immigrant Services Society of BC	Vancouver	5 June 2006
Beth Davis	Public librarian and book club leader of a marginalized group from the Downtown Eastside	VPL	Vancouver	9 June 2006
Wayson Choy, Todd Wong, Larry Wong	Author of *The Jade Peony*, which was chosen for the inaugural program in 2002; supporters and members of the Chinese-Canadian community	n/a	Vancouver	12 June 2006
Susan, Jinder, Jane, Corinne, Barbara	Staff producers' committee	VPL	Vancouver	13 June 2006
Beverley Ranger	President, Beyond Words Book Club	n/a	Vancouver	20 June 2006
Patrick Lane	Author of *There Is a Season: A Memoir*, which was chosen for the program in 2006	X	Victoria via telephone	20 June 2006

[1] While visiting Kenwood High School, we spoke with the book club members but were not allowed to tape or collect demographic data.

For a usual period of six weeks during each MRE, the online survey was "live." Table A3 illustrates the data collection period, the language of the survey, and the number of respondents.

Participants were recruited through bookmarks left in bookstores and libraries, community centers, and other public places. We also purchased advertisements in local and arts newspapers, and the questionnaire for the RJBC was promoted via GoogleAds. The producers of *Richard & Judy* also promoted our survey via a link on their webpage. Additionally, we invited survey participation through our own professional and social networks and those of the local assistant and key figures. Respondents, who elected to do so, were entered into a draw for a $50 gift certificate at the bookstore of their choice. In some locations, the response was disappointingly low and in these cases, we are careful not to use the data and only combine across datasets whenever it is statistically valid to do so. For example, we combine datasets to illustrate the genre preferences of all readers we surveyed. In all cases, throughout the book, we make clear which site and which dataset our conclusions are based on. Because we used snowball and referral sampling procedures, we cannot generalize our findings to the general reading public, but we can make conclusions

Table A3 Quantitative Datasets

Research site	Language(s) of survey	Data collection period	Number of respondents
Bristol (The Great Reading Adventure)	English	5 January to 15 March 2006	75
Birmingham (the Birmingham Readers Festival- the RJBC)	English	25 September to 6 November 2006	228
Liverpool (Liverpool Reads)	English	19 February to 2 April 2007	134
Chicago (OBOC Chicago)	English, French, and Spanish	13 October to 24 November 2006	125
Huntsville (OBOC Huntsville-NEA sponsored event)	English, French, and Spanish	2 April to 12 May 2007	75
Seattle (Seattle Reads)	English, French, and Spanish	12 May to 23 June 2007	153
Vancouver (OBOC Vancouver)	English, French, and Spanish	15 May to 20 June 2006	235
Canada (Canada Reads)	English, French, and Spanish	10 April to 10 May 2006	961
UK (the RJBC)	English	8 January to 19 February 2007	1,559

based on those *who did* respond (Locke, Silverman, and Spirduso 2004, 126). In several instances throughout the book when we do want to contemplate reading in general, we make note of other reader surveys and compare them to our own findings. We were interested in people who identified as readers, and we believe that the survey data provides "a truthful reflection of what the study is intended to examine" (Locke, Silverman, and Spirduso, 2004, 127). In other words, we used the survey as part of our efforts to better understand why people come together to share reading, to evaluate whether or not marginalized communities participate, and whether new reading practices and/or social change is enabled through MREs.

There are some obvious advantages and limits involved in employing an online survey. The online administration was flexible because it offered twenty-four-hour access, assured anonymity, and no time limitation for completion once a participant had begun it. However, we recognize that conducting the survey online meant that those who were not comfortable in that environment or who did not have access to the Internet were not given the opportunity to participate. In addition, those with uncertainty about the meanings of questions were not able to communicate with us in order to dispel any confusion.

Once the questionnaire was no longer live, the data set was saved to an SPSS file. A case analysis method was used to manage the data. Variable labels were confirmed. Cases in which more than 20 percent of the categorical responses were missing were removed from the set. Because there was not a large number of cases that were missing more than 20 percent of their responses, a mean or median replacement method was not used. "Cleaning" the data also included removing all identifying factors of the respondents, including names, addresses, and e-mail addresses. Three team members coded a sample of the open-ended responses independently and then compared the results, forcing them into categories after extensive team discussions (see Fuller and Rehberg Sedo, 2012). The code books were updated after these discussions and the remaining open-ended responses were coded.

The quantitative portion of our study is largely descriptive. That is, we employ statistical analysis, but we limit those analyses to the orthodox methods of frequencies, cross tabulations, and regression analysis to gauge correlations between ethnicity, gender, age, class, and reading behaviors.

OUR SURVEY READERS

The majority of the readers who responded to our online questionnaire could be described as keen readers. Most respondents claimed to read between two to five hours per week (42 percent; 1,471) with another 32 percent (1,120) reading between six and ten hours per week. We did not distinguish in the survey between "reading for pleasure" and "reading for work," but we did ask about the genres of books that readers most prefer, and contemporary fiction (31 percent; 1,100), followed by mysteries (14 percent; 481) and science fiction (11 percent; 377) were the most popular. Levels of education were high, and there was little variation across the three nation-states. Many respondents (32 percent; 1,002) had completed a university degree, and an additional 26 percent (824) had obtained a graduate degree (known as a postgraduate degree in the UK). Across all datasets (N = 3,060), 53 percent (1,608) identified as "middle class." In the UK, 47 percent (787) identified themselves as such, and in Canada, the percentage was much higher at 62 percent (657). In the US, 54 percent (164) chose that classification when asked. Notions of class stratification and class identity operate in subtly different ways within the three nation-states of our study, so the category "middle class" does not necessarily have the same properties or cultural connotations for British, Canadian, and American respondents. During focus groups, British participants often queried their own self-identifications, wondering aloud, for example, whether their "working-class roots" were cancelled out by their current profession or their relatively comfortable lifestyle. Americans were more prone to define class in terms of their current income and material possessions, and did not concern themselves about the fine-grained distinctions that British readers were prone to make between "lower middle class" and "middle class." Such distinctions may account for the difference in our quantitative data between the percentage of British and Canadian readers who selected "middle class." Canadians who participated in our focus groups generally referred to their job, income, and levels of education as markers of class.

Across our combined datasets, the readers who responded to our online survey were predominantly women (61 percent; 1,919), and approximately one-third of respondents (39 percent; 1,219) were men. Of the 3,009 survey respondents who noted their ethnicity, 42 percent (1,273) identified as "White," while 35 percent (1059) marked "British." Other categories, such as African American, Asian, or Québécois, each accounted for a little more than 1 percent of our survey respondents. Of our survey respondents, 85 percent (3,030) read in English as their first language, while another 9 percent (310) read in French and nearly 2 percent (58) read in Spanish. Since the MREs that we were investigating focused on texts originally written in or translated into English, it is not surprising that we received so few responses from readers whose first language for reading is Spanish or French, despite making our questionnaire available in these languages. Adult readers were the primary focus of our research, and of those who responded to the online survey, the largest percentages in each nation-state were in the thirty to thirty-nine age range. In the UK, 25 percent (421) of respondents were aged between twenty and twenty-nine years old, a larger group than in the US and Canada, which might reflect the type of MREs we selected in the UK rather than a greater enthusiasm for pleasure reading among British readers in their twenties (Figure A2). Both Liverpool Reads and Bristol's Great Reading Adventure have consistently selected books, themes, and activities that appeal to younger readers as well as adults, while the RJBC was well

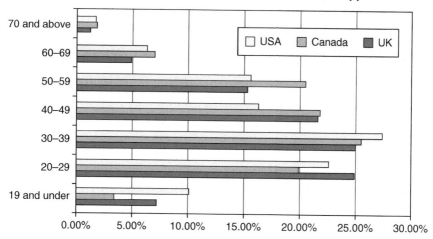

Figure A2 Age Category Chart
Percentage of all surveyed readers. N = 2,938

known among the university student population who, as television producer Amanda Ross (pers. comm., 2006) noted, made up a sizeable proportion of the show's daily audience.

OBSERVATION—PARTICIPANT OBSERVATION

Borrowed from cultural anthropology, participant observation offered us as researchers the opportunity to experience the local events during intense periods of fieldwork.[2] While readers ourselves, we were always researchers and never able to immerse ourselves fully because of our role as researchers and because of time and travel constraints. We used a standard observation protocol (see Figure A3) for all public events that we attended, and adapted it for semiprivate events such as book club meetings. In most cases, attending the events allowed us to experience the events as other readers might but, of course, always acknowledging our positions of power as researchers in our analysis.

OBSERVATIONAL PROTOCOL
Notes about my EXPERIENCES, HUNCHES, LEARNINGS
Record:

- portraits of attendees (includes age, gender, ethnicity obvious to the eye). Include the author and producers.
- the setting
- particular activities
- my reactions

Potential categories:
Verbal: tone, content, silences of attendees
Non-verbal: kinesics (body), proxemic use of space (props), appearance (of attendees), engagement and feedback
Combined verbal, non-verbal: touching, greeting one another
Global: positioning of attendees, hand gestures, use of objects, amount of time each person speaks, content of the talk, formal/informal leader(s), who seems to have power? Why? Who is recognised to speak? What norms are evident? Resisted?

Topics discussed:

Time

Situation–Description	Reflection-Self

Illustration A3 Observation Protocol

Notes

NOTE TO THE INTRODUCTION

1. No complete record of OBOC programs exists, but the Center for the Book at the Library of Congress in Washington, D.C., registers some that have taken place in the US, Canada, Australia, and the UK; see www.read.gov/resources. By July 2012, the NEA had awarded more than 1,000 grants to community programs since the launch of the Big Read initiative in 2007, and each year at least 30 percent of the grants fund new OBOC programs. We estimate, then, that there are around 300 OBOCs annually in the US alone. See www.neabig-read.org/.

NOTES TO CHAPTER 1

1. Further examples of reading and publishing histories include: in Australia and New Zealand, see Eggert and Webby (2004); Liebich (2011) and, for South Africa under apartheid, C. Davis (2011), and McDonald (2009).
2. See especially, Altick ([1957] 1998); Augst (2003); F. Black, Fleming, and Lamonde (2005); Boyarin (1992a); Casper, Chiason, and Groves (2002); Davidson (2004); Finkelstein and McCleery (2002); Fleming, Gallichan, and Lamonde (2004); Gerson and Michon (2007); Kaestle and Radway (2009); McKitterick (2009); Nord, Rubin, and Schudson (2009); Suarez and Wouhuysen (2010); R. J. Zboray and M. Zboray (2006). For an up-to-date list of resources, see the Society for the History of Authorship, Reading and Publishing at www.sharpweb.org.
3. A recent exception to the focus on contemporary book groups is Adam Reed's (2011) investigation of a set of solitary readers who belong to a single literary society, the Henry Williamson Society.
4. Here, "realist" and "interpretative" refer to two of the dominant traditions of thought and practice within the social sciences. The "realist" paradigm, which, broadly speaking, underpins the employment of quantitative methods, conceptualizes the social world as knowable via the verifiable investigation of its properties and relations (cf. the scientific investigation of the natural world). The "interpretative" paradigm, traditionally associated with the employment of qualitative methods, operates from the assumption that the social world is accessed via its (mediated) representations. Knowledge is thus contingent on and constitutive of particular contextual and discursive factors.

NOTES TO CHAPTER 2

1. Cole Moreton's article appeared in the newspaper on November 25, 2001, but is no longer accessible online. http://www.independent.co.uk/news/people/profiles/richard-and-judy-the-golden-couple-617972.html (Last accessed 9 March 2012).
2. The "You Say, We Pay" scandal took place in the spring of 2007, and was a result of call-in contestants' complaints that they were told to phone a premium-rate number even after contestants had already been chosen to participate in a visual guessing game competition. Finnigan and Madeley claimed innocence in the entire affair and were vocal in their support of the allegedly cheated viewers.
3. See Grindstaff (2002) for an interesting history of the American talk show. Relevant to our argument about the emotive style of program hosts, Grindstaff highlights the commercial move to create para-intimate programs with one name titles such as "Donahue" and "Geraldo" (50).
4. Wednesday is known in the UK media industry as the day for "lifestyle" programming.
5. Squires quotes Hattersley, who is quoted below. *Cloud Atlas* appeared on the Winter 2005 series of the book club. It was written by David Mitchell, and published in the UK by Sceptre in 2004.
6. The wine club launched in the fall of 2004 with segments running for six weeks. The publicity around the project "aimed to debunk wine snobbery and ensure everyone gets more enjoyment out of wine." The public relations agency website, and this quotation, can be found at: http://www.taylorherring.com/richardandjudy_case.html (Last accessed 1 December 2012).
7. The entire segment is available on Adichie's webpage at: http://www.halfofayellowsun.com/content.php?page=author_gallery&n=1&f=2 (Last accessed 1 December 2012).
8. The website for *Half of a Yellow Sun* includes reader responses to the novel among other interesting information about the book and its author. http://www.halfofayellowsun.com/public/yourstory/guestbook.php (Last accessed 1 December 2012).
9. While our survey did not isolate participation in the live chats, 45 percent of respondents had visited the website, but only 4 percent had registered, which was a requirement to take part in the live chats. Fifty-one percent of those who visited the website found it "useful."
10. Both of these readers work in industries that Bourdieu (1984) called "cultural facilitation" in which they might enjoy "intellectual solidarity with the dominated classes" but because of their work tasks and the general economic milieu of cultural production, they are, according to Bourdieu, condemned to seek "narcissistic self-absorption" (f.n. 365–66).
11. Readers will notice different interviewers quoted throughout our book. As outlined in our Methods Appendix, our focus groups were conducted by two out of three members of the core research team: namely, the authors and the post-doctoral fellow, Dr. Anouk Lang. When all three researchers were involved, as was the case in several sites, the extra member acted as a silent observer and note taker.
12. Because of BBC rules, advertising would not be possible in any case.
13. Our online readers self-identified their class positions. The range of class among the participants who specifically identified as *Richard & Judy* viewers was varied (1,034): 32 percent identified as lower class; 18 percent as lower middle class; 43 percent as middle class; 7 percent identified as upper middle class or upper class. Respondent ethnicity was an open-ended question on the survey. Most of the respondents (90 percent) identified as "white" or "British." Women participate in the program more so than do men (90 percent).

NOTES TO CHAPTER 3

1. The 2011 season aired in one-hour segments.
2. In 2004 and 2005, *Canada Reads* was also televised. For more discussion on why the translation of the series across media failed due to underfunding and crucial differences in communicative strategies between radio and television, see Fuller and Rehberg Sedo (2006). The article also includes a discussion of Société Radio Canada's *Le combat des livres* and its place in Canadian broadcast book programming.
3. Mackenzie King was Prime Minister from 1921 to 1930, except during a short hiatus, and again from 1935 to 1948.
4. Consider, as illustration, that large television networks are required to broadcast eight hours per week of Canadian programming during peak viewing periods (http://www.crtc.gc.ca/eng/archive/1999/PB99-97.HTM#t11) and that "Commercial radio stations . . . have to ensure that at least 35% of the Popular Music broadcast between 6:00 a.m. and 6:00 p.m. Monday to Friday is Canadian content" (ibid.). The CBC is required "to ensure that at least 50% of their Popular Music selections" are Canadian-made (2002).
5. As of 2 February 2011, there was a webpage that covered news about the CBC at www.themothercorp.com. It is no longer accessible.
6. National (Canadian) radio and television ratings can be found at: http://www.bbm.ca. *The Globe and Mail* reporter Andrew Ryan (2010) provides a glimpse into the Canadian viewer psyche in an article claiming that Canadian television viewers appreciate CBC television but that they do not necessarily watch it.
7. The "CBC Arts & Culture Research Study" (Créatec and Canadian Heritage 2005), which asked 1,900 English-speaking Canadians about their radio listening habits, puts listenership for Radio1 at 35 percent (2).
8. CBC Television also sells advertisements, as we noted above. CBC television is a more commercial endeavor than CBC radio because of this business model. It is difficult for CBC television to compete with the other two major networks (Global Television and CTV) because of the influence of American programming. For example, Canadian viewers are not likely to watch Canadian content over American content when the Canadian popular press highlights the lineup of the US-made television series *Dancing with the Stars*. See also n 4.
9. Participation includes listening or watching the program, participating in local events, such as panel discussions or movie screenings. Participation could also mean going to the website and reading at least one of the *Canada Reads* picks. It may also include watching the televised version that ran in 2004–2005.
10. Thanks to Simone Murray who brought these discussions to our attention.
11. The introductory segment is no longer available online; however, the five-day program itself is accessible at: http://www.cbc.ca/books/canadareads/2006/10/listen-to-canada-reads-2006.html#more.
12. The 2009 season even continued with an online book club that highlighted the "winner" of the competition: *The Book of Negros* by Lawrence Hill.
13. *A Complicated Kindness* won the 2004 Governor General's Award for English Language fiction and *Three Day Road* was nominated for the 2005 Governor General's Award. That year Boyden's novel won both the McNally Robinson Aboriginal Book of the Year Award and the Rogers Writers' Trust Fiction Prize. In 2006, it won Amazon/Books in Canada First Novel Award.
14. Comparisons across the two studies should be made with caution because the sampling procedures and questions were different.
15. Some of the selected titles over the years could be considered crossover genres, such as *The Outlander* by Gil Adamson and Nalo Hopkinson's *Brown Girl in the Ring*, which blend the elements of mystery and science fiction, respectively. Interestingly, the 2011 season of *Canada Reads* was limited to only nonfiction titles.

16. For instance, Bristol's "Great Reading Adventure" chose *Day of the Triffids* (Michael Joseph), first published in 1951, and in 2005, *Hominids* (Tor Books Lead Science), published in 2002, was the OBOC Kitchener-Waterloo-Cambridge selection.

17. *Young Canada Reads* is a CBC Halifax-produced radio program that sees youth aged between ten and fourteen mimic *Canada Reads*.

18. Sampling procedures for the online survey included snowball sampling, which might explain the high level of education of our respondents. See our Methods Appendix. A Créatec study on Canadian reading notes that "a substantial majority of those who have completed college (59 percent) and a large majority of those who have completed university (66 percent) are regular readers . . . [and, there] is a clear trend toward reading literary materials and reading diligently that becomes evident as soon as university studies are completed: half of university graduates (50 percent) are mainly literary readers (versus 43 percent in the other categories) and 20 percent are heavy readers (versus 14 percent on average in the other categories)" (Créatec and Canada Heritage 2005, 49–50).

19. The internal CBC study echoes this finding (CBC/Radio-Canada 2005).

20. Two years later, Garner recycled the same article in another magazine: "The Phony Cult of Canned Canadianism," *Maclean's* (21 May 1960): 8, 58, 60.

21. Transliteracies is a term often associated with the transfer of literacy from print to digital environments. See, for example, Lotherington 2005; Liu 2009.

NOTES TO CHAPTER 4

1. Although we are not conceptualizing moral power as a kind of capability performed by individual social actors as sociologists Jal Metha and Christopher Winship have done, their emphasis on moral power as "highly relational and socially constructed" is pertinent here (2010, 425). Winship's and Metha's (2010) model also proposes that certain individuals may have the ability "to persuade and influence others by asserting the correctness of particular moral positions" (435), but that this ability often requires other resources, such as economic and social capital, access to the media and education.

2. For specific case studies and a discussion of trade disputes between Canada and the US involving the cultural industries, see, for example, Acheson and Maule (2001).

3. In the UK, the current nomenclature is the Department of Culture, Media and Sport, while the Canadian federal government counterpart is the Department of Canadian Heritage.

4. Formerly known as the Scottish Arts Council, Creative Scotland is a "development body for the arts, culture and creativity" established in July 2010. See http://www.creativescotland.com/ (Last accessed 3 December 2012).

5. In his preface to the "Reading at Risk" report, Chairman Dana Gioia (2004) strongly echoes Putnam's (2000) language of civic responsibility and his lament about the decline of associational behavior and its social, political, and moral consequences: "More than reading is at stake. As this report unambiguously demonstrates, readers play a more active and involved role in their communities. The decline in reading, therefore, parallels a larger retreat from participation in civic and cultural life. The long-term implications of this study not only affect literature but all the arts—as well as social activities such as volunteerism, philanthropy, and even political engagement" (NEA 2004, vii).

6. Although the figures quoted here for the UK and the US both include digital products, Bowker (2010) also reported that print titles increased by 5 percent from 2009–2010.

7. Statistics Canada states the population of the Vancouver "census metropolitan area" (as defined by the 2006 census boundaries) as 2,231,500 for 2007

and 2,391,300 for 2010. One of top three destinations for new immigrants to Canada, the population of the Vancouver metropolitan area increased by about 50,000 each year during the first decade of the twenty-first century (Statistics Canada, http://www.statcan.gc.ca/tables-tableaux/sum-som/l01/cst01/demo05a-eng.htm, Last accessed 3 December 2012).

8. In 2009, the Minister for Canadian Heritage and responsible for Official Languages announced that the Book Publishing Industry Development Program (known as the BPIDP) was being "streamlined and renamed" the Canada Book Fund, in an attempt to reflect a "shift in its focus from developing the industry to providing support to a mature industry that will help bring Canadian books to readers" (http://www.pch.gc.ca/pgm/padie-bpidp/index-eng.cfm, Last accessed 3 December 2012). Of course, "streamlined" is often "NewLiberalSpeak" for standardization and cutbacks (Bourdieu and Wacquant 2001). Given the realities of the English-language publishing field that we have outlined in this chapter, the funds available to publishers in Canada cannot combat the biggest difficulties posed by industry structures, although government grants do have the effect of legitimating the Canadian industry and overtly encourage (oblige) Canadian operators to keep "publishing Canadian."

9. In Williams's (1961) early work, "structures of feeling" refers to the general organization of emotion and experience in a given period. It describes the ways that common values or shared generational experiences shape subjective experience (e.g., *The Long Revolution* 1961). There is a sense in *The Country and the City* (1973) that the lived experience of a community is visible or traceable in its social and textual practices, including art and literature. Much of Williams's (1961, 1977, 1983) work brackets ideology off from experience, perhaps because his notion of culture describes a dynamic process rather than one that can be fully accounted for by the ideas and structures associated with institutions, and also because he is arguing against the Marxist structure/superstructure paradigm. John Higgins offers a thoughtful critical account of the emergence and development of the concept in Williams's work (1999, 37–39), noting that it is as "shifting and unstable" (37) as any of the terms Williams (1977, 1983) explored in *Keywords* (1976).

10. Not knowing about the event was the top reason for not participating across all datasets (37 percent; 625).

11. LibraryThing is an online self-styled "book club" with over one million members, which enables readers to catalogue their books, write reviews and blogs, and contribute to discussions. See http://www.librarything.com/ (Last accessed 3 December 2012).

12. Some of the earlier GRA evaluation reports are no longer available online. The Small Island Read evaluation report is at: http://www.bristolreads.com/small_island_read/index.html (Last accessed 3 December 2012).

13. Scholars who have assessed the benefits and failures of Liverpool's "cultural moment" as European Capital of Culture 2008 and the "extreme makeover" of the city's infrastructural redevelopment and image rebranding include McGuigan (2010, 126–28) and Patterson (2010).

14. Brunel 200 was "supported by funding from the National Lottery, including over £500,000 from the Urban Cultural Programme (Arts Council England and the Millennium Commission) and a grant of £980,000 from the Heritage Lottery Fund" (Brunel 200, http://www.brunel200.com/, Last accessed 3 December 2012)).

15. Levy's editor at Hodder originally offered the special edition books to the BCDP for just £0.29 per copy, but this figure most likely increased to around £0.49 per copy by the time they were produced (B. Colley, pers. comm., 2006).

16. The authors interviewed a group of cultural workers involved with the NEA's Big Read at the NEA headquarters in Washington, D.C., May 25, 2006. The group consisted of Maryrose Flanigan, David Kipen, Hope O'Keefe, Tom Bradshaw,

and Kate Kaiser, all of whom were working for the NEA at the time, and Karen Motylewski, Evaluation Officer, and Marsha L. Semmel, Deputy Director for Museums and Director for Strategic Partnerships, the IMLS.

NOTES TO CHAPTER 5

1. "Cultural mediators" is a deliberate choice of term, since Bourdieu's (1993) term "cultural intermediaries" has been applied by media and cultural studies scholars to such a wide range of cultural production roles that its precision and original meaning has been lost. For a fuller discussion of this problem, see Hesmondhalgh (2006, 226–27; [2002] 2007, 66–67).
2. "Ruling relations of power" is a term first employed by Dorothy Smith (1987) and widely adopted by feminist standpoint epistemologists (e.g., Harding 1991; Stanley and Wise 1990). Ruling relations of power include the political, legal, economic, and institutional structures that organize society. For an application of feminist standpoint theory to literary-cultural production, particularly with regards to women's writing and publishing communities, see Fuller (2004, esp. 16–29).
3. These words were used to introduce Pearl at an OBOC event in Seattle, 17 May 2007.
4. See http://www.mcphee.com/shop/products/Librarian-Action-Figure.html (Last accessed 3 December 2012). As befits a radio and television host, and a best-selling author with her own calendar, Pearl induces fan-type behaviors even from academic researchers. We took "Nancy" with us on some of our fieldwork trips, setting up our Nancy icon like a shrine on top of our hotel room TV to bring us luck and guidance. The research team also obtained the obligatory hardcore fan "meet your hero" photograph.
5. Others include whichbook.net; DearReader; BookLetters; and NextReads.
6. US Census Data estimate at 1 July 2007.
7. Drawing from a variety of available data resources, the "America's Most Literate Cities" study ranks the largest cities (population 250,000 and above) in the United States. This study focuses on six key indicators of literacy: newspaper circulation, number of bookstores, library resources, periodical publishing resources, educational attainment, and Internet resources. In other words, this study focuses "not on whether their citizens can read, but whether they do" (Marklein 2005).
8. Although Pearl (pers. comm., 2006) describes a secular scene of shared reading, there are parallels with the goals and practices of faith-based reading groups past and present. Significantly for our analysis in this book, Pearl's liberal conceptualization echoes the moral and religious symbolic meanings that reading held within Judeo-Christian cultures prior to the "industrialization of the book" (see, for example, Bonfil 1999 and Parkes 1999) that began in the early 1800s (Banham 2009) and the advent of widespread literacy via national policies of education that enabled the expansion of literacy in the second half of the nineteenth century. The text selection increased but the association of reading books with the spiritual and moral life of the reader persisted as leisure reading became a possibility for more people. For example, Joan Shelley Rubin examines the reading of poetry by Christian Americans of the early twentieth century for devotional purposes, edification, and pleasure (2007, 287–335). Cathy N. Davidson points out, however, that by the late eighteenth century, the Bible was no longer the central text for many American readers (2004, 141).
9. We have interviewed Jane and her coworkers on several occasions (e.g., 22 April 2005, 27 June 2006, 22 February 2007), and have met with some of the participants in GIR groups, including a small group of 17-year-olds (Rocket Training group, 20 February 2007) and one of adult male asylum seekers (Asylum Link,

21 February 2007). Additionally, GIR facilitators made presentations at the "Beyond the Book" conference in September 2007. The Reader Organisation introduces Get Into Reading, some of the groups that it runs, its training, and research projects at http://reachingout.thereader.org.uk/get-into-reading.html (Last accessed 3 December 2012).

10. In Phil Davis's own words in a 2009 University of Liverpool staff profile, his "interests concern the relation of writing and reading to living" and this socially engaged but aesthetically informed approach to texts inflects his interdisciplinary research into the "acts of reading" as well as his published examinations of Shakespeare, Victorian British literature, and Jewish-American writing (http://www.liv.ac.uk/english/staff/philipdavis.htm). (The page contents have since changed.)

11. For testimonies from GIR members, see, the "Why It Works" section of the GIR website, at: http://reachingout.thereader.org.uk/what-is-get-into-reading.html (Last accessed 3 December 2012).

NOTES TO CHAPTER 6

1. The prizes that Ricci won for *Lives of the Saints* included the Governor General's Award, The Books in Canada First Novel Award, The F. G. Bressani Prize, The Betty Trask Award, and the Winifred Holtby Prize. The novel was published in the US as *The Book of Saints*. (See http://ninoricci.com/. Last accessed 3 December 2012.)

2. Huntsville is more economically prosperous than rural areas of the state, and its high-tech industries (NASA, Redstone Arsenal, and the industries that support the military-industrial complex) require a skilled and highly qualified workforce (especially of engineers). Cummings Research Park, which forms part of a research hub, is the second largest in the United States. However, our focus group participants' perceptions about literacy and education in Alabama may have been influenced by past realities rather than the contemporary situation. For example, Alabama's adult literacy rates actually improved in sixty-six out of sixty-seven counties between 1992 and 2003. Based on a report from the National Center for Educational Statistics (NCES), *The Birmingham News* stated, "Alabama's [adult illiteracy] rate dropped from 21 percent to 15 percent, bringing it far closer to the national rate, which was 14.5 percent, down from 14.7 percent in 1992" (Ray 2009).

3. For further analysis of book group discussions about Small Island that took place in Liverpool and elsewhere in the UK, and also of readers' comments submitted to the Small Island Reads 2007 website, see Benwell (2009) and Lang (2009a, 2009b).

NOTE TO CHAPTER 7

1. Literature for All of Us (literatureforallofus.org) is a Chicago-based, not-for-profit literacy group that facilitates book clubs in high schools across the city. In 2007, we hosted an international conference as part of the "Beyond the Book" project. Two young book club moderators from Chicago, and Jane Davis and her team from Liverpool, met at that conference.

NOTES TO METHODS APPENDIX

1. For a full discussion, see Fuller and Rehberg Sedo (2012).

2. In Huntsville, Vancouver, and Birmingham, our research assistants were trained in observation methods and attended events outside of our fieldwork schedules.

References

Acheson, Keith, and Christopher Maule. 2001. *Much Ado About Culture: North American Trade Disputes*. Ann Arbor: University of Michigan Press.

Adams, Douglas. 1979. *The Hitchhiker's Guide to the Galaxy*. London: Pan Books.

Adamson, Rondi. 2005. "Just Pull the Plug on the CBC Already." *Christian Science Monitor*, October 11. http://www.csmonitor.com/2005/1011/p09s02-coop.html. (Accessed 7 September 2012.)

Adichie, Chimamanda Ngozi. 2006. *Half of a Yellow Sun*. London: Harper Perennial.

Ahmed, Sara. 2004. *The Cultural Politics of Emotion*. Edinburgh: Edinburgh University Press.

Allen, Katie. 2009. "Ross Confident of Book Club Future." *The Bookseller*, May 17. http://www.thebookseller.com/news/ross-confident-book-club-future.html. (Accessed 21 December 2010.)

Allen, Robert C. 1992. "More Talk About TV." In *Channels of Discourse, Reassembled: Television and Contemporary Critics*, edited by Robert Allen, 1–30. London: Routledge.

Allington, Daniel, and Joan Swann. 2009. "Researching Literary Reading as Social Practice." *Language and Literature* 18 (3): 219–30.

Altick, Richard Daniel. [1957] 1998. *The English Common Reader: A Social History of the Mass Reading Public, 1800–1900*. Columbus: Ohio State University Press.

Ang, Ien. 1985. *Watching Dallas: Soap Opera and the Melodramatic Imagination*. Translated by Della Couling. London and New York: Methuen.

———. 1990. "Culture and Communication: Towards an Ethnographic Critique of Media Consumption in the Transnational Media System." *European Journal of Communication* 5 (2/3): 239–60.

———. 1996. "Feminist Desire and Female Pleasure: On Janice Radway's *Reading the Romance*." In *Living Room Wars: Rethinking Media Audiences for a Postmodern World*, 98–108. London: Routledge.

Anonymous. 1997. "ALA—Oprah's Book Club Gets the Country Reading." *American Libraries* 28 (3): 6.

Argenti, Paul, and Courtney Barnes. 2010. *Digital Strategies for Powerful Corporate Communications*. New York: McGraw-Hill.

Armstrong, Robert. 2010. *Broadcasting Policy in Canada*. Toronto: University of Toronto Press.

Attallah, Paul. 2000. "Public Broadcasting in Canada: Legitimation Crisis and the Loss of Audience." *Gazette* 62 (3–4): 177–203.

Augst, Thomas. 2003. "Introduction: American Libraries and Agencies of Culture." In *Libraries as Agencies of Culture*, edited by Thomas Augst and Wayne A. Wiegand, 5–22. Madison: University of Wisconsin Press.

Augst, Thomas, and Kenneth E. Carpenter, eds. 2007. *Institutions of Reading: The Social Life of Libraries in the United States.* Amherst and Boston: University of Massachusetts Press.

Banham, Rob. 2009. "The Industrialization of the Book (1800–1970)." In *A Companion to the History of the Book*, edited by Simon Eliot and Jonathan Rose, 273–90. Malden: Wiley-Blackwell.

Banks, Mark. 2007. *The Politics of Cultural Work.* Houndmills: Palgrave Macmillan.

———. 2009. "Fit and Working Again? The Instrumental Leisure of the 'Creative Class'." *Environment and Planning A* 41 (3): 668–81.

Barber, Karin. 2007. *The Anthropology of Texts, Persons and Publics: Oral and Written Culture in Africa and Beyond.* Cambridge: Cambridge University Press.

Beck, Andrew. 2003. "Introduction: Cultural Work, Cultural Workplace—Looking at the Cultural Industries." In *Cultural Work: Understanding the Cultural Industries*, edited by Andrew Beck, 1–11. London and New York: Routledge.

Beckett, Sandra L. 2009. *Crossover Fiction: Global and Historical Perspectives.* New York: Routledge.

Belfiore, Eleonora, and Oliver Bennett. 2010. *The Social Impact of the Arts: An Intellectual History.* Houndmills: Palgrave Macmillan.

Bennett, Tony. 1987. "Texts in History: The Determination of Readings and Their Texts." In *Post-Structuralism and the Question of History*, edited by Derek Attridge, Geoff Bennington, and Robert Young, 63–81. Cambridge: Cambridge University Press.

———. 2006. "Distinction on the Box: Cultural Capital and the Social Space of Broadcasting." *Cultural Trends* 15 (2–3): 193–212.

Bennett, Tony, Mike Savage, Elizabeth Silva, Alan Warde, Modesto Gayo-Cal, and David Wright. 2009. *Culture, Class, Distinction.* London and New York: Routledge.

Benwell, Bethan. 2009. "'A Pathetic and Racist and Awful Character': Ethnomethodological Approaches to the Reception of Diasporic Fiction." *Language and Literature* 18 (3): 300–15.

Benwell, Bethan, James Procter, and Gemma Robinson. 2011. "Not Reading Brick Lane." In *New Formations, Special Issue: Reading After Empire*, edited by Bethan Benwell, James Procter, and Gemma Robinson, 73: 90–116.

Berg, Temma. 2008. "'What Do You Know?': Or, The Question of Reading in Groups and Academic Authority." *LIT: Literature Interpretation Theory* 19 (2): 123–54.

Berlant, Lauren. 2008. *The Female Complaint: The Unfinished Business of Sentimentality in American Culture.* Durham: Duke University Press.

Birkerts, Sven. 1996. "The Time of Reading: A Meditation on the Fate of Books in an Impatient Age." *Boston Review.* http://bostonreview.net/BR21.3/Birkerts.html. (Accessed 12 November 2011.)

Birmingham City Council. 2012. "Big City Read." http://www.birmingham.gov.uk/bigcityread. (Accessed 20 August 2012.)

Black, Alistair. 1996. *A New History of the English Public Library: Social and Intellectual Contexts, 1850–1914.* London: Leicester University Press.

———. 2000. *The Public Library in Britain, 1914–2000.* London: British Library.

Black, Fiona, Patricia Fleming, and Yvan Lamonde, eds. 2005. *History of the Book in Canada, Volume 2: 1840–1918.* Toronto: University of Toronto Press.

Blair, Amy. 2011. *Reading Up: Middle-Class Readers and the Culture of Success in the Early Twentieth-Century United States.* Philadelphia: Temple University Press.

Bleich, David. 1975. *Readings and Feelings: An Introduction to Subjective Criticism.* Urbana: National Council of Teachers of English.

———. 1978. *Subjective Criticism.* Baltimore: The John Hopkins University Press.

Bloom, Harold. 2000. *How to Read and Why.* New York and Toronto: Scribner.

————. 2011. *The Anatomy of Influence: Literature as A Way of Life*. New Haven: Yale University Press.

Böhm, Steffen, and Chris Land. 2009. "No Measure for Cultural Value? Value in the New Economy." *Capital & Class* 33 (1): 75–98.

Bonfil, Robert. 1999. "Reading in the Jewish Communities of Western Europe in the Middle Ages." In *A History of Reading in the West*, edited by Guglielmo Cavallo and Roger Chartier, translated by Lydia G. Cochrane, 149–78. Cambridge: Polity Press.

Born, Daniel. 2011. "Utopian Civic-Mindedness: Robert Maynard Hutchins, Mortimer Adler, and the Great Books Enterprise." In *Reading Communities from Salons to Cyberspace*, edited by DeNel Rehberg Sedo, 81–100. Houndmills: Palgrave Macmillan.

Born, Georgina. 2003. "Strategy, Positioning and Projection in Digital Television: Channel Four and the Commercialization of Public Service Broadcasting in the UK." *Media, Culture & Society* 25 (6): 774–99.

Botshon, Lisa, and Meredith Goldsmith, eds. 2003. *Middlebrow Moderns: Popular American Women Writers of the 1920s*. Boston: Northeastern University Press.

Bourdieu, Pierre. [1979] 1984. *Distinction: A Social Critique of the Judgement of Taste*. Translated by Richard Nice. Cambridge: Harvard University Press.

————. 1993. *The Field of Cultural Production: Essays on Art and Literature*. Edited by Randal Johnson. New York: Polity Press.

Bourdieu, Pierre, and Loïc Wacquant. 2001. "NewLiberalSpeak—Notes on the New Planetary Vulgate." *Radical Philosophy* 105: 2–3.

Bowker. 2010. "Bowker Reports Traditional U.S. Book Production Flat in 2009." http://www.bowker.com/index.php/press-releases/616-bowker-reports-traditional-us-book-production-flat-in-2009. (Accessed 12 December 2010. No longer available.)

Boyarin, Jonathan. 1992a. *The Ethnography of Reading*. Berkeley: University of California Press.

————. 1992b. "Voices Around the Text: The Ethnography of Reading at Mesivta Tifereth Jerusalem." In *The Ethnography of Reading*, edited by Jonathan Boyarin, 212–37. Berkeley: University of California Press.

Boyd, William. 2006. *Restless*. London: Bloomsbury Publishing.

Boztas, Senay. 2008. "Richard and Judy 'Treat Their Readers as Stupid'." The *Guardian*, August 17. http://www.guardian.co.uk/books/2008/aug/17/edinburghbookfestival.fiction. (Accessed 20 August 2008.)

Brandt, Deborah. 1998. "Sponsors of Literacy." *College Composition and Communication* 49 (2): 165–85.

————. 2004. "Drafting U.S. Literacy." *College English* 66 (5): 485–502.

Brantlinger, Patrick. 1998. *The Reading Lesson: The Threat of Mass Literacy in Nineteenth-Century British Fiction*. Bloomington: Indiana University Press.

Breakenridge, Deirdre. 2008. *PR 2.0 New Media, New Tools, New Audiences*. Upper Saddle River: FT Press.

Bremner, Robert. 1988. *American Philanthropy*. 2nd ed. Chicago: University of Chicago Press.

Bristol Cultural Development Partnership (BCDP). 2006. Brunel 200. http://www.brunel200.com/ (Accessed 18 November 2012.)

Brooke, James. 2000. "Al Purdy, Poet, Is Dead at 81; A Renowned Voice in Canada." *The New York Times*, April 26. http://www.nytimes.com/2000/04/26/arts/al-purdy-poet-is-dead-at-81-a-renowned-voice-in-canada.html. (Accessed 4 July 2011.)

Brooker, Will. 2001. "Living on *Dawson's Creek*: Teen Viewers, Cultural Convergence and Television Overflow." *International Journal of Cultural Studies* 4 (4): 456–72.

Brouillette, Sarah. 2007. *Postcolonial Writers in the Global Literary Marketplace*. Houndmills: Palgrave Macmillan.

Brunsdon, Charlotte. 1990. "Problems with Quality." *Screen* 31 (1): 67–90.

———. 2000. *The Feminist, the Housewife, and the Soap Opera*. Oxford: Clarendon Press.

———. 2003. "Lifestyling Britain." *International Journal of Cultural Studies* 6 (1): 5–23.

Burkeman, Oliver. 2002. "It's a Novel Idea, but Nothing Can Get New York Reading from the Same Page." The *Guardian*, February 27. http://www.guardian.co.uk/world/2002/feb/27/books.booksnews. (Accessed 26 May 2012.)

Buschmann, John E. 2003. *Dismantling the Public Sphere: Situating and Sustaining Librarianship in the Age of the New Public Philosophy*. Westport: Libraries Unlimited.

Carey, John. 1992. *The Intellectuals and the Masses: Pride and Prejudice Among the Literary Intelligentsia, 1880–1939*. London: Faber and Faber.

Casey, Bernadette, Neil Casey, Ben Calvert, Liam French, and Justin Lewis, eds. 2008. *Television Studies: The Key Concepts*. London: Routledge.

Casper, Scott E., Joanne D. Chaison, and Jeffrey D. Groves, eds. 2002. *Perspectives on American Book History: Artifacts and Commentary*. Amherst and Boston: University of Massachusetts Press.

CBC. 2003. "Press Release: Canada Reads 2003." http://www.cbc.ca/books/canadareads/. (Accessed 9 September 2012.)

CBC/Radio-Canada. 2005. *CBC Arts and Culture Research Study: Summary Report*. http://earsay.com/standonguardforcbc/printme/ CBC-SummaryReport-Radio-Apr05.pdf. (Accessed 8 May 2012.)

CBC/Radio-Canada. 2012. *Explore CBC/Radio-Canada*. http://cbc.radio-canada.ca/en/explore/. (Accessed 19 November 2012.)

Chabot Davis, Kimberly. 2004. "Oprah's Book Club and the Politics of Cross-Racial Empathy." *International Journal of Cultural Studies* 7 (4): 399–419.

———. 2008. "White Book Clubs and African American Literature: The Promise and Limitations of Cross-Racial Empathy." *LIT: Literature Interpretation Theory* 19 (2): 155–86.

Charmaz, Kathy. 2006. *Constructing Grounded Theory: A Practical Guide Through Qualitative Analysis*. London: Sage.

Chartier, Roger, and J. A. González. 1992. "Laborers and Voyagers: From the Text to the Reader." *Diacritics* 22 (2): 49–61.

Choy, Wayson. 1995. *The Jade Peony*. Toronto: Douglas & McIntyre.

Chui, Tina W. L., Kelly Tran, Hélène Maheux, and Canada Statistics. 2007. *Immigration in Canada: A Portrait of the Foreign-born Population, 2006 Census*. Ottawa: Statistics Canada/Statistique Canada. http://www12.statcan.gc.ca/census-recensement/2006/as-sa/97-557/index-eng.cfm. (Accessed 23 November 2012.)

Clee, Nicholas. 2005. "The Book Business: The Rise of Book Clubs Has Coarsened Literary Debate." *New Statesman*, 134 (4732): March 21. http://www.newstatesman.com/node/150243. (Accessed 9 September 2012.)

Coleman, Daniel. 2009. *In Bed With the Word: Reading, Spirituality, and Cultural Politics*. Edmonton: University of Alberta Press.

Collins, Jim. 2002. "High-Pop: An Introduction." In *High-Pop: Making Culture Into Popular Entertainment*, edited by Jim Collins, 1–31. Malden and Oxford: Blackwell Publishers.

———. 2010. *Bring on the Books for Everybody: How Literary Culture Became Popular Culture*. Durham: Duke University Press.

Collinson, Ian. 2009. *Everyday Readers: Reading and Popular Culture*. London and Oakville: Equinox.

Conrath, Chris. 2001. "Reminiscing with Radio from Days Gone By." *itWorld Canada*. http://www.itworldcanada.com/news/reminiscing-with-radio-from-days-gone-by138025/138025. (Accessed 7 September 2012.)

Coser, Lewis A., Charles Kadushin, and Walter W. Powell. 1982. *Books: The Culture and Commerce of Publishing*. New York: Basic Books.

Cousins, Helen. 2011. "A Good Authentic Read: Exoticism in the Post-Colonial Novels of the Richard & Judy Book Club." In *The Richard & Judy Book Club Reader: Popular Texts and the Practices of Reading*, edited by Jenni Ramone and Helen Cousins, 137–53. Farnham: Ashgate.

Créatec and Canadian Heritage. 2005. *Reading and Buying Books for Pleasure: 2005 National Survey Final Report*. Montreal: Canadian Heritage.

Crisell, Andrew. 1994. *Understanding Radio*. London: Taylor & Francis.

———. 2006. *A Study of Modern Television: Thinking Inside the Box*. Houndmills: Palgrave Macmillan.

Culler, Jonathan. 1980. "Literary Competence." In *Reader-Response Criticism: From Formalism to Post-Structuralism*, edited by Jane P. Tompkins, 101–17. Baltimore: The Johns Hopkins University Press.

Daley, Richard M. 2002. "Introduction." In *One Book, One Chicago Resource Guide for "My Antonia" by Willa Cather*. Chicago: Chicago Public Library. http://www.chipublib.org/eventsprog/programs/oboc/02f_myantonia/oboc_02f_intro.php. (Accessed 12 September 2012.)

Davidson, Cathy. 2004. *Revolution and the Word: The Rise of the Novel in America*. Expanded ed. New York: Oxford University Press.

Davis, Caroline. 2011. "Histories of Publishing Under Apartheid: Oxford University Press in South Africa." *Journal of Southern African Studies* 37 (1): 79–98.

Davis, Jane. 2009. "Silver Threads Among the Dross." *The Reader* 33: 99–103.

DeMaria, Robert Jr. 2009. "Book Collecting and the Book as Object." In *A History of the Book in America, Volume 5: The Enduring Book, Print Culture in Post-War America*, edited by David Paul Nord, Joan Shelley Rubin, and Michael Schudson, 485–502. Chapel Hill: University of North Carolina Press.

DCMS. 2003. *Framework for the Future: Libraries, Learning and Information in the Next Decade*. London: Department for Culture, Media and Sport.

DCMS. 2010. *A Place for Culture: Developing a Local Culture Offer for All Children and Young People*. London: Department for Culture, Media and Sport. http://webarchive.nationalarchives.gov.uk/20100407120701/http://www.culture.gov.uk/images/publications/place_for_culture.pdf. (Accessed 28 June 2011.)

Desai, Ian. 2011. "Books Behind Bars: Mahatma Ghandi's Community of Captive Readers." In *The History of Reading, Volume 1: International Perspectives, c. 1500–1990*, edited by Shafquat Towheed and W. R. Owens, 178–91. Houndmills: Palgrave Macmillan.

Dick, Archie L. 2011. "Remembering Reading: Memory, Books and Reading in South Africa's Apartheid Prisons, 1956–1990." In *The History of Reading, Volume 1: International Perspectives, c. 1500–1990*, edited by Shafquat Towheed and W. R. Owens, 192–207. Houndmills: Palgrave Macmillan.

Dilevko, Juris, and Candice F. C. Magowan. 2007. *Readers' Advisory Service in North American Libraries, 1870–2005: A History and Critical Analysis*. Jefferson and London: McFarland.

DiMaggio, Paul, and Becky Pettit. 1999. "Public Opinion and Political Vulnerability: Why Has the National Endowment for the Arts Been Such an Attractive Target?" *Working Papers Series* 7: 1–54.

Driscoll, Beth. 2008. "How Oprah's Book Club Reinvented the Woman Reader." *Popular Narrative Media* 1 (2): 139–50.

———. 2011. "'Not the Normal Kind of Chicklit'?: Richard & Judy and the Feminized Middlebrow." In *The Richard and Judy Book Club Reader: Popular Texts and the Practices of Reading*, edited by Jenni Ramone and Helen Cousins, 109–20. Farnham: Ashgate.

Driscoll, Catherine, and Melissa Gregg. 2011. "Convergence Culture and the Legacy of Feminist Cultural Studies." *Cultural Studies* 25 (4–5): 566–84.

Druick, Zoë. 2006. "International Cultural Relations as a Factor in Postwar Canadian Cultural Policy: The Relevance of UNESCO for the Massey Commission." *Canadian Journal of Communication* 31 (1): 177–95.

Dudley, Michael. 2008. "Place Matters." *Winnipeg Free Press*, March 16. http://www.winnipegfreepress.com/historic/32768089.html. (Accessed 12 September 2012.)

Dugdale, John. 2006. "Sofa, so Good: Many of This Year's Top Selling Authors Owe Their Fortunes to Richard and Judy." The *Guardian*, December 30. http://www.guardian.co.uk/books/2006/dec/30/bestbooksoftheyear.bestbooks2. (Accessed 12 August 2009.)

Dunbar-Odom, Donna. 2007. *Defying the Odds: Class and the Pursuit of Higher Literacy*. Albany: State University of New York Press.

Duxbury, Nancy. 1995. *The Reading and Purchasing Public: The Market for Trade Books in English Canada 1991*. Toronto: The Association of Canadian Publishers.

Eco, Umberto. 1979. *The Role of the Reader: Explorations in the Semiotics of Texts*. Bloomington: Indiana University Press.

Eddy, Jacalyn. 2003. "'We Have Become Too Tender-Hearted': The Language of Gender in the Public Library, 1880–1920." In *Libraries as Agencies of Culture*, edited by Thomas Augst and Wayne A. Wiegand, 155–72. Madison: University of Wisconsin Press.

Edwards, Brendan Frederick R. 2005. *Paper Talk: A History of Libraries, Print Culture, and Aboriginal Peoples in Canada Before 1960*. Lanham and Toronto: Scarecrow Press.

Eggert, Paul, and Elizabeth Webby, eds. 2004. *Books and Empire: Textual Production, Distribution and Consumption in Colonial and Postcolonial Countries*. Wagga Wagga: Bibliographical Society of Australia and New Zealand.

Elliott, Jane. 2002. "O Is for the Other Things She Gave Me: Jonathan Franzen's *The Corrections* and Contemporary Women's Fiction." http://bitchmagazine.org/article/franzen. (Accessed 8 May 2012.)

Ellis, John. 2003. "Channel Four: Innovation in Form and Content?" In *The Television History Book*, edited by Michele Hilmes, 93–98. London: British Film Institute.

Epstein, Jason. 2002. *Book Business: Publishing Past, Present and Future*. New York and London: W. W. Norton.

Falconer, Rachel. 2009. *The Crossover Novel: Contemporary Children's Fiction and Its Adult Readership*. New York: Routledge.

Farndale, Nigel. 2007. "The Best Seller." *The Daily Telegraph*, March 25. http://www.telegraph.co.uk/culture/3664052/The-best-seller.html. (Accessed 17 November 2009.)

FCM. 2002. "Bridging the Innovation Gap: Count Cities." *Federation of Canadian Municipalities*. www.fcm.ca/newfcm/Java/gap.pdf. (Accessed 8 May 2012.)

Felski, Rita. 2008. *Uses of Literature*. Malden and Oxford: Blackwell Publishing.

Fenton, Natalie. 2009. "My Media Studies: Getting Political in a Global, Digital Age." *Television and New Media* 10 (1): 55–57.

Filion, Michel. 1996a. "Broadcasting and Cultural Identity: The Canadian Experience." *Media, Culture & Society* 18 (3): 447–67.

———. 1996b. "Radio." In *The Cultural Industries in Canada: Problems, Policies, and Prospects*, edited by Michael Dorland, 118–41. Toronto: James Lorimer.

Finkelstein, David, and Alistair McCleery. 2002. *The Book History Reader*. London and New York: Routledge.

Fischer, Steven R. 2003. *A History of Reading*. London: Reaktion Books.

Fish, Stanley. 1980. *Is There a Text in This Class? The Authority of Interpretive Communities*. Cambridge: Harvard University Press.

Fiske, John. 1987. "Film, TV and the Popular." *Continuum: Journal of Media & Cultural Studies* 12 (1): 16–17.

Fister, Barbara. 2011. "One Book, One College: Common Reading Programs." *College and Research Libraries* 72 (5): 474–95.

Fleming, Patricia Lockhart, Gilles Gallichan and Yvan Lamonde, eds. 2004. *History of the Book in Canada, Volume 1: Beginnings to 1840.* Toronto: University of Toronto Press.

Florida, Richard. 2002. *The Rise of the Creative Class: And How It's Transforming Work, Leisure, Community and Everyday Life.* New York: Basic Books.

———. 2005. *Cities and the Creative Class.* New York and London: Routledge.

———. 2008. *Who's Your City? How the Creative Economy Is Making Where to Live the Most Important Decision of Your Life.* New York: Basic Books.

Frampton, Edith. 2010. "From the Nobel to Oprah: Toni Morrison, Body Politics, and Oprah's Book Club." In *Stories of Oprah: The Oprahfication of American Culture,* edited by Trystan T. Cotten and Kimberly Springer, 145–60. Jackson: University Press of Mississippi.

Fraser, Robert. 2008. *Book History Through Postcolonial Eyes: Rewriting the Script.* London and New York: Routledge.

Friends of Canadian Broadcasting. 2010. "CBC Radio Audience." http://www.friends.ca/news-item/9768. (Accessed 12 January 2011.)

Frith, Simon. 2001. "The Popular Music Industry." In *The Cambridge Companion to Pop and Rock,* edited by Simon Frith, Will Straw, and John Street, 26–52. Cambridge: Cambridge University Press.

Frow, John. 1995. *Cultural Studies and Cultural Value.* Oxford and New York: Clarendon Press.

———. 2002. "Signature and Brand." In *High-Pop: Making Culture into Popular Entertainment,* edited by Jim Collins, 56–74. Malden and Oxford: Blackwell Publishers.

Fuller, Danielle. 2004. *Writing the Everyday: Women's Textual Communities in Atlantic Canada.* Montreal and Kingston: McGill-Queen's University Press.

———. 2007. "Listening to the Readers of 'Canada Reads'." *Canadian Literature* 193 (Summer): 11–34.

———. 2008. "Reading as Social Practice: The Beyond the Book Research Project." *Popular Narrative Media* 1 (2): 211–16.

———. 2011. "Citizen Reader: Canadian Literature, Mass Reading Events and the Promise of Belonging." *The Fifth Eccles Centre for American Studies Plenary Lecture,* 25. London: The Eccles Centre for American Studies & The British Library. http://www.bl.uk/eccles/pdf/bacs2010.pdf. (Accessed 23 November 2012.)

———. 2012. "Beyond CanLit(e): Reading. Interdisciplinarity. Trans-Atlantically." In *Shifting the Ground of Canadian Literary Studies,* edited by Smaro Kamboureli and Robert Zacharias, 77–100. TransCanada Series. Waterloo: Wilfrid Laurier University Press.

Fuller, Danielle, and James Procter. 2009. "Reading as 'Social Glue'?: Book Groups, Multiculture, and Small Island Read 2007." *Moving Worlds: A Journal of Transcultural Writings* 9 (2): 26–41.

Fuller, Danielle, and DeNel Rehberg Sedo. 2006. "A Reading Spectacle for the Nation: The CBC and 'Canada Reads'." *Journal of Canadian Studies* 40 (1): 5–36.

———. 2011. "Suspicious Minds: Richard & Judy's Book Club and Its Resistant Readers." In *The Richard & Judy Book Club Reader: Popular Texts and the Practices of Reading,* edited by Jenni Ramone and Helen Cousins, 21–42. Farnham: Ashgate.

———. 2012. "Mixing It Up: Using Mixed Methods Research to Investigate Contemporary Cultures of Reading." In *From Codex to Hypertext: Reading at the Turn of the Twenty-First Century,* edited by Anouk Lang, 234–51. Amherst and Boston: University of Massachusetts Press.

Fuller, Danielle, DeNel Rehberg Sedo, and Claire Squires. 2011. "Marionettes and Puppeteers? The Relationship Between Book Club Readers and Publishers." In *Reading Communities: From Salons to Cyberspace*, edited by DeNel Rehberg Sedo, 181–99. Houndmills: Palgrave Macmillan.

Fuller, Danielle, DeNel Rehberg Sedo, and Amy Thurlow. 2009. More Than 'Just a Little Library Program'." *Logos* 20 (1–4): 228–40.

Gamson, Joshua. 2007. "The Assembly Line of Greatness: Celebrity in Twentieth-Century America." In *Stardom and Celebrity: A Reader*, edited by Sean Redmond and Su Holmes, 141–55. London: Sage.

Garnham, Nicholas. 1998. "Media Policy." In *The Media: An Introduction*, edited by Adam Briggs and Paul Cobley, 210–23. Harlow: Addison Wesley Longman.

———. 2005. "From Cultural to Creative Industries." *International Journal of Cultural Policy* 11 (1): 15–29.

Gentikow, Barbara. 2005a. *Hvordan Utforsker Man Medieerfaringer?: Kvalitativ Metode*. Kristiansand: IJ forlaget.

———. 2005b. "Exploring Media Experiences: A New Approach to Reception Theory and Empirical Studies." Paper presented at the First European Communication Conference, Amsterdam.

Gere, Anne Ruggles. 1997. *Intimate Practices: Literacy and Cultural Work in U.S. Women's Clubs, 1880–1920*. Urbana: University of Illinois Press.

Gerson, Carole, and Jacques Michon, eds. 2007. *History of the Book in Canada, Volume 3: 1918–1980*. Toronto: University of Toronto Press.

Gertler, Meric S., Richard Florida, Gary Gates, and Tara Vinodrai. 2002. *Competing on Creativity: Placing Ontario's Cities in the North American Context*. Toronto: Ontario Ministry of Enterprise, Opportunity and Innovation. http://creativeclass.com/rfcgdb/articles/2002-Competing_on_Creativity.pdf. (Accessed 23 November 2012.)

Giles, David. 2000. *Illusions of Immortality: A Psychology of Fame and Celebrity*. Houndmills: Palgrave Macmillan.

———. 2002. "Parasocial Interaction: A Review of the Literature and a Model for Future Research." *Media Psychology* 4 (3): 279–305.

———. 2003. *Media Psychology*. Mahwah: Lawrence Erlbaum Associates.

Gill, Rosalind, and Andy Pratt. 2008. "In the Social Factory? Immaterial Labour, Precariousness and Cultural Work." *Theory, Culture and Society* 25 (7–8): 1–30.

Gladwell, Malcolm. 2001. *The Tipping Point: How Little Things Can Make a Big Difference*. London: Abacus.

Glazer, Nathan. 2008. "The Best Addresses." *The New Republic* 239 (10) (December 3): 46–47. http://www.tnr.com/article/books/the-best-addresses. (Accessed 2 June 2011.)

Glynn, Kevin. 2000. *Tabloid Culture: Trash Taste, Popular Power, and the Transformation of American Television*. Durham: Duke University Press.

Godard, Barbara. 1999. "Privatizing the Public: Notes from the Ontario Culture Wars." *Fuse* 22 (3): 27–33.

———. 2000. "Notes from the Cultural Field: Canadian Literature from Identity to Commodity." *Essays on Canadian Writing* 72: 209–47.

———. 2002. "Upping the Anti: Of Poetic Ironies, Propaganda Machines and the Claims for Public Sponsorship of Culture." *Fuse* 25 (3): 12–19.

Goldstein, Philip, and James L. Machor. 2008. "Introduction: Reception Study: Achievements and New Directions." In *New Directions in American Reception Study*, edited by Philip Goldstein and James L. Machor, xi–xxviii. New York: Oxford University Press.

Grams, Diane. 2008. "Creative Reinvention: From 'One Book' to 'Animals on Parade,' How Good Ideas Spread Like Wildfire." In *Entering Cultural Communities: Diversity and Change in the Nonprofit Arts*, edited by Diane Grams and Betty Farrell, 194–220. New Brunswick: Rutgers University Press.

Gray, Jonathan. 2008. *Television Entertainment*. New York: Routledge.

Greco, Albert N. 2004. *The Book Publishing Industry*. 2nd ed. New York: Routledge.

Greenwood, Dara N., and Christopher R. Long. 2009. "Psychological Predictors of Media Involvement: Solitude Experiences and the Need to Belong." *Communication Research* 36 (5): 637–54.

Griffin, Linda. 1999. "An Analysis of Meaning Creation through the Integration of Sociology and Literature: A Critical Ethnography of a Romance Reading Group." PhD diss., University of Houston.

Grindstaff, Laura. 2002. *The Money Shot: Trash, Class and the Making of TV Talk Shows*. Chicago: University of Chicago Press.

Griswold, Wendy. 2008. *Regionalism and the Reading Class*. Chicago: University of Chicago Press.

Griswold, Wendy, McDonnell Terry, and Wright Nathan. 2005. "Reading and the Reading Class in the Twenty-First Century." *Annual Review of Sociology* 31: 127–41.

Grossberg, Lawrence. 2010. "Affect's Future: Rediscovering the Virtual in the Actual." In *The Affect Theory Reader*, edited by Melissa Gregg and Gregory J. Seigworth, 309–38. Durham: Duke University Press.

Gruzd, Anatoliy, and DeNel Rehberg Sedo. 2012. "*#1b1t:* Investigating Reading Practices at the Turn of the Twenty-first Century." *Mémoires Du Livre/Studies in Book Culture* 3 (2). New Studies in the History of Reading / Nouvelles Études En Histoire De La Lecture. http://www.erudit.org/revue/memoires/2012/v3/n2/1009347ar.html. (Accessed 8 May 2012.)

Haag, Laurie L. 2003. "Oprah Winfrey: The Construction of Intimacy in the Talk Show Setting." *Journal of Popular Culture* 26 (4): 115–22.

Haberman, Clyde. 2002. "NYC: One City, One Book, Zero Chance." *The New York Times*, May 15. http://www.nytimes.com/2002/05/15/nyregion/nyc-one-city-one-book-zero-chance.html. (Accessed 26 May 2012.)

Hall, Geoff. 2009. "Texts, Readers—and Real Readers." *Language and Literature* 18 (3): 333–39.

Hall, Mark R. 2003. "The 'Oprahfication' of Literacy: Reading 'Oprah's Book Club'." *College English* 65 (6): 646–67.

_____. 2008. "Oprah's Book Selections: Teleliterature for *The Oprah Winfrey Show*." In *The Oprah Effect: Critical Essays on Oprah's Book Club*, edited by Cecilia Konchar Farr and Jaime Harker, 89–118. Albany: State University of New York Press.

Hall, Stuart. 1980. *Culture, Media, Language?: Working Papers in Cultural Studies, 1972–79*. Centre for Contemporary Cultural Studies, University of Birmingham and London: Hutchinson.

———. 2012. "The Neoliberal Revolution." In *Soundings: The Neoliberal Crisis*, edited by Jonathan Rutherford and Sally Davison, 8–26. London: Lawrence Wishart.

Harding, Sandra. 1991. *Whose Science? Whose Knowledge? Thinking from Women's Lives*. Milton Keynes: Open University Press.

Harker, Jaime. 2007. *America the Middlebrow: Women's Novels, Progressivism, and Middlebrow Authorship Between the Wars*. Amherst and Boston: University of Massachusetts Press.

———. 2008. "Afterword: Oprah, James Frey, and the Problem of the Literary." In *The Oprah Effect: Critical Essays on Oprah's Book Club*, edited by Cecilia Konchar Farr and Jaime Harker, 321–33. Albany: State University of New York Press.

Harris, Jennifer, and Elwood Watson. 2007. "Introduction: Oprah Winfrey as Subject and Spectacle." In *The Oprah Phenomenon*, edited by Jennifer Harris and Elwood Watson, 1–34. Lexington: University Press of Kentucky.

Hartley, Jenny with Sarah Turvey. 2001. *Reading Groups*. Oxford: Oxford University Press.

———. 2011. "Nineteenth-Century Reading Groups in Britain and the Community of the Text: An Experiment with *Little Dorrit*." In *Reading Communities: From Salons to Cyberspace*, edited by DeNel Rehberg Sedo, 44–59. Houndmills: Palgrave Macmillan.

Hartley, Jenny, and Sarah Turvey. 2008. "What Can a Book Do Behind Bars?" *The Reader* 32: 60–68.

———. n.d. "Reading Together: The Role of the Reading Group Inside Prison." http://www.prisonerseducation.org.uk/index.php?id=230. (Accessed 14 June 2012.)

Harvey, David. 2007. *A Brief History of Neoliberalism*. Oxford: Oxford University Press.

Hattersley, Giles. 2006. "She's Choosing Your Books," *The Times*, August 13. http://www.timesonline.co.uk/tol/news/article607041.ece. (Accessed 12 August 2009.)

Hermes, Joke. 1995. *Reading Women's Magazines: An Analysis of Everyday Media Use*. London: John Wiley & Sons.

Hesmondhalgh, David. 2006. "Bourdieu, the Media and Cultural Production." *Media Culture Society* 28: 211–31.

———. 2007. [2002]. *The Cultural Industries*. 2nd ed. London: Sage.

Hesmondhalgh, David, and Sarah Baker. 2008. "Creative Work and Emotional Labour in the Television Industry." *Theory, Culture & Society* 25 (7–8): 97–118.

———. 2011. *Creative Labour: Media Work in Three Cultural Industries*. London and New York: Routledge.

Hesmondhalgh, David, and Andy C. Pratt. 2005. "Cultural Industries and Cultural Policy." *International Journal of Cultural Policy* 11 (1): 1–13.

Higgins, John. 1999. *Raymond Williams: Literature, Marxism and Cultural Materialism*. London: Routledge.

Hochman, Barbara. 2008. "Sentiment Without Tears: Uncle Tom's Cabin As History in the 1890s." In *New Directions in American Reception Study*, edited by Philip Goldstein and James L. Machor, 255–76. New York: Oxford University Press.

Hochschild, Arlie Russell. 1983. *The Managed Heart: The Commercialization of Human Feeling*. Berkeley: University of California Press.

———. 1997. *The Time Bind: When Work Becomes Home and Home Becomes Work*. New York: Metropolitan Books/Holt.

Hofmeyr, Isabel. 2004. *The Portable Bunyan: A Transnational History of The Pilgrim's Progress*. Princeton: Princeton University Press.

Holden, John. 2004. *Capturing Cultural Value*. London: DEMOS. http://www.demos.co.uk/publications/culturalvalue. (Accessed 2 April 2011.)

Holderman, Lisa B. 2003. "Media-constructed Anti-intellectualism: The Portrayal of Experts in Popular US Television Talk Shows." *New Jersey Journal of Communication* 11 (1): 45–62.

Holland, Norman Norwood. 1968. *The Dynamics of Literary Response*. New York: Oxford University Press.

———. 1975. *Readers Reading*. New Haven: Yale University Press.

Holmwood, Leigh. 2008. "Multichannel TV Ratings—October 8: Ratings Dive for Richard and Judy Show." The *Guardian*, October 9. http://www.guardian.co.uk/media/2008/oct/09/tvratings.television1. (Accessed 29 May 2012.)

Homes, A. M. 2006. *This Book Will Save Your Life*. New York: Penguin Books.

Hosseini, Khaled. 2007. *A Thousand Splendid Suns*. London: Bloomsbury.

Howard, Vivian. 2011. "The Importance of Pleasure Reading in The Lives of Young Teens: Self-Identification, Self-Construction and Self-Awareness." *Journal of Librarianship and Information Science* 43 (1): 46–55.

Howie, Linsey. 1998. "Speaking Subjects: A Reading of Women's Book Groups." PhD diss., La Trobe University, Bundoora.

———. 2011. "Speaking Subjects: Developing Identities in Women's Reading Communities." In *Reading Communities from Salons to Cyberspace*, edited by DeNel Rehberg Sedo, 140–58. Houndmills: Palgrave Macmillan.

Howsam, Leslie. 2006. *Old Books & New Histories: An Orientation to Studies in Book & Print Culture*. Toronto: University of Toronto Press.

Ingarden, Roman. 1973. *The Literary Work of Art: An Investigation on the Borderlines of Ontology, Logic and Theory of Literature*. Translated by George G. Grabowicz. Evanston: Northwestern University Press.

Iser, Wolfgang. 1978. *The Act of Reading: A Theory of Aesthetic Response*. Baltimore: The Johns Hopkins University Press.

———. 1980. "The Reading Process: A Phenomenological Approach." In *Reader-Response Criticism: From Formalism to Post-structuralism*, edited by Jane P. Tompkins, 50–70. Baltimore: The Johns Hopkins University Press.

Ivey, Bill. 2008. *Arts, Inc.: How Greed and Neglect Have Destroyed Our Cultural Rights*. Berkeley: University of California Press.

Ivy, Anna S. 2011. "Leading Questions: Interpretative Guidelines in Contemporary Popular Reading Culture." In *Reading Communities from Salons to Cyberspace*, edited by DeNel Rehberg Sedo, 159–80. Houndmills: Palgrave Macmillan.

Jackson, John D. 2004. "Canadian Radio & Multiculturalism." In *The Museum of Broadcast Communications Encyclopedia of Radio*, edited by Christopher H. Sterling and Michael C. Keith, 275–77. New York: Fitzroy Dearborn.

Jeannotte, Sharon, M. 2000. *Cultural Symbiosis: Cultural Participation and Cohesive Communities*. Hull, Québec: Strategic Research and Analysis (SRA), Strategic Planning and Policy Coordination, Department of Canadian Heritage. http://www.socialsciences.uottawa.ca/governance/eng/documents/cultural_symbiosis.pdf. (Accessed 23 November 2012.)

Jeannotte, Sharon M. 2003. "Singing Alone? The Contribution of Cultural Capital to Social Cohesion and Sustainable Communities." *The International Journal of Cultural Policy* 9 (1): 35–49.

Jeffries, Stuart. 2009. "Richard & Judy: Where Did It All Go Wrong?" The *Guardian*, February 9. http://www.guardian.co.uk/culture/2009/feb/09/richard-judy-show-bookclub. (Accessed 23 November 2012.)

Jenkins, Barbara. 2009. "Cultural Spending in Ontario, Canada: Trends in Public and Private Funding." *International Journal of Cultural Policy* 15 (3): 329–42.

Jenkins, Henry. 2006. *Convergence Culture: Where Old and New Media Collide*. New York: New York University Press.

———. 2007. *The Wow Climax: Tracing the Emotional Impact of Popular Culture*. New York: New York University Press.

Jones, Philip. 2008. "Retailers Still Back Richard & Judy." *The Bookseller*, August 15. http://www.thebookseller.com/news/retailers-still-back-richard-judy.html. (Accessed 19 July 2012.)

Joshi, Priya. 2008. "Futures Past: Books, Reading, Culture in the Age of Liberalization." In *Books without Borders, Volume 2: Perspectives from South Asia*, edited by Robert Fraser and Mary Hammond, 85–99. Houndmills: Palgrave Macmillan.

Jowell, Tessa. 2004. *Government and the Value of Culture*. London: Department for Culture, Media and Sport.

Kaestle, Carl F., and Janice A. Radway, eds. 2009. *A History of the Book in America, Volume 4: Print in Motion, The Expansion of Publishing and Reading in the United States, 1880–1940*. Chapel Hill: University of North Carolina Press.

Kelley, Mary. 2003 "'A More Glorious Revolution': Women's Antebellum Reading Circles and the Pursuit of Public Influence." *New England Quarterly* 76 (2): 163–96.

Kellner, Douglas. 1990. *Television and the Crisis of Democracy*. Boulder: Westview Press.

———. 2003. "Introduction: Media Culture and the Triumph of the Spectacle." In *Media Spectacle*, by Douglas Kellner, 1–33. London and New York: Routledge.

Kelly, Melanie. 2007. *Small Island Read 2007 Evaluation Report*. Bristol: Bristol Cultural Development Partnership. http://www.bristolreads.com/small_island_read/downloads/small_island_evaluation.pdf. (Accessed 23 November 2012.)

Kiernan, Anna. 2011. "The Growth of Reading Groups as a Feminine Leisure Pursuit: Cultural Democracy or Dumbing Down?" In *Reading Communities from Salons to Cyberspace*, edited by DeNel Rehberg Sedo, 123–39. Houndmills: Palgrave Macmillan.

Kinsella, Bridget. 1997. "The Oprah Effect—How TV's Premier Talk Show Host Puts Books over the Top." *The Publishers Weekly* 244(3): 276.

Kirkpatrick, David D. 2002. "Want a Fight? Pick One Book for All New Yorkers." *The New York Times*, February 19. http://www.nytimes.com/2002/02/19/nyregion/want-a-fight-pick-one-book-for-all-new-yorkers.html. (Accessed 4 February 2012.)

Kitchener Public Library. 2011. "About One Book, One Community." http://www.kpl.org/books_more/oboc.html#events. (Accessed 3 November 2011.)

Knight, Lorna. 2004. "Reaching Out to Isolated Readers." In *History of the Book in Canada, Volume 3: 1918–1980*, edited by Carole Gerson and Jacques Michon, 491–96. Toronto: University of Toronto Press.

Knoch, Jen. 2010. "Civilians Read 2011: The Line-up". Blog. *The Keepin' It Real Book Club*. http://kirbc.com/2010/11/26/civilians-read-2011-the-line-up/. (Accessed 7 September 2012.)

Kogawa, Joy. 1981. *Obasan*. Toronto: Lester & Orpen Dennys.

Konchar Farr, Cecilia. 2005. *Reading Oprah: How Oprah's Book Club Changed the Way America Reads*. Albany: State University of New York Press.

———. 2008. "Talking Readers." In *The Oprah Effect: Critical Essays on Oprah's Book Club*, edited by Cecilia Konchar Farr and Jaime Harker, 33–54. Albany: State University of New York Press.

Konchar Farr, Cecilia, and Jaime Harker, eds. 2008. *The Oprah Effect: Critical Essays on Oprah's Book Club*. Albany: State University of New York Press.

Krueger, Richard A., and Mary Anne Casey. 2009. *Focus Groups: A Practical Guide for Applied Research*. 4th ed. Thousand Oaks: Sage.

Kuffert, Len. 2003. *A Great Duty: Canadian Responses to Modern Life and Mass Culture in Canada, 1939–1967*. Montréal and Kingston: McGill-Queen's University Press.

———. 2009. "'What Do You Expect of This Friend?' Canadian Radio and the Intimacy of Broadcasting." *Media History* 15 (3): 303–19.

Lamonde, Yvan, Peter F. McNally, and Andrea Rotundo. 2005. "Libraries and Their Publics." In *History of the Book in Canada, Volume 2: 1840–1918*, edited by Fiona A. Black, Patricia Lockhart Fleming, and Yvan Lamonde, 250–89. Toronto: University of Toronto Press.

Landau, Emily. "The Walrus Blog | Canada Reads." *Walrus Magazine*. http://walrus-magazine.com/blogs/tag/canada-reads/. (Accessed 7 September 2012.)

Lang, Anouk. 2009a. "Reading Race in Small Island: Discourse Deviation, Schemata and the Textual Encounter." *Language and Literature* 18 (3): 316–30.

———. 2009b. "'Enthralling but at the Same Time Disturbing': Challenging the Readers of Small Island." *The Journal of Commonwealth Literature* 44 (2): 123–40.

———. 2010. "'A Dirty Little Secret': Taste Hierarchies and Richard and Judy's Book Club." *Particip@tions: Journal of Audience & Reception Studies* 7 (2). http://www.participations.org/Volume%207/Issue%202/lang.htm. (Accessed 23 November 2012.)

———. 2012. "Transforming Reading." In *From Codex to Hypertext: Reading at the Turn of the Twenty-First Century*, edited by Anouk Lang, 1–26. Amherst and Boston: University of Massachusetts Press.

Langley, William. 2007. "Profile of the Bookmaker: Amanda Ross." *The Daily Telegraph*, December 30. http://www.telegraph.co.uk/comment/3645031/Profile-of-the-bookmaker-Amanda-Ross.html. (Accessed 23 November 2012.)

Lansens, Lori. 2005. *The Girls*. Toronto: Alfred A. Knopf Canada.

Larsson, Mariah, and Ann Steiner, eds. 2011. *Interdisciplinary Approaches to Twilight: Studies in Fiction, Media and a Contemporary Cultural Experience.* Lund: Nordic Academic Press.

Latham, Sheila. 2007. "CBC Radio and Anglophone Authors." In *History of the Book in Canada, Volume 3: 1918–1980,* edited by Carole Gerson and Jacques Michon, 154–56. Toronto: University of Toronto Press.

Lavender, Terry. 2010. "One Book, One Vancouver Loses Its Local Connection." *The Vancouver Observer,* October 9. http://www.vancouverobserver.com/blogs/megabytes/2010/10/09/one-book-one-vancouver-loses-its-local-connection. (Accessed 23 November 2012.)

Laycock, John. 1992. "Gzowski=Canada." *Continuum: The Australian Journal of Media & Culture* 6 (1): 69–74.

Lewis, Justin, and Toby Miller. 2003. "Introduction." In *Critical Cultural Policy Studies: A Reader,* edited by Justin Lewis and Toby Miller, 1–9. Malden and Oxford: Blackwell.

Liebich, Susann. 2011. "Connective Readers: Reading Practices and Communities Across the British Empire, C. 1890–1930." PhD diss., University of Wellington, Victoria, NZ.

Liu, Alan. 2009. "Digital Humanities and Academic Change." *English Language Notes* 47 (1): 17–35.

Livingstone, Sonia. 1992. "The Resourceful Reader: Interpreting Television Characters and Narratives." *Communication Yearbook* 15: 58–90.

Livingstone, Sonia, and Peter Lunt. 1994. *Talk on Television: Audience Participation and Public Debate.* London and New York: Routledge.

Locke, Lawrence F., Stephen J. Silverman, and Waneen Wyrick Spirduso. 2004. *Reading and Understanding Research.* 2nd ed. Thousand Oaks: Sage.

Long, Elizabeth. 1986. "Women, Reading and Cultural Authority: Some Implications of the Audience Perspective in Cultural Studies." *American Quarterly* 38: 591–612.

———. 1992. "Textual Interpretation as Collective Action." In *The Ethnography of Reading,* edited by Jonathan Boyarin, 180–212. Berkeley: University of California Press.

_____. 2003. *Book Clubs: Women and the Uses of Reading in Everyday Life.* Chicago: University of Chicago Press.

Lorimer, James. 1981. *The Readership and Distribution of Books in Canada: An Analysis of the Readers of English-Language Books in Canada: What They Read, Where They Get Their Books, and How They Find Out About Books.* Ottawa: Book Publishing and Public Policy.

Lorimer, Roland. 1992. "TV, Radio, Books, Film: Government Support for Culture." *Social Policy* 23 (1): 73–79.

Lotherington, Heather. 2005. "Writing Postmodern Fairy Tales at Main Street School: Digital Narratives and Evolving Transliteracies." *McGill Journal of Education* 40 (1): 109–19.

Low, Gail. 2010. *Publishing the Postcolonial: Anglophone West African and Caribbean Writing in the UK, 1948–1968.* New York: Routledge.

Luey, Beth. 2009. "The Organization of the Book Publishing Industry." In *A History of the Book in America, Volume 5: The Enduring Book, Print Culture in Postwar America,* edited by David Paul Nord, Joan Shelley Rubin, and Michael Schudson, 29–54. Durham: North Carolina University Press.

———. 2010. *Expanding the American Mind: Books and the Popularization of Knowledge.* Amherst and Boston: University of Massachusetts Press.

Lyons, Martyn. 1999. "New Readers in the Nineteenth Century: Women, Children, Workers." In *A History of Reading in the West,* edited by Guglielmo Cavallo and Roger Chartier, translated by Lydia G. Cochrane, 313–44. Cambridge: Polity Press.

———. 2001. "Reading Models and Reading Communities." In *A History of the Book in Australia, 1891–1945: A National Culture in a Colonised Market*, 370–88. St Lucia: University of Queensland Press.

MacLennan, Anne F. 2005. "American Network Broadcasting, the CBC, and Canadian Radio Stations During the 1930s: A Content Analysis." *Journal of Radio Studies* 12 (1): 85–103.

MacSkimming, Roy. 2003. *The Perilous Trade: Publishing Canada's Writers*. Toronto: McClelland & Stewart.

Maggiore, Matteo. 2011. "The BBC, Public Value and Europe." *Public Value* 2: 229–44. http://www.springerlink.com/content/w573632121433023/. (Accessed 4 September 2012.)

Manga, Julie Engel. 2003. *Talking Trash: The Cultural Politics of Daytime TV Talk Shows*. New York: New York University Press.

Marklein, Mary Beth. 2005. "Seattle Reaches Literacy Peak." *USA Today*, November 28. http://www.usatoday.com/news/nation/2005-11-28-seattle-literate_x.htm. (Accessed 23 November 2012.)

Max, D. T. 1999. "The Oprah Effect." *New York Times Magazine*, 26 December. http://people.lis.illinois.edu/~unsworth/courses/bestsellers/Max.Oprah-Effect. pdf. (Accessed 21 December 2010.)

McAdam, Doug, John D. McCarthy, and Mayer N. Zald. 1988. "Social Movements." In *Handbook of Sociology*, edited by Neil J. Smelser, 695–737. Newbury Park: Sage.

McCrum, Robert. 2006. "Our Top 50 Players in the World of Books." The *Guardian*, March 5. http://observer.guardian.co.uk/review/story/0,,1723568,00.html#article_continue. (Accessed 21 December 2010.)

McDonald, Peter D. 2009. *The Literature Police: Apartheid Censorship and Its Cultural Consequences*. Oxford: Oxford University Press.

McGinley, William, and Conley Katanna Conley. 2001. "Literary Retailing and the (Re)making of Popular Reading." *Journal of Popular Culture* 35: 207–21.

McGuigan, Jim. 2005. "Neo-liberalism, Culture and Policy." *International Journal of Cultural Policy* 11 (3): 229–41.

———. 2009a. *Cool Capitalism*. Cambridge: Pluto Press.

———. 2009b. "Doing a Florida Thing: The Creative Class Thesis and Cultural Policy." *International Journal of Cultural Policy* 15 (3): 291–300.

———. 2010. *Cultural Analysis*. London: Sage.

McGuigan, John. 1996. *Culture and the Public Sphere*. London and New York: Routledge.

McHenry, Elizabeth. 2002. *Forgotten Readers: Recovering the Lost History of African-American Literary Societies*. Durham: Duke University Press.

McKenzie, Donald F. 2002. "The Book as an Expressive Form." In *The Book History Reader*, edited by David Finkelstein and Alistair McCleery, 27–38. London and New York: Routledge.

McKitterick, David, ed. 2009. *The Cambridge History of the Book in Britain, Volume 6: 1830–1914*. Cambridge: Cambridge University Press.

McLean, Gareth. 2000. "Saint Judy: Why We Can't Help Loving TV's Accidental Heroine." The *Guardian*, October 12. http://www.guardian.co.uk/media/2000/oct/12/tvandradio.g2. (Accessed 21 December 2010.)

McLuhan, Marshall. 1964. *Understanding Media: The Extensions of Man*. New York: Mentor.

McNally, Peter F. 2004. "Education for Library Staff." In *History of the Book in Canada, Volume 2: 1840–1918*, edited by Fiona A. Black, Patricia Lockhart Fleming, and Yvan Lamonde, 285–89. Toronto: University of Toronto Press.

McQueen, Craig. 2006. "How the Richard & Judy 'Effect' Is Worth £50m to Book Trade." *Daily Record*, June 20. http://www.dailyrecord.co.uk/news/2006/06/20/

how-the-richard-and-judy-effect-is-worth-50m-to-book-trade-86908–17258117/. (Accessed 4 July 2011.)

McRobbie, Angela. 2002. "From Holloway to Hollywood: Happiness at Work in the New Cultural Economy." In *Cultural Economy: Cultural Analysis and Commercial Life*, edited by Paul du Gay and Michael Pryke, 97–114. London: Sage.

———. 2006. "Creative London—Creative Berlin: Notes on Making a Living in the New Cultural Economy." *Atelier Europa*. www.ateliereuropa.com/doc/creative-londberlin.pdf. (Accessed 23 November 2012.)

———. 2007. "The Los Angelisation of London: Three Short-waves of Young People's Micro-economies of Culture and Creativity in the UK." *Transversal* (January). Creativity Hypes. http://eipcp.net/transversal/0207/mcrobbie/en. (Accessed 23 November 2012.)

———. 2013. *Be Creative: Making a Living in the New Culture Industries*. London: Sage.

Meehan, Eileen R. 2002. "Gendering the Commodity Audience: Critical Media Research, Feminism and Political Economy." In *Sex and Money: Feminism and Political Economy in the Media*, edited by Eileen R. Meehan and Ellen Riordan, 209–22. Minneapolis: University of Minnesota Press.

Mehta, Jal, and Christopher Winship. 2010. "Moral Power." In *Handbook of the Sociology of Morality*, edited by Steven Hitlin and Stephen Vaisey, 425–38. New York: Springer.

Miller, Colin. 2004. "Canadian Broadcasting Corporation". In *The Museum of Broadcast Communications Encyclopedia of Radio*, edited by Christopher H. Sterling and Michael C. Keith, 271–75. New York: Fitzroy Dearborn.

Miller, John W. 2008. "America's Most Literate Cities, 2008." http://web.ccsu.edu/amlc/. (Accessed 23 November 2012.)

Miller, Laura J. 2006. *Reluctant Capitalists: Bookselling and the Culture of Consumption*. Chicago: University of Chicago Press.

———. 2009. "Selling the Product." In *A History of the Book in America, Volume 5: The Enduring Book, Print Culture in Postwar America*, edited by David Paul Nord, Joan Shelley Rubin, and Michael Schudson, 91–106. Chapel Hill: North Carolina University Press.

Mitchell, David. 2004. *Cloud Atlas*. London: Sceptre.

Moody, Nickianne. 2011. "Entertainment Media, Risk and the Experience Commodity." In *The Richard & Judy Book Club Reader: Popular Texts and the Practices of Reading*, edited by Jenni Ramone and Helen Cousins, 43–58. Farnham: Ashgate.

Moore, Ellen, and Kira Stevens. 2004. *Good Books Lately: The One-Stop Resource for Book Groups and Other Greedy Readers*. New York: St. Martin's Griffin.

Moran, Albert, and Justin Malbon. 2006. *Understanding the Global TV Format*. Bristol and Portland: Intellect Books.

Morley, David, and Charlotte Brunsdon. 1978. *Everyday Television: Nationwide*. London: British Film Institute.

———. 1980. *The Nationwide Audience: Structure and Decoding*. London: British Film Institute.

Moreton, Cole. 2001. "Richard and Judy: The Golden Couple," *The Independent*, 25 November. http://www.independent.co.uk/news/people/profiles/richard-and-judy-the-golden-couple-617972.html. (Accessed 9 March 2012.)

Murdock, Graham. 2003. "Back to Work: Cultural Labour in Altered Times." In *Cultural Work: Understanding the Cultural Industries*, edited by Andrew Beck, 15–36. London: Routledge.

Murray, Heather. 2002. *Come, Bright Improvement!: The Literary Societies of Nineteenth-Century Ontario*. Toronto: University of Toronto Press.

Murray, Simone. 2011. *The Adaptation Industry: The Cultural Economy of Contemporary Literary Adaptation*. New York and London: Routledge.

Murray, Simone, and Alexis Weedon. 2011. "Beyond Medium Specificity: Adaptations, Cross-media Practices and Branded Entertainments." *Convergence: The International Journal of Research into New Media Technologies* 17 (1): 3–5.

NEA. 2004. *Reading At Risk: A Survey of Literary Reading in America.* Washington, DC. http://www.nea.gov/news/news04/ReadingAtRisk.html. (Accessed 23 November 2012.)

_____. 2005. "National Endowment for the Arts Announces the Big Read." http://www.nea.gov/news/news05/BigReadAnnounce.html. (Accessed 23 November 2012.)

_____. 2007. "How the United States Funds the Arts." http://www.arts.gov/pub/how.pdf. (Accessed 11 August 2010.)

———. 2009. *Reading on the Rise: A New Chapter in American Literacy.* http://www.nea.gov/research/ReadingonRise.pdf. (Accessed 21 December 2010.)

_____. 2012. "The Big Read." http://www.neabigread.org/. (Accessed 23 November 2012.)

Newell, Stephanie. 2006a. *The Forger's Tale: The Search for Odeziaku.* Athens: Ohio University Press.

———. 2006b. *West African Literatures: Ways of Reading.* Oxford: Oxford University Press.

Niedzviecki, Hal. 2002. "The Story of O." *This Magazine.* (July/August): 15–17.

Nielson Book. 2011. *Nielson Book Releases 2010 Book Production Figures.* Woking: The Nielsen Company. http://www.isbn.nielsenbook.co.uk/uploads/press/1NielsenBook_2010ProductionFigures_Feb11.pdf. (Accessed 21 February 2011.)

Nord, David Paul, Joan Shelley Rubin, and Michael Schudson, eds. 2009. *A History of the Book in America, Volume 5: The Enduring Book, Print Culture in Postwar America.* Chapel Hill: University of North Carolina Press.

Norvel, George Whitefield. 1973. *The Reading Interests of Young People.* East Lansing: Michigan State University Press.

Ommundsen, Wenche. 2007. "From the Altar to the Market-Place and Back Again: Understanding Literary Celebrity." In *Stardom and Celebrity: A Reader*, edited by Sean Redmond and Su Holmes, 244–55. London: Sage.

Pagé, Pierre- C., and David R. Spencer. 2004. "Canadian Radio Programming." In *The Museum of Broadcast Communications Encyclopedia of Radio*, edited by Christopher H. Sterling and Michael C. Keith, 266–71. New York: Fitzroy Dearborn.

Parkes, M. B. 1999. "Reading, Copying and Interpreting a Text in the Middle Ages." In *A History of Reading in the West*, edited by Guglielmo Cavallo and Roger Chartier, translated by Lydia G. Cochrane, 90–102. Cambridge: Polity Press.

Patterson, Anthony. 2010. "Extreme Cultural and Marketing Makeover: Liverpool Home Edition." In *Marketing the Arts: A Fresh Approach*, edited by Daragh O'Reilly and Finola Kerrigan, 240–56. London: Routledge.

Pawley, Christine. 2002. "Seeking 'Significance': Actual Readers, Specific Reading Communities." *Book History* 5 (1): 143–60.

———. 2003. "Reading Versus The Red Bull: Cultural Construction of Democracy and the Public Library in Cold War Wisconsin." In *Libraries as Agencies of Culture*, edited by Thomas Augst and Wayne A. Wiegand, 87–104. Madison: University of Wisconsin Press.

———. 2007. "Blood and Thunder on the Bookmobile: American Public Libraries and the Construction of 'the Reader,' 1950–1995." In *Institutions of Reading: The Social Life of Libraries in the United States*, edited by Thomas Augst and Kenneth Carpenter, 264–82. Amherst and Boston: University of Massachusetts Press.

———. 2009. "Beyond Market Models and Resistance: Organizations as a Middle Layer in the History of Reading." *Library Quarterly* 79 (1): 73–93.

———. 2010. *Reading Places: Literacy, Democracy, and the Public Library in Cold War America.* Amherst and Boston: University of Massachusetts Press.

Pearce, Lynne. 1997. *Feminism and the Politics of Reading*. London: Hodder Education.

Pearl, Nancy. 2003. *Book Lust: Recommended Reading for Every Mood, Moment, and Reason*. Seattle: Sasquatch Books.

———. 2005. *More Book Lust: Recommended Reading for Every Mood, Moment, and Reason*. Seattle: Sasquatch Books.

———. 2008. Keynote Address. The PAGES Forum. Stanley A. Milner Library, Edmonton, Alberta, November.

Peck, Jamie. 2005. "Struggling with the Creative Class." *International Journal of Urban and Regional Research* 29 (4) (December): 740–70.

Peck, Janice. 2008. *The Age of Oprah: Cultural Icon for the Neoliberal Era*. Boulder: Paradigm.

———. 2010. "The Secret of Her Success: Oprah Winfrey and the Seductions of Self-Transformation." *Journal of Communication Inquiry* 34 (1): 7–14.

Pecoskie, Jen (J.L.). 2009. "The Solitary, Social, and 'Grafted Spaces' of Pleasure Reading: Exploring Reading Practices from the Experiences of Adult, Self-Identified Lesbian, Gay, Bisexual, and Queer Readers and Book Club Members." PhD diss., University of Western Ontario.

Pedersen, Sarah. 2008. "Now Read This: Male and Female Bloggers' Recommendations for Further Reading." *Particip@tions: Journal of Audience & Reception Studies* 5 (2). http://www.participations.org/Volume%205/Issue%202/5_02_pedersen.htm. (Accessed 23 November 2012.)

Penfield Lewis, Kelley. 2008. "The Trouble with Happy Endings: Conflicting Narratives in Oprah's Book Club." In *The Oprah Effect: Critical Essays on Oprah's Book Club*, edited by Cecilia Konchar Farr and Jaime Harker, 211–34. Albany: State University of New York Press.

Penney, Louise. 2010. *Bury Your Dead*. London: Sphere.

Pinder, Julian. 2012. "Online Literary Communities: A Case Study of Library Thing." In *From Codex to Hypertext: Reading at the Turn of the Twenty-First Century*, edited by Anouk Lang, 68–87. Amherst and Boston: University of Massachusetts Press.

Pogrebin, Robin. 2009. "New Endowment Chairman Sees Arts as Economic Engine." *The New York Times*, August 7. http://www.nytimes.com/2009/08/08/arts/08rocco.html. (Accessed 3 March 2011.)

Price, Leah. 2004. "Reading: The State of the Discipline." *Book History* 7 (1): 303–20.

———. 2012. *How to Do Things with Books in Victorian Britain*. Princeton: Princeton University Press.

Procter, James. 2011. "Introduction: Reading After Empire." *New Formations* 73 (1): 5–10.

Putnam, Robert D. 2000. *Bowling Alone: The Collapse and Revival of American Community*. New York: Simon & Schuster.

Putnam, Robert D., and Lewis M. Feldstein. 2003. *Better Together: Restoring the American Community*. New York: Simon & Schuster.

Raboy, Marc, and David Taras. 2007. "On Life Support: The CBC and the Future of Public Broadcasting in Canada." In *How Canadians Communicate II: Media, Globalization and Identity*, edited by David Taras, Maria Bakardjieva, and Frits Pannekoek, 83–103. Calgary: University of Calgary Press.

Radway, Janice. 1988. "Reception Study: Ethnography and the Problems of Dispersed Audiences and Nomadic Subjects." *Cultural Studies* 2 (3): 359–76.

———. 1991. *Reading the Romance: Women, Patriarchy, and Popular Literature*. 2nd ed. Chapel Hill: University of North Carolina Press.

———. 1996. "The Hegemony of 'Specificity' and the Impasse in Audience Research: Cultural Studies and the Problem of Ethnography." In *The Audience and Its Landscape*, edited by James Hay, Lawrence Grossberg, and Ellen Wartella, 235–45. Boulder: Westview Press.

————. 1997. *A Feeling for Books: The Book-of-the-Month Club, Literary Taste, and Middle-Class Desire*. Chapel Hill: University of North Carolina Press.

————. 2007. "The Library as Place, Collection, or Service: Promoting Book Circulation in Durham, North Carolina, and at the Book-of-the-Month Club, 1925–1945." In *Institutions of Reading: The Social Life of Libraries in the United States*, edited by Thomas Augst and Kenneth Carpenter, 231–63. Amherst and Boston: University of Massachusetts Press.

————. 2008. "What's the Matter with Reception Study? Some Thoughts on the Disciplinary Origins, Conceptual Constraints, and Persistent Viability of a Paradigm." In *New Directions in American Reception Study*, edited by Philip Goldstein and James L. Machor, 327–52. New York: Oxford University Press.

Rak, Julie. 2010. "Insecure Citizenship: Michael Ignatieff, Memoir, Canada." *Biography* 33 (1): 1–23.

Ramone, Jenni. 2011. "'What Really Counts Is the Story': Interview with Andrew Smith, Author of *Moondust*, (February 10, 2010)." In *The Richard & Judy Book Club Reader: Popular Texts and the Practices of Reading*, edited by Jenni Ramone and Helen Cousins, 175–89. Farnham: Ashgate.

Ramone, Jenni, and Helen Cousins, eds. 2011. *The Richard & Judy Book Club Reader: Popular Texts and the Practices of Reading*. Farnham: Ashgate.

Ray, Tiffany. 2009. "Illiteracy Declines in 66 Out of Alabama's 67 Counties." *The Birmingham News*, March 13. http://www.al.com/news/birminghamnews/metro.ssf?/base/news/12369340078860.xml&coll=2. (Accessed 23 May 2012.)

The Reader Organisation. 2010. "Get into Reading." http://reachingout.thereader.org.uk/get-into-reading.html. (Accessed 23 November 2012.)

Reed, Adam. 2011. *Literature and Agency in English Fiction Reading: A Study of the Henry Williamson Society*. Manchester: Manchester University Press.

Rehberg Sedo, DeNel. 2003. "Readers in Reading Groups: An Online Survey of Face-to-Face and Virtual Book Clubs." *Convergence: The International Journal of Research into New Media Technologies* March (9): 66–90.

————. 2004. "Badges of Wisdom, Spaces for Being: A Study of Contemporary Women's Book Clubs." PhD diss., Simon Fraser University.

————. 2007. "Reading and Study Clubs." In *History of the Book in Canada, Volume 3, 1918–1980*, edited by Carole Gerson and Jacques Michon, 509–13. Toronto: University of Toronto Press.

————. 2008. "'Richard & Judy's Book Club' and 'Canada Reads': Readers, Books and Cultural Programming in a Digital Era." *Information, Communication and Society* 11 (2): 188–206.

————. 2010. "Cultural Capital and Community in Contemporary City-wide Reading Programs." *Mémoires Du Livre / Studies in Book Culture* 2 (1). Book Networks and Cultural Capital: Space, Society and the Nation / Réseaux Du Livre et Capital Culturel: Territoire, Société et Nation. http://www.erudit.org/revue/memoires/2010/v2/n1/045314ar.html. (Accessed 23 November 2012.)

Rehberg Sedo, DeNel, ed. 2011a. *Reading Communities from Salons to Cyberspace*. Houndmills: Palgrave Macmillan.

————. 2011b. "An Introduction to Reading Communities: Processes and Formations." In *Reading Communities from Salons to Cyberspace*, edited by DeNel Rehberg Sedo, 1–24. Houndmills: Palgrave Macmillan.

————. 2011c. "'I Used to Read Anything That Caught My Eye, but . . .': Cultural Authorities and Intermediaries in a Virtual Young Adult Book Club." In *Reading Communities from Salons to Cyberspace*, edited by DeNel Rehberg Sedo, 101–22. Houndmills: Palgrave Macmillan.

————. 2011d. "Twentieth- and Twenty-first-Century Literary Communities." In *The Cambridge History of the American Novel*, edited by Leonard Cassuto, Clare Virginia Eby, and Benjamin Reiss, 1154–67. New York: Cambridge University Press.

Reinking, David. 2009. "Valuing Reading, Writing, and Books in a Post-Typographic World." In *A History of the Book in America, Volume 5: The Enduring Book, Print Culture in Post-War America*, edited by David Paul Nord, Joan Shelley Rubin, and Michael Schudson, 485–501. Chapel Hill: University of North Carolina Press.

Rhys Jones, Griff. 2006. *Semi-Detached*. London: Michael Joseph.

Ricci, Nino. 1990. *Lives of the Saints*. Toronto: Cormorant Books.

———. 1993. *In A Glass House*. Toronto: McClelland & Stewart.

———. 2012. "Nino Ricci." http://ninoricci.com/. (Accessed 23 November 2012.)

Robbins, Sarah. 2007. "Making Corrections to Oprah's Book Club: Reclaiming Literary Power for Gendered Literacy Management." In *The Oprah Phenomenon*, edited by Jennifer Harris and Elwood Watson, 227–57. Lexington: University Press of Kentucky.

Roberts, Gillian. 2011. *Prizing Culture: The Celebration and Circulation of National Culture*. Toronto: University of Toronto Press.

Robertson, James. 2006. *The Testament of Gideon Mack*. London: Penguin Books.

Rodriguez, Ana Patricia. 2008. "'Did Isabel Allende Write This Book for Me?': Oprah's Book Club Reads *Daughter of Fortune*." In *The Oprah Effect: Critical Essays on Oprah's Book Club*, edited by Cecilia Konchar Farr and Jaime Harker, 189–210. Albany: State University of New York Press.

Rohrer, Finlo. 2009. "How Richard and Judy Changed What We Read." *BBC News Magazine*. http://news.bbc.co.uk/2/hi/uk_news/magazine/8128436.stm. (Accessed 19 July 2012.)

Rojek, Chris. 2007. "Celebrity and Religion." In *Stardom and Celebrity: A Reader*, edited by Sean Redmond and Su Holmes, 171–80. London: Sage.

Rose, Jonathan. 2001. *The Intellectual Life of the British Working Classes*. New Haven: Yale University Press.

Ross, Andrew. 2009. *Nice Work If You Can Get It: Life and Labor in Precarious Times*. New York: New York University Press.

Rubenfeld, Jed. 2006. *The Interpretation of Murder*. London: Headline Review.

Rubin, Joan Shelley. 1992. *The Making of Middlebrow Culture*. Chapel Hill: University of North Carolina Press.

———. 2007. *Songs of Ourselves: The Uses of Poetry in America*. Cambridge: Harvard University Press.

———. 2009. "The Enduring Reader." In *A History of the Book in America, Volume 5: The Enduring Book, Print Culture in Postwar America*, edited by David Paul Nord, Joan Shelley Rubin, and Michael Schudson, 412–31. Chapel Hill: University of North Carolina Press.

Rubin, Rebecca B., and Michael P. McHugh. 1987. "Development of Parasocial Interaction Relationships." *Journal of Broadcasting & Electronic Media* 31 (3): 279–92.

Ryan, Andrew. 2010. "What Canadians Like to Watch on TV." *The Globe and Mail*, September 30. http://www.theglobeandmail.com/news/arts/television/andrew-ryan/what-canadians-like-to-watch-on-tv/article1732917/. (Accessed 8 August 2011.)

Ryan, Barbara, and Amy M. Thomas, eds. 2002. *Reading Acts: U.S. Readers' Interactions with Literature, 1800–1950*. Knoxville: University of Tennessee Press.

Ryan Hyde, Catherine. 2007. *Love in the Present Tense*. London: Black Swan.

Ryan, James D. 1998. "Analysis of the National Endowment of the Arts Using SAS (R)/STAT." In *Proceedings of the Twenty-Third Annual SAS Users Group International Conference*, 1137–42. http://www2.sas.com/proceedings/sugi23/Posters/p210.pdf. (Accessed 23 November 2012.)

Savage, Philip. 2009. "Canada: Local Content in the New Media Broadcasting Environment." Paper presented at the Annual Meeting of the International Communication Association, Chicago.

——. 2010. "Identity Housekeeping in Canadian Public Service Media." In *Reinventing Public Service Communication: European Broadcasters and Beyond*, edited by Petros Iosifidis, 273–86. Houndmills: Palgrave Macmillan.

Schellenberg, Betty. 2011. "Reading in an Epistolary Community in Eighteenth-Century England." In *Reading Communities from Salons to Cyberspace*, edited by DeNel Rehberg Sedo, 25–43. Houndmills: Palgrave Macmillan.

Schiffrin, André. 2001. *The Business of Books: How International Conglomerates Took Over Publishing and Changed the Way We Read*. London and New York: Verso.

Shattuc, Jane. 2008. "The Confessional Talk Show." In *The Television Genre Book*, edited by Glen Creeber, 167–70. 2nd ed. London: British Film Institute and Palgrave Macmillan.

Sheldrick Ross, Catherine, Lynne McKechnie, and Paulette M. Rothbauer. 2006. *Reading Matters: What the Research Reveals About Reading, Libraries, and Community*. Westport: Libraries Unlimited.

Shep, Sydney J. 2008. "Books Without Borders: The Transnational Turn in Book History." In *Books Without Borders: The Cross-National Dimension in Print Culture*, 13–37. Houndmills: Palgrave Macmillan.

Sicherman, Barbara. 2007. "Ideologies and Practices of Reading." In *A History of the Book in America, Volume 3: The Industrial Book, 1840–1880*, edited by Scott E. Casper, Jeffrey D. Groves, Stephen W. Nissenbaum, and Michael Winship, 279–302. Chapel Hill: University of North Carolina Press.

——. 2010. *Well-Read Lives: How Books Inspired a Generation of American Women*. Chapel Hill: University of North Carolina Press.

Siebert, Maria Verena. 2011. "Kidult Readers: The Cross-Generational Appeal of Harry Potter and Twilight." In *Interdisciplinary Approaches to Twilight?: Studies in Fiction, Media, and a Contemporary Cultural Experience*, edited by Mariah Larsson and Ann Steiner, 213–28. Lund: Nordic Academic Press.

Singh, J. P. 2010. "Introduction: Global Cultural Policies and Power." In *International Cultural Policies and Power*, edited by J. P Singh, 1–15. Houndmills: Palgrave Macmillan.

Skains, Lyle R. 2010. "The Shifting Author-Reader Dynamic: Online Novel Communities as a Bridge from Print to Digital Literature." *Convergence: The International Journal of Research into New Media Technologies* 16 (1): 95–111.

Skeggs, Beverley. 2004. *Class, Self, Culture*. London and New York: Routledge.

Smith, Alisa, and J. B. MacKinnon. 2007. *The 100-Mile Diet: A Year of Local Eating*. Toronto: Vintage Canada.

Smith, Dorothy E. 1987. *The Everyday World as Problematic: A Feminist Sociology*. Boston: Northeastern University Press.

Smith, Erin. 2007. "'Jesus, My Pal': Reading and Religion in Middlebrow America." *Canadian Review of American Studies* 37 (2): 147–81.

——. 2008. "The Religious Book Club: Print Culture, Consumerism and the Spiritual Life of American Protestants Between the Wars." In *Religion and the Culture of Print in America*, edited by Charles L. Cohen and Paul S. Boyer, 217–42. Madison: University of Wisconsin Press.

Smith, Russell. 2004. "CBC Showing Its Age in Sook-Yin Lee Tempest." *The Globe and Mail*, January 15, R1.

Snape, Robert. 1995. *Leisure and the Rise of the Public Library*. London: Library Association Publishing.

——. 2011. "Reading Across Empire: The National Home Reading Union Abroad." In *Reading Communities from Salons to Cyberspace*, edited by DeNel Rehberg Sedo, 60–80. Houndmills: Palgrave Macmillan.

Spry, Graham. 1931. "A Case for Nationalized Broadcasting." *Queen's Quarterly* 38: 169.

Squire, Corinne. 1997. "Empowering Women? The Oprah Winfrey Show." In *Feminist Television Criticism: A Reader*, edited by Charlotte Brunsdon, Julie D'Acci, and Lynn Spigel, 98–113. Oxford and New York: Clarendon Press.

Squires, Claire. 2007. *Marketing Literature: The Making of Contemporary Writing in Britain*. Houndmills: Palgrave Macmillan.

Staggenborg, Suzanne. 2008. *Social Movements*. Toronto: Oxford University Press.

Stanley, Liz, and Sue Wise. 1990. "Methodology and Epistemology in Feminist Research Processes." In *Feminist Praxis: Research, Theory and Epistemology in Feminist Sociology*, edited by Liz Stanley, 20–60. London: Routledge.

Statistics Canada. 1998. *Canadians' Reading Habits 1998*. http://www.statcan.ca/english/Pgdb/People/Culture/arts13a.htm. (Accessed 22 January 2001.)

Statistics Canada. 2007. *Kitchener, Ontario. 2006 Community Profiles—Census Subdivision*. http://www12.statcan.ca/census-recensement/2006/dp-pd/prof/92–591/details/Page.cfm?Lang=E&Geo1=CSD&Code1=3530013&Geo2=PR&Code2=35&Data=Count&SearchText=kitchener&SearchType=Begins&SearchPR=35&B1=All&Custom=. (Accessed 1 July 2009.)

———. 2008. *Educational Attainment*. http://www12.statcan.ca/census-recensement/2006/rt-td/edct-eng.cfm. (Accessed 1 July 2009.)

Steiner, Ann. 2008. "Private Criticism in the Public Space: Personal Writing on Literature in Readers' Reviews on Amazon." *Particip@tions: Journal of Audience & Reception Studies* 5 (2). http://www.participations.org/Volume%205/Issue%202/5_02_steiner.htm. (Accessed 23 November 2012.)

Stevenson, Deborah, Kieryn McKay, and David Rowe. 2010. "Tracing British Cultural Policy Domains: Contexts, Collaborations and Constituencies." *International Journal of Cultural Policy* 16 (2): 159–72.

Stewart, David W., Prem N. Shamdasani, and Dennis W. Rook. 2007. *Focus Groups: Theory and Practice*. 2nd ed. Thousand Oaks: Sage.

St-Laurent, Fanie. 2007. "Case Study: Société d'étude et de Conférences." In *History of the Book in Canada, Volume 3: 1918–1980*, edited by Carole Gerson and Jacques Michon, 513–14. Toronto: University of Toronto Press.

Stow, Simon. 2008. "The Way We Read Now: Oprah Winfrey, Intellectuals, and Democracy." In *The Oprah Effect: Critical Essays on Oprah's Book Club*, edited by Cecilia Konchar Farr and Jaime Harker, 277–94. Albany: State University of New York Press.

Straw, Will, and Richard Sutherland. 2007. "The Canadian Music Industry at a Crossroads." In *How Canadians Communicate II: Media, Globalization and Identity*, edited by David Taras, Maria Bakardjieva, and Frits Pannekoek, 141–65. Calgary: University of Calgary Press.

Street, John. 2005. "Luck, Power, Corruption, Democracy? Judging Arts Prizes." *Cultural Politics* 1 (2): 215–32.

Striphas, Theodore G. 2003. "A Dialectic With the Everyday: Communication and Cultural Politics on Oprah Winfrey's Book Club." *Critical Studies in Media Communication* 20 (3): 295–316.

———. 2009. *The Late Age of Print: Everyday Book Culture from Consumerism to Control*. New York: Columbia University Press.

Suarez, Michael F. S. J. and Michael L. Turner, eds. 2009. *The Cambridge History of the Book in Britain, Volume 5: 1695–1830*. Cambridge: Cambridge University Press.

Suarez, Michael Felix, and H. R. Woudhuysen. 2010. *The Oxford Companion to the Book*. Oxford and New York: Oxford University Press.

Sweeney, Megan. 2010. *Reading Is My Window: Books and the Art of Reading in Women's Prisons*. Chapel Hill: University of North Carolina Press.

Taylor, Joan Bessman. 2007. "When Adults Talk in Circles: Book Groups and Contemporary Reading Practices." PhD diss., University of Illinois at Urbana-Champaign.

Taylor, Kate. 2005. "Cultural Contests Out of Control." *The Globe & Mail*, February 23: R1.

Teather, David. 2002. "Chat Queen Oprah Shelves Her TV Book Club." The *Guardian*, April 8. http://www.guardian.co.uk/world/2002/apr/08/media.books. (Accessed 20 June 2012.)

The Work Foundation, and NESTA. 2007. *Staying Ahead. The Economic Performance of the UK's Creative Industries*. London: The Work Foundation Alliance Limited. http://www.theworkfoundation.com/Reports/176/Staying-Ahead-The-economic-performance-of-the-UK39s-creative-industries-overview. (Accessed 23 November 2012.)

Thompson, John B. 2010. *Merchants of Culture: The Publishing Business in the Twenty-First Century*. Cambridge: Polity Press.

Thurling, Chris. 2009. "Interview with Andrew Kelly, Head of Bristol's Cultural Development Partnership." http://community.brandrepublic.com/blogs/frombristol/archive/2009/05/12/interview-with-andrew-kelly-head-of-bristol-s-cultural-development-partnership.aspx. (Accessed 25 April 2011.)

Tinic, Serra. 2010. "Walking a Tightrope: The Global Cultural Economy of Canadian Television." In *How Canadians Communicate III: Contexts of Canadian Popular Culture*, edited by Bart Beaty, Derek Briton, Gloria Filax, and Rebecca Sullivan, 95–115. Edmonton: Athabasca University Press.

Tivnan, Tom. 2008. "Last Hurrah or New Beginning?" *Bookseller.com*, August 15. http://www.thebookseller.com/in-depth/feature/65076-last-hurrah-or-new-beginning.html. (Accessed 21 December 2010.)

Tompkins, Jane P. 1980. *Reader-Response Criticism: From Formalism to Post-Structuralism*. Baltimore: The Johns Hopkins University Press.

Toynbee, Polly. 2011. "Viewpoint: Why the Class Struggle Is Not Dead." *BBC News UK Politics*. http://www.bbc.co.uk/news/uk-politics-14721315. (Accessed 19 July 2012.)

Travis, Trysh. 2003. "Divine Secrets of the Cultural Studies Sisterhood: Women Reading Rebecca Wells." *American Literary History* 15 (1): 134–61.

———. 2007. "'It Will Change the World If Everybody Reads This Book': New Thought Religion in Oprah's Book Club." *American Quarterly* 59 (3): 1017–41.

———. 2009. *The Language of the Heart: A Cultural History of the Recovery Movement from Alcoholics Anonymous to Oprah Winfrey*. Chapel Hill: University of North Carolina Press.

Turner, Graeme. 2010. *Ordinary People and the Media: The Demotic Turn*. London: Sage.

Turner-Riggs. 2008. *Book Distribution in Canada's English-Language Market*. Ottawa: The Department of Canadian Heritage. http://www.pch.gc.ca/pc-ch/org/sectr/ac-ca/pblctns/bk_dstrbtn_lv/dst_eng/pdf-eng.pdf. (Accessed 23 November 2012.)

Urquhart, Jane. 2001. *The Stone Carvers*. Toronto: McClelland and Stewart.

Urry, John. 1990. *The Tourist Gaze*. London: Sage.

Valentine, Lynn. 1992. "Gender, Technology and Democracy at Work." In *Information Technology and Workplace Democracy*, edited by Martin Beirne and Harvie Ramsay, 193–211. London and New York: Routledge.

Van Slyck, Abigail Ayres. 1995. *Free to All: Carnegie Libraries and American Culture, 1890–1920*. Chicago: University of Chicago Press.

Vipond, Mary. 2004. "Canada." In *The Museum of Broadcast Communications Encyclopedia of Radio*, edited by Christopher H. Sterling and Michael C. Keith, 257–61. New York: Fitzroy Dearborn.

———. 2009. "Whence and Whither: The Historiography of Canadian Broadcasting." In *Communicating in Canada's Past: Essays in Media History*, edited by Gene Allen and Daniel J. Robinson, 233–56. Toronto: University of Toronto Press.

Viswanathan, Gauri. 1989. *Masks of Conquest: Literary Study and British Rule in India*. New York: Columbia University Press.

Van der Vlies, Andrew E. 2007. *South African Textual Cultures: White, Black, Read All Over*. Manchester: Manchester University Press.

Walsh, Kimberly. 2010. "CBC Live at IFOA." http://eastcoastbychoice.ca/2010/10/21/cbc-live-at-ifoa/. (Accessed 23 November 2012.)

Ward, Philip, and Graham Dolphin. 2011. "Funding the Arts: Standard Note for the Home Affairs Section." Houses of Parliament. www.parliament.uk/briefing-papers/SN05706.pdf. (Accessed 1 June 2011.)

Watson, Patrick. 1999. "Save CBC Radio." *Time Canada* 53 (13): 61.

Wheatley, Helen. 2003. "ITV 1955–89: Populism and Experimentation." In *The Television History Book*, edited by Michele Hilmes, 76–81. London: British Film Institute.

Wiegand, Wayne A. 2009. "The American Public Library: Construction of a Community Reading Institution." In *A History of the Book in America, Volume 4, Print in Motion: The Expansion of Publishing and Reading in the United States, 1880–1940*, edited by Carl F. Kaestle and Janice A. Radway, 431–51. Chapel Hill: University of North Carolina Press.

———. 2011. *Main Street Public Library: Community Places and Reading Spaces in the Rural Heartland, 1876–1956*. Iowa City: University of Iowa Press.

Williams, Raymond. 1961. *The Long Revolution*. London: Chatto and Windus.

———. 1973. *The Country and the City*. Oxford: Oxford University Press.

———. 1976. *Keywords*. Oxford: Oxford University Press.

———. 1977. *Marxism and Literature*. Oxford: Oxford University Press.

Wirtén, Eva Hemmungs. 2009. "The Global Market 1970–2000: The Producers." In *A Companion to the History of the Book*, edited by Simon Eliot and Jonathan Rose, 395–405. Chichester: Wiley-Blackwell.

Wright, David. 2007. "Watching 'The Big Read' with Pierre Bourdieu: Forms of Heteronomy in the Contemporary Literary Field." Centre for Research on Socio-Cultural Change (CRESC). http://www.cresc.ac.uk/publications/watching-the-big-read-with-pierre-bourdieu-forms-of-heteronomy-in-the-contemporary-literary-field. (Accessed 23 November 2012.)

Wyszomirski, Margaret Jane. 2008. "Field Building: The Road to Culture Policy Studies in the United States." In *Understanding the Arts and Creative Sector in the United States*, edited by Joni Maya Cherbo and Ruth Ann Stewart, 39–59. Piscataway: Rutgers University Press.

Ytre-Arne, Brita. 2011. "'I Want to Hold It in My Hands': Readers' Experiences of the Phenomenological Differences Between Women's Magazines Online and in Print." *Media, Culture & Society* 33 (3): 467–77.

Yúdice, George. 2003. *The Expediency of Culture: Uses of Culture in the Global Era*. Durham: Duke University Press.

Zboray, Ronald J., and Mary Saracino Zboray. 2006. *Everyday Ideas: Socioliterary Experience Among Antebellum New Englanders*. Knoxville: University of Tennessee Press.

Zeitchik, Steven. 2002. "Winfrey Provokes Range of Reaction and Speculation." *The Publishers Weekly*. http://www.publishersweekly.com/pw/print/20020415/26175-winfrey-provokes-range-of-reaction-and-speculation-.html. (Accessed 19 July 2012.)

Index